WRITER'S DIGEST

GRAMMAR DESK REFERENCE

The definitive source for clear and correct writing

WRITER'S DIGEST
BOOKS

WritersDigest.com
Cincinnati, Ohio

D1005111

**GARY LUTZ &
DIANE STEVENSON**

Writer's Digest Grammar Desk Reference. Copyright © 2010 by Gary Lutz & Diane Stevenson. Manufactured in the United States of America. All rights reserved. No other part of this book may be reproduced in any form or by any electronic or mechanical means including information storage and retrieval systems without permission in writing from the publisher, except by a reviewer, who may quote brief passages in a review. Published by Writer's Digest Books, an imprint of F+W Media, Inc., 4700 East Galbraith Road, Cincinnati, Ohio 45236. (800) 289-0963. First paperback edition.

For more resources for writers, visit www.writersdigest.com/books.

To receive a free weekly e-mail newsletter delivering tips and updates about writing and about Writer's Digest products, register directly at http://newsletters.fwpublications.com.

15 14 13 12 11   5 4 3 2 1

Distributed in Canada by Fraser Direct
100 Armstrong Avenue
Georgetown, Ontario, Canada L7G 5S4
Tel: (905) 877-4411

Distributed in the U.K. and Europe by F+W Media International
Brunel House, Newton Abbot, Devon, TQ12 4PU, England
Tel: (+44) 1626-323200, Fax: (+44) 1626-323319
E-mail: postmaster@davidandcharles.co.uk

Distributed in Australia by Capricorn Link
P.O. Box 704, Windsor, NSW 2756 Australia
Tel: (02) 4577-3555

The Library of Congress has catalogued the hardcover edition as follows:
Library of Congress Cataloging-in-Publication Data
Lutz, Gary
        The Writer's Digest grammar desk reference : the definitive source for clear
        and correct writing / Gary Lutz & Diane Stevenson.
          p. cm.
        Includes index.
        ISBN 1-58297-335-0 (alk. paper)
        1. English language—Grammar—Handbooks, manuals, etc. 2. English language—Rhetoric—Handbooks, manuals, etc. 3. English language—Usage—Handbooks, manuals, etc. I. Stevenson, Diane II. Title.
PE1112.L88 2005
428.2—dc22   2004063750

ISBN-13 978-1-59963-220-9 (pbk:alk.paper)
ISBN-10 1-59963-220-9 (pbk:alk.paper)

Edited by: Kelly Nickell and Melissa Wuske
Designed by: Claudean Wheeler, based on the first edition design by Lisa Kuhn
Production coordinated by: Debbie Thomas

ABOUT THE AUTHORS

Gary Lutz is the author of the short-story collections *Stories in the Worst Way* (published in hardcover by Alfred A. Knopf in 1996 and in paperback by 3rd bed in 2002) and *I Looked Alive* (published by Black Square Editions/Four Walls Eight Windows in 2004). His chapbook, *Partial List of People to Bleach*, was released by Future Tense Books in 2007. His work has appeared in several anthologies, including *The Random House Treasury of Light Verse* and *The Anchor Book of New American Short Stories*. He has been awarded grants from the National Endowment for the Arts and the Foundation for Contemporary Performance Arts.

Diane Stevenson is the editor of two collections of newspaper columns by best-selling novelist Carl Hiaasen, *Kick Ass: Selected Columns of Carl Hiaasen* and *Paradise Screwed: Selected Columns of Carl Hiaasen*. She has been the recipient of grants from the Ohio Arts Council and the Florida Humanities Council. Her work has appeared in *Poetry*, *The American Poetry Review*, and elsewhere. She teaches at the University of Florida.

Table of Contents

INTRODUCTION

Books about grammar tend to fall into two categories. In the first category are books that describe the operations of the English language and explain how words go about performing their uncanny business in sentences. The approach of such books, unfortunately, is often far removed from the workaday urgency with which we fit words together into sentences and get our hands dirty in the entanglements of syntax and usage. In the second category are books that present a set of rules enabling writers to avoid conspicuous or subtle errors. Such books are practical, but they often leave readers yearning for a larger, clarifying context or reasons why a particular construction is deemed correct or not.

Our book attempts to integrate the two approaches by providing both a macrogrammar and a microgrammar—first, a systematizing of the often perplexing behaviors of words and, second, a how-to guide that will help you produce sentences free of the kinds of errors that distract readers.

Some readers might think that the formulation of rules is an arbitrary or elitist act. The rules and principles set forth in this book, however, are not decrees issued from on high. Instead, the conventions we present here have been induced from a very close inspection of how professional writers and the editorial departments of distinguished newspapers, magazines, and book publishers handle the intricate and sometimes vexatious matters of grammar, punctuation, mechanics, and usage. Such wordsmiths deserve our emulation. They err so rarely that their errors are unusually instructive.

Rather than invent our own sentences to illustrate what can go wrong on the page, therefore, we have extracted erroneous sentences from lively published sources, mostly newspapers and magazines we enjoy reading. (You are likely to notice that some of the illustrative sentences are weakened by more than one kind of error.) The sentences are included to demonstrate that even the most gifted writers can bend or even break the rules of grammar, punctuation, and usage, especially when a deadline looms and the pressure is intense. The errors sometimes slip past even the most vigilant and conscientious editors, copy editors, and proofreaders.

That our very best writers now and then commit errors should deepen our appreciation of just how demanding the craft of writing is—from drafting, composing, and revising to editing, proofreading, and printing. We are certain that, despite diligent proofreading, we ourselves are likely to have committed our share of blunders in the production of this book. We therefore invite readers to alert us to our lapses. (Diane Stevenson wrote Part I; Gary Lutz wrote Parts II–IV.) You can e-mail Diane at part1grammar@yahoo.com and Gary at grammardeskref@aol.com.

Throughout the book, we emphasize the importance of having a good dictionary close by as you write. The desk dictionaries that we recommend (each includes about 160,000 words) are *Webster's New World College Dictionary* and *Merriam-Webster's Collegiate Dictionary*. The unabridged dictionary that we recommend is *Webster's Third New International Dictionary* (published by Merriam-Webster).

For those of you who become interested in reading further about grammar, punctuation, mechanics, and usage, we recommend ten thorough, revered, authoritative, and altogether extraordinary books that shaped our own sensibilities: *Garner's Modern American Usage*, by Bryan A. Garner (Oxford University Press, 2003); *Modern American Usage: A Guide*, by Wilson Follett and revised by Erik Wensberg (Hill and Wang, 1998); *The Careful Writer*, by Theodore M. Bernstein (Free Press, 1995); *The Handbook of Good English*, by Edward D. Johnson (Washington Square Press, 1991); *Understanding Grammar*, by Paul Roberts (Harper, 1954); *Rhetorical Grammar: Grammatical Choices, Rhetorical Effects*, third edition, by Martha Kolln (Allyn and Bacon, 1998); *Right Words, Right Places*, by Scott Rice (Wadsworth Pub. Co., 1993); *Merriam-Webster's Manual for Writers and Editors* (Merriam-Webster, 1998); *Words into Type* (Prentice Hall, 1974); and *The Chicago Manual of Style*, fifteenth edition (University of Chicago Press, 2003).

PART I:
GRAMMAR: AN OVERVIEW

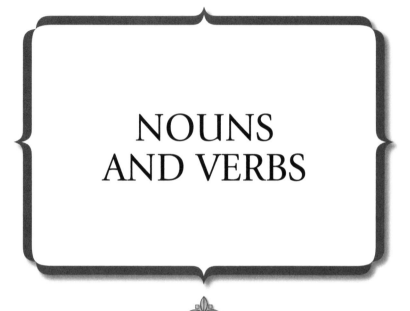

CHAPTER 1

NOUNS AND VERBS

While there are eight parts of speech, the two most essential parts are nouns and verbs. Nouns name the things of the world, and verbs tell what those things do. Everything else in a sentence accompanies, embellishes, assists, and refines those two major sentence understructures, without which there would be no meaning—just random words like *the quickly because yes red they*. Nouns and verbs convey all sense and substance; they are the parts of speech that allow us to express thoughts, ideas, statements, questions, facts, and opinions. Shaped and directed by other parts of speech, nouns and verbs are the most elemental components of speech in any language.

1A NOUNS: TYPES AND FORMS

A noun is typically thought of as the name of a person, place, or thing (and an idea or emotion can be considered a thing). This traditional definition covers all possibilities in the world, as it should, for nouns name our reality. Everything we see, think, have, feel, hope, and know can be called something, and that something will take the form of a noun that tells what it is. In fact, you first learned language by discovering the names of objects and people, single words identifying *mama* or *dog* or *milk*. Because the material world and the less tangible world of thoughts, ideas, and emotions constitute a complicated array of possibilities, nouns themselves can be classified according to what they name. Nouns can be classified, for instance, as specific, general, concrete, abstract, singular, or plural. As you strive in your writing for precision and accuracy of meaning, grammar, and style, keep in mind the definitions and treatments of the basic noun classes listed here.

Proper nouns vs. common nouns: A proper noun names one specific person, thing, or place (*Woofy, Mount Everest*), whereas a common noun names a class or group (*dog, mountain*).

Concrete nouns vs. abstract nouns: A concrete noun refers to a material object (*the table, a dog*), whereas an abstract noun refers to something intangible (*love, art*).

Count nouns vs. noncount (or mass) nouns: A count noun identifies something that can be preceded by *many* or *fewer*, and can become plural with the addition of *-s: fewer coins, many rivers*. A noncount noun designates something that cannot become divisible, such as *money, tuberculosis*, or *happiness*. Noncount nouns can be preceded by *much* and *less*. Thus *He ate fewer cookies today* is correct, not *less cookies*, and *I prefer less cream in my coffee* is correct, not *fewer cream*. Often, abstract nouns are noncount nouns as well: *honor, duty, authority, love.*

Proper Nouns

These words name specific, particular things or persons and therefore are always capitalized. For example, Tallahassee is the one and only capital of Florida (and there is only one state named *Florida*); Aunt Betty is one person—a specific relative (she's not Aunt Mary or Uncle Joe)—and a Dirt Devil is a certain kind of handheld vacuum cleaner. Proper nouns are the most restrictive category of nouns because they name so specifically. All books, magazines, plays, movies, paintings, cities, countries, people, and brands have names unique to themselves alone: *The Orchid Thief; Good Housekeeping; The Taming of the Shrew; Starry Night; Braveheart;* and so forth. As in the example above, if a certain person with a title is referred to (Aunt Betty), then the title itself is also capitalized. Proper nouns, because they name one specific individual or type, ordinarily cannot be made plural: *Aunt Bettys* would be possible only if there existed two distinct people who were aunts to the person calling them Aunt Betty. Even so, each Aunt Betty would be one individual (although there might be many Dirt Devils in the garage, along with several Fords, but those garages wouldn't be located in several Clevelands).

Over time, proper nouns, especially those that originally designate a particular brand or trademarked product, can evolve into common nouns, which are not capitalized—for example *French fry* has evolved into the accepted *french fry;* however, certain proper nouns remain proper (consult your dictionary when unsure): *Internet* (not *internet*); *World Wide Web* (not *worldwide web* or *world wide web*); *Lycra* (not *lycra*).

Common Nouns (Noncount)

The other very broad category of noun is called *common,* meaning that such a noun names an entire class or kind or group. Many common nouns are noncount nouns—that is, they refer to something whole that cannot be separated into individual units and counted separately. Noncount nouns can also be classified as abstract nouns because the indivisible whole they refer to is also a nonphysical quality, characteristic, or attribute—positive, negative, or neutral. Thus *bravery, loneliness, humor, strength, wisdom, greed, sloth, anger, stress, frustration, anxiety,* and *alienation* are all noncount abstract nouns. However, noncount nouns can also designate types of abstractions other than those of qualities, characteristics, and attributes—abstractions in the form of institutions, conditions, or states of being : *marriage, wealth, hunger, fame, masculinity, fatigue, romance, exercise, business, leisure, activity, motion, quietude, clarity, speed,* and *opinion.*

Notice that some of the noncount nouns above can be preceded by *a, an, or the,* and some can be made plural, while others cannot. In the above group of noncount abstract nouns designating qualities and attributes, all nouns can be preceded with *the,* but only *strength, stress, frustration,* and *anxiety* can be preceded by *a* or *an.* Those same nouns are the only ones that can be pluralized: *stresses, strengths, frustrations, anxieties.* In the group of noncount nouns designating institutions and conditions, most nouns can be preceded by both *a (an)* or *the,* but only *wealth, hunger, fame, masculinity, fatigue,* and *quietude* can be preceded by *the.* Those same nouns are the only ones that cannot be pluralized.

Why are there such differences? It would seem there are degrees or kinds of abstraction. In the examples that can be pluralized, specific instances of the abstraction itself exist: In other words, the institution of marriage is an abstraction, yet specific people get married. Likewise, the concept of romance is abstract, yet that concept can be instantiated with flesh-and-blood people; the idea of exercise is abstract, yet there are particular exercises. On the other hand, there are no possible instantiations of *wealth, hunger, fame, masculinity, fatigue,* and *quietude:* these nouns represent abstractions that have only degree or kind—as in *severe fatigue* or *great wealth.*

Certain distinctions made at the very beginning of this chapter—between *much/less* and *many/fewer,* as they apply to noncount and count nouns—don't derive from such an in-depth examination: According to the *much/less* and *many/fewer* litmus test, the difference between *romance* and *wealth* would hinge on whether the things they designate could be counted. Thus *romance* might be considered in terms of *much* or *less,* as in *There was less romance possible on the porch than under the stars.* But romance might also be thought of in terms of number through sequence: *She has had many unsuccessful romances.* In the first case, *romance* would be a noncount noun, and in the second, a count noun. This distinction is a valuable one, but neither *romance* nor *wealth* is divisible and both are concepts, so the basic characteristic defining them as noncount nouns still pertains. Therefore, the essential difference between *romance* and *wealth* seems clearer when they are considered in terms of degree vs. instantiation, as discussed above.

Noncount nouns may also be concrete—that is, the things they designate may possess dimension and physical characteristics that allow for verification through the senses. Such noncount concrete nouns include the following: *clothing, silverware, stationery, bruise, fruit, money, jewelry, music, crop, lawn,* and *sky.* These nouns represent aspects of the world that can be seen, touched, smelled, tasted, and heard, yet they cannot be broken into constituent parts; therefore, these nouns are both concrete and noncount. (Words like *fruit* and *money* can be broken down into constituent parts, but there are specific words for those parts: *apples* and *pennies,* for example; likewise, *music* can be specified as *sonata, jazz, barbershop quartet,* and so forth.) Notice that the previous discussion about pluralization and type of abstraction does not apply here: only *bruise, crop, lawn,* and *sky* can become plural. Those same nouns can be preceded by *a* or *an,* while the other concrete nouns listed cannot—we don't think in terms of *a clothing,* but visualizing *a bruise* is quite possible. Likewise, there may be many bruises or three bruises, but not many clothings or two clothings.

Common Nouns (Count)

Common count nouns can *always* be pluralized: simply put, there can be one of something, or many. There are straightfoward rules governing the pluralization of common count nouns.

1. To form a plural, add -*s*.
   - cat/cats
   - house/houses
   - flower/flowers

2. To form the plural of a noun ending in -*s*, -*sh*, -*ch*, *or* -*x*, add -*es*. Note that the -*es* adds a syllable to the singular form.
   - peach/peaches
   - hex/hexes
   - flash/flashes
   - ditch/ditches
   - dish/dishes
   - mess/messes
   - ax/axes

3. To form the plural of a noun ending in a -*y* that is preceded by a consonant, change the -*y* to -*i* and add -*es*.
   - lady/ladies
   - berry/berries
   - cry/cries

4. To form the plural of a noun ending in a -*y* that is preceded by a vowel, add -*s*.
   - toy/toys
   - monkey/monkeys
   - bay/bays
   - play/plays.

5. To form the plural of most nouns ending in -*f* or -*fe*, change the -*f* or -*fe* to a -*v* and add -*s* or -*es*.
   - knife/knives
   - leaf/leaves
   - scarf/scarves
   - sheaf/sheaves
   - wife/wives

6. To form the plural of certain nouns ending in -*f* or -*fe*, add -*s*.
   - roof/roofs
   - belief/beliefs
   - chief/chiefs
   - hoof/hoofs (or hooves)

7. To form the plural of a noun that ends in an -*o* that is preceded by another vowel, add -*s*; to form a plural with a noun that ends in an -*o* that is preceded by a consonant, add -*es*.
   - radio/radios
   - cameo/cameos
   - hero/heroes
   - tomato/tomatoes
   - solo/solos
   - piano/pianos

8. To form the plural of a noun ending in an *-o* that is preceded by a consonant, add either *-es* or *-s*.
   - cargo/cargos/cargoes
   - motto/mottos/mottoes
   - mosquito/mosquitos/mosquitoes
   - zero/zeros/zeroes

9. To form the plural of a compound noun (two nouns that have been joined together), add *-s* or *-es* to the last word.
   - checkbook/checkbooks
   - doghouse/doghouses
   - housekeeper/housekeepers

10. To form the plural of a noun that has an attached modifier, add *-s* or *-es* to the first noun, not to a noun in the attached modifying phrase.
    - mother-in-law/mothers-in-law
    - lady-in-waiting/ladies-in-waiting
    - passer-by/passers-by
    - editor-in-chief/editors-in-chief

CAUTION

Some plurals are formed irregularly: *tooth/teeth, man/men, foot/feet, child/children, mouse/mice, goose/geese*. Some nouns are the same in singular and plural form: *sheep, deer, trout, elk, fish, rice, wheat, pheasant, quail*.

Plural-Only Nouns

Some nouns have an automatically plural form, even though they are not themselves plural in meaning: *measles, physics, economics, linguistics, mathematics, mumps, civics*. Others can be either singular or plural, depending on the context: *acoustics, athletics, gymnastics, tactics, hysterics*. Notice that this last group of words ends in *-ics*. Check your dictionary if you are unsure of the correct usage for a term.

Nouns and Case (Possessive)

Nouns show possession by the addition of an apostrophe and an *-s: Tom's car, today's weather, a cat's meal, the child's school*. Anytime you can mentally create a construction containing *of* or *belongs to* there is an implicit possessive: *the car of* (or *belonging to*) *Tom; the weather of* (or *belonging to*) *today; the school of* (or *belonging to*) *the child*.

Notice that the apostrophe is added after the *-s* in a plural noun: *cats', houses', dishes', Joneses', briefcases'*. For a complete discussion of possessives, see chapter 21 on apostrophes.

Nouns and Gender

Nouns also display gender—that is, they refer to people, places, or things that are masculine, feminine, or neuter. This distinction is often conveniently built into the words themselves (with the male designation preceding the female in the following examples: *man/woman, boy/girl, father/mother, fiancé/fiancée, actor/actress, duke/duchess, waiter/waitress, host/hostess, hero/heroine, blond/blonde, king/queen, lion/lioness, goose/gander, rooster/hen, pig/sow* (*sow* is actually the word for several female animals, including bears).

Notice that these nouns often fall into one of three categories: nouns for humans, titular nouns, and nouns for animals. Frequently, a title is made female by adding the suffix *-ess:* thus *prince* and *princess,* or *steward* and *stewardess.* Many of those distinctions are now considered superfluous, as are the automatically male-gendered titles with *-man* as a suffix: *policeman, fireman, chairman, congressman, mailman.* Since such suffixes do not apply to women in the professions, other terms are used: *police officer, firefighter, chair (or chairperson), congressperson, mail carrier.*

Collective Nouns

Collective nouns are similar to noncount concrete nouns because they refer to a group as a unit: *audience, class, orchestra, jury, team, family,* to name a few. Although their purpose is clear, collective nouns can pose grammatical challenges when the individual members of a group need to be emphasized. This topic will be addressed thoroughly in chapters 5 and 11, which focus on subject-verb agreement and pronoun agreement.

1B THE FUNCTIONS OF NOUNS IN SENTENCES

Nouns can be *subjects, subjective complements (predicate nominatives), objective complements, direct objects, indirect objects,* or *objects of prepositions,* as well as *modifiers* for other nouns. Remember, a noun names a person, place, or thing—and a thing can be an object, an idea, or an emotion.

Subjects

A noun as a subject performs the action of a sentence, and it can be expanded on or explained with additional nouns or modifiers. Whether simple or elaborately modified, the subject is what the sentence is about. A single noun acting as a subject is called a simple subject. In the following sentences, the noun simple subject, without its modifiers, has been underlined.

- The lonely old dog howled at the moon.
- Dick's anger caused him to lash out at people.
- Cars clog the road at rush hour.
- Physics is a difficult subject.
- The deer ate all the corn we put out for them.
- Art can be appreciated by everyone.

Nouns can be joined into compound subjects with the use of a coordinating conjunction, in the following examples with *and.* The simple subjects—single nouns—have been underlined. The coordinating conjunction *and* appears in italics.

- The lonely old dog *and* the homeless cat howl at the moon every night.
- Dick's anger and Bob's frustration cause them to lash out at people.
- Cars and buses clog the road at rush hour.
- Physics and mathematics are difficult subjects.
- The deer and the elk always eat all the corn we put out for them.

Nouns as Modifiers or Appositives

Modifiers, as the term suggests, are words that modify other words. In the phrase *the wide trailer, wide* is an adjective modifying *trailer.* In the phrase *the very wide trailer, very* is an adverb modifying *wide.* (The next chapter will discuss adjectives and adverbs in more detail.)

Adjectives and adverbs aren't the only types of words that can act as modifiers: Nouns can modify other nouns. For example, if you wanted to refer to the house belonging to the Smiths, you might use the possessive—*the Smiths' house*—but you might also have occasion to call it *the Smith house*. In this case, a proper noun is modifying a common noun, but common nouns can also modify other nouns.

When two nouns are used together (one modifying the other), the result is a compound. Compound nouns can be open, with one space and no punctuation between the words (*convenience store, computer desk, trailer park*); they can be hyphenated (*great-grandfather, triple-header, two-piece*); or they can be closed—run together as one word (*houseplant, homework, hairspray, doghouse, shoeshine*). A good dictionary and the guidelines in chapter 24 will help you determine when a compound noun should be open, hyphenated, or closed.

In the sentences below, the noun modifiers have been italicized.

- What are you going to wear to the *spring* formal?
- The *train* wreck resulted in only minor injuries.
- Lisa, the *flower* girl at her sister's wedding, was much too young.

Too many individual noun modifiers can also create a hard-to-read sentence.

- The *winter homecoming neighborhood block* party is about to begin.
- Our *car show party* reception was a great success.
- Bill's *nightmare executive job interview* questions were actually asked at the meeting.

Nouns can also modify, in a sense, by being in apposition to another noun. An appositive is a noun, or group of words generally including a noun, that renames a different noun (or pronoun) by providing another way to look at or describe it. If the appositive is needed to identify the noun—if it's restrictive, in other words—then no comma is used. However, if the appositive provides only additional, incidental information about the noun, punctuation is used, and the appositive is said to be nonrestrictive.

Appositives can appear at the beginning, middle, or end of a sentence. They can be set off with commas, em dashes, colons (but only if the appositive is at the end of a complete sentence), and parentheses.

In the following examples, the appositives have been italicized and the nouns they modify have been underlined.

- Ben's brother *Bob* helped him build the house.

  If Ben has more than one brother, the name *Bob* would be necessary to identify which brother is being discussed—in other words, to restrict the meaning of the word *brother*. If Ben has only one brother, the name *Bob* would be additional information not essential to the meaning of the sentence; *Bob* would be a nonrestrictive appositive. Nonrestrictive appositives are always set off by punctuation. Since no punctuation surrounds the appositive Bob in this example, we know that Bob is a restrictive appositive (and that Ben has more than one brother).

- My sister, *Sandy*, is the most organized person I know.

  The appositive in this sentence, Sandy, is set off by commas. This example contrasts with the first example—the appositive here is nonrestrictive: It adds information, but it is not vital to the identity of *sister* because there is only one sister, Sandy.

- Margaret's mother, *an artistic soul from Naples*, received first place.

  An *artistic soul from Naples* is additional information about the person who received first place, but we don't need that information to identify the winner, because *Margaret's mother* already does that for us.

- My dog won a contest that earned him a new doghouse—*an elaborately carpeted two-story affair with an accompanying white picket fence.*

    The appositive is set off with a dash and appears at the end of the sentence. This appositive is nonrestrictive: *an elaborately carpeted two-story affair with an accompanying white picket fence* isn't necessary to distinguish this prize doghouse from another prize doghouse, but it is certainly delightful information to have.

- *A tale of intrigue and terror,* Scream at Dark isn't a novel you want to read when you're alone.

    The appositive is introductory: *a tale of intrigue and terror* describes the novel, but *Scream at Dark* is so specific that nothing else is needed to identify it. The appositive is nonrestrictive and therefore has accompanying punctuation, in this case only one comma because it is an introductory group of words.

In the following examples, the italicized appositives have been set off with em dashes, which are more emphatic than commas (the noun each appositive renames has been underlined).

- The rancher—*a weather-beaten, toughened-up, no-nonsense man known for his kind heart*—nursed the premature, motherless lamb to adulthood.

- *Great generosity, unusual insight into complex problems, devotion to the task at hand*—these attributes distinguished Loretta from the other candidates.

    The appositive in this example introduces the single noun described by the group of nouns that precedes it.

- Nora overpaid for the dress—*an ill-fitting bit of badly dyed fluff.*

    The use of a single em dash and the emphatic sentence position of the appositive emphasize the biting criticism of the dress.

In the examples below, the appositives introduced by a colon come at the end of a sentence. Note how the parenthetical appositives have the quality of asides.

- John got what he wanted most: *admission to Harvard.*
- He lacked the one ability needed most for this job: ruthless self-interest.
- The jeweled-fruit cheesecake (my own favorite dessert) was eagerly devoured by all guests.
- Steve's greatest fear (a deeply rooted, vaguely understood horror of all creatures even remotely arachnid) kept him from traveling to distant, jungly places.

The appositives below are not accompanied by punctuation, because they cannot be removed from the sentence (i.e., they are restrictive). Each is followed by a title that must be included for the purpose of identification.

- The film *Don't Look Now* gave me nightmares for weeks.

    Unless *Don't Look Now* were named, *the film* as a generic term would be meaningless.

- Margot set sail on the yacht *Sea Scallop* at dawn.

Subjective Complements

Nouns can also be complements. A complement, like an appositive, is a noun that completes meaning. A subjective complement (also called a predicate nominative) is always necessary in a certain construction—it is not optional, but required.

For example, in the sentence *John is president,* the word *president* can't be removed without leaving the nonsensical *John is,* a grammatical unit acceptable only as a truncated response to a question like *Who's here?* The pattern of a sentence like *John is president* is called SVC—subject, verb, complement—and the verb in this pattern is always a linking verb, as will be discussed later in this chapter. For now, think of the subjective complement (or predicate nominative) as one side of an equation, with the verb as the equal sign. In the following examples, the subject has been underlined, the verb has been italicized, and the subjective complement appears in boldface.

- Mom *is* a **lawyer**.
- The dog *has been* a **champion**.
- The children *are* little **monsters** today.

In the above examples, you can see that Mom = lawyer, dog = champion, and children = monsters. Thus a subjective complement is a noun that is equivalent to the subject, but renames it in different terms. (Objective complements, which rename objects, are discussed on page 13.)

Direct Objects

A direct object is a noun that receives the action of the verb. For example, in *Hillary aced the test*, the subject is *Hillary*, the verb is *aced*, and *the test* is what was aced. *Test* is the direct object. The sentence would not make sense if *test* were removed: *Hillary aced*. In a sense, a direct object shows the outcome of the action of the verb. Therefore, SVO (subject-verb-object) is a sentence pattern with required elements, just as SVC (subject-verb-complement) is, and all components within either pattern are necessary if the sentence is to function as a complete grammatical unit. (SV is also a pattern, though a less typical one, because sentences conforming to this pattern are unusually terse: *Mom agrees.*)

To determine whether a sentence contains a direct object, ask *what* or *whom* after the verb (*Bob kicked* [what?] *the door*). In the following examples, the noun subject has been underlined, the verb has been italicized, and the noun direct object—sometimes singular, sometimes plural or compound—has been boldfaced.

- Lucy *wanted* a new **car**.
- Nick *typed* the **story** quickly.
- The storm *destroyed* our **trees and shrubs**.
- Tom and Jerry *ate* the entire **pie**.
- Kids never *appreciate* their **parents**.

Indirect Objects

Nouns as indirect objects appear in sentences with direct objects and are identified by imagining a *to* or *for* in front of them. While the direct object expresses the outcome or the recipient of the action of the verb, the indirect object shows for whom or for what the action was undertaken.

The best way to identify an indirect object is to notice its position in the sentence (it comes before the direct object), and then imagine a *to* or *for* in front of it: *Bob gave* (to) *me* [what?] *a new watch*. It's important to note that if the *for* or *to* actually appears (*Bob gave to me a new watch*), then the sentence contains a prepositional phrase (*to me*) and not an indirect object.

In the following sentences, the subjects have been underlined, the verbs have been italicized, the direct objects have been boldfaced, and the indirect objects appear in brackets.

- The strange man *told* the [girls] a **story**.
- Mom *gave* the [dogs] our leftover **meatloaf**.
- The teacher *made* the [class] a batch of **cookies**.

It's easy to identify the noun subject of each sentence, partly because the subject most often comes first, but also because it indicates the agent of the action: The subject, remember, is what the sentence is about: *man, mom, teacher*. What did those subjects do? *Man told; mom gave; teacher made*. What did the man tell? What did mom give? What did the teacher make? By asking these questions, you arrive at the direct object: *a story, meatloaf, a batch of cookies*. And for whom were those actions performed? The *girls*, the *dogs*, the *class*. Those are the indirect objects.

Objective Complements

Objective complements, like subjective complements, complete or add to the meaning of a noun—in this case, a noun used as an object, rather than as a subject. Objective complements usually follow the noun or nouns they modify. In the following examples, the direct objects have been italicized, and the objective complements have been boldfaced.

- Dad called the *salesperson* a **charlatan** and a **fraud**.

    The objective complement in this example is compound (i.e., it consists of more than one noun). A *charlatan* and a *fraud* renames *salesperson*, the direct object of the verb, *called*. Note that, in this case, the objective complement is necessary to make the sentence grammatically complete.

- The mechanic considered the *car* a **lemon**.

    The objective complement (*lemon*) renames the direct object (*car*) of the verb (*considered*). In this case, the objective complement is necessary to make the sentence grammatically complete.

- Our committee elected *Mr. Greene* **president**.

    President renames *Mr. Greene*, the direct object of the verb *elected*. In this sentence, unlike in the previous two examples, the objective complement is not necessary to make the sentence grammatically complete. However, the objective complement does add information important to the meaning of the sentence.

- We made the *children* model **citizens**.

    In this example, the objective complement, *citizens*, is modified by the adjective *model*. The objective complement is necessary to make the sentence grammatically complete.

- My sister nicknamed *me* Smart **One**.

    In this sentence, *Smart* modifies the objective complement, *One*. The objective complement in this example is not necessary to make the sentence grammatically complete, but it does add information important to the meaning of the sentence.

Objects of Prepositions

A noun can be an object of a preposition—that is, in a phrase beginning with a preposition and ending with a noun, the noun is the object of that preposition. Some common prepositions indicate location: *of, on, to, in, near, below, beneath, beside, over, under, and across*, for example.

In the following examples, the noun objects appearing in prepositional phrases have been italicized.

in the right *mood*	under the *hills*	over the *top*
on the *table*	near the *river*	to a *store*
across the *room*	beneath the *chair*	below the *trees* and *bushes*

Notice that objects of prepositions can have modifiers (*right mood*), they can be plural (*hills*), and they can be compound (*trees and bushes*).

1C VERBS AND TENSES

Verbs are complicated parts of speech. Their parts, forms, and attributes can be categorized and classified in many ways. At the most basic level, verb stems (*be* in *to be, run* in *to run*) change—or, are conjugated—to match the subject in number (singular or plural) and to indicate the time (past, present, or future) when the action of the verb occurs.

The verb attributes that indicate agreement with the subject are *person* and *number*. Examine the present-tense conjugation of the verb *to like*. The columns indicate number, or whether the subject is singular or plural. The rows indicated *person*, or the point of view of the subject.

	Singular	Plural
First Person	I like	we like
Second Person	you like	you like
Third Person	he, she, it likes	they like

A subject is singular in number if it represents one person or thing (as in *I like tomatoes,* or *You [Erica] like tomatoes*). The subject is plural if it represents more than one person or thing (as in *We like tomatoes,* or *You [Erica and Nick] like tomatoes,* or *They like tomatoes*). A first-person subject is either *I* or *we* (*I* plus at least one other person). A second-person subject is either *you* (as one person) or *you* (as more than one person). A third-person subject is one that can be represented by the pronouns *he, she, it,* or a combination—*they.* (Note that in future examples, only *he* [instead of *he, she, it* as illustrated above] will be used to represent the third-person singular.)

The third-person-plural present tense of the verb *to like,* therefore, is *like.* But the third-person-singular present tense of *to like* is *likes.* In order to construct clear and grammatically correct sentences, you must be able to think of verbs in terms of person and number.

The Meaning of Tenses

You must also be able to identify the tenses of verbs. The tense of a verb indicates the point in time when the action of the verb occurs. The conjugation of *to like,* above, was given in present tense—that is, the action of the verb takes place in the present. There are three broad and general tenses—present, past, and future—and, within them, more specific tenses that narrow the time frame and sometimes show its relationship to another time frame.

Present Tense

The present tense is used to indicate an action or event occurring now, at the present time, either immediately (in the present-progressive tense) or as a rule. There are some very fine distinctions to be made regarding *present tense.*

Present tense can indicate habitual action, as in *He eats a hearty breakfast,* or *I play tennis.* It can also express action in the immediate present through the present-progressive form: *He is eating a hearty breakfast,* meaning he is eating *right now* and has not yet finished. Present tense also expresses what are known as general truths, such as *Home is where the heart is,* or *The United States is in North America.*

- This weather feels wonderful.
  This sentence means the weather is great at the moment.

- I live here.
  > This sentence means that this is where I have lived and do live and will live for the foreseeable future.

The present-progressive tense is used to indicate action happening at the very moment the statement is being made.

- I am working hard.
  > In other words, at this very moment, as we speak, I am working hard.
- He is planting flowers.
  > In other words, he can be observed putting flowers into the ground right now.

TIP: All third-person present-tense verbs end in -s, even verbs like *goes, does,* and *is.* Consider the following examples, all of which have correctly conjugated third-person singular verbs.

- John *mows* the lawn each Friday.
- The dog often *howls* at the moon.
- It *looks* like summer.
- Mom *wants* roses.

Past Tense

The past tense is used to indicate an action or event that occurred in the past but did not extend into the present. The action expressed by the verb ended at a particular time and is not ongoing.

- I worked at the restaurant during the holidays.
  > In other words, the holidays are past, and so is my work experience at the restaurant.

Past-Progressive Tense

The past-progressive tense is used to indicate past action that occurs at the same time another past action takes place, or past action that does not have a specific endpoint in time. There is a sense of ongoing, continuing action with all progressive-tense verbs.

- I was eating breakfast when the phone rang.
  > In other words, this morning, as I ate breakfast, someone called on the phone.

Future Tense

The future tense is used to indicate an action or event that hasn't happened yet but is expected to occur sometime after the statement—five minutes from now, next year, etc. The future tense is formed by adding *will* or *shall* to the simple, or base, form of the verb (that is, the infinitive without the *to*).

- I will work in the library after school.
  > This sentence means that right now it's noon, but when school ends three hours from now, I intend to do a particular thing: work in the library.

TIP: Traditionally, the distinction between will and shall is one of volition (*will*) as opposed to obligation (*shall*). Thus *I will do my best on the exam* indicates the speaker's determination to perform well, whereas *I shall attend the funeral* indicates the speaker's

---

articulation of a duty. This distinction can be further illustrated by the way certain questions are posed. If one person invites another to an event, the invitation is expressed as *Shall we go?* not *Will we go?* Thus *shall* functions in a very precise way in relation to the future, a way that incorporates a suggestion of duty almost synonymous with *should*.

Perfect Tenses

Within, or related to, the three major tenses are perfect tenses: present perfect, past perfect, and future perfect.

Present-Perfect Tense

The present perfect is used to indicate an action or event that began at an unspecified time in the past and extends into the present, with no clear boundary that terminates the event or action. It is formed using the present tense auxiliary verb *to have* (*has* or *have*).

A sentence in present-perfect tense sometimes, but not always, specifies the point in time at which the action of the verb originated. The verb stays the same whether or not the beginning point of the action is indicated.

- I have worked here for six weeks.
    In other words, I began working here six weeks ago, and I am still working here. In this example, the phrase *for six weeks* tells us when the past action started.
- I have often gone to that park.
    In other words, I visited that park many times and may do so again. In this example, the point in time at which the past action began is nonspecific.

Past-Perfect Tense

The past-perfect tense is used to indicate an action or event completed in the past *before* some other past action or event. Often, the past-perfect tense is used in a sentence to show a relationship between two or more events in the past. It is formed using the past tense auxiliary verb *to have* (*had*).

- After I had worked for a week, I asked for my pay.
    This sentence means that I started a new job, then, seven days later, I asked for my pay.
- Once I had gotten over the fight, I called to apologize.
    In other words, I got in a fight; I then recovered from the fight. After that, I called to apologize.
- I had painted for about an hour when I started to get muscle cramps.
    In other words, I was still painting an hour later, when I got muscle cramps.

Future-Perfect Tense

The future-perfect tense is used to indicate an action or event that will be completed in the future before some other future action or event. It is formed using *will* or *shall* (indicating future time) and the auxiliary verb *have* (indicating a perfect tense). The auxiliary verb *will* in the future tense does not change according to person or number as verbs ordinarily do in other tenses.

- By the time school starts, I will have worked here eight weeks.
    This sentence means that I am now working here, and when school starts, my working time will total eight weeks.

- At four o'clock, I will have practiced for two hours.

    In other words, I am now practicing, and when four o'clock comes, my practice time will total two hours.

The Formation of Tenses

So far, we have broadly examined verb tenses and how they are used to convey specific meanings associated with occurrences or actions taking place in the past, present, or future. Now we will look at how those tenses are formed.

All verbs have principal parts: the infinitive (which is the tenseless, unconjugated form of the verb as in *to go* or *to sleep*), the present participle, the past tense, and the past participle. The present participle of all verbs always ends in *-ing*. The past tense ends in *-d, -t*, or *-ed* (if the verb is regular), or changes internally (if the verb is irregular, as in *know, knew*). If the verb's present tense ends in *-y* (*obey, deny, play*), add *-ed* directly if the *-y* is preceded by a vowel: *play/played*. If the *-y* is preceded by a consonant, change the *-y* to *-i* before adding the final *-ed*: *deny/denied*.

The past participle of regular verbs is identical to the past tense; in the case of irregular verbs, the past participle may also change internally. Let's look at a few examples, the first three based on regular verbs, the others on irregular verbs.

Infinitive	Present Participle	Past Tense	Past Participle
to hope	hoping	hoped	hoped
to want	wanting	wanted	wanted
to believe	believing	believed	believed
to know	knowing	knew	known
to think	thinking	thought	thought
to begin	beginning	began	begun

Present- and Past-Progressive Tenses

Present- and past-progressive tenses, as we have seen, are versions of the present or past tense, and they suggest either immediate or contemporaneous action. A present-progressive verb conveys a sense of something happening *right now*: *I am eating breakfast*, or *The dog is sleeping*. A past-progressive verb is often combined with another past-tense verb to show simultaneous past action: *The team was winning until Denton tripped and lost the ball*.

Progressive tenses are formed with the present participle, which always ends in *-ing*, and a conjugated form of the auxiliary verb *to be*, in present or past tense, depending on whether the verb is present or past progressive. Present participles, though they are derived from verbs, cannot function as verbs in a sentence, as the following examples show: *I eating breakfast. He looking healthy. They wanting a vacation.* The auxiliary verb is what makes the construction a verb.

Consider the difference between the present- and past-progressive verb, as indicated by the conjugation of the auxiliary verb in the chart below.

Present Progressive		Past Progressive	
I am going	we are going	I was going	we were going
you are going	you are going	you were going	you were going
he is going	they are going	he was going	they were going

The verb *to be*, which is the auxiliary verb in progressive tenses, can be and is used alone as a linking verb. It is conjugated in the present and past tenses below, with complements in parentheses.

I am/was (tired.)   We are/were (here.)
You are/were (handsome.)   You are/were (happy.)
He is/was (clever.)   They are/were (sick.)

Present- and Past-Perfect Tenses

While progressive tenses are formed using the present participle and an auxiliary verb, perfect tenses are formed using the past participle and a different auxiliary verb, a conjugated form of *to have*. Progressive tenses seldom present any difficulty, but perfect tenses can cause confusion, especially when an irregular verb is involved.

A regular verb is one that forms its past tense and past participle by adding -*t* (*keep, kept*), -*d* (*believe, believed*), or -*ed* (*blend, blended*) to the base form of the verb—the form of the verb once the *to* of the infinitive has been omitted. The first verb examined in this section on verb tense, *to like*, is a regular verb. Its past tense is formed by adding -*ed* (*I liked that film*), and so is its past participle (*I have liked that actor for a long time*).

Irregular verbs, on the other hand, form their past tense and/or past participle by changing the verb internally rather than by adding -*ed:cling/clung, meet/met, light/lit, choose/chose.*

UNDERSTANDING IRREGULAR VERBS

Since the past tenses and past participles of irregular verbs are formed in a variety of ways, it is important to know their principal parts (base [or stem], past form, and past participle). Following is a list of common irregular verbs.

Base Verb	Past	Past Participle
arise	arose	arisen
awake	awoke	awakened
bear	bore	borne
beat	beat	beaten
begin	began	begun
bite	bit	bitten
blow	blew	blown
break	broke	broken
bring	brought	brought
burst	burst	burst
catch	caught	caught
come	came	come
creep	crept	crept
dive	dived	dived
do	did	done
draw	drew	drawn
drink	drank	drunk
drive	drove	driven
eat	ate	eaten
fall	fell	fallen
fling	flung	flung

fly	flew	flown
freeze	froze	frozen
give	gave	given
go	went	gone
know	knew	known
lay	laid	laid
lead	led	led
lend	lent	lent
lie	lay	lain
ride	rode	ridden
ring	rang	rung
rise	rose	risen
see	saw	seen
set	set	set
shake	shook	shaken
shine	shone	shone
sink	sank	sunk
sit	sat	sat
speak	spoke	spoken
steal	stole	stolen
sting	stung	stung
swear	swore	sworn
swim	swam	swum
take	took	taken
tear	tore	torn
throw	threw	thrown
write	wrote	written

The past participle and the auxiliary verb *to have* combine to form a complete perfect tense. In the present-perfect tense, the auxiliary verb is in the present tense, while the participle remains unchanged. Consider the following examples of present-perfect verbs.

Forms of the auxiliary verb *to have* are in bold, and the past participles have been italicized.

- I **have** *gone* fishing there many times.
- The dog **has** *fallen* asleep.
- Your snoring **has** *kept* me awake for a week now.
- They **have** *run* that marathon before.
- We **have** *gotten* lazy in our old age.

Sometimes a past participle is mistakenly used alone as the past tense.

Faulty: I seen her walking by.
Correct: I saw her walking by.

Faulty: She begun the job.
Correct: She began the job.

Faulty: He drunk milk.
Correct: He drank milk.

Faulty: He come here yesterday.
Correct: He came here yesterday.

The helping verb *to have* is used with past participles to form perfect tenses. The present-prefect tense is formed by combining the present tense of *to have* with a past participle, as shown in the following examples of the verbs *to see* and *to go*.

I have seen	we have seen	I have gone	we have gone
you have seen	you have seen	you have gone	you have gone
he has seen	they have seen	he has gone	they have gone

Just as it's incorrect to use the past participle as the past tense of a verb (*I seen her walking by*), it's incorrect to combine the past tense of an irregular verb with the helping verb to have to create a perfect tense. Here are some examples of mistakenly combining the past tense, and not the past participle, with a helping verb to create a perfect tense: *He has went to the doctor. They've tore up the land. She's ate all she wants.*

Similarly, you want to make sure you use the auxiliary verb *to have* and not another auxiliary verb to create the present-perfect tense. Sometimes, in speech, you hear an utterance like *He done gone and bought that expensive car,* or *They done ate the peanuts.* In the first example, the past participle of the verb *to do* (*done*) is used as the auxiliary verb, rather than the correct auxiliary verb for a perfect tense, *to have*; in the second case, the same error occurs, with the added error of a past tense (*ate*) used as past participle.

THE AUXILIARY VERB *TO DO*

The verb *to do* is correctly used as an auxiliary verb to establish emphasis. In fact, it is often referred to as the emphatic form.

- She does want to see that film.
- But Billy does brush his teeth.

Notice that the use of the emphatic form changes the conjugation of the main verb: in the examples above, which are both in the third-person singular, *to do* is conjugated, but the main verb appears in simple or base form, without the -s it would ordinarily need. Here are more examples of the emphatic form created by the auxiliary verb *to do*, with additional sentences that show other uses of the emphatic form—to pose a question or create a negation.

- Carla does say what's on her mind.
- She does not know.
- Does he think that he can get away with this crime?

The formation of the past-perfect tense is very simple and consistent: the past tense of *to have* is combined with the past participle. Below are past-perfect conjugations for *to go* and *to write*.

Past Perfect		Past Perfect	
I had gone	we had gone	I had written	we had written
you had gone	you had gone	you had written	we had written
he had gone	they had gone	he had written	they had written

Below is a comparison of present-perfect and past-perfect tenses for the verb *to get*.

Present Perfect		Past Perfect	
I have gotten	we have gotten	I had gotten	we had gotten

| you have gotten | you have gotten | you had gotten | you had gotten |
| he has gotten | they have gotten | he had gotten | they had gotten |

Perfect-Progressive Tenses

Having seen examples of some of the more complicated tenses, we will now conjugate both a regular and an irregular verb in all their tenses, first *to look* and then *to ride*. The more complicated tenses, such as future-perfect progressive, are formed by following the rules already set forth: progressive tenses require a present participle (ending in *-ing*), and perfect tenses require a *to have* auxiliary verb and the past participle. Therefore perfect-progressive tenses employ both.

Present Tense		**Present Progressive**	
I look	we look	I am looking	we are looking
you look	you look	you are looking	you are looking
he looks	they look	he is looking	they are looking

Past		**Past Progressive**	
I looked	we looked	I was looking	we were looking
you looked	you looked	you were looking	you were looking
he looked	they looked	he was looking	they were looking

Present Perfect		**Past Perfect**	
I have looked	we have looked	I had looked	we had looked
you have looked	you have looked	you had looked	you had looked
he has looked	they have looked	he had looked	they had looked

Future		**Future Perfect**	
I will look	we will look	I will have looked	we will have looked
you will look	you will look	you will have looked	you will have looked
he will look	they will look	he will have looked	they will have looked

Present-Perfect Progressive	
I have been looking	we have been looking
you have been looking	you have been looking
he has been looking	they have been looking

Past-Perfect Progressive	
I had been looking	we had been looking
you had been looking	you had been looking
he had been looking	they had been looking

Future-Perfect Progressive	
I will have been looking	we will have been looking
you will have been looking	you will have been looking
he will have been looking	they will have been looking

To ride:

Present Tense		**Present Progressive**	
I ride	we ride	I am riding	we are riding
you ride	you ride	you are riding	you are riding
he rides	they ride	he is riding	they are riding

Past		Past Progressive	
I rode	we rode	I was riding	we were riding
you rode	you rode	you were riding	you were riding
he rode	they rode	he was riding	they were riding

Present Perfect		Past Perfect	
I have ridden	we have ridden	I had ridden	we had ridden
you have ridden	you have ridden	you had ridden	you had ridden
he has ridden	they have ridden	he had ridden	they had ridden

Future		Future Perfect	
I will ride	we will ride	I will have ridden	we will have ridden
you will ride	you will ride	you will have ridden	you will have ridden
he will ride	they will ride	he will have ridden	they will have ridden

Future Progressive	
I will be riding	we will be riding
you will be riding	you will be riding
he will be riding	they will be riding

Present-Perfect Progressive	
I have been riding	we have been riding
you have been riding	you have been riding
he has been riding	they have been riding

Past-Perfect Progressive	
I had been riding	we had been riding
you had been riding	you had been riding
he had been riding	they had been riding

Future-Perfect Progressive	
I will have been riding	we will have been riding
you will have been riding	you will have been riding
he will have been riding	they will have been riding

The verb *to be* plays a prominent role in our language, as an auxiliary verb in a progressive tense or as a linking verb. A conjugation of it in all tenses follows, though some tense formations would not ordinarily be employed in speech or in writing; indeed, some are comical. (Remember: *been* is the past participle; *being* is the present participle.)

Present		Past	
I am	we are	I was	we were
you are	you are	you were	you were
he is	they are	he was	they were

Present Perfect		Past Perfect	
I have been	we have been	I had been	we had been
you have been	you have been	you had been	you had been
he has been	they have been	he had been	they had been

Present Progressive		Past Progressive	
I am being	we are being	I was being	we were being

| you are being | you are being | you were being | you were being |
| he is being | they are being | he was being | they were being |

Future (*shall* can substitute for *will*)   Future Perfect

I will be	we will be	I will have been	we will have been
you will be	you will be	you will have been	you will have been
he will be	they will be	he will have been	they will have been

Future Progressive

I will be being	we will be being
you will be being	you will be being
he will be being	they will be being

Future-Perfect Progressive

I will have been being	we will have been being
you will have been being	you will have been being
he will have been being	they will have been being

Modals

Modals are words that combine with unconjugated main verbs—verbs in their simple or base form—to suggest conditions like need, ability, probability, obligation, likelihood, and permission. Modals include such auxiliary verbs as *can, could, may, might, should, would, must,* and the related *ought to* and *used to*. Modals do not derive from an infinitive (there is no such thing as *to can* or *to must*). Furthermore, modals lack both a present and past participle and cannot be conjugated. Consider the sentences below and note the absence of the third-person-singular -*s*.

- He *must go* to the store right now.
    This sentence suggests need.

- She *can do* that job for you.
    This sentence suggests ability.

- If he *could mow* the lawn, he *would mow* the lawn.
    This sentence (in both its clauses) suggests a lack of ability.

- She *may call* you.
    This sentence suggests possibility or probability.

- He *ought to visit* his mother.
    This sentence suggests obligation.

Modals are often thought of in pairs: *may/might, can/could, will/would,* and *shall/should,* for example. Some definitions hold that *might* is the past tense of *may* and that *could* is the past tense of *can,* though the distinction between *might* and *may* is more often considered one of degree of probability. Generally, *might* is said to convey greater uncertainty than *may: Glenda may go to the show,* in other words, indicates a greater likelihood that Glenda will go to the show than the statement *Glenda might go to the show.* This distinction is a very fine one, and both examples can be interpreted as present or future tense. Past tense can be created by adding *have* before the past participle of the main verb: *Glenda [may/might] have gone to the show.*

The tense difference between *can* and *could* is a bit clearer: *We can hear the choir singing* suggests present tense, whereas *We could hear the choir singing* suggests the action is past. *Could* is most often used to express doubt or possibility (*I could borrow his car if I had to*) or as a synonym for *might: I [might/could] survive without seeing her again.*

The distinction between *can* and *may* is also a fine one. *Can* refers more to ability (*He can carry those heavy boxes*), while *may* refers more to possibility (*He may carry those heavy boxes*). Both *can* and *may* are capable of implying permission.

Modals are commonly used to express nuances. The most important points to remember are that modals, on their own, have no tense, person, or number, and that they are connected, even through their name, to mood. Modals are therefore suggestive and connotative and used in combination with an unconjugated main verb to economically convey such things as contingencies, possibilities, needs, requirements, and abilities.

Mood

Mood is traditionally defined as the quality of a verb that conveys the speaker's attitude toward a subject. To put it another way, mood is the form of the sentence that makes it a statement, a command, or a type of conjecture. There are three types of mood.

Indicative Mood

Indicative mood refers to the expression of a fact or a question. Most statements or questions about real events or things are in indicative mood.

- I went to the store.
- Did you buy milk?
- No, I forgot, but I did get the grapefruit.

Imperative Mood

Imperative mood refers to the expression of a command, an order, or a direct request. Often the subject in an imperative expression is understood—that is, it is omitted—and the verb is in the simple or base form.

- [you] Set the table.
- [you] Eat your dinner.

Subjunctive Mood

Subjunctive mood refers to the expression of wishes, contingencies, conjectures, desires, recommendations, requirements, uncertainties, or anything else contrary to fact. In this respect, its use resembles that of a modal verb, and modals are often used in subjunctive constructions: *If only I could [not can] become president*, or *I wish that they would [not will] call.* The use of the subjunctive is diminishing in our language, particularly in its unconjugated *to be* form: *It is essential that he be present during the ceremony* (not the conjugated *he is*).

The subjunctive has a present and a past tense. The present tense uses the simple or base form of the verb, regardless of person or number.

- I ask that she *refrain* from making those rude remarks.
- Mom requires that Mary clean her room once a week.
- Bob insisted that Mona remove her name from the ballot.
- It is necessary that he be courteous and respectful.

Third-person-singular verbs reveal essential differences in usage. Notice how, in the examples above, the subjunctive appears in a *that* clause following a present- or past-tense main verb and expresses a request, a requirement, or a need. In the examples below, you can see that the expected -s ending is removed from the present-tense examples of the subjunctive.

Indicative (present tense)	Subjunctive (present tense)
he hopes	he hope
he thinks	he think

In the following chart showing the present tense of the verb *to be*, notice how the subjunctive, as a verb in a *that* clause, is unconjugated.

Indicative		Subjunctive	
I am	we are	(that) I be	(that) we be
you are	you are	(that) you be	(that) you be
he is	they are	(that) he be	(that) they be

Here are further examples in sentences of the present-tense subjunctive.

- He asked that she *be informed* of her rights.
- The parents insisted that their daughter *be contacted* immediately.
- They requested that their terminally ill dog *be humanely euthanized*.
- Whether it *be* true or not, the fact remains that he is considered guilty.
- It is important that Bob *arrive* on time.

The subjunctive past tense uses the same past tense as a conjugated verb. Often, past-tense sub-junctives appear in clauses beginning with *if*. This use of the subjunctive is still fairly common, though also fairly formal. Below is a chart showing past-tense indicative and subjunctive.

Indicative		Subjunctive	
I was	we were	I were	we were
you were	you were	you were	you were
he was	they were	he were	they were

Notice that the past subjunctive of *to be* is *were* throughout person and number (in other words, *If he were here, he would say so himself*, is correct, rather than *If he was here, he would say so himself*). As in the present subjunctive, past subjunctive expresses the conditional, contrary-to-fact, conjectural nature of certain statements, and in the past tense is often found in clauses that begin with *if, as if, as though,* or *unless*. Consider the sentences below.

- If the event were not so formal, I would attend.
- It's not as if I were wealthy.
- He behaved as though truth were foreign to him.

1D TYPES OF VERBS: ACTION AND LINKING

Outside of tense, verbs can also be classified according to whether they are action verbs or link-ing verbs. To do so, consider verbs in direct relation to other words within a sentence.

Action Verbs

There are two types of action verbs: transitive and intransitive. Some verbs can be both, and you should always consult your dictionary when in doubt (the dictionary might designate transitive verbs with *tr* or *vt*, and intransitive verbs with *intr* or *vi*).

Transitive Verbs

A transitive verb expresses an action and is followed by an object (a noun or pronoun) that receives the action of the verb or shows the results of the verb's action. For example, in the sentence *John kicked the ball*, the verb indicates an action, *kicked*, and something was kicked, *the ball*. The ball therefore *receives* the action of being kicked. *Kicked*, in this case, is a transitive verb. The *ball* is the direct object.

- The organizers planned the event with great care.
    The *event* receives the action of being planned, so it is the direct object. A very simple way of identifying the direct object is to ask *what?* or *who?* or *whom?* immediately after the verb. If you can answer the question with a noun (a person, place, or thing) or a pronoun, then the verb is transitive—it has a direct object. A prepositional phrase can never be an object (because it is not a noun).

In the sentences below, the verb has been underlined, and the direct object has been italicized.

- Rita <u>washed</u> [what?] the *car* every Saturday.
- The hungry dog <u>ate</u> [what?] the *pizza*.
    Notice that this sentence would be complete without the addition of the object: *The hungry dog ate.* Thus the verb *to eat* is both transitive and intransitive—it can take an object or not.

- He <u>took</u> [whom?] his *brother* to the carnival.
- Justin <u>threw</u> [what?] the *newspaper* into the trash can.
- I accidentally <u>hit</u> [whom?] my *cousin* with a fly ball.

Intransitive Verbs

Intransitive verbs, even though they express action, do not have direct objects. If you apply the *what?* test to an intransitive verb, you can tell immediately that an object cannot follow.

- The child cried [what?] for its mother.
    Clearly, nothing receives the action of the child's crying, though a prepositional phrase modifier, *for its mother*, is present.

In each of the following sentences, the verb has been italicized.

- Mike *laughed* loudly at the joke.
- The children *ran* quickly up the hill and down the neighboring street.
- The wind *strengthened*, howling through the trees and bending the saplings.
- A sinkhole *is opening* underneath the Dades' house.
- The students *have worked* hard on their group project.

Many verbs can be both transitive and intransitive. In the following paired sentences with identical verbs, the direct object of the transitive verb is italicized.

- John kicked wildly as he finished the 100-meter backstroke event.
- John kicked *the ball* down the field.
- The unlucky self-employed consultant filed for bankruptcy.
- Jane filed *the taxes* by April 1.
- The kind gentleman sang to his grandchild.
- *The kind gentleman* sang the song to his grandchild.
    In this example, *to his grandchild* is a prepositional phrase and not an indirect object. (A prepositional phrase can never be an object [or a subject], because it is not a noun.)

Although you probably would not mistakenly use a transitive verb as an intransitive verb (*I am hitting with my brother*), there are certain verbs that typically do cause confusion: *lay* and *lie*, *sit* and *set*, and *rise* and *raise*. To avoid misusing these verbs, distinguish them according to meaning.

Lie denotes a state of being in a certain position—reclining, or stretching out on the couch or in bed—and *lay* denotes the act of placing an item somewhere. Therefore, *lie* is an intransitive verb, and *lay* is a transitive verb—and both happen to be irregular. Their tense formation overlaps, and hence the confusion: *lay* is the past tense of to *lie*, which is an intransitive verb, and *lay* is also the present tense of *to lay*, a transitive verb. Let's first examine *to lie* in its tenses, recalling that it is an intransitive verb.

Present Tense		Past Tense (Past Participle: lain)	
I lie	we lie	I lay	we lay
you lie	you lie	you lay	you lay
he lies	they lie	he lay	they lay

To express the action of someone who reclined on a couch yesterday, you would say *Bob lay on the couch all afternoon.* However, if Bob regularly and habitually spends the afternoon on the couch, you would say, *Bob lies on the couch.* To show that Bob sometimes does and will continue to lie on the couch, the present perfect would be used: *Bob has lain on the couch.* In none of these sentences, however, was anything (including Bob) *put* on the couch.

Now let's consider the conjugation of *to lay*.

Present Tense		Past Tense (Past Participle: laid)	
I lay	we lay	I laid	we laid
you lay	you lay	you laid	you laid
he lays	they lay	he laid	they laid

The statement *I lay the book on the table every day* contains a transitive verb in the present tense, with *the book* as the direct object. If placing the book on the table occurred yesterday, the sentence would read *I laid the book on the table.* In all cases, *to lay* must have an object, and *to lie* must not. The following sentences illustrate how confusion can arise.

- The mason lays brick for a living.
  The verb is transitive, present tense: *to lay*.

- The mason regularly lies down to rest.
  The verb is intransitive, present tense: *to lie*.

- The bricks lie on the ground until the mason lays them.
  The first verb is *to lie*: present tense, intransitive; the second verb is *to lay*: present tense, transitive.

Similarly, *to sit* is an irregular intransitive verb, and its principal parts (present, past form, and past participle) are *sit*, *sat*, and *sat*, whereas *to set* is an irregular transitive verb, and its principal parts are *set*, *set*, and *set*. Compare the following sentences, which have their past tenses in parentheses.

- I sit (or sat) on the bench, waiting for the bus.
- I set (or set) [what?] lunch out for the boys.

Likewise, the distinction between *rise* and *raise* is one of transitivity. *To rise* is intransitive (and irregular), with the principal parts *rise, rose, risen; to raise* is transitive (and regular), with the principal parts *raise, raised,* and *raised*. Compare the following sentences, which have their past tenses in parentheses.

- I raise (raised) [whom?] my children to be polite and considerate.
- I rise (or rose or have risen) early.

SVO SENTENCE PATTERN

As noted in section 1B, sentence patterns are often designated by the initials of the major sentence elements. Thus a sentence containing only a subject and a verb would be labeled *SV*.

- The dog snored loudly.
  In this sentence, *dog* is the subject and *snored* is the verb (modified by the adverb *loudly*).

Sentences containing a subject, a verb, and an object would be labeled SVO. This type of sentence pattern is more common than the skeletal SV pattern.

- The kids played kick-the-can until bedtime.
  In this sentence, the subject is *kids*, the verb is *played*, and *kick-the-can* is the object of the verb *to play* (a verb which can also be intransitive).

However, as mentioned earlier, sentences with specifically transitive verbs *must* be completed by an object. The following sentences show the problem with omitting an object from a sentence containing a transitive-only verb.

- He devoted.
- They brought.
- We eulogized.

Linking Verbs

If a verb—with or without an object—does not communicate an action, then it expresses a state of being by connecting the subject of the sentence to the subjective complement. Such a verb is a linking verb, and although *to be* is the most common, other verbs also function to link the subject with the complement: *appear, seem, become, feel, sound, taste, grow, look, remain.*

A complement is either a noun or an adjective following the verb and is equivalent in identity to the subject of the sentence. In the sentence *She is president,* the term *president* identifies her—in other words, *president* is what she *is*. To determine whether a verb links the subject with the complement, imagine the verb as an equal sign. Consider the following sentences, which have *to be* as a linking verb in various tenses. The linking verbs have been underlined and the complements have been italicized.

- Roger has been *depressed* lately.
- The tree is *greener and leafier* this year than last.
- They were *happy* with the results of the election.
- Maria was *an athlete* in high school.
- Norma and I are *cochairs* of the committee next week.

In the first three sentences, the complements are adjectives called predicate adjectives. In the last two sentences, the complements are nouns called predicate nominatives. Whether an adjective or a noun, the complement shares an identity with the subject: *depressed* describes what Roger *is; greener and leafier* describes what the tree *is; an athlete* describes what Maria *was*.

1E ACTIVE AND PASSIVE VOICE

Another characteristic of verbs is *voice*, a term referring to the agent of action within the sentence. A verb is said to be in *active voice* if the subject of the sentence performs the action expressed by the verb, as in *John hit the ball. John* is the subject, and he is also performing the action of hitting. However, if the sentence were constructed *The ball was hit by John*, John would no longer be the subject, though he is still performing the action of hitting. In this case, the verb is said to be in *passive voice*, because the actual subject is not performing the action expressed by the verb. In passive voice, the performer of the action (John) has been tucked into a prepositional phrase—*by John*—and the object of the verb, *ball*, from the active-voice sentence, has been bumped into the subject position. Is the second sentence therefore incorrect? No, it isn't, but it creates a strange and unnecessary sense of disembodied action.

In some cases, the agent of action is not known or cannot be named.

- It is going to rain.
- The product was recalled because of contamination.

Sometimes in scientific writing, the agent of the action is not as important as the action itself, and therefore passive voice is used.

- The experiment was performed using four gallons of milk.

The following sentence pairs are constructed first in active voice, then in passive voice, so that you can compare the constructions.

- The youngsters ate all the pie before the party.
- The pie was eaten by the youngsters before the party.

- My son wrecked the car late last night.
- The car was wrecked by my son late last night.

- The storm damaged the crops and tore up the land.
- The crops were damaged and the land torn up by the storm.

In each pair, the sentence in active voice is shorter and more direct. Notice also that each active-voice verb has a direct object that is converted, in the second sentence of the pair, to the subject. Therefore, only transitive verbs can be converted to passive voice.

Finally, note that the actual verb in the passive-voice construction has its own unique form: a conjugation of *to be*, followed by a past participle: *was eaten, was wrecked, were damaged*.

Notice that the *to be* verb can appear in various tenses.

- Maria has been chosen.
  The verb is in the present-perfect tense with passive voice.

- Maria had been chosen.
  The verb is in the past-perfect tense with passive voice.

- Maria will have been chosen.
  The verb is in the future-perfect tense with passive voice.

- I am being cheated.
  The verb is in the present-progressive tense with passive voice.

- Roger was being scolded.
  The verb is in the past-progressive tense with passive voice.

A variation on all the sentences above involves the *get* form of the passive.

- Maria got chosen.
- I got cheated.
- Roger got scolded.

CHAPTER 2

MODIFIERS AND OTHER PARTS OF SPEECH

Now that we have examined the building blocks of sentences—nouns and verbs—we can move on to the embellishments that either limit meaning or add further information (as well as direction, color, and detail to the basic grammatical unit).

2A ADJECTIVES

An adjective modifies a noun or a pronoun by providing information that describes, clarifies, expands, or limits it. Most adjectives can appear before or after the word modified, and adjectives answer these questions: *what kind? which one? how many?* An adjective describes by contributing specific characteristics to a person, place, or thing in order to help the reader visualize or appreciate it.

In the following examples, the adjectives have been italicized and the nouns they are modifying have been boldfaced.

- Smith's *oblong* **pond**
- a *spindly* **redwood**
- his *hideous* **lie**
- the *bloodshot* **eye**
- *guilty* **pleasures**
- my *spectacular* **view**

Notice that certain of the preceding adjectives were purely descriptive, whereas others added an element of subjective perception. Notice also that the italicized descriptive word was often accompanied by another modifier—an article (*the, a*), a pronoun (*his, my*), or the possessive form of a proper noun (*Smith's*). All those words function as adjectives because they tell something about the noun they're attached to. Below are words that modify nouns or pronouns, classified according to parts of speech.

Definite and Indefinite Articles

The definite article—*the*—points to only one particular example or instance of something: *the dog, the answer, the spaghetti*. An indefinite article—*a* or *an*—is more general because it points to any example of something: *a dog, an answer* (*spaghetti* can't be preceded by *an* indefinite article because it is a noncount concrete noun). Articles are sometimes referred to as *noun determiners* because they signal that a noun is about to appear; they are also termed "limiting adjectives" because their presence before a noun eliminates the possibility that the noun could be misconstrued as something else: *the dog* means one specific dog, not another; *a child* means child, not monkey.

Pronouns

Many pronouns also function as adjectives because they tell something about the noun (or pronoun) they modify: *my book, their house, your money*. The preceding examples are of possessive pronouns, but other types of pronouns can also act as adjectives: demonstrative pronouns (*this, these, that, those*); indefinite pronouns (*several, all, any, few, each, both, many, either, neither, some*); interrogative pronouns (*what, which, whose*); and relative pronouns (*who, which, that, whose, whatever, whichever*). Words that function as cardinal or ordinal numbers are also adjectives: *one, first, two, second,* and so forth. The following sentences show how these pronouns (italicized), frequently referred to as limiting adjectives, modify the nouns to which they are attached.

- *This* car is fast.
- The *first* person in line will be admitted early.
- *Many* people prefer lasagna to macaroni.
- I am unsure *which* film you are referring to.
- *Both* dogs are sleeping on the porch.

An adjective can appear before or after the noun it modifies. In the typical sequence, an adjective appears before a noun: *the full moon, an ordinary evening, this distressing event.* However, an adjective can also appear post-position—that is, following the noun it modifies: *the sky so blue, the man possessed, a land unexplored.* Adjectives can also be compound or in series (see Chapter 18 for a full discussion of this topic).

Multiple adjectives modifying the same noun or pronoun are considered either coordinate or cumulative; if coordinate, each adjective could modify the noun separately, so commas are used, as in any series: *The overripe, bursting, odiferous mangoes seeped onto the countertop.* Notice that the arrangement of these adjectives has no particular order or rationale; each modifier might appear elsewhere in the series, and *and* could be placed between them: *The bursting and odiferous and overripe mangoes seeped onto the countertop.*

Cumulative adjectives, on the other hand, are not equivalent to a punctuated series because the first adjective in the group is not individually modifying the noun but is instead modifying the noun-modifier combination that follows. For example, in the phrase *obsolete desktop computer, obsolete* modifies *desktop computer* and *desktop* modifies *computer.* These adjectives cannot appear in a different order (*the desktop obsolete computer*), nor can they be connected with and (*the desktop and obsolete computer*).

Adjectives following the noun they modify can also be set off by commas, as in a typical noun-appositive pattern, here presented with compound adjectives: *The children, muddy and shivering, finally came inside for hot chocolate.* Notice that *shivering* is a present participle. Both past and present participles are very common modifiers.

In the sentences that follow, the past and present participles have been italicized.

- *Crying* and *exhausted*, the young child got out of bed.
- The *howling* dog broke my heart.
- Our *skidding* car bumped a stalled bus.
- The *leaping, spinning* clown amused our bored children.

Subjective and Objective Complements

Adjectives also appear as complements, either subjective or objective (see Chapter 1 for a discussion of complements). Complements are nouns sharing an identity with either the subject or the object, but complements can also be adjectives sharing that identity. In the following examples, the complements have been italicized.

- She is *president*.
    In this sentence, the complement is a noun (a predicate nominative).

- She is *wealthy*.
    In this sentence, the complement is a predicate adjective.

Predicate adjectives modify the noun subject, as the following sentences illustrate, often in conjunction with a greater variety of linking verbs than the forms of *to be* most often used with predicate nominatives. In the sentences below, the predicate adjectives have been italicized.

- The dog seems *listless* and *ill*.
- He felt *abused, lost*, and *overwhelmed*.
- The parrot finally grew *quiet*.

As objective complements, adjectives follow the direct or indirect object, just as nouns functioning as objective complements do. In each of the following pairs, the first sentence contains a noun objective complement, and the second, an adjective. The objective complements have been italicized.

- She called her boyfriend an *idiot*.
- She called her boyfriend *idiotic*.

- She thought the film a *bore*.
- She thought the film *boring*.

- She considered him an *incompetent*.
- She considered him *incompetent*.

Notice that in the last pair, an adjective is used as a noun: an *incompetent*. Similarly, other adjectives can function as nouns: *the rich, the poor, the young, the restless, the beautiful, the smart, the disadvantaged, the good, the bad, the ugly.*

Comparative and Superlative Adjectives

One of the most important characteristics of adjectives is that they express degree—comparative and superlative. For example, the sky may be blue, but it also may be bluer in Florida than in

Ohio (according to someone's perception), and it may be bluest of all in the Bahamas (again, according to a comparison of blue skies made by a particular viewer). All adjectives are capable of evolving from their original descriptive form to a more intense form of themselves, with the superlative indicating either the greatest degree or a comparison among more than two things.

Adjective	Comparative	Superlative
nice	nicer	nicest
good	better	best
friendly	friendlier	friendliest
many	more	most
bad	worse	worst
clean	cleaner	cleanest
thankful	more thankful	most thankful
little	less	least
few	fewer	fewest

Thus you would say of two choices that one of them was *better* than the other, not *best*, and if you received *bad* news that was worse than other bad news, it would be the *worst* news of all. If parents have two children, and one behaves better than the other, then that child is the *better* behaved, not the *best* behaved. If three people were to present arguments for claiming the same prize, the *strongest*, *clearest* argument would prevail; but if only two people claimed the prize, then the *stronger*, *clearer* argument would win.

The general rule for creating the comparative and the superlative is to add *-er* or *-est* to the original modifier (*pink, pinker, pinkest*). However, there are exceptions and additional rules.

1. When the adjective ends in *-y*, drop the *-y* and add *-ier* or *-iest* (*lovely, lovelier, loveliest*).

2. When the adjective has three or more syllables, you generally add *more* or *most* to the original modifier: *considerate, more considerate, most considerate*.

3. Be aware of exceptions, as with two-syllable adjectives ending in *-ful, -less, -ish, -able, -al*, and *-some*, for example: *more grateful/most grateful, more worthless/most worthless, more stylish/ most stylish, more sinkable/most sinkable, more venal/most venal, more loathsome/most loathsome*.

4. *More* and *most* should never be paired with an adjective that has a changed form in the comparative or superlative: *more worse, more uglier, most friendliest, most cleanest*.

In all cases of negative rather than positive comparison, *less* or *fewer* is comparative, and *least* or *fewest* is superlative.

- There are *fewer* cookies in this jar than there were yesterday.
- Nick is *less* sympathetic than his brother.
- My husband and I are *least* impressed with that particular candidate's positions.
- In fact, he received the *fewest* votes of all.

Few in all its forms is used to modify only a plural (and therefore count) noun, whereas *less* in all its forms is used to modify noncount nouns: *I have fewer pairs of shoes than you do. There is less sand on Fernandina Beach this year. The few apples remaining were rotten. Nick likes Bob least of all.* In addition, *less* and its forms can be adjectives or adverbs, but *few* and its forms can only be adjectives.

Adjectives may appear in hyphenated form, as discussed thoroughly in Chapter 24. Whenever several adjectives combine to make a single-word modifier, that combination is hyphenated all the way to the last word constituting the modifier. The hyphenated modifiers in the examples below have been italicized.

- His *over-the-top* approach to sales is driving customers away.
- The spoiled child's *give-me-what-I-want-right-now* attitude alienates other children.
- The *Spanish-speaking* population of Florida is quite large.
- His reaction to her *ill-timed* remark made everyone laugh.
- My *well-developed, fast-paced* argument won the debate.

WORD FORMS

Many words have more than one form, and can be used as several different parts of speech.

Verb	Noun	Adjective
comply	compliance	compliant
obey	obedience	obedient
deduce	deduction	deductive
rely	reliance	reliable
care	care	careful
act	action	active, actionable
accept	acceptance	acceptable
recommend	recommendation	recommendable
analyze	analysis	analytical
recognize	recognition	recognizable

In some instances, the noun form of a word ends in *-ness: ugly/ugliness, holy/holiness, great/greatness, flat/flatness, earnest/earnestness, hopeful/hopefulness, cheerful/cheerfulness,* and so forth.

2B ADVERBS

Adverbs are flexible, all-purpose modifiers providing detail and information about verbs, adjectives, and other adverbs. Many adverbs are clearly and easily recognizable because they describe how an action was performed—that is, they modify a verb as opposed to a noun. Many end in *-ly: ran quickly, ate heartily, slept soundly, fought valiantly.* Often, adverbs follow the verb they modify, whereas adjectives often appear before the noun they modify: *The man ran awkwardly* vs. *The awkward man ran.*

Adverbs also modify adjectives. In the following examples, the adjectives have been bold-faced and the adverbs have been italicized.

- a *very* **bright** color
- a *seemingly* **insignificant** event
- an *easily* **misplaced** item
- a *distinctly* **loud** voice
- a *sharply* **focused** argument
- a *wonderfully* **complete** analysis

Finally, adverbs modify other adverbs. In each of following sentences, the adverb being modified has been boldfaced and the adverb modifying that adverb has been italicized.

- She writes *remarkably* **slowly**.
- He moved *quite* **deliberately**.

- They drove *somewhat* **erratically**.
- The young child paints *rather* **hesitantly**.

By answering the questions *when? where? to what extent? how? how often? how much? and why?*, adverbs provide information about time and duration, place, degree, manner, and cause. Adverbs that stipulate time or duration (*when? how long? how often?*) include *always, early, finally, late, never, next, now, often, seldom, sometimes, soon, still, subsequently, then, tomorrow,* and *yesterday.* Certain of the words in that list are nouns that can act as adverbs—*tomorrow* and *yesterday,* for example: *Tomorrow is another day* vs. *I will call mom tomorrow.* An individual word functions grammatically within the context of the sentence according to its relationship with other words.

Adverbs that stipulate place (*where?*) include *above, around, behind, below, down, elsewhere, everywhere, here, in, inside, off, out, outside, over, somewhere, there,* and *up.* When these words are single-word modifiers, they function as adverbs: *Barbara looked inside,* or *He was cut off in traffic.* However, these same words designating location can be prepositions when they begin a phrase.

Another type of adverb doesn't have the *-ly* suffix and is identical in form to an adjective—that is, the same word can be used to modify both nouns and verbs (and adjectives and other adverbs): *far, fast, hard, slow, little, loose, early, quick, near, long, high, late, straight, ill,* and *well* are examples. In each of the sentence pairs below, the italicized word acts as an adjective in the first sentence, but as an adverb in the second.

- John thought the test was *hard*.
- John ran so *hard* he was out of breath.

- Her *late* arrival stunned us.
- Nick arrived *late*.

- John drew a *straight* line.
- John walked *straight* into the line of fire.

It is important to note that some adjectives end in *-ly,* just as some adverbs do: *ghastly, ghostly, friendly, costly, deadly, homely, likely, ugly, timely, lonely,* and *sisterly,* for example. In the sentences below, the nouns have been boldfaced, and the *-ly* adjectives modifying them have been italicized.

- The company replied to my request in a *timely* **fashion**.
- I like *homely, lonely* **dogs**.
- The *friendly* **neighbor** brought newcomers a pie.
- What a *ghastly* **shirt**!

In some cases, the adjectival form of a word can be converted to an adverb by adding an *-ly* suffix.

Adjective	Adverb
magnificent	magnificently
beautiful	beautifully
soft	softly
neat	neatly
cold	coldly
strong	strongly

Some adverbs have two forms: *loud/loudly, near/nearly, tight/tightly, clean/cleanly, deep/deeply, quick/quickly, and slow/slowly,* for example.

- The child cried *loudly* for his mother.
- Robert spoke *loud* and clear.

- Margot *nearly* won the election.
- The plane flew uncomfortably *near* ours.

- I care *deeply* for you.
- They must have dug *deep* to find that oil.

Certain of these dual-form adverbs can be used interchangeably.

- Come *quick!*
- Come *quickly.*

- Hold the rope *tight.*
- Hold the rope *tightly.*

Others, however, have only one appropriate usage. You would not, for example, use *clean* in the following sentence: *The cut was cleanly defined.* Nor would you use *cleanly* in this sentence: *He was cut clean to the bone.*

Comparative and Superlative Adverbs

Adverbs, like adjectives, have comparative and superlative forms: When two items are being compared, the comparative is used, and when more than two items are being compared, the superlative is used. The rules for creating those forms resemble the rules for creating degree in adjectives. Most adverbs ending in *-ly* form their comparative and superlative by using *more* and *most.*

Adverb	Comparative	Superlative
soundly	more soundly	most soundly
valiantly	more valiantly	most valiantly
slowly	more slowly	most slowly

Most adverbs having one syllable or ending in *-y* form the comparative by adding *-ier* or *-er* and the superlative by adding *-iest* or *-est.*

Adverb	Comparative	Superlative
easy	easier	easiest
early	earlier	earliest
fast	faster	fastest
slow	slower	slowest
high	higher	highest

Others form comparatives and superlatives irregularly, just as certain adjectives do.

Adverb	Comparative	Superlative
badly	worse	worst
little	less	least
much	more	most
well	better	best

You may have noticed that the comparative and superlative forms of *badly, well,* and *much* are the same as the comparative and superlative forms of the adjectives *bad, good,* and *many.* These terms are often mistakenly used interchangeably. *Bad* is an adjective, and therefore as a complement would correctly express the self-state described in a sentence that uses the linking verb *to feel: I feel bad.*

The difference between *good* and *well* is complicated, largely because *good* is always an adjective, but *well* can be either an adjective or an adverb. As an adjective, *well* can suggest a state of health opposite to *ill: Dad's been feeling well for a week now.* Well can also suggest a state of being: *All's well that ends well.* (In this sentence, *well* is used first as an adjective and then as an adverb.)

As an adverb, *well* can be combined with another modifier to form a pre-noun modifier that conveys a degree of success: *well-considered, well-dressed, well-manicured.* Also as an adjective, *well* conveys a successful performance: *John played that sonata very well.* It would be inaccurate to say *John played that sonata good,* although this error is a common one. Similarly, stating *I don't feel good* is akin to saying *I feel badly*—because *good* is an adjective. Such a sentence would be saying that the feel of you—to someone performing the act of feeling—was unpleasant. In other words, someone touching you wouldn't find the experience a positive one. Likewise, if you said *We ran the race good,* you would be erroneously using an adjective, *good,* to modify a verb, *ran.*

Less and *least* are the comparative and superlative of *little: I eat very little. She eats less than Mark does. He eats least at breakfast.* A common usage error involves *few* and *less* and *fewer* and *less.* As adjectives or adverbs, the forms of *less* indicate that the thing being modified cannot be counted—it is an indivisible unit, a whole, something like *water, respect, hope, grass.*

On the other hand, *few* and its forms apply to things that can be individually counted and therefore pluralized: *dogs, chairs, raisins.* Likewise, the use of *much* and *many* depends on whether the word being modified is a count or noncount noun: *Much of the lemonade was simply too sour* vs. *Many of the lemons were simply too sour.*

Conjunctive Adverbs

There is a form of adverb that connects ideas on the sentence level or beyond by showing such relationships as cause, addition, contrast, and emphasis. The following conjunctive adverbs, which, as their name suggests, are also a type of conjunction, are used to provide transition between independent clauses: *accordingly, also, anyhow, besides, consequently, finally, furthermore, hence, however, indeed, instead, likewise, meanwhile, moreover, nevertheless, nonetheless, otherwise, still, then, therefore,* and *thus.* Conjunctive adverbs can provide transition at the beginning of a sentence—*Meanwhile, Rome was burning*—and they can also join clauses internally, as the following sentences illustrate (notice the punctuation).

- Marty chaired the meeting successfully; *however*, doing so left him exhausted.
- Donna prefers small vehicles; *consequently*, she purchased an English SmartCar.

2C PREPOSITIONS

We have just examined single-word modifiers: adjectives and adverbs. Sometimes whole phrases function as adjectives and adverbs.

A preposition is used to introduce a prepositional phrase, which contains additional modifying words and an object (either a noun or pronoun, single or compound). The following sentence pairs illustrate how single-word modifiers—in this case, adjectives—can be expanded into prepositional phrases. In the examples below, the adjectives and prepositional phrases have been italicized.

- Donna loves *tomato-based* pasta sauces.

- Donna loves pasta *with red sauce*.
- Dick recently bought a *lakeside* cabin.
- Dick recently bought a cabin by the lake.

The following sentence pairs illustrate how single-word modifiers—in this case, adverbs—can also be expanded into prepositional phrases.

- Nick lives *recklessly*.
- Nick lives *with reckless abandon*.

- She worked *hurriedly*.
- She worked *in a hurry*.

The difference between these sentence pairs is largely rhetorical—that is, one sentence would be chosen over another for purposes of style or economy. Many words that function as single-word adverbs become prepositions when followed by additional words including a noun or pronoun object.

- *in* the river
- *out of* luck
- *as well as* the scores

The following is a list of single-word prepositions: *about, above, across, after, against, along, amid, among, around, as, at, before, behind, below, beneath, beside, besides, between, beyond, by, concerning, despite, down, during, except, for, from, in, inside, including, into, like, of, off, on, onto, out, over, near, past, regarding, since, through, throughout, to, toward, under, underneath, until, unto, up, upon, while, with, within,* and *without*. (Many of the single-word prepositions listed above [such as *about, across, since*] can also be adverbs. The words are designated certain parts of speech depending on their function within a sentence.)

Compound prepositions are formed by combining single-word prepositions: *across from, alongside of, ahead of, apart from, by means of, down by, down under, in case of, in favor of, in front of, in regard to, in spite of, inside of, on account of, regardless of, such as,* and *together with*.

Because prepositional phrases can substitute for single-word modifiers, they can take the position in a sentence of a single word modifier—a subjective complement (a predicate adjective) or an objective complement. In each of the following sentences, the prepositional phrase used as a predicate adjective has been italicized.

- Robert was *in a snit*.
- Joe is *beneath contempt*.
- Physics is *over my head*.

The following sentences contain prepositional phrases that function as objective complements—they modify the object.

- Physics is a subject *beyond my mental abilities*.
- He considered himself *in trouble* and *out of luck*.
- He found her *out of sorts*.

It is often said that prepositions should never fall at the end of a sentence, that it is incorrect to write something like *Who should I give this book to?* Only in formal circumstances, however, would a person feel obliged to write or say *To whom should I give this book?* Even then, someone would be unlikely to write *About what are you upset?* instead of *What are you upset about?* Typically, sentences such as the following, all of which end in prepositions, are perfectly acceptable.

- Where do you come from?
- I don't know what the utensil is used for.
- They don't fully understand the predicament they're in.
- He uttered words to live by.
- Their solution was an outcome we could live with.

In fact, there is a famous quotation that comically illustrates the difficulty with trying to avoid ending a sentence with a preposition: *This is something up with which I will not put.* Even though it's acceptable to end a sentence with a preposition, you should always be careful not to double up unnecessarily on prepositions anywhere (or to use them redundantly), especially at the end of the sentence.

- Bob is going to jump *off of* the bridge using a parachute.
   Off indicates direction, so *of* is not needed.
- Where are my glasses *at*?
   At repeats the request for location already articulated by *where*.

Sometimes prepositional phrases cause confusion that can be avoided if you remember that modifying phrases can never function as nouns—if they are modifiers, then they must tell more about a noun or pronoun. However, when a prepositional phrase begins a sentence, it can be tempting to identify it as the subject. Consider the following.

- In the tropical foliage croaked a newborn tree frog.

We are so accustomed to expecting an SVO (subject-verb-object), SVC (subject-verb-complement), or even an SV (subject-verb) construction, that the first word or group of words automatically seems to be the subject. However, a prepositional phrase can't function as a noun, so *In the tropical foliage* cannot be the subject. In cases of inverted construction—that is, constructions that don't follow a typical and expected progression—identify the verb first: What is the action or state of being expressed by the sentence? The answer is *croaked*. Ask yourself then who or what was performing the action of croaking. The answer is *a newborn tree frog*. Recast, then, into an SV construction, the sentence reads: *A newborn tree frog croaked in the tropical foliage.* In inverted constructions, the verb comes before the subject, subverting all our expectations.

2D CONJUNCTIONS

All conjunctions serve to connect parts of sentences—words with other words in compounds and series, phrases with similar phrases, clauses with clauses, etc. The three types of conjunctions are coordinating, correlative, and subordinating.

Coordinating Conjunctions

Coordinating conjunctions create balanced structures because they join similar sentence components. They can easily be remembered by the mnemonic device *fanboys: for, and, nor, but, or, yet, so.*

- John ate fruit, *and* Nick ate a sandwich for lunch.
- The children ran, skipped, screamed, *and* played all afternoon.
- He asked, *but* no one answered.

- Sam didn't speak, *nor* did Ralph.
- I will eat pie, *or* I will eat cake.
- He is angry, *so* he will not speak.

Correlative Conjunctions

These conjunctions are especially tricky and are discussed at length in chapter 7, which looks at parallelism. Correlative conjunctions include the following.

> not only … but also
> either … or
> neither … nor
> both … and

These conjunctions must join items that are alike: *not only my mother but also my father; not only his feelings but also his intellect; not only the house but also the car; neither the cats nor the dogs; either my brother or my sister.*

Subordinating Conjunctions

Subordinating conjunctions introduce dependent clauses, and therefore, unlike coordinating conjunctions, they join sentence elements that are not balanced grammatically: one is dependent on the other. Subordinating conjunctions include *after, although, as, as if, as long as, as though, because, before, even though, if, in order that, provided that, once, since, so that, that, though, unless, until, when, where,* and *while.* Notice the difference between these two sentences.

- After the rain, we went shopping.
     After is a preposition introducing a prepositional phrase.
- After the rain had stopped, we went shopping.
     After is a subordinating conjunction introducing a dependent clause.

Adverbs have a form that serves as a conjunction—that is, conjunctive adverbs join two independent clauses when used with the proper punctuation. Conjunctive adverbs include *moreover, however, therefore, thus, hence, consequently, furthermore, nevertheless, instead,* and *then.*

Many people believe that it is improper or incorrect to begin a sentence with a conjunction. However, it is acceptable to do so. Beginning a sentence with a conjunction ties it to the previous sentence.

- John failed his final exams. *But* what the heck, he didn't care.
- Ellen called frequently. *Not only* did she attempt to communicate, *but also* she sent gifts.
- I dislike your behavior. *Furthermore,* I dislike the attitudes behind the behavior.

2E INTERJECTIONS

Interjections are the simplest part of speech. In a nutshell, they include abrupt additions to conversation or writing: *oops! whoops! ouch! yikes!* Interjections are often accompanied by exclamation marks, a form of punctuation that should be used sparingly.

2F PRONOUNS

Pronouns take the place of nouns or other pronouns and help us avoid redundancies such as *Sara left Sara's purse on Sara's bed because Sara was in a hurry.* Instead of awkwardly repeating ourselves, we have the language to make our meaning clear using other parts of speech: *Sara left her purse on her bed because she was in a hurry.*

Despite their seemingly simple function, however, pronouns are complicated parts of speech; so much so, in fact, that we devote three chapters to examining them. For our purposes here, then, we will just briefly consider different kinds of pronouns: personal (and possessive), reflexive/intensive, relative, interrogative, indefinite, reciprocal, and demonstrative.

One of the complications regarding pronouns is case—the form of pronoun that identifies how it is used within the sentence. For example, we would use one case of pronoun for a subject—*We like tomatoes*—but another case for an object—*Bob gave us tomatoes.* Although it is unlikely that you will make errors in case (*Us like tomatoes* and *Bob gave we tomatoes*) it is important that you understand this basic difference.

SUBJECTIVE CASE		OBJECTIVE CASE	
Singular	Plural	Singular	Plural
I	we	me	us
you	you	you	you
he, she, it	they	him, her, it	them

Notice how some pronouns are used as subjects and some are used as objects in the following sentences.

- *We* elected *them* to office, so *we*'d better get used to excess.
- *They* wanted *us* to give you a call.
- *She* contacted *him* to apologize.
- *He* believed that *I* deceived *him*.
- *You* chose *her* as a companion?

Personal pronouns also have a possessive form—that is, a form that is adjectival and signals ownership of an item, a trait, or an idea. These pronouns are modifiers and do not have case.

Singular	Plural
my, mine	ours
your, yours	your, yours
his, her, hers, its	their, theirs

Reflexive and Intensive Pronouns

Personal pronouns that have the suffix *-self* or *-selves* attached perform highly specific functions in sentences, though they are mistakenly used in other ways. When used reflexively, these pronouns must follow a previously used pronoun and refer back directly to it in an instance of shared identity: *I shot myself in the foot. Nick found a message on his answering machine that he had left for himself earlier.*

Singular	Plural
myself	ourselves
yourself	yourselves
himself, herself, itself	themselves

Never combine a plural pronoun with the singular suffix: *themself.*

Relative Pronouns

Relative pronouns introduce clauses that are used as either adjectives or nouns. These pronouns (in some instances referred to as relative adjectives or relative adverbs) are not broken down according to person and number. They include *who, which, that, whom, what,* and *whose.* In the sentences below, the adjectival and nominative clauses have been italicized, and the relative pronouns that introduce these clauses have been boldfaced.

- The man **who** *told me the story* lives down the street.
- **That** *I love pizza* is a well-known fact.
- Lola forgot **whose** *book it was.*

Interrogative Pronouns

Interrogative pronouns are fairly simple, and many are identical to relative pronouns. Again, their classification depends on how they are used within a sentence. An interrogative pronoun begins a question: *Who went to the party? What did you bring? Which couples showed up late? Whose house was it held at?*

Demonstrative Pronouns

Demonstrative pronouns, which, like possessive pronouns, are modifiers, are also fairly simple, though they often are used incorrectly. The four demonstrative pronouns are *this,* which has *these* as its plural, and *that,* which has *those* as its plural. In all instances, these pronouns point: *this book, these books; that house, those houses.* Errors arise when personal pronouns are used as demonstrative pronouns: *them books, them houses.* Errors also arise when demonstrative pronouns are used to point sweepingly to entire sentences, paragraphs, ideas, or concepts—to anything more than a specific object or abstraction: *This is true.*

Indefinite Pronouns

There are many indefinite pronouns; some are singular, some are plural, and some can be both. Although many typical singular indefinite pronouns sound as if they represent more than one person, when paired with a verb it is clear they don't. Indefinite pronouns include *anybody, anyone, each, either, everybody, everyone, neither, nobody, no one, one, somebody,* and *someone.* The sentences *Everybody are here* and *Someone are in the yard* clearly show that these pronouns are singular. On the other hand, *both, few, many,* and *several* are plural, and *some* and *all* can be either, as shown in the following paired sentences.

- All of the golf clubs are stored in the garage.
- All of the equipment is stored in the garage.

- Some of the lemons are too sour.
- Some of the lemonade is too sour.

Reciprocal Pronouns

Reciprocal pronouns refer to the separate elements of a plural antecedent. For example, in the sentence *Bob and I respect each other, each other* is the reciprocal pronoun signifying a relationship between the two antecedents. The other reciprocal pronoun is *one another.*

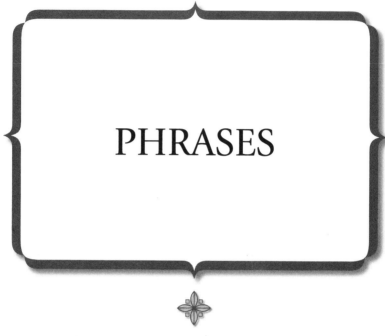

CHAPTER 3

PHRASES

Phrases are groups of words that share a very important characteristic: the absence of both a subject and a verb. Sometimes it may seem that a phrase has a subject because it includes a noun, and sometimes it may seem that a phrase has a verb because it includes a word that conveys action. Those nouns and verb-like words in a phrase are not subjects and functioning verbs. If they were, the phrase would not be able to function, as a single word does, as a noun or a modifier.

There are many kinds of phrases, and the ability to distinguish one type from another requires an understanding of how a phrase functions in a sentence. Phrases can modify, but phrases can also act like nouns. One of the most important characteristics of any phrase is its ability to behave as though it were a single word.

- The flower garden is beautiful.
    In this sentence, *flower* functions as a single-word modifier answering the question *what kind?*
- The garden of flowers is beautiful.
    In this sentence, *of flowers*, a prepositional phrase, also modifies *garden* by answering the same question.

The examples below illustrate the same principle: single words modify, and phrases function in the same way single words do—as adjectives telling more about the noun or as adverbs telling more about the verb (or adjective).

- The *ghost* story frightened him.
    The noun *ghost* is functioning as a modifier of *story*.
- The story *about ghosts* frightened him.
    The phrase *about ghosts* is acting like a single-word modifier of the word *story*.

Phrases can be difficult to understand and manage because so many different kinds can be used in so many different ways and in so many different combinations. Within one sentence there can be compound phrases (or phrases with compound objects) and phrases embedded within other phrases. Perhaps the most common kind of phrase is the prepositional phrase, an all-purpose modifier (functioning either adjectivally or adverbially) that can appear by itself, in combination with other phrases, or as part of other phrases.

3A PREPOSITIONAL PHRASES AND MODIFICATION

A prepositional phrase begins with a preposition and contains additional words, most often an article followed by a single-word noun (or a pronoun) called the object of the preposition. Modifying words may precede the object of the preposition. Sometimes two nouns form a compound object of the preposition, as in *The cat hid under the table and chairs.* (See section 3K for a thorough examination of the internal structures of various types of phrases.) Prepositional phrases can function as adjectives or adverbs. Remember that an adjective answers the questions *which? what kind? how many? whose?* An adverb answers the questions *how? in what manner? when? where? how often? to what extent or degree?* In each of the following examples, the prepositional phrase has been underlined.

- The song about loneliness moved him to tears.
    Which song? The phrase provides descriptive information about the song and is adjectival because it modifies a noun.

- The house in the forest had been abandoned.
    This phrase seems to answer two questions: *which house? where?* If the phrase answers the first question, it is adjectival; if it answers the second, it is adverbial. To determine which question is answered, ask whether the phrase provides information about the house itself or about the fact it *had been abandoned.* You will see that the phrase provides information about the noun *house* and is functioning as an adjective.

- Tom ran into the woods.
    Where? The phrase answers that question with *into the woods* and is therefore an adverb modifying *ran.*

- He placed the book next to the door.
    Where? The phrase begins with the phrasal preposition *next to* and functions as an adverb modifying *placed.*

- As the dog's owner, Nancy was required to report the incident.
    The phrase identifies Nancy as the dog's owner and functions as an adjective.

Many prepositions indicate location: *in, on, into, beneath, below, through, beside, and inside,* to name a few. Accordingly, many prepositional phrases function as adverbs in answering the question *where?* Because adverbs modify not only verbs but also other adverbs and adjectives, it might seem quite difficult to determine what is modifying what. Properly identifying modifiers and their relationship to other sentence elements is important when determining their placement in a grammatically correct sentence, however. (See the further discussion of this point at the end of this chapter and in chapter 8, which looks at misplaced and dangling modifiers.)

3B APPOSITIVE PHRASES AND MODIFICATION

An appositive phrase provides additional information about the noun or pronoun it directly precedes or follows. An appositive renames that noun by referring to another aspect of its identity. In the following sentences, a noun is immediately preceded or followed by additional information in the form of an appositive phrase.

- Jack, a man admired for his integrity and unflinching devotion to duty, got married today to Sally Barnes.

  The phrase *a man admired for his integrity and unflinching devotion to duty* is an appositive phrase modifying the subject, *Jack*.

- The patient, Lorene Smith, recovered quickly from gallbladder surgery.

  In this sentence, *patient* is the subject and *Lorene Smith* is the appositive. The commas around the appositive identify it as nonessential information. In other words, *Lorene Smith* is a nonrestrictive appositive and the sentence would be complete both grammatically and in meaning without the appositive. You can infer from the punctuation of this example that only one patient is under discussion.

- A woman of infinite patience, my mother has been an inspiration to me.

  The appositive phrase in this sentence, *A woman of infinite patience*, precedes the noun it modifies, *mother*.

- He has three favorite foods—spaghetti, lasagna, and macaroni.

  In this sentence, the appositive phrase *spaghetti, lasagna, and macaroni* modifies the direct object, *foods*, and has been set off with an em dash rather than with a comma.

Notice that an appositive can come between a subject and a verb, it can precede a subject, or it can follow an object. Appositives can appear anywhere as long as they are immediately adjacent to the nouns they modify and as long as they are punctuated correctly.

There are two types of appositive phrases. If a phrase merely adds additional information or renames its noun by using several descriptive words, then it is nonessential to the meaning of the sentence or to the identity of that noun—it is nonrestrictive. But if a phrase is instrumental in helping us understand *who* or *which,* then it is essential, or restrictive.

Because appositives are an economical way of supplying additional information, they are generally not essential to the identification of the noun they modify. Most appositives could be removed without damaging a sentence's construction or altering its meaning. Some appositives, however, are crucial to a sentence's meaning.

- Your sister Marge voted today.

  Marge is needed to identify which sister. If the sentence read *Your sister, Marge, voted today*, the sister's name wouldn't be necessary because we would infer from the commas surrounding it that there is only one sister.

- His friend Joe claimed the prize.

  The punctuation indicates that Joe is one of many friends, so his name is essential in identifying which friend claimed the prize.

Most errors with appositives occur because writers automatically insert commas around any word that renames the subject. However, as we've seen, the need for commas is not automatic; they are used to indicate a particular relationship between the appositive and the element it modifies. (See also the discussion of appositives in section B of chapter 1.)

3C VERBAL PHRASES AND MODIFICATION

Verbal phrases can enrich your writing by helping create variety in sentence structure as well as vigorous, compact prose. They can also result in sentence fragments (if you misuse one for a verb), or in awkward and erroneous statements (if you misplace one in a sentence).

A verbal phrase begins with a verb that is followed by additional words, just as a prepositional phrase begins with a preposition that is followed by additional words. A verbal is related to a verb—that is, a verbal also communicates action. There are three types of verbal:

participles (past, present, and perfect tense), gerunds, and infinitives. The verbal can be followed by a noun, which functions as the object of the verbal, by other single-word modifiers, or by other types of phrases.

As you learn to use and identify verbal phrases, keep in mind the various characteristics and roles of participles, gerunds, and infinitives. (See chapter 1 for further discussion of each.) A present participle ends in *-ing* (*hoping, thinking, wanting, knowing*) and cannot function by itself as a verb: in the statement *I eating breakfast,* something is obviously missing—the helping verb *am* or *was,* which creates, in combination with the present participle, either the present- or past-progressive tense, as in *I am* (*was*) *eating breakfast.* Participles can also function as single-word modifiers, just like the adjectives *red* or *big.*

- The <u>screaming</u> monkey scared visitors away from the zoo.
- <u>Barking</u> loudly, the loyal bulldog alerted its family to danger.

Present participles and gerunds both end in *–ing,* but in verbal phrases, all participles function as modifiers, and all gerunds function as nouns.

Consider the following phrases: *running up the hill, hopping on his left leg, thinking of money.*

The words at the beginning of all these phrases are verbals, but we cannot identity them as participles (modifiers) or gerunds (nouns) until we see them functioning in sentences. If the phrase *running up the hill* is used as a participle, it will modify.

- Running up the hill, Tom felt his nose grow cold.
    The phrase tells more about Tom, and therefore modifies as an adjective.

But if the phrase is used as a gerund, it will function as a noun.

- Running up the hill is something Tom does every morning.
    The gerund phrase is the subject of the sentence, and the verb is *is.*

Compare the following.

- Hopping on his left leg, the child managed to bounce the ball.
- Hopping on his left leg caused Lester to develop cramps in his right.

- Thinking of money, the college student accepted three part-time jobs.
- Thinking of money made the young couple nervous.

The first sentence of each pair contains a verbal-phrase modifier beginning with a participle: *hopping* and *thinking.* The second sentence of each pair contains an identical phrase, but the entire phrase functions as a noun—as the subject of the sentence—and the first word is a therefore a gerund.

There are obvious differences between the sentences in each pair. First, notice the use of commas. Each modifying verbal phrase begins the sentence and is therefore introductory, and each modifying verbal phrase is also followed by a comma. A comma rule to remember, therefore, is that all introductory-phrase modifiers are followed by commas. However, when the phrase functions as a gerund, it is not followed by a comma. The comma rule here is simple: Subjects and verbs are never separated by only one comma.

Second, notice the placement of the modifying phrases. They are right next to the words they modify. A confusing sentence would result if the modifier were too far away: *The child managed to bounce the ball hopping on his left leg.* (It sounds as if a ball is hopping on a leg.)

Third, notice that a phrase is classified by its first word, even though it may contain additional phrases. The participial or gerund phrase *Hopping on his left leg* contains a prepositional phrase, *on his left leg*. But because the phrase begins with a participle or a gerund, depending on its use in a sentence, it would be considered a participial or gerund phrase, not a prepositional phrase.

3D PRESENT-PARTICIPIAL PHRASES: RHETORICAL USE

Inexperienced writers often use two or three sentences to express an idea or related ideas that could easily and more economically be expressed by one sentence that makes use of modification. Remember that modification supplies some extra bit of information. While the inexperienced writer gives equal weight and therefore equal emphasis to every idea by putting every piece of information into a separate sentence, the more experienced and language-savvy writer determines the main idea and incorporates additional details of lesser importance into the same sentence by using phrase modifiers and other strategies. Consider these two sentences.

- Tom walked into the room. He looked lonely.

Two things are happening simultaneously: A person walks into a room, and the observer notes something about that person. Should those two events be distanced by placement in two separate sentences that cause the reader to stop and start over again? Should both sentences carry the same grammatical weight and significance? If we assume that the writer of these two sentences did not have a particular stylistic purpose in mind, the answer to both questions is probably no. Rewritten using a present-participial-phrase modifier, the sentence would more economically read:

- Looking lonely, Tom walked into the room.

Using participal phrases for modification achieves a number of effects. First, it makes writing more concise: Fewer words are used to say the same thing. This economy makes reading easier and more engaging. Second, modifying phrases allow the writer to vary the typical sentence structure of subject, verb, object (SVO). Although repetitive structure might help achieve clarity in technical reports, such redundancy otherwise defeats the purpose of using language to entertain and delight. Suppose you had written the following.

- The dog sat on the porch. He scratched his ear. He looked back into the house. Suddenly, he felt hungry.

In twenty words and four sentences, a sequence of events is related, although exactly how those events are related in time is unclear. One event presumably follows another because one sentence follows another. In both revisions below, however, one sentence of eighteen words not only conveys the same sequence but also clarifies the temporal relationship between the events.

- The dog sitting on the porch scratched his ear and, suddenly feeling hungry, looked back into the house.
  In this example, the verb *sat* from the first sentence of the original has been converted into the participle *sitting*. The verb *felt* from the fourth sentence of the original has been converted to the participle *feeling*. Each participle introduces a verbal phrase that adds variety to the new sentence and makes the new sentence more concise.

- Scratching his ear and suddenly feeling hungry, the dog sitting on the porch looked back into the house.
  The verbs *scratched* and *felt* from the original sentences are now participles that increase the economy and complexity of the sentence.

It is also important to note that the same modifying phrase can often appear in a number of different positions within a given sentence, as long as it is next to the words it modifies. In the following sentence, for instance, the phrase *tying his shoelaces tightly* can appear before the subject or between the subject and the verb.

- Tying his shoelaces tightly, the runner prepared for the race.
- The runner, tying his shoelaces tightly, prepared for the race.

3E ESSENTIAL (RESTRICTIVE) AND NONESSENTIAL (NONRESTRICTIVE) PHRASES

A phrase that comes between a subject and a verb is called an interrupter, and it is most often set off by a pair of commas. It is important to distinguish between essential and nonessential phrases, however, when deciding whether to place commas around a phrase. A nonessential phrase adds information but is not required to establish the identity of the word it modifies. But an essential phrase cannot be removed from the sentence, because it establishes the identity of the word it modifies. In each of the following sentences, the participial phrase adds detail, but it can be removed from the sentence without either altering the sentence's meaning or removing vital information.

- The young woman, appearing to be serenely indifferent, picked red flowers.
    Although the young woman's attitude might be worth mentioning, it does not single her out in any way.
- The wind, blowing hard from the east, damaged the palm.
    We would never need to distinguish one wind direction from another, because two winds most likely wouldn't be blowing at the same time in different directions.

Now consider these sentences.

- The man looking at Mary remembered he had seen her before.
    We wouldn't know which man remembered Mary unless the phrase *looking at Mary* was there to tell us.
- The dog scratching his ear is the one needing a new home.
    We wouldn't know which dog needs a new home without the identifying phrase *scratching his ear*.

Some phrases can be either essential or nonessential. For example, when a person or thing being modified is already identified, the modifying phrase is unlikely to be essential. If we return to the earlier sentence about the dog and give that dog a name, Billy, then the sentence will read: *Billy, scratching his ear, is the dog needing a new home*. The phrase *scratching his ear* now merely provides additional information unnecessary for the purpose of identification—so it is now nonessential. Compare these two sentences.

- The girl walking slowly toward the house felt uneasy.
    We know which girl felt uneasy only because she is the one identified as *walking slowly toward the house*. Therefore, the phrase is essential and not set off by commas.
- Leah, walking slowly toward the house, felt uneasy.
    We know Leah felt uneasy walking toward the house because her name is given, so the modifying phrase is nonessential and set off by commas: We don't need it to identify Leah.

A phrase can be either essential or nonessential depending on the context and the writer's intention.

- The young child crying his heart out looks lost.
    In this sentence, the information that the child was crying his heart out is needed to distinguish him, perhaps from other children.

- The young child, crying his heart out, looks lost.
  > In this sentence, it would appear that he is the only young child, he looks lost, and by the way, he is crying his heart out.

The difference between essential and nonessential phrases is usually clear. However, many errors occur because writers make essential phrases nonessential—that is, they unnecessarily add commas rather than mistakenly omit them. (It's difficult to imagine anyone writing the following sentence: *Joe skating too fast on his new Rollerblades crashed into the picket fence.*)

3F VERBAL PHRASES: TENSE AND PARTICIPLES

We have thus far been examining modifying phrases that begin with present participles only. However, there are different kinds of participial phrases.

Past-Participial-Phrase Modifiers

Past participles, like present participles, can modify as single words, or they can introduce phrase modifiers. (See section C in Chapter 1 for a more detailed discussion of past and present participles.) In *The fugitive wanted in four states hid in the woods for a month*, the essential phrase beginning with the past participle *wanted* modifies *fugitive* and thus functions as an adjective, as do all participial phrases. The following sentences all contain past-participial modifying phrases.

- Cupped in Paul's hand, the butterfly looked faded.
- Sal felt frozen to the bone.
- The audience, moved by the senator's speech, clapped enthusiastically.

Like any modifying phrase, a past-participial phrase can be placed at the beginning, in the middle, or at the end of the sentence, as long as it is next to the word it is intended to modify.

Present-Perfect and Past-Perfect Participial-Phrase Modifiers

Although verbals, strictly speaking, don't have tenses in the same way that functioning verbs within sentences do, they nevertheless have tenses based on their relationship to the main verb; those tenses are formed by combining participles and helping verbs. A present-perfect participial-phrase modifier is formed by combining the present participle of *to have* and a past participle; the past-perfect participial-phrase modifier is formed by combining the present participle of *to have*, the past participle of *to be*, and another past participle—in other words, by combining *having been* and a past participle.

Suppose you wanted to convey two events in the past, one of which happened before the other. You could express each event in a separate sentence.

- She thought it over carefully. Then she decided not to apply.

You could express both events in one sentence, using two clauses and two separate verb tenses to establish the order in which the events occurred.

- Although she had thought it over carefully, she decided not to apply.

You could also use a phrase modifier, making sure that the tense of the participle indicated the same order of action.

- Having thought it over carefully, she decided not to apply.

In this sentence, the present participle *having* has been combined with the past participle *thought* to form a present-perfect participial-phrase modifier. It is clear that the decision not to apply came after the action of thinking.

Compare the uses of present- and past-perfect participial-phrase modifiers in the following examples.

- Having been depressed for years, the man finally sought treatment.
  The present participle *having* has been combined with *been* (the past participle of *to be*) and the past participle *depressed* to form the past-perfect participial-phrase modifier *having been depressed*. The phrase starting with *having* contains another phrase, the adverbial phrase *for years*.

- The child ate the salad, having been satisfied with its taste before.
  The present participle *having* has been combined with the past participles *been* and *satisfied* to form a past-perfect participial-phrase modifier.

- The sun, having risen, heated the ice until it melted.
  Having risen is a present-perfect participial-phrase modifier.

- Having had enough of Martin's moods, his wife went to the movies.
  The present participle *having* has been combined with *had*, the past participle of *to have*. The result is the present-perfect participial-phrase modifier *having had*.

3G MISPLACED AND DANGLING MODIFIERS

A modifying phrase needs to be placed as close as possible to the noun it is modifying. When the modifier is too far away, it is called misplaced.

Awkward: Not completely finished with the exam, the teacher told the students to put their pencils down anyway.
  The introductory phrase modifies the word next to it, *teacher*, but the teacher wasn't taking the exam—the students were.
Better: Not completely finished with the exam, the students put their pencils down at the request of the teacher.
Better: Not completely finished with the exam, the students were told by the teacher to put down their pencils anyway.
  Notice that this revision converts an active verb to a passive verb.

If the word being modified is only implied, then the modifier is said to dangle. In either case, the consequences can be amusing or absurd. Remember: Whether you intend it to or not, a modifier will always modify the word it is closest to.

Awkward: Driving his car recklessly, the convertible hit a streetlight.
  The introductory-phrase modifier appears to tell more about *convertible*, but the car couldn't be driving itself. Because there is no person present in the sentence who could be *driving his car recklessly*, the word being modified is only implied.
Better: Driving his car recklessly, the motorist in the convertible hit a streetlight.

Misplaced and dangling modifiers are discussed in further detail in chapter 8.

3H GERUNDS

A gerund is a word formed by adding the suffix *-ing* to a base verb and therefore looks exactly like a present participle. (In fact, if you saw the word *playing* outside the context of a sentence, you would know only that the word was a verbal. You would not know whether it was a single-word participial modifier or a gerund capable of doing what a noun does in a sentence—functioning as a subject, an object, or a complement.)

A gerund, like a present participle, can appear as a single word. In each of the following sentences, the single-word gerund serves as a subject.

- Swimming is his favorite sport.
- Hiking requires great stamina.

A single-word gerund can also function as an object. In each of the following two sentences, the gerund is the object of a preposition.

- Before eating, the old dog licked his chops.
- John stretched while writing.

A single-word gerund can also function as the object of a verb.

- The first person in line has finished showering.
- Dietary restrictions prohibit his eating meat.

A single-word gerund can function as a complement in a sentence with a linking verb.

- Her main responsibility is teaching.
- Joe's only pleasure was eating.

Gerund Phrases as Subjects

Like gerunds themselves, multiword phrases beginning with a gerund (gerund phrases) can be used as subjects, as objects of prepositions and verbs, and as complements. In the following example, the gerund phrase is the subject of the sentence.

- Going to work every day takes a lot of effort.

When you are trying to locate the subject of a sentence, look first for the verb. In the example above, *takes* is clearly the verb. If you then ask yourself *what takes?*, the answer is *Going to work every day*. The entire phrase is the subject of the sentence, just as a single word can be the subject. Remember that phrases function as if they were single words. Below are several sentences with gerund phrases (underlined) as subjects.

- Baking for others is fun.
- Listening to sad romantic tunes stirred old memories.
- Talking about people behind their backs can get you into trouble.

Like participial phrases, gerund phrases can contain prepositional phrases. In fact, a gerund phrase and a participial phrase are identical when they are removed from the context of a sentence.

- running on the balls of his feet
- walking with his nose in the air
- speaking to her son
- thinking about dinner

Until we see how those phrases function within sentences, we can't tell whether they begin with gerunds or with participles. In each of the sentence pairs below, the introductory phrase of the first sentence is a gerund phrase. Each gerund phrase contains one or more prepositional phrases.

- Running on the balls of his feet allowed the sprinter to increase his speed.
- Running on the balls of his feet, Raymond sped toward the finish line.

- Walking with his nose in the air made the young man appear conceited.
- Walking with his nose in the air, Raymond failed to notice the rock in his path.

- Speaking to her son saddened the older woman.
- Speaking to her son, the older woman grew sad.

- Thinking about dinner caused Raymond to salivate.
- Thinking about dinner, Raymond salivated.

Notice that the gerund phrases and the participial phrases are identical in form. Notice also that introductory-phrase modifiers are followed by commas, while gerund phrases are not.

As we saw earlier, inserting a comma after a gerund-phrase subject would separate the subject from its verb, an error that the following sentences without gerund subjects clearly illustrate.

- The tree, was blown to the ground.
- The building, needed to be demolished.

Gerund Phrases as Objects of Prepositions

Identifying gerunds that are functioning as objects can be difficult, because there are several types of objects: objects of prepositions, objects of verbs, and objects of participles and other gerunds. Just remember that every time you see a word ending in -*ing,* it will be functioning in one of three ways: (a) as part of a verb, (b) as a single-word participial modifier or the first word in a participial phrase, or (c) as a single-word gerund or the first word in a gerund phrase. Let's first examine gerunds serving as objects of prepositions. Recall that an object of a preposition is a noun at the end of a prepositional phrase. In the following examples, the object of the preposition has been underlined.

- of his dog
- after noon
- despite Mary's misgivings

The underlined objects are single words, but gerund phrases can function like single words. We can therefore replace the single-word noun objects above with gerund phrases.

- of watching his dog
- after waiting until noon
- despite understanding Mary's misgivings

These phrases take their places in the sentences below.

- Nick grew tired of watching his dog.
- After waiting until noon, the angry man stomped out of the restaurant.
- Despite understanding Mary's misgivings, her lawyer advised her to sue.

Gerund Phrases as Objects of Verbs

In the sentence *He threw the ball,* the action verb *threw* is followed by a word (the direct object) that benefits from or receives the action of the verb. To determine the direct object, you would ask *He threw what?* The answer is *ball.* Phrases can also function as direct objects. If the sentence above read *He enjoys throwing the ball,* the object would be the entire gerund phrase *throwing the ball.* You identify direct objects by asking *what?* or *whom?* after the verb.

- We recommend placing your order by noon on Friday.
    We recommend *what?* Answer: *placing your order by noon on Friday.* The gerund phrase is the object of the verb.

- The teacher's strict rules forbid talking in class.
    Forbid *what?* Answer: *talking in class.*

- Her mother still likes swimming in the ocean at dawn.
  - Likes *what*? Answer: *swimming in the ocean at dawn*.
- They discussed going to the mountains for vacation this year.
  - Discussed *what*? Answer: *going to the mountains for vacation this year*.

A gerund phrase can even be the object of a gerund or a participle, but the resulting construction is awkward.

- Quitting smoking now greatly reduces risks to your health.
  - The subject of the sentence is *quitting*, and the verb is *reduces*. If you ask the question *quitting what?*, the answer is *smoking*, a gerund.

Gerund Phrases as Complements

A complement is a noun or a modifier equated to the subject of a sentence by a linking verb.

- I am sad.
- Bill was treasurer of that organization.

Both sentences include forms of the verb *to be,* the first in the present tense, the second in the past tense. The linking verb establishes an equivalence between the subject and the word or words following the verb. *Sad,* therefore, *is* what *I* am. Similarly, *treasurer is* what *Bill* was. A shared identity exists between the subject and what follows the verb. The words following the verbs in these examples are different in kind: *sad* is a modifier, and *treasurer* is a noun. In both cases, however, the word following the linking verb is a subjective complement—that is, it is equivalent to the subject of the sentence. If the word is a noun, it is called a predicate nominative; if the word is an adjective, it is called a predicate adjective. Gerunds and gerund phrases are always nouns, so they are always predicate nominatives when used as complements. Do be careful to distinguish progressive-tense verbs from gerunds used as subjective complements.

- Tom was washing his car.
  - Is *was washing* a past-progressive-tense verb, or is *was* a linking verb and *washing his car* a complement? If you ask yourself what Tom is doing, what the action of the sentence is, the answer will be *washing his car*, with *car* as the direct object, the noun receiving the action of being washed.
- Tom's greatest joy in life was washing his car.
  - Is *was washing* still the verb? It can't be, or the sentence would mean that *joy* was performing an action, *washing his car*. *Was* alone is the verb—a linking verb—connecting *joy* to what that joy is or involves: *washing his car*, a gerund phrase functioning as the predicate nominative.
- Her last occupation was professional gardening.
  - The subject is *occupation*. An occupation cannot garden. In this sentence, *occupation* is equivalent to, or shares an identity with, *gardening*; they are the same thing, connected by the linking verb *was*. *Gardening* is therefore a predicate nominative, a noun reflecting the identity of the subject.

To distinguish between progressive-tense verbs and gerund phrases used as predicate nominatives, you must first determine the subject of the sentence.

- His greatest fear was failing the exam.
  - The subject is *fear*, but can a fear fail? A fear can't do anything like that, so *was* must be connecting *fear* with its equivalent on the other side. What is the fear? Answer: *failing the exam*. The fear is a fear of failure.
- Tom was failing the exam.
  - In this sentence, *Tom*, the subject, is indeed performing an action, *failing the exam*.

Gerund phrases and infinitive phrases used as complements are often interchangeable. Sometimes it is difficult to distinguish between a progressive-tense verb and a gerund used as a predicate nominative.

- Sally's job was making Nick's life miserable.
  Is it the case that Sally's job required that she make Nick's life miserable? In other words, was Sally hired to torment Nick so that he became miserable? Or is it instead the case that Sally's line of work caused Nick to become miserable? Clearly, the more plausible interpretation is the second—Nick was miserable because of Sally's job.

Keep in mind that if a sentence requires you to stop and reread it in order to be sure you've understood its meaning, then chances are the ambiguity should have been avoided in the first place.

31 INFINITIVES

An infinitive begins with *to* and is the formal designation of an unconjugated verb—that is, a verb having no functional tense, as in the following: *to run, to hope, to know, to have*. Infinitives are verbals and therefore can function as modifiers and as nouns, alone or in phrases. *To be, or not to be* is perhaps the most famous infinitive construction—a compound infinitive used as the appositive subject of the sentence *To be, or not to be: That is the question*. An infinitive cannot function as a verb, as is made clear by the following sentence: *I to go to the store soon*. Although infinitives never function as verbs *within* a sentence, they do have a perfect tense, as we will see later in this section.

Sometimes infinitives are confused with prepositional phrases beginning with the preposition *to*, as in the sentence *He went to Europe*. *To Europe*, however, could never be conjugated, because *Europe* is a proper noun, not a verb. One cannot say *He Europed through the yard*.

An infinitive phrase is identified as such by the infinitive that begins it. Like all phrases, an infinitive phrase may contain additional words—more phrases or a combination of objects, single-word modifiers, and other phrases: *to know something about this subject, to hope for the best*.

Infinitive Phrases as Subjects

That infinitives and gerunds are sometimes interchangeable is illustrated by the subjects of the following sentences.

- To bake an apple pie requires both patience and the right ingredients.
- Baking an apple pie requires both patience and the right ingredients.

- To tell the truth isn't always easy.
- Telling the truth isn't always easy.

- To want it all is the trademark of youth.
- Wanting it all is the trademark of youth.

Determining where a phrase stops can be difficult, but in cases in which the subject precedes the verb, you know the subject is complete once you encounter the verb. In each of these sentences, the infinitive has an object.

- To lift impossibly heavy objects with ease requires the strength of Superman.
  To lift is followed by *impossibly heavy objects*, its object.

- To demonstrate his absolute loyalty necessitated that Roger sign an oath.
  To demonstrate is followed by *his absolute loyalty*, its object.

- To earn a great fortune these days means that you must have great luck.
  To earn is followed by *a great fortune*, its object.

An infinitive can have an infinitive as its object, but the construction may be awkward.

- To hope to win was foolish at this point.
  To win is the object of *to hope*.

Infinitive Phrases as Objects of Verbs

An infinitive can also function as an object of a verb. In the following examples, the infinitive or infinitive phrase is the direct object of the sentence.

- He wanted to go.
  He wanted *what? To go.*
- Monica remembered to open the mail.
  Monica remembered *what? To open the mail.*
- Roberto wished to excel in math.
  Robert wished *what? To excel in math.*

As these examples illustrate, you can recognize an infinitive as the object of a verb simply by asking *what?* or *whom?* after the verb. There are virtually no examples, however, of infinitives functioning as objects of prepositions.

Infinitive Phrases as Objects of Gerunds and Participles

Just as infinitives can function as objects of a verb, they can also function as objects of a participle or as objects of a gerund.

- Known to be ruthless, the great warrior took no prisoners.

The past-participial phrase *known to be ruthless* modifies *the great warrior*. The object of the participle *known* is *to be ruthless*. In the examples below, the infinitive phrase is underlined.

- Thought to be lost, the missing hiker arrived at camp a month overdue.
- Meant to be taken as a joke, the tasteless comment instead offended many.
- Hoping to discover the truth, she relentlessly asked questions.

In each sentence above, the infinitive functions as the object of a participle, past or present. Similarly, an infinitive can function as the object of a gerund, as in the examples below. Notice that in the first three sentences, the infinitive object also has an object itself. In each sentence, the gerund phrase has been underlined, the verb has been italicized, the infinitive-phrase object has been parenthesized, and any object of the infinitive has been boldfaced.

- Wanting (to win the game) *became* an obsession.
- Remembering (to lock the door) required all her concentration.
- Hoping (to earn a million dollars) is a waste of energy.
- The child's constant crying (to be picked up) annoyed the bystanders.
- Asking (to be excused from the conversation) made the youth seem callow.

Infinitive Phrases as Complements

Infinitive phrases can sometimes be substituted for gerund-phrase subjects and for gerund-phrase complements. In the sentence *His lifelong desire is seeing her again,* a gerund phrase serving as the subjective complement can be translated into an infinitive phrase, possibly to better effect: *His lifelong desire is to see her again.*

Infinitive phrases can also function as objective complements. Like subjective complements, objective complements rename, identify, or describe a noun—in this case a noun functioning as an object. Objective complements can be single words, gerunds, participles, or infinitives—in other words, they can function as modifiers or as nouns, just as subjective complements can be either predicate adjectives or predicate nominatives.

- I regard him to be the best candidate for the job.
- I regard him to be selfishly indulgent.

In each case, *him* is the direct object of the verb, and the infinitive phrase that follows renames *him* as a noun (*the best candidate*) or describes *him* adjectivally (*selfishly indulgent*).

Infinitive Phrases as Modifiers

Just as the phrase *going to the store* can be either a present-participial phrase modifier or a gerund, depending on how it functions in a sentence, so can the infinitive phrase *to understand myself* be either a modifier—an adjective or adverb—or a noun subject, an object, or a complement. In the sentences below, *to understand myself completely* is the infinitive phrase.

- To understand myself completely will take more effort than I'm willing to invest.
    The infinitive phrase is the subject.

- To understand myself completely, I entered therapy.
    The infinitive phrase is a phrase modifier.

- My goal is to understand myself completely.
    The infinitive phrase is the predicate nominative.

- I want to understand myself completely.
    The infinitive phrase is the object of the verb.

When an infinitive phrase functions as a modifier, it must be placed as close as possible to the word being modified; and when an infinitive phrase is an introductory element, it must be followed by a comma. Compare the following.

- To solve the problem, they employed a full-time security guard.
    The infinitive phrase is an introductory modifier and is therefore followed by a comma. The phrase answers the question *why?* and is thus an adverb modifying *employed*. A simple way to determine whether an infinitive phrase is functioning as an adverb is to ask whether the words *in order* can be inserted before the infinitive. If they can, the infinitive must be an adverb answering *why?* (In this example, the phrase could just as well appear at the end of the sentence: *They employed a full-time security guard* [why?] *to solve the problem.*)

- To solve the problem required a full-time security guard.
    The infinitive phrase is used as the subject of the sentence and is therefore not followed by a comma.

The Infinitive "Clause"

Infinitive phrases, as we have seen, can function as nouns or as modifiers. Unlike other verbals, however, infinitives can be said to have their own subjects, as well as typical modifiers and complements. When a pronoun is the subject of an infinitive, the pronoun must be an objective pronoun, because this construction follows a transitive verb. Some grammarians refer to the construction thus formed as an infinitive clause because the infinitive appears to have a subject, even though a pronoun in this position is not in the subjective case and the infinitive itself is not a conjugated verb. Other grammarians simply refer to the infinitive as having a subject. Consider the following examples.

- My mother expects me to paint my room.

    Expects is a transitive verb with *me* as its object. *Me* is also considered to be the subject of the infinitive phrase that follows it, *to paint my room*. The combination of *me* and *to paint my room* is considered the infinitive clause.

- Bob wants his brother to buy fish for dinner.

    The word *brother* is the object of the verb *wants*. It is also the subject of the infinitive phrase *to buy fish for dinner*. The combination of *his brother* and *to buy fish for dinner* is the infinitive clause.

- I asked Ellen to arrange the flowers.

    Ellen is the object of the verb asked and the subject of the infinitive phrase *to arrange the flowers*. *Ellen to arrange the flowers* is the infinitive clause.

Remember, however, that when trying to determine how a phrase is functioning within a sentence, you identify this entire group of words (the infinitive clause) as the direct object of the verb.

Another interpretation might hold that the single-word direct objects are actually indirect objects.

- My mother expects for me to paint my room.
- Bob wants for his brother to buy fish for dinner.
- I asked for Ellen to arrange the flowers.

If this interpretation were the case, then each infinitive phrase would be the direct object: *to paint my room* would be what the mother wants. Similarly, what the *I* in the third sentence wants is that the flowers be arranged by Ellen. This interpretation becomes especially pertinent in relation to objective complements.

Infinitive Phrases in Present-Perfect and Past-Perfect Tenses

Infinitive phrases have tenses. This is not to say that they are conjugated verbs, but rather that they appear in forms other than the simple *to go, to think, to sleep*, and so forth. Infinitives may appear in the perfect tense, as in *to have gone, to have thought, to have slept*. The use of the perfect tense in an infinitive is often determined by the tense of the verb in the sentence itself. (The sequencing of tenses is discussed in Chapter 1.) In the examples above, the infinitive is introduced with *to*, but instead of being followed by only the simple or base form of the verb, it is followed by the present tense of *to have*, along with a past participle. The sentences below illustrate some of the uses of perfect-tense infinitives.

- To have considered such a drastic step indicates his level of desperation.

    In this sentence, the infinitive phrase *to have considered such a drastic step* is the subject. The infinitive is in the present-perfect tense.

- To have been chosen for this job, she needed to have shown more consistent and overt aggressiveness.

    In this sentence, the infinitive phrase *to have been chosen for this job* is a modifier in the past-perfect tense.

- To have gone to such lengths only to lose at the last moment must have been very discouraging.

    In this sentence, the entire phrase *to have gone to such lengths only to lose at the last moment* is the subject.

- John was pleased to have met his very first goal.

    In this sentence, the infinitive phrase *to have met his very first goal* is a modifier and is in the present-perfect tense.

- The white-haired lady hoped to have been his first love.
    > In this sentence, the past-perfect infinitive phrase *to have been his first love* is the object of the verb *hoped*.
- To have been captured so soon would have meant certain defeat.
    > *To have been captured so soon* is a past-perfect infinitive phrase and the subject of the sentence.
- To have been thought at fault would have destroyed her confidence.
    > The past-perfect infinitive phrase *to have been thought at fault* is the subject of the sentence.

3J ABSOLUTE PHRASES

An absolute phrase is a rather formal construction and, unlike other phrases, functions independently within the sentence—that is, an absolute phrase does not modify only one word but instead qualifies an entire clause or sentence. The absolute phrase must always have a noun and a modifier. In the sentence *The weather being balmy for January, we went for a long walk,* the absolute phrase appears before the comma and consists of a noun (*weather*) and a participial-phrase modifier (*being balmy for January*).

If the modifying phrase within the absolute construction is a participial, the participial phrase can be in any tense—present, past, present perfect, or past perfect. Other types of verbal phrases, such as infinitives, can also be part of the absolute construction, as can a prepositional phrase: *His hands under the table, the little boy played cat's cradle while the teacher explained long division.* The placement of an absolute phrase depends on other words within the sentence. Consider these sentences with absolute phrases. (The absolute phrases have been underlined.)

- Today being Monday, we reluctantly got up and dressed for work.
- Their tasks having been accomplished, the committee adjourned for the day.
- Sheila and Frank will go to Spain this summer, finances permitting.
- The child cried pitifully, his head beneath the pillow.

3K INSIDE THE PHRASE

The internal structure of phrases can be complicated, because all phrases can include objects and complements as well as additional phrases. You already know how to identify phrases functioning *within* sentences—gerund phrases and infinitive phrases used as objects of verbs, for example, as well as gerund phrases used as objects of prepositions. The internal structure of the phrase is much the same as that of the phrase operating within a sentence: A gerund, an infinitive, and a participle can each have an object. You first have to identify the phrase within the sentence, because you won't be able to identify an object as, say, the object of a gerund unless you know it is a gerund and not a participle (which can also have an object). In the following sentences, the phrases under discussion have been underlined.

- Lester suggested using oatmeal.
    > The underlined phrase is a gerund phrase functioning as the object of the verb *suggested*. But how is *oatmeal* functioning? Remember, all you need to do is ask the question *what* or *whom?* after a verb or verbal to identify objects. Lester suggested *what?* Using oatmeal. Oatmeal is the object of the gerund *using*.

- Knowing the truth about recipes cost Lester his job.
    > The underlined phrase is a gerund phrase functioning as the subject, and *cost* is the verb of the sentence. The gerund is *knowing*. If you ask *knowing what?*, you get the object *truth*, which is thus the object of the gerund. It is followed by the prepositional phrase *about recipes*.

- Lester dreaded getting flour stuck to his fingers.

  What did Lester dread? The answer is *getting flour stuck to his fingers*, so the verb has an object, and that object has to be a gerund phrase. What is the function of *flour*? It is the object of the gerund *getting*.

- The flames shot up, searing the bottoms of Mary's cherry pies.

  The underlined word group is a present-participial phrase modifying *flames*, with *searing* as the participle. Once you know it's a participial phrase, you can look to see whether the phrase includes an answer to the question *searing what?* The answer is *bottoms*, which is the object of the participle.

- Happily humming a tune, Lester carried the cherry pies inside.

  The phrase is participial—it modifies *Lester*—and the participle *humming* has an object—*humming what?* The answer is *tune*.

- Mary had no fear of striking the match to light the fire.

  Of introduces a prepositional phrase, and the underlined word group that follows is a gerund-phrase object of that preposition.

In examining how both participles and gerunds can have objects, we have been considering only single-word nouns as objects. But the internal structure of phrases becomes even more complicated when we start to look at gerund phrases as objects, especially considering that a participial phrase or a gerund phrase can have a gerund phrase as an object.

Let's pause for a moment to consider the rest of the last example, which contains an infinitive, *to light*. Infinitives are easy to spot, and fortunately, it doesn't matter whether they are functioning as nouns or as modifiers—they are still infinitives, so their objects will always be the objects of infinitives. Infinitives, like gerunds and participles, can also have gerund phrases as objects.

In the last example, the prepositional phrase has a gerund phrase as its object, and the gerund, *striking*, also has an object. Striking what? The match. *Match* is therefore the object of the gerund. But what about the function of the rest of the phrase? *To light* is clearly an infinitive, and in this case, because you can mentally add *in order* to *to light*, you know that the infinitive is functioning adverbially. If you ask *what?* after *to light*, you arrive at *the fire* as the object of the infinitive.

Here are a few more examples of how infinitives are used.

- Mary decided to bake cakes instead, after examining her alternatives.

  The underlined word group begins with a preposition, so it is a prepositional phrase, and the gerund phrase *examining her alternatives* is the object of the preposition. Contained within that gerund phrase is an object of the gerund *examining: alternatives*. The sentence also includes an infinitive phrase, *to bake*, which, if followed by the question *what?*, yields *cakes* as the object of the infinitive.

- To have so many ruined pies to throw out upset Lester.

  The infinitive phrase is functioning as the subject. If the infinitive itself is followed by the question *what?* the answer is *so many ruined pies to throw out*, which is the object of the infinitive.

- Lester hoped to cook the pies over the charcoal.

  Here the infinitive is the object of the verb, and the infinitive has an object. *To cook* what? *Pies*.

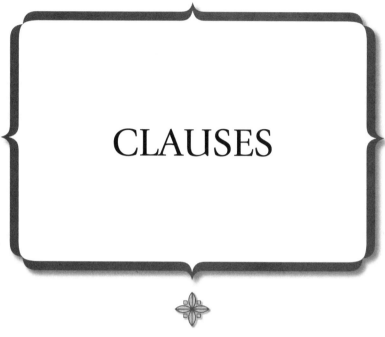

CHAPTER 4

CLAUSES

A phrase is a group of words without a subject and a verb: *in the tree, looking tired, about three o'clock, to be ripped to shreds*. A clause is a group of words that does contain a subject and verb. There are two major types: independent clauses and dependent clauses. An independent clause can stand alone as a sentence, beginning with a capital letter and ending with terminal punctuation such as a period. A dependent clause cannot stand alone as a sentence; instead, it must be attached to an independent clause. Consider the following groups of words.

- he often went to the beach
- because tomatoes taste good
- the young woman liked studying psychology
- although Laura wanted to ride the horse
- the committee voted to censure the attorney's behavior

Each of these unpunctuated groups of words is a clause, but some are independent and some are dependent. You can probably tell which could begin with a capital letter and end with a period. Those are the independent clauses, and the fact that they can stand alone as sentences is what makes them independent. The term *sentence* is often defined according to meaning conveyed—that is, a sentence is considered to be a grammatical unit that expresses a complete thought. But what is a complete thought? Consider the word group *The wig is in the tree*. This group of words conveys no readily comprehensible meaning—unless it is understood in the context of, say, a storm that blew a wig off someone's head. But sentences do not depend on context to be grammatically correct, though we typically expect such word groups to communicate effectively. Therefore, what makes a sentence a complete grammatical structure is the presence of a subject and a verb.

To return to the earlier definition, then, a clause is a group of words containing at least one subject and one conjugated verb. An independent clause (also known as a main clause) can stand alone as a sentence; a dependent clause (also known as a subordinate clause) cannot stand alone, because it begins with a word that renders it dependent.

In the examples above, only the first, third, and fifth clauses can stand alone as sentences. The second and fourth examples are also clauses, but they cannot begin with capital letters and end with periods, because they are dependent clauses. A dependent clause can begin with a subordinating conjunction or a relative pronoun, depending on what kind of dependent clause it is, but as the second and fourth examples illustrate, a dependent clause cannot be punctuated as a stand-alone, complete sentence.

- He often went to the beach.
- Because tomatoes taste good.
- The young woman liked studying psychology.
- Although Laura wanted to ride the horse.
- The committee voted to censure the attorney's behavior.

The second and fourth examples show the error known as a sentence fragment—a part of a sentence mistakenly punctuated as a sentence.

4A INDEPENDENT CLAUSES

When two or more independent clauses are joined, the result is a compound sentence. (The four sentence types will be discussed later in this chapter.) Independent clauses can be joined in the following ways. More patterns for joining such clauses are discussed in chapter 25.

Pattern 1: independent clause + comma + coordinating conjunction + independent clause. Note that the comma does not follow the coordinating conjunction. Coordinating conjunctions are easy to remember if you think of the mnemonic device *fanboys: for, and, nor, but, or, yet, so*. In the examples below, the coordinating conjunctions have been boldfaced.

- The room was hot, **and** Joe had a headache.
- He wanted to leave, **but** he also was required to attend the lecture.
- Joe knew nothing about birds, **nor** did he care much for them.
- He listened closely, though, **so** he'd pass the quiz.
- Joe's head throbbed, **yet** he was beginning to appreciate birds.
- Maybe he'd get himself a canary, **or** perhaps he'd buy a finch.
- At last Joe felt better, **for** he had developed an avian interest.

Pattern 2: independent clause + semicolon + independent clause.

- The room was hot; Joe had a headache.
- He wanted to leave; he was required to stay.
- Joe knew nothing about birds; he did not care much for them.
- He listened closely; he had a quiz to pass.
- Joe's head throbbed; he was beginning to appreciate birds.
- Maybe he'd get himself a canary; perhaps he'd buy a finch.
- Joe felt better; he had developed an interest in birds.

Pattern 3: independent clause + semicolon + conjunctive adverb + comma + independent clause. Common conjunctive adverbs include *consequently, furthermore, however, indeed, instead, meanwhile, moreover, nevertheless, next, then, therefore,* and *thus.* You will find a more thorough list in Chapter 25. Phrases like *on the other hand* and *in fact* also function as conjunctive adverbs. These words and phrases create more than just a grammatically correct sentence when used to join independent clauses—they also create a relationship between those clauses. *Consequently* indicates that a conclusion is forthcoming, and so do *hence* and *therefore. Furthermore* suggests that another point is about to be made, and so does *moreover.* In the following examples, the conjunctive adverbs have been boldfaced.

- The room was hot; *consequently*, Joe had a headache.
- He wanted to leave; *however*, he was required to attend the lecture.
- Joe knew nothing about birds; *moreover*, he didn't care much for them.
- He listened closely; *thus*, he'd pass the quiz.
- Joe's head throbbed; *nevertheless*, he was beginning to appreciate birds.
- Maybe he'd get himself a canary; *on the other hand*, perhaps he'd buy a finch.
- At last Joe felt better; *indeed*, he had developed an avian interest.

When you decide how to connect independent clauses, you make some very fine distinctions regarding the relationship between ideas within those clauses. The following list suggests the relationships that are created by the use of specific conjunctive adverbs.

Addition: also, besides, furthermore, moreover

Contrast: conversely, however, instead, nevertheless, nonetheless, on the other hand, otherwise, still

Comparison: likewise, similarly

Result, Conclusion, Summary: accordingly, therefore, thus, hence, then

Time: finally, meanwhile, next, subsequently, then
Emphasis: certainly, indeed, in fact

4B DEPENDENT CLAUSES

Every clause has both a subject and a verb. An independent (or main) clause has a subject and a verb, and it can be presented as a complete sentence and punctuated accordingly. A dependent (or subordinate) clause also has a subject and a verb, but it cannot stand alone as a sentence. To punctuate it as such would create a sentence fragment.

There are two types of dependent clauses: noun clauses (nominative dependent clauses) and modifying clauses. Modifying clauses can be either adverbial or adjectival. Furthermore, if the modifying clause is adverbial, it is introduced by a subordinating conjunction; if the modifying clause is adjectival, it is introduced by a relative pronoun (*who, whom, whose, which* or *that*), or by a relative adverb (*when, where, why*).

4C ADVERBIAL DEPENDENT CLAUSES

Adverbial dependent clauses modify verbs, verbals, adjectives, and adverbs. They provide information explaining *how, when, where, why, to what extent, under what conditions,* or *in what manner.* The subordinating conjunctions that begin this type of modifying clause express logical relationships, just as conjunctive adverbs do. Below is a list of subordinating conjunctions grouped according to the relationships they express.

Time: after, as, before, once, since, until, when, whenever, while

Place: where, wherever

Concession: although, even though, while, since, unless, whereas

Cause: because, since

Purpose: in order that, provided that, so that

Comparison: as if, as though, than

Condition: as long as, whether, if

To create an adverbial dependent clause, then, you place a subordinating conjunction in front of a group of words containing both a subject and verb.

- he often went to the beach
- because he often went to the beach

- the young woman liked studying psychology
- although the young woman liked studying psychology

- the committee voted to censure the attorney's behavior
- before the committee voted to censure the attorney's behavior

Subordinating conjunctions economically join otherwise independent clauses by creating relationships between them—relationships of time, purpose, result, place, condition, concession, contrast, manner, and cause. Examine the independent clauses below joined by a subordinating conjunction.

- Howard hates mowing the lawn
- it's raining outside
- Howard hates mowing the lawn when it's raining outside.

Some subordinating conjunctions can express more than one kind of relationship. *Since* can indicate time (*Things have changed since you arrived*) or reason (*Since you asked, the answer is no*).

Some subordinating conjunctions can also be used as different parts of speech. *After*, for instance, can connect independent clauses, rendering one of them subordinate (*The game resumed after the storm ended*), but it can also function as a preposition if it's followed not by a clause, but by an object of a preposition (*after the storm*).

Consider the following pairs of independent clauses and how they might be joined by subordinating conjunctions.

- the snake slithered quickly into the bushes
- it heard the approach of an enemy

- the cow seemed distressed
- Madge hesitated

There are many possibilities for combining these pairs of independent clauses, depending on which subordinating conjunction is used and which clause is subordinated. In the first pair, the snake might have slithered away *when* it heard an enemy approach or *because* it heard an enemy approach. One independent clause expresses a temporal relationship, the other a causal relationship.

Let's consider the second pair at length. Did Madge hesitate *because* the cow seemed distressed, or did the cow seem distressed *because* Madge hesitated? Notice the several possible meanings, each of which depends on the choice of the subordinating conjunction.

- When the cow seemed distressed, Madge hesitated.
- Because the cow seemed distressed, Madge hesitated.
- Although the cow seemed distressed, Madge hesitated.
- Whenever the cow seemed distressed, Madge hesitated.
- Madge hesitated as if the cow seemed distressed.
- When Madge hesitated, the cow seemed distressed.
- As long as Madge hesitated, the cow seemed distressed.

The relationship between Madge and the cow is established by the choice of the subordinating conjunction. If you tried to combine the two independent clauses with coordination instead of subordination, that subtle relationship would not be expressed.

- Madge hesitated, and the cow seemed distressed.
- Madge hesitated, yet the cow seemed distressed.

The meaning achieved by combining clauses also depends on which clause is subordinated. The independent (or main) clause carries the central, emphasized idea, and the subordinate clause attaches to, and significantly contributes to, that main idea. In the example above, either the cow's distress or Madge's hesitation can be the main idea, depending on what you want to emphasize.

Subordinating conjunctions are thus the workhorses of our language: They create meaning by clarifying the relationship between ideas, and they do so economically and precisely.

TIP: Adverbial-clause modifiers can substitute for either single-word adverbs or phrase modifiers.

- She likes to plant tomatoes at night.
    The underlined adverbial prepositional phrase tells *when.*

- She likes to plant tomatoes when the moon is full.
    The underlined adverbial dependent clause tells *when.*

- Mickey plays tennis everywhere.
    The underlined word, an adverb, tells *where.*

- Mickey plays tennis wherever he goes.
    The underlined adverbial dependent clause tells *where.*

- Shauna swims every day for exercise.
    The underlined adverbial prepositional phrase tells *why.*

- Shauna swims every day because she wants the exercise.
    The underlined adverbial dependent clause tells *why.*

Placement and Punctuation of Adverbial Clauses

An adverbial dependent clause can precede or follow the independent clause of a sentence. An adverbial dependent clause can also be inserted between the subject and the verb of the independent clause. The placement of dependent clauses most often depends on the stylistic effect you want to achieve. Compare the following sentences.

- Because Gloria likes tomatoes, she eats them every day.
- Gloria eats tomatoes every day because she likes them.

In these examples, it doesn't matter whether the independent clause or the dependent clause comes first. However, the way the sentences are punctuated does matter. Chapter 18 thoroughly discusses the principles governing the punctuation of dependent clauses, but here are two important rules to keep in mind when it comes to adverbial dependent clauses.

1. An adverbial dependent clause at the start of a sentence should be followed by a comma.

- Because he often spent time at the beach, his grades suffered.

2. An adverbial dependent clause following an independent clause is not usually preceded by a comma.

- His grades suffered because he spent so much time at the beach.

ERRORS TO AVOID IN PUNCTUATING ADVERBIAL DEPENDENT CLAUSES

A dependent clause mistakenly punctuated as a sentence is called a fragment, because it is only part of a sentence.

- Before they voted to censure the attorney.
- Because he went to the beach so often.

Sentence fragments most often result when the writer separates phrases or clauses that belong together. In other words, the writer punctuates with a period instead of a comma at the end of an introductory phrase or clause. The erroneously punctuated phrases below introduce the independent clauses that follow.

- Hoping her mother would let her go to the beach for the weekend.
- Hoping her mother would let her go to the beach for the weekend, Lola worked hard to finish her homework ahead of time.
- Exhausted by the effort they'd expended and by the defeat they had suffered at the hands of their rivals.
- Exhausted by the effort they'd expended and by the defeat they had suffered at the hands of their rivals, the hockey players found it very difficult to psych themselves up for the next game.

4D ADJECTIVAL DEPENDENT CLAUSES

An adjectival dependent clause—also called a relative clause—begins with a relative pronoun: *who, whom, whose, which,* or *that.* A clause beginning with a relative pronoun modifies a noun in the same way a single-word adjective does, or in the same way an adjectival prepositional phrase or a participial phrase does.

- Tom's car needs expensive repairs.
      This sentence employs a single-word adjective, *Tom's,* to modify *car.*
- The car belonging to Tom needs expensive repairs.
      This sentence uses a participial phrase, *belonging to Tom,* to modify *car.*

- The car that belongs to Tom needs expensive repairs.
    This sentence uses an adjectival dependent clause, *that belongs to Tom*, to modify *car*.

Adjectives tell more about nouns and pronouns by presenting descriptive details that answer the questions *what kind? which one? how many? which? whose?* In the following sentences, the adjectival dependent clauses have been underlined.

- Lavinia is a person who knows her own mind.
    The dependent clause answers the question *what kind of person?*
- The man who sat next to Clarissa lives next door to me.
    The dependent clause answers the question *which man?*
- The suitcase that Herbert had brought along burst open on the plane.
    The dependent clause answers the question *which suitcase?*

As you were reading over the above examples, a few questions probably occurred to you: When do you use commas, and when don't you use commas? Is there a difference between *that* and *which,* or are they interchangeable? Where does an adjectival clause actually end? When should *whom* be used instead of *who?*

Before we answer those questions, we need to observe that all the dependent clauses in the sentences above are embedded—that is, unlike the adverbial dependent clauses you were working with before (most of which appeared at the beginning or the end of a sentence), an adjectival dependent clause is frequently lodged somewhere deep inside a sentence. For this reason, such clauses are easily overlooked as dependent clauses, and sometimes the relative pronoun itself is dropped at the beginning of a clause, as in the third sentence, which can be rewritten: *The suitcase Herbert had brought along burst open on the plane.* The relative pronoun *that* can be dropped before *Herbert,* because the pronoun is understood or implied; that is, the reader can easily supply it.

Consider the following sentences in which the relative pronouns are implied at the beginning of adjectival dependent clauses.

- The flowers [that] she picked in the garden are beautiful.
- The house [that] the Smiths built collapsed in the hurricane.
- The bike [that] he bought was bright blue.
- The box [that] Mordecai set on the table was filled with fragile items.

When we're speaking, we frequently omit the relative pronoun from such clauses because there is little chance that we will be misunderstood.

Restrictive and Nonrestrictive Adjectival Dependent Clauses

Whether or not you use a comma to set off an adjectival dependent clause depends on what you intend your clause and sentence to mean. If the clause can be removed without changing the meaning or diminishing the readability of the sentence, the clause should be set off with punctuation. But if the clause is essential to the identification of the noun it modifies, the clause must not be punctuated.

- John, who sat next to Mary on the bus, looked sleepy and rather sick.
- The man who sat next to Mary on the bus looked sleepy and rather sick.

In the first sentence, you know the name of the person who looked sleepy and rather sick. It was John, who happened to be sitting next to Mary on the bus, but the detail about seating is not necessary to identify him. The adjectival dependent clause, *who sat next to Mary on the bus*, merely adds supplementary information about John, but it doesn't identify him in the same way his name does. The clause is thus a nonrestrictive (or nonessential) adjectival clause.

In the second sentence, you need a way to identify *which* man looked sleepy and rather sick. It wasn't the man who sat next to Bill or the man who sat next to Sally; it was the man who sat next to Mary. Because you need that information in order to identify the man who sat next to Mary on the bus, you do not put commas around the adjectival dependent clause. The clause contains essential information needed to identify *which* man. In fact, you know who looked sleepy and sick only because you're told it was the man sitting next to Mary. The meaning of the subject is therefore restricted—made specific and precise—by the presence of the clause. Restrictive adjectival dependent clauses are also known as *essential clauses*—because the information they provide is crucial to the meaning of a sentence.

A nonrestrictive clause can be removed from a sentence without harming the grammatical structure of the sentence, but a different sentence results. Ideally, everything in a sentence should count—whether it clarifies, adds, modifies, limits, expands, connects, explains, describes, or defines. The best way to determine whether an adjectival clause is restrictive or nonrestrictive, therefore, is not by asking whether you can delete the clause, but by asking whether you intend the clause to narrow down or restrict the meaning of the noun or pronoun being modified by it.

The following examples further illustrate the difference between restrictive and nonrestrictive clauses.

- The dog that Tom found belongs to Roger Smith.
    The adjectival clause *that Tom found* does not provide disposable, incidental information. The clause provides important information that enables us to understand which dog is being discussed. If we eliminate the dependent clause, we're left with only *The dog belongs to Roger Smith*. You can see how essential the adjectival dependent clause is to the intended meaning once you try to remove it from the sentence.

- Kim, who arrived early, helped arrange the event.
    Although it might be interesting that Kim arrived early, this fact is not vital to the meaning of the sentence. The clause *who arrived early* is thus nonrestrictive and has been set off by a pair of commas.

Understanding the distinction between restrictive and nonrestrictive elements and then punctuating them appropriately will add precision to your sentences. If you intend your readers to regard an element as restrictive but you punctuate otherwise, your sentence will not communicate your intended meaning.

For example, the adjectival dependent clause in the sentences below can be either restrictive or nonrestrictive, depending upon which of two possible meanings the writer wants to communicate.

- The box that Mordecai set carefully on the table next to the door is filled with fragile items.
    The reader needs to know that a *particular* box is filled with fragile items, so the clause is restrictive.

- The box, which Mordecai set carefully on the table next to the door, is filled with fragile items.
    In this sentence, the box itself is emphasized, and its location is secondary. That is, one particular box is not being distinguished from other boxes. Only one box is under consideration, therefore, the clause is nonrestrictive.

That and *which* differ in function and in usage. *Which* is often used to introduce a non-restrictive clause.

- The candy, which Mrs. Fitzgibbon told Eddie not to eat, was mysteriously gone when she returned.

That introduces restrictive clauses.

- The safe that contained those important documents seems to have been stolen.

That can refer to human beings, but *who* and *whom* are preferred. *Which* should never refer to human beings. Finally, *who* and *that* are commonly used to begin adjectival clauses that modify nouns naming animals. The choice of *who* or *that* depends on how close you feel to the creature being described.

- My Persian cat, who eats nothing but chopped liver, needs to diet.
- The cow that gave the most milk won the Bessie Award.

Inside the Adjectival Dependent Clause

A relative pronoun can function as the subject of an adjectival clause when another subject is not present.

- The man who ate sushi was rushed to the hospital.
    The pronoun *who* is the subject of the adjectival clause, and *ate* is the verb.

- The test that Barbara took was extremely difficult.
    In this sentence, a subject (*Barbara*) follows a relative pronoun (*that*) that introduces an adjectival clause, and *took* is the verb.

All relative pronouns except *whom* can function as the subjects of their clauses. (Remember that *whom* is an objective-case, rather than a subjective-case, pronoun.)

Reducing Adjectival Dependent Clauses to Phrases

Adjectival dependent clauses provide an important kind of modification, but their excessive use results in wordiness. Achieving economy in one's style—saying the most, most effectively, with the fewest words—is one of the goals of good writing. Consider the following sentence.

- The man *who was walking down the street* was the one *who delivered the mysterious package.*

The sentence includes two adjectival clauses (one modifying *man* and the other modifying *one*), and it consists of sixteen words. If you reduce the first dependent clause to a participial phrase and delete the relative pronoun from the beginning of the second dependent clause, you get a streamlined sentence requiring only ten words to communicate the same message.

- The man walking down the street delivered the mysterious package.

Below is a series of sentences containing adjectival dependent clauses. Notice how each wordy dependent clause can be reduced to a phrase.

- Melinda, who was a junior psychology major, told her depressed friend to seek counseling.
- Melinda, a junior psychology major, told her depressed friend to seek counseling.
- Kelly looked at the clock, which was ticking slowly, and wished for English class to end.

- Kelly looked at the slowly ticking clock and wished for English class to end.
- The thought that irritated him most revolved around an unanswerable question.
- The thought irritating him most revolved around an unanswerable question.

- The children who were playing in the street didn't see the car that was speeding toward them.
- The children playing in the street didn't see the car speeding toward them.

Clauses that include *to be* verbs (*is, are, was, were*) are most easily reducible to phrases. In the final series, for example, eliminating *who were* and *that was* results in a more economical sentence. But the reduction of adjectival dependent clauses to phrases can be accomplished with verbs other than *to be*. You can make use of apposition in order to economize, as in the first series.

4E NOUN CLAUSES

A gerund phrase can function as the subject of a sentence, as the object of a preposition or a verb, and as a subjective complement (a predicate nominative) or an objective complement. Dependent clauses can also function as nouns, but it is often very difficult to discern their use as such. Because clauses contain subjects and verbs, the temptation is to locate the verb within the noun clause and identify it as the verb of the main clause of the sentence.

Dependent clauses functioning as nouns are called noun clauses or nominative clauses. They are introduced by *that, which, who, whoever, what, whatever, whichever, whomever, whether, where, when, how*. A noun clause, because it is not a modifier, will not limit, expand on, add to, or embellish another noun in the sentence. Instead, nominative clauses function as single-word nouns do—as subjects, objects, and complements.

Noun Clauses as Subjects

In each of the the paired sentences below, the first sentence has a single-word noun (perhaps with a modifier) as the subject; the second sentence has a noun clause as the subject. In each pair, the subjects have been italicized and the verbs have been underlined.

- The *person* who took my debit card <u>should return</u> it.
- *Whoever* took my debit card <u>should return</u> it.

- Her snide *remark* <u>angered</u> me.
- *What she said* <u>angered</u> me.

- *His devotion* to his mother <u>is known</u> by everyone.
- *That he is devoted to his mother* <u>is known</u> by everyone.

In the first sentence of each pair, the core of the subject is easily recognized: *person, remark, devotion*. Each of those single words can be expanded into a noun clause without changing the meaning of the sentence. But a writer should never expand a noun into a noun clause without good reason, such as the desire to achieve a particular stylistic effect (securing more emphasis on the subject, for instance, or varying the sentence structure), because the transformation will increase the number of words in the sentence.

The easiest way to identify a noun clause functioning as the subject of a sentence is to locate the verb of the independent clause. In the sentences below, the independent-clause verbs have been underlined, so finding the noun clauses is simply a matter of examining the words leading up to the verbs.

- Whatever you want is all right with me.

  Whatever you want is the subject of the sentence. The subject of the noun clause is *you*, and the verb is *want*.

- Whoever locates the lost child will be hailed as a hero.

  Whoever locates the lost child is the subject of the sentence. The subject of the noun clause is *whoever*, and the verb of the noun clause is *locates*.

- Whose book this is remains a mystery.

  This sentence is more complicated because there is a complement within the noun clause. The entire clause reads *Whose book this is*. The verb of the noun clause is *is*, but what is the subject? Ask yourself what is? in order to arrive at the answer: *this is*. *Whose book* therefore becomes the complement (or predicate nominative) of the pronoun *this*. The interrogative structure of *Whose book is this?* has been inverted.

Noun Clauses as Complements

A complement, as you may recall from section B in Chapter 1, is a noun connected to the subject by a linking verb, often a conjugated form of *to be*. The complement shares an identity with the subject. In the sentences below, the complements have been underlined.

- This has been his position for years.
- She is president.

In both sentences above, the complement is a noun, but remember that adjectives can also be complements, as in *The baby looked happy*. Below are paired sentences that include complements. In the first sentence of each pair, the italicized complement is a single word; in the second sentence, the single-noun complement has been expanded into a noun-clause complement, also italicized.

- The blue house is her *home*.
- The blue house is *where she lives*.

  The subject of the noun clause is *she*, and the verb is *lives*.

- Winning the award is her *goal*.
- Winning the award is *what she hopes to achieve*.

  The subject of the noun clause is *she*, and the verb is *hopes*. This sentence also contains two verbals: *winning the award* (the gerund subject) and *to achieve* (the infinitive object of the noun-clause verb *to hope*).

- Mercy Hospital is Stephen's *place of birth*.
- Mercy Hospital is *where Stephen was born*.

  Stephen is the subject of the noun clause, and *was born* is the noun-clause verb.

- This is her *profession*.
- This is *what she does for a living*.

  The subject of the noun clause *what she does for a living* is *she*, and the verb is *does*.

- This is *their method for finishing so quickly*.
- This is *how they finish so quickly*.

  The subject of the noun clause *how they finish so quickly* is *they*, and the verb is *finish*.

Notice that a comma is never used to separate a noun-clause subject from the rest of a sentence, nor is a comma used to set off a noun clause that functions as a complement. A fundamental principle of punctuation is that a single comma never separates a subject from a verb. Sometimes, however, an entire phrase or clause is inserted as an interruptive element between a subject and a verb. Such an interruptive element must then be set off with commas or other appropriate punctuation at both ends.

Noun Clauses as Objects

A nominative dependent clause can function as a direct object and as an object of a preposition.

- Tom appreciated her remark.
    The verb *appreciated* takes a direct object because it demands that the question *whom?* or *what?* be answered. Tom appreciated *what?* Her remark. Therefore *remark* is a noun used as a direct object.

- Tom appreciated what she had said.
    What she had said functions the same way the noun *remark* did in the first sentence—it answers the question *what?* It, too, is a direct object.

Noun clauses often serve as objects of prepositions. Compare the following sentences.

- Please listen to my remarks.
    Remarks is the object of the preposition *to.*

- Please understand my remarks.
    Remarks is the direct object of the verb.

- Please listen to what I'm saying.
    What I'm saying is the object of the preposition *to.*

- Please understand what I'm saying.
    What I'm saying is the direct object of the verb.

When you are identifying a noun clause functioning as the direct object of a verb, you need to recognize that such a clause is an object *within the sentence itself*. The noun clause is a major element in the sentence. When you are identifying a noun clause functioning as an object of a preposition, however, you are first identifying a modifying phrase—a prepositional phrase. The noun clause takes the place of a single word (a noun) as the object of the preposition, but the clause is still *inside* the prepositional phrase, and the entire phrase itself, not the clause, is a minor, modifying element in the sentence.

There is a significant difference, then, between a noun clause serving as a direct object and a noun clause serving as the object of a preposition. A direct object, like an indirect object, is a major sentence element—so major, in fact, that a common sentence pattern is SVO (subject-verb-object). When you identify a noun clause as an object, therefore, you are working with an essential component of the sentence as a whole. When you identify a noun clause as the object of a preposition, however, you are dealing with a less important component of the sentence—a modifying phrase—even though the noun clause within the phrase may be lengthy and complicated.

In short, a noun clause used as a direct object must be considered in relation to the entire sentence, but a noun clause functioning as the object of a preposition need not be considered in relation to the sentence as a whole, because such a noun clause is tucked away inside a phrase.

Noun Clauses as Objects in Participial Phrases

A noun clause has been used as the object of the participle in the sentence below.

- Knowing that he was being followed, Roger crept softly toward the door.

In order to identify whether the noun clause is the object in a participial phrase or in a gerund phrase, you must identify the phrase itself. The phrase in the sentence above begins with a word ending in *-ing* and obviously modifies *Roger*, so it is a participial phrase. The participle is *knowing,* and if you ask *knowing what?*, your answer will yield the object: *that he was being followed,* a noun clause. Inside the noun clause itself, the subject is *he,* and the verb is *was being followed.* If the participial phrase were converted to a gerund phrase, the noun clause itself would be the same, but it would be the object of the gerund.

- Knowing that he was being followed gave Roger the creeps.

Whether a noun clause is an object of a participle or an object of a gerund depends entirely on whether the phrase itself is a participial phrase or a gerund phrase. Consider two more examples.

- Thinking that no one would notice, the young couple kissed behind the bushes.
- Thinking that no one would notice was naive.

In both sentences, *that no one would notice* is the noun clause, with *no one* as the subject and *would notice* as the verb. In the first sentence, the phrase is an introductory participial modifier, so the noun clause is the object of the participle. In the second sentence, *thinking* is a gerund, so the noun clause *that no one would notice* is the object of the gerund. The entire gerund phrase is the subject of the sentence. Here are a few more examples of participial phrases containing noun-clause objects.

- Lucinda, hoping that the horse would not throw her, held the reins tightly.
    Here, *hoping* is a participle introducing a phrase that modifies *Lucinda*. The noun clause *that the horse would not throw her* is therefore the object of the participle.
- Having always understood that someday her secret would be revealed, Elizabeth calmly met with angry relatives.
    Having always understood is the present-perfect participle. What did Elizabeth understand? The answer is *that someday her secret would be revealed*, the noun-clause object of the phrase modifying Elizabeth.
- The lonely dog, realizing that its owner wasn't coming back, headed toward the hills.
    In this case, *realizing* is the participle, and its object is the noun clause *that its owner wasn't coming back*. The participial phrase modifies *the lonely dog*.
- Rupert sat in the rain, thinking that everyone he loved had abandoned him.
    This is particularly difficult. There are two dependent clauses—*that everyone had abandoned him* and *that he loved*. The *that* in the second, modifying dependent clause is understood.

If you recall, the implied, understood *that* is common, particularly in speech. In the following sentences, the optional *that* has been parenthesized.

- The man (that) Lucas saw reminded him of his father.
- Terry hoped (that) the girl next door would be home.

Noun Clauses as Objects in Gerund Phrases

The type of phrase—participial or gerund—must first be identified in order to determine whether the clause inside it is functioning as the object of a gerund or the object of a participle. The following sentences contain gerund phrases with noun clauses as the objects. In the sentences below, the gerund phrases have been underlined and the noun clauses have been bracketed.

- Knowing [that you can always go home] relieves anxiety.
- Recalling [how much his mother liked artichokes] often amused Elbert.
- Understanding [who is responsible for the tragedy] will prevent a similar event.
- Buying [whatever struck his fancy] occupied most of the wealthy man's time.
- Finding out [when she would arrive] obsessed Gerald.

4F CLAUSES EMBEDDED IN OTHER CLAUSES

Sometimes one dependent clause can be embedded in another clause, particularly if two different kinds of clauses are present. Examine the following sentence.

- Richard hoped that although Barbara was angry she would still attend the meeting.

The subordinating conjunction *although,* which begins an adverbial clause, follows *that,* which begins a noun clause. Both clauses are dependent. When you see a construction like this, pick it apart word by word. Unraveling dependent clauses becomes easy if you determine where one clause ends and another begins. First, *although Barbara was angry* is easily identifiable as an adverbial modifier. If you mentally bracket that clause, you see that it interrupts a noun clause, *that she would still attend the meeting.* This clause answers the question *what?* following the verb *hoped.* The clause functioning as a noun is the object of the verb, and the adverbial clause modifies the same verb.

Consider the following example.

- John believed that, even though Sally often fibbed, she was basically an honest person.
  Even though Sally fibbed is an adverbial-clause modifier that interrupts the noun clause *that she was basically an honest person.* Once again, the verb takes an object: What did John believe? The answer (in the form of a noun clause) is *that she was basically an honest person.*

Sometimes a noun clause can even serve as the subject of another noun clause, as in this sentence.

- That whatever he does is fine with Mom really irritates me.
  That whatever he does is fine with Mom is the subject of the sentence, and *irritates* is the verb. The subject of the noun clause functioning as the subject is *whatever he does,* and the verb for the subject of the noun clause is *is.* So a noun clause is the subject of the sentence, and another noun clause is the subject of the noun clause.

A noun clause can also function as the subject of a noun clause used as an object, as in the following.

- Robert thinks that whatever he says pleases people.
  The object of the verb *thinks* is the noun clause *that whatever he says pleases people.* This clause has as its subject *that whatever he says,* and the verb for this subject is *pleases.*

4G SENTENCE TYPES

The four sentence types are defined according to the number and kinds of clauses that appear between the initial capital letter and the terminal punctuation. A simple sentence consists of one independent clause and no dependent clauses. A compound sentence consists of two or more independent clauses and no dependent clauses. A complex sentence consists of one independent clause and one or more dependent clauses. A compound-complex sentence consists of two or more independent clauses and one or more dependent clauses.

4H SIMPLE SENTENCES

A simple sentence is often mistakenly defined according to its length, just as the term *sentence* itself can be mistakenly defined according to the completeness of the *thought* it conveys. Simple sentences are thus believed to be short and uncomplicated, along the lines of *The dog ate its dinner,* or *She slept until noon.*

The *simplicity* of a sentence, however, has nothing to do with the completeness or content of the thought expressed, or with the number of words used to express that thought. How simple, for instance, is the following short sentence?

- A flow of negative energy into the black hole therefore reduces its mass.

(Stephen Hawking, *The Theory of Everything*, Beverly Hills, CA: New Millennium Press, 2003, p. 84).

This sentence conveys a complete thought, yet that thought is far from simple. This sentence is, however, a simple sentence, because it contains only one independent clause and no dependent clauses.

A simple sentence, no matter how long, no matter how intellectually dense, has only one independent clause. While the sentence above illustrates the problem with defining a simple sentence in terms of the thought contained within it, the sentence below illustrates the problem with defining a simple sentence in terms of its length.

- Having been disappointed by love in the past, Lucas, his head bowed and burdened with grief, his arms limp and heavy by his sides, walked slowly and haltingly away from the woman sobbing in the doorway, her cries and tears a sign for him to return and give her a chance to show love and devotion.

Even though the sentence is fifty-six words long, it is a simple sentence, because it contains only one independent clause—along with many, many modifying words and phrases.

Simple sentences can have compound subjects and compound verbs, which make the sentences appear to be more than simple. The following sentence, for instance, has a compound subject.

- The dog and the cat ate dinner side by side.

Both animals did the same thing—ate dinner.

Let's combine the compound subject with a compound predicate.

- The dog and the cat ate dinner side by side and slept peacefully together, too.

In this sentence, both animals did two things: ate and slept. A compound verb is thus attached to a compound subject, yet there is still only one independent clause, and therefore the sentence is simple.

Consider a few more examples of simple sentences with compound subjects or compound verbs, or both compound subjects and compound verbs.

- Her mother and her father separately advised against joining the sorority.
- Robert and his friend went sailing and then ate dinner at the club.
- The tree, weakened by parasites, fell sideways and crashed into the garage.
- Albert thought the matter over and decided to speak to his brother.

4I COMPOUND SENTENCES

A compound sentence consists of two or more independent clauses joined in one of three ways: (a) by a comma, a coordinating conjunction, and a semicolon; (b) by a semicolon, conjunctive adverb, and comma; (c) by a semicolon alone. (See pages 62–63 for further discussion.) Use a coordinating conjunction or a semicolon when the independent clauses joined to form a compound sentence are considered coordinate—that is, when you want to connect them in a way that suggests they are equal, balanced, or logically related to each other in one intact grammatical unit. Use a conjunctive adverb when you want to express a different kind of relationship between the two independent clauses. Neither clause is more significant than the other, and therefore the typical compound sentence builds by showing addition, contrast, comparison, cause, result, conclusion, or emphasis.

- Tom likes tomatoes, José likes eggplant, and Elaine likes green peppers.
- He drives an expensive car; he has money to burn.
- The lawn turned brown and died; consequently, it had to be replaced with sod the following season.
- She doesn't study much, but she gets good grades.
- Nick will finish the race, or he will die trying.

4J COMPLEX SENTENCES

A complex sentence contains one independent clause and at least one clause made dependent by a subordinating conjunction or a relative pronoun. Dependent clauses beginning with subordinating conjunctions are adverbial, and dependent clauses beginning with relative pronouns are adjectival. When you are identifying types of sentences, it is important to know that certain words can function as either subordinating conjunctions or as prepositions, depending on whether they are followed by groups of words containing subjects and verbs. Compare the following sentences.

- <u>After the heavy rain</u>, trees seemed to turn greener.
  In this sentence, *after* is not followed by a subject and verb; therefore, it functions as a preposition with *rain* as its object.
- <u>After the heavy rain had stopped</u>, trees seemed to turn greener.
  Here, *after* begins a dependent clause: *rain* is the subject, and *had stopped* is the past-perfect verb.

Remember also that any independent clause can be made dependent by preceding it with a subordinating conjunction. Consider the following independent clauses.

- the flowers had bloomed
- the man ate his lunch
- my friend ran four miles

If you place a subordinating conjunction before each of the clauses above, you create dependent clauses.

- because the flowers had bloomed
- as the man ate his lunch
- although my friend ran four miles

Nominative Clauses and Sentence Type: Simple or Complex?

Most grammar books define a simple sentence as having a subject and a verb—that is, having only one independent clause and no dependent clauses. The presence of a dependent clause in fact does generally classify a sentence as complex. What is seldom explored, however, is the status of the sentence if a noun clause functions as a subject, an object, or a complement. Remember that a noun clause can function in the same way a single word does—as a subject, as an object (of a verb, participle, gerund, or preposition), or as a complement; but a noun clause must also be dependent, since it cannot be punctuated as a sentence. You can therefore have the rather peculiar instance of a dependent clause (which would ordinarily establish a sentence as complex) functioning as a major element in a sentence containing only an independent clause. Consider the following, paying particular attention to the underlined words.

- Whoever keeps a journal is rewarded with a record of ongoing life and its many changes.
  The underlined noun clause is the subject of this sentence.

- That Rudy enjoys his new job makes his parents very happy.
  This sentence also has a noun clause for its subject.

- Your life is whatever you make of it.
  In this sentence, the noun clause is a complement.

- She made a copy of what Bob wrote.
  The noun clause *what Bob wrote* is the object of the preposition *of*.

- They maintain that faith can move mountains.
  The noun clause is the object of the verb *maintain*.

Each sentence is simple according to the accepted definition that a simple sentence has only an independent clause; yet each is also complex according to the accepted definition that a complex sentence has a dependent clause.

The fourth sentence is less problematic than the others, because its dependent clause is contained within a modifying phrase, and the phrase can be *eliminated*. In other words, the entire prepositional phrase can be removed without gutting the sentence grammatically. But a subject, or a necessary complement or object, cannot be removed: Each of the other four sentences above would become a fragment if the noun clause were deleted.

Despite the special circumstances discussed in this section, it is generally safe to assume that the presence of any kind of dependent clause anywhere in a sentence makes the sentence complex.

4K COMPOUND-COMPLEX SENTENCES

Compound-complex sentences begin with at least two independent clauses legitimately joined.

- The dog waiting patiently for his dinner wagged his tail, and the cat paced nervously.
- John ordered from the menu quickly, so Luther followed suit by choosing the first item on the list.
- On the beach near Miami, we found a rare shell, but we left it in the motel by mistake.

To those independent clauses, a dependent clause may simply be added, or a phrase can be turned into a dependent clause.

- The dog waiting patiently for his dinner wagged his tail, but the cat paced nervously because it hadn't eaten for days.
- John ordered from the menu quickly, so Luther followed suit by choosing the first item he saw.
- On the beach near Miami, we found a rare shell, but we left it in the motel by mistake when we checked out.

Below are three compound sentences. Each is followed by a dependent clause that can be attached to the compound sentence to make a complex sentence. The third sentence in each set is an example of a compound-complex sentence that can be formed by the combination of the compound sentence with the dependent clause.

- John got great grades, and he was very proud of his accomplishment.
- because he worked diligently
- Because he worked diligently, John got great grades, and he was very proud of his accomplishment.

- The young artist struggled with adversity; ultimately, he became famous in his field.
- who never anticipated such success
- The young artist, who never anticipated such success, struggled with adversity; ultimately, he became famous in his field.

    [Note: This sentence has redundant elements.]

- Nick hated to eat at restaurants; therefore, he seldom went out for dinner.
- even though his friends wanted him to
- Nick hated to eat at restaurants; therefore, he seldom went out for dinner even though his friends wanted him to.

PART II:

GRAMMAR: RULES, CONVENTIONS, AND ERRORS TO AVOID

CHAPTER 5

AGREEMENT OF SUBJECTS AND VERBS

The principle of subject-verb agreement seems simple: A singular subject requires a singular verb, and a plural subject requires a plural verb. But errors in subject-verb agreement are the most common grammatical errors in newspapers and magazines. The thirty-six rules in this chapter will help you avoid such blunders.

Most errors in subject-verb agreement result from the writer's failure to locate the subject of the clause in which the verb appears. Before we discuss the rules of subject-verb agreement, therefore, let's master eight easy methods for finding a subject.

5A FINDING THE SUBJECT OF A CLAUSE

1. You will never find the subject of a clause within a prepositional phrase. That is, an object of a preposition never functions as a subject. Therefore, you need to disregard all prepositional phrases when you are seeking the subject. In the sentence below, the subject has been boldfaced, and the prepositional phrases have been underlined.

   - **One** of every four people in the workforce lacks health insurance. (See rule 4 in section 5B.)
     The noun *insurance* is the direct object of the transitive verb *lacks*.

2. The subject of a clause is not necessarily the most conspicuous noun (or pronoun) in the clause. The subject of the sentence below has been boldfaced, and the prepositional phrases have been underlined.

   - A **few** of the employees of the food court at the Southland Mall won a three-week vacation to Europe.

All but one of the most conspicuous nouns are functioning as objects of prepositions. (The exception is *vacation*, which is functioning as the direct object of the transitive verb *won*.) The two most conspicuous nouns (*Southland Mall* and *Europe*) are proper nouns.

3. Direct and indirect objects of transitive verbs never function as subjects of clauses. In the following sentence, the subject has been boldfaced, the direct object has been underlined, and the indirect object has been italicized.

   • The **mayor** gave her *assistant* a difficult task.

4. Do not mistake a complement for the subject of a clause. In a clause with a linking verb, a subject is being equated with a complement. In the following sentence, the subject has been boldfaced, the prepositional phrase has been underlined, and the complement has been italicized.

   • **Another** of her favorite rock bands is *Luna*. (See rule 11 in section 5B.)

5. In an inverted clause, the subject will follow the verb rather than precede it. Inverted sentences often begin with one or more prepositional phrases. In the following sentence, the subject has been boldfaced, and the prepositional phrases have been underlined.

   • Across the street from the restaurant was a new **supermarket**. (See rule 29A in section 5B.)

6. Many inverted clauses begin with the expletive *there*, which never functions as the subject of a clause. The subject of the following sentence has been boldfaced, and the prepositional phrase has been underlined.

   • There were several **magazines** in the mailbox. (See rules 29B–D in section 5B.)

7. Do not mistake the object of a gerund (a verbal noun ending in *-ing*) for the subject of a clause. In the sentence below, the gerund, which is serving as the subject, has been boldfaced, and the object of the gerund has been italicized.

   • **Losing** the first three *games* was a big setback. (See rule 7 in section 5B.)
     The noun *setback* is a complement.

8. An entire dependent clause can function as the subject of a clause. In the sentence below, the subject, which has been boldfaced, is a nominative dependent clause. The complement has been italicized, and the prepositional phrase has been underlined.

   • **What she wants** is a fresh *start* in life. (See rule 34 in section 5B.)

5B SUBJECT-VERB AGREEMENT: THE BASICS

1. Subjects in the Form of *A and B* (Compound-Additive Subjects)

Compound-additive subjects usually take the form *A and B*. Such subjects require a plural verb if *A* and *B* name distinct entities or qualities. (The coordinating conjunction *and* joining *A* and *B* functions like a plus sign.) A compound-additive subject can also take the form of a series of three or more elements joined by *and*.

The elements of the compound-additive subjects in the following sentences have been underlined. Erroneous verbs are followed by bracketed, boldfaced corrections.

   • Small wonder vaccine production and research has [**have**] suffered so badly of late, leading to repeated shortages of flu and childhood vaccines.
     ("Action on Anthrax," editorial, *Wall Street Journal*, 2 Jan. 2004, p. A8)

- The absence of chemical and biological weapons and our failure thus far to create a stable, secular democracy makes [make] it extremely difficult for Americans to justify the price in blood paid by coalition soldiers and by Iraqi civilians.
  (Timothy Noah, "Assassination Porn," Slate.com, 5 Aug. 2004, paragraph 5)

- Shock and titillation in popular culture is [are] nothing new.
  (David Bauder, "TV Hastens to Cover After Jackson Uproar," for Associated Press, in *Pittsburgh Post-Gazette*, 7 Feb. 2004, p. B8)

- Their [the Velvet Underground's] disillusionment, exhaustion and ache is [are] explosive, and the churning rhythm guitar in "What Goes On" could shame lead guitarists.
  ("The Five Hundred Greatest Albums of All Time," *Rolling Stone*, 11 Dec. 2003, p. 154)

Compound-Additive Subjects and Singular Verbs

There are six categories of compound-additive subjects for which singular verbs are usually preferred.

A. Choose a singular verb if the second element of a compound-additive subject is a synonym (or near synonym) of the first element—that is, if the second element restates, renames, or duplicates the first element. The subject *wear and tear,* for instance, should take a singular verb.

  - The moaning and groaning has increased.

B. Choose a singular verb if the meanings of the nouns in a compound-additive subject overlap considerably. As subjects, standard phrases such as *the sum and substance* and *my pride and joy* call for singular verbs. And singular verbs are defensible in the following sentences, whose compound-additive subjects have been underlined.

  - The extent and severity of the problem is worse than we could have predicted.
  - The size and scope of the problem continues to alarm us.

(Deciding whether a compound-additive subject is singular in meaning can be difficult. When in doubt, prefer the plural verb.)

C. Choose a singular verb if the two elements of a compound-additive subject emphasize the double nature of a single thing or person, as in the following sentences: *Its blessing and its curse is its accessibility. The long and short of it is this: We need new leadership. My best friend and next-door neighbor is a website designer.*

D. Choose a singular verb if the two elements of a compound-additive subject together constitute a single unit or entity in your mind. As subjects, *macaroni and cheese, fish and chips, pasta and meat sauce, chicken and dumplings,* and *oil and vinegar* should each take a singular verb.

E. Choose a singular verb if the elements of a compound-additive subject are parts of a single process, idea, etc. As a subject, *forgiving and forgetting* must take a singular verb, and so must the subjects of the following sentences.

  - Buying and selling kitsch on eBay is an amusing way to make money.

F. Choose a singular verb if one or all of the elements of a compound-additive subject are preceded by the adjective *every* or *each*. If the pronoun *each* follows the two or more elements in a compound-additive subject (and thus functions as an appositive), however, the verb must be plural.

- Every language and skin color are [is] represented, but we have one thing in common and we all know it: a relative is having a cancer operation, and we are waiting.

  (Denise Grady, "Waiting for News in a Room of Death and Miracles," *New York Times*, 9 Mar. 2004, p. D5)

- He cited Monica Lewinsky and Kathleen Willey as two victims whose every transgression and flaw have [has] been exposed.

  (Helen Kennedy, "She's Not Miss-ing [sic] Bill Probe," *New York Daily News*, 22 Mar. 1998, p. 4)

The following sentences are correct.

- Each supervisor and employee is required to attend the meeting.
- The supervisor and the employee each are required to attend the meeting.
- Every supervisor and every employee is required to attend the meeting.
- Every Tom, Dick, and Harry seems to be a Monday-morning quarterback.
- Everybody and his mother seems to be on a low-carbohydrate diet these days.

CAUTION

Do not confuse the prepositions *plus, in addition to, along with,* and *as well as* with the coordinating conjunction *and. And* is the only word that can unite two or more nouns or pronouns to form a compound-additive subject. The nounal or pronominal contents of a prepositional phrase beginning with *plus, in addition to, along with,* or *as well as* have no influence on the singularity or plurality of the verb of a clause (see rule 4), and any such prepositional phrase is almost always set off with commas at both ends. The subjects of the following sentences have been underlined, and erroneous verbs are followed by bracketed, boldfaced corrections.

- That plan, plus Plans B and C, have [has] come and gone, and the challenge of renewal remains.

  (photo caption, *Pittsburgh Post-Gazette*, 8 Feb. 2004, p. G1)

- White, as well as her successor Gustave Lobrano, were [was] remarkably successful in finding new young writers—often enough New York writers—who gave the magazine an original kind of vitality and its readers something mysterious and lasting to hold on to as the weekly issues came and went.

  (David Remnick, "Introduction," *Wonderful Town* [New York: Random House, 2000], p. xi)

---

2. Subjects in the Form of *A or B; A nor B; either A or B;* and *neither A nor B* (Compound-Alternative Subjects)

Compound-alternative subjects take the forms *A or B; A nor B; either A or B;* and *neither A nor B.* The words constituting the *A* and *B* elements in a compound-alternative subject can both be nouns, can both be pronouns, or can be a combination of a noun and a pronoun. Sometimes both *A* and *B* will be singular; sometimes both *A* and *B* will be plural; sometimes *A* will be singular and *B* plural; and sometimes *A* will be plural and *B* singular. But despite the array of possibilities, conjugating the verb is easy: The verb always agrees in number with the part of the compound-alternative subject closer to the verb. That is, the singularity or plurality of the *B* element determines the singularity or plurality of the verb.

A compound-alternative subject will sometimes consist of three or more elements, though many editors insist that *neither … nor* constructions be limited to two elements.

- Traditional Arab shoppers may occasionally be spotted wearing headscarves with designer logos, but neither Prada nor Missoni nor Christian Dior, a unit of LVMH Moet Hennessy Louis Vuitton, produce [**produces**] them.

  (Cecilie Rohwedder, "The Chic of Arabia," *Wall Street Journal*, 23 Jan. 2004, p. A13)

TIP: When a compound-alternative subject consists of one singular element and one plural element, it is stylistically preferable for the plural element to be positioned closer to the verb.

- It does not appear that the senator or his friends have committed an impropriety.

In the following examples, the *B* elements have been underlined. Erroneous verbs are followed by bracketed, boldfaced corrections.

- And he or his publisher seem [**seems**] to hope that such an opening might hook the reader and justify the silly, hype-inducing embargo of this book.

  (Michiko Kakutani, "'Hollywood Animal': Screenplay by Schadenfreude, from a Story by Angst," *New York Times* online, 27 Jan. 2004, paragraph 2)

- Dessert options offer fewer fireworks, but the financier with pear and ginger or the raspberry napoleon with Thai basil syrup are [**is**] irreproachable—the perfect exclamation to Robins's bravura performance.

  (Brad Goldfarb, "All the Dish," *Interview*, Apr. 2004, p. 99)

- Their passion is all the stronger because one or both of them is [**are**] permanently boozed up, bruised, or flushed with fury.

  (Anthony Lane, "Arms and the Woman," *New Yorker*, 8 Sept. 1997, p. 91)

- Neither Leno nor Letterman were [**was**] available for comment.

  (Adam Buckman, "It's 'Late Fight,'" *New York Post*, 20 June 2000, p. 83)

- Neither Lobel Brothers Prime Meats on Madison Avenue, which has grass-fed beef, nor Fairway on Broadway, which carries organic meat, have [**has**] noticed an uptick in orders.

  (Marian Burros, "Eating Well: Warily Searching for Safer Beef," *New York Times*, 31 Dec. 2003, p. D4)

- Last fall, he [Mel Gibson] insisted: "Neither I nor my film are [**is**] anti-Semitic."

  ("Papal Audience," editorial, *Pittsburgh Post-Gazette*, 23 Jan. 2004, p. A16)

- Neither lost innocence nor the Metropolitan Opera were ever priorities [**was ever a priority**] in their worlds.

  (Greg Tate, "The Resurrection and the Light," *Village Voice*, 8–14 Sept. 2004, p. 44)

- Lt. Bob Woolridge, a public-relations officer for the Knoxville Police Department, said Friday that the police were awaiting the results of an autopsy to determine whether drugs or alcohol were [**was**] involved in the crash.

  (Frank Litsky, "John Tate, 43, Troubled Heavyweight Champ," *New York Times*, 11 Apr. 1998, p. D11)

TIP: When the second element in a compound-alternative subject is a pronoun, choose the verb appropriate to that pronoun.

- They or he is likely to arrive early. She or they are certain to reconsider. Either you or I am responsible for the mix-up. Neither she nor you are right this time.

---

3. Plural Subjects Followed by *each*

A plural subject followed by the appositive *each* takes a plural verb.

- The stores each have their own returned-merchandise policies.
- The employees each are late with submitting their reports.
- The stockboys are each deserving of a raise.

4. Subjects Followed by One or More Prepositional Phrases

A verb agrees with the subject of a clause—not with the object of a preposition in any prepositional phrase that appears in the clause. Never mistake the object of a preposition for the subject. In many clauses, one or more prepositional phrases will follow the subject, and each of those prepositional phrases will include at least one noun or pronoun as the object of the preposition. Each of those objects can distract you into regarding it as the subject. The subject of the clause, however, will never be found in a prepositional phrase—so mentally cross out the prepositional phrases as you are searching for the subject with which the verb must agree.

Not all of the prepositions in the English language are single words. Be alert to multiword prepositions—such as *along with, as well as,* and *in addition to.* Furthermore, remember that *plus* is a preposition, not a conjunction like *and.*

(There are four exceptions to the rule that the object of a preposition has no influence on the verb of a clause. Those exceptions will be discussed in rules 9E, 9F, 10C, and 12.)

In the following sentences, the subjects of clauses with erroneous verbs have been underlined. Correct verbs have been bracketed and boldfaced.

- The winning combination of style, importance and star power have [**has**] made Face the Issue one of the most talked-about ad campaigns of the fall.
  (Alyson Ward, "What Gives Public Service Ads Punch," for *Fort Worth Star-Telegram,* in *Seattle Post-Intelligencer,* 20 Jan. 2004, p. C1)

- The rarefied air of its sleekly modern buildings have [**has**] produced a long list of hallowed names including Miles Davis, Philip Glass, Yo-Yo Ma, Itzhak Perlman, Nina Simone and Robin Williams.
  (N. R. Kleinfield and Ian Urbina, "For Shining Light at Juilliard, a Tragic End in a Remote Spot," *New York Times* online, 27 May 2004, paragraph 4)

- The tension between the social and spiritual sides of the Army on display in New York have [**has**] occurred in Salvation Army divisions elsewhere in the nation, officials said.
  (Daniel J. Wakin, "Renewed Emphasis on Religion Puts Salvation Army Under Fire," *New York Times,* 2 Feb. 2004. p. A20)

- Unseasonably warm temperatures in most of the nation has [**have**] left fall and winter gear, from sweaters to snow blowers, sitting in stores.
  (Lorrie Grant, "Bargain Hunters Proliferate," *USA Today,* 21 Dec. 2001, p. 2B)

- Vanity Fair's lineup of political and world affairs pieces this month are [**is**] even better than usual.
  ("On the Newsstand," *New York Post* online, 8 Dec. 2003, paragraph 7)

- They said yesterday that they want to know whether warnings were ignored during the summer of 2001, when intelligence about terror prospects were [**was**] pouring in to the CIA.
  (Ann McFeatters, "Bush, Cheney to Meet 9/11 Panel in Private," *Pittsburgh Post-Gazette,* 29 Apr. 2004, p. A8)

- The General Accounting Office warned in 2002 that the nation's food supply was quite vulnerable to mad-cow disease, given that bans on feeding infected mad-cow tissue to other animals was [**were**] not being enforced by the Food and Drug Administration.
  (Phillip Morris, "Cow Consumers Have a Right to Get Mad, Too," *Cleveland Plain Dealer,* 6 Jan. 2004, p. B9)

- While the exact nature of Madonna's songwriting contributions have [**has**] never been clear, no one disputes that she's in complete control of every aspect of her career.
  (Jennifer Egan, in the Dec. 2002 issue of *GQ*—cited in Sasha Frere-Jones, "When Critics Meet Pop," Slate.com, 22 Aug. 2003, paragraph 7)

- More readers are listeners these days, as the price of MP3 players have [has] decreased and commute times have risen.

  (Kaya Laterman, "MP3 Players Fit the Bill," *New York Post*, 20 June 2004, p.-34)

In the lengthy sentence below, the subject of an adjectival dependent clause is followed not only by a prepositional phrase but also by a long interruptive element consisting of an appositive to which an adjectival dependent clause has been attached—and by the time the writers are ready for a verb, they seem to have forgotten their subject. (The subject of the misagreeing verb has been underlined.)

- In the hundred and forty years since Antietam, the technologies of depiction have advanced to the point where our <u>experience</u> of a comparable horror—the more than three thousand murders that took place at the southern tip of Manhattan, at the Pentagon, and in Pennsylvania on the morning of September 11, 2001—are [is] infinitely, and inescapably, more immediate.

  (David Remnick and Hendrik Hertzberg, "A Year After," *New Yorker*, 16 Sept. 2002, p. 31)

An especially pervasive error appears in clauses in which the subject *one* is followed by a prepositional phrase whose object is a plural noun.

- In fact, an estimated <u>one</u> out of eight people in the United States are [is] owed money.

  (Mellody Hobson, "Find a Hidden Fortune (Yours!)," *Good Housekeeping*, Feb. 2004, p. 67)

- ... even among the most successful food brands, only about <u>one</u> in a hundred have [has] that kind of conversion rate.

  (Malcolm Gladwell, "The Ketchup Conundrum," *New Yorker*, 6 Sept. 2004, p. 129)

- Fewer than <u>one</u> in 10 high school seniors want [wants] to teach in the future, according to a study released by the ACT testing service last week.

  ("Teacher Shortage Spreads As Schools Paper Over Problem," editorial, USA Today, 26 Aug. 1999, p. 16A)

It is not always quick and simple to fix this kind of error.

- About <u>one</u> in six American women have [has] enough facial hair—usually growing above their [her] lips, on their [her] chin or on their [her] cheeks—that they remove [she removes] it at least once a week.

  (Phil Galewitz, "Gillette, Partner Create Cream to Stop Female Facial Hair," for Associated Press, in *Pittsburgh Post-Gazette*, 3 Nov. 1999, p. E1)

TIP: A subject in the form of *X after X* takes a singular verb.

- Commercial after commercial shows thin, beautiful young women.

---

5. Subjects Followed by Participial Phrases

A participial phrase is a phrase beginning with a participle—an adjective formed from a verb. The nouns or pronouns within a participial phrase have no influence on the singularity or plurality of the verb of a clause.

In the following sentences, the subjects of clauses with misconjugated verbs have been underlined, and the participial phrases have been italicized. Erroneous verbs are followed by bracketed, boldfaced corrections.

- The administration's reported <u>contemplation</u> of postponing the elections, *coupled with this election strategy*, inevitably raise [raises] the question of its intentions with respect to the smooth functioning of American democracy.

  ("Campaign of Contempt," editorial, *Pittsburgh Post-Gazette*, 14 July 2004, p. A18)

- A general physical examination, *followed by a more focal examination of the upper extremity*, specifically the hand and wrist, also help [**helps**] in the diagnosis.

  (Dr. Rock Positano, "Be on Wrist Watch for Pain," *New York Daily News*, 11 Jan. 2004, p. 28)

- Bob Hope's birth May 29, 1903, *coupled with his survival* make [**makes**] him the oldest living major star.

  (Ed Blank, "On Video," *Greensburg [PA] Tribune Reivew*, 2 Mar. 2002, p. A16)

- A satiny corset *paired with chiffon* make [**makes**] for pretty polar opposites.

  (Amy Diluna, "The Ties Have It," *New York Daily News*, 11 Jan. 2004, p. Lifeline7)

- But if society—*meaning banks, government and, yes, the buyers who sign on the dotted line*—aren't [**isn't**] prepared to support and sustain the biggest single purchase a person makes in a lifetime, then it is playing a cruel joke on itself.

  ("Broken Dreams," editorial, *Pittsburgh Post-Gazette*, 13 June 2004, p. E6)

The greater the distance between a verb and its subject, the more likely the writer will misconjugate the verb. But sometimes the substitution of the correct verb for the incorrect verb is not enough to set a sentence right.

> **Faulty:** The urgent need to control—to make sure you see what he sees, with no room for dissent—*coupled with a desire to seduce* are [**is**], of course, the traits of a comedian as well as those of a critic, and of course the hallmark of Peck's style is a ferocious sense of humor that, in wildness, parodic ferocity, and machine-gun willingness to hit or miss[,] is indeed Aristophanic.

(Daniel Mendelsohn, "Nailed!," *New York Review of Books* online, 15 July 2004, paragraph 12)

> Replacing *are* with *is* following the participial phrase *coupled with a desire to seduce* will not result in a grammatically sound sentence, because the singular verb will then clash with the plural noun *traits* and the plural pronoun *those*.
>
> **Correct:** The urgent need to control—to make sure you see what he sees, with no room for dissent—*and a desire to seduce* are, of course, the traits of a comedian as well as those of a critic. . . .
>
> Substitute *and* for *coupled with*, and recast the subject as a compound-additive subject legitimately taking the plural verb.

6. Subjects Followed by Infinitive Phrases

An infinitive phrase is a phrase beginning with an infinitive (the word *to* followed by the stem of a verb). The nouns or pronouns within an infinitive phrase have no influence on the singularity or plurality of the verb of a clause.

The subject of the following sentence is underlined, the infinitive phrase has been italicized, and the correct verb has been bracketed and boldfaced (the noun *reasons* has been singularized as well).

- The administration's refusal *to put in place cost-saving measures* were [**was**] the reasons [**reason**] that some finance department employees left their jobs.

  (Mark Mustio, "Tough Love for the City," *Pittsburgh Post-Gazette*, 1 Jan. 2004, p. A17)

7. Gerunds as Subjects

A gerund is a verbal form ending in *-ing* and functioning as a noun. The verb of a clause whose subject is a gerund must agree in number with the gerund—not with the object of the gerund. In the sentence *Planning family get-togethers is often difficult when both parents work and the children are busy with extracurricular activities*, the subject, *planning*, is a gerund. Its singularity determines the singularity of the verb. (The noun *get-togethers* is the object of the gerund and has no influence on the verb.)

In the following sentences, the gerunds are underlined, the objects of the gerunds have been italicized, and the correct verbs have been bracketed and boldfaced.

- As a psychology major in college, Evan realizes that reading *journals* he kept as a boy allow [**allows**] him to reenter the past.

  (Barbara Vancheri, "'Butterfly Effect' Blacks Out on the Logic," *Pittsburgh Post-Gazette*, 23 Jan. 2004, p. W14)

- "Sending large volumes of e-mail involve [**involves**] costs that are paid for by the I.S.P.'s and eventually by consumers," said Linda Beck, executive vice president for operations at Earthlink.

  (Saul Hansell, "Speech by Gates Lends Visibility to E-mail Stamp in War on Span," *New York Times*, 2 Feb. 2004, p. C3)

- "Folding *virtue* and *criminality* around profit are [**is**] [John] Laroche's specialty," Orlean writes of the oddly likable felon who's the subject of her latest book.

  (*Publishers Weekly* review of Susan Orlean's *The Orchid Thief* at Amazon.com)

8. Subjects Followed by Appositives

An appositive is a noun or noun phrase that follows another noun and provides further information about it. The verb of a clause whose subject is followed by an appositive must agree in number with the subject—not with the appositive or with the combination of the subject and the appositive. In the sentence *Another source of revenue, private funds, includes the ticket surcharges recommended by the councilman,* the subject is *source,* and its singularity determines the singularity of the verb. The appositive (*private funds*) has no influence on the verb.

In the following sentence, the subject has been underlined, the appositive has been italicized, and the correct verb has been bracketed and boldfaced.

- Plus-size apparel—*clothes larger than the average U.S. size range of 2 to 12 for women*—make [**makes**] up more than 90 percent of the market for all goods sold to the overweight, according to retail analyst Marshal Cohen of Port Washington, N.Y.-based NPD.

  (Patrick Cole, "Obese Americans Spur Demand in 'Plus Size' Industry," for Bloomberg News, in *Pittsburgh Post-Gazette*, 4 July 2004, p. C1)

9. Subjects Beginning with *a/the number of; an/the average of; a/the total of; a/the variety of; a/the majority/minority of; a/the percent of; a/the percentage of;* and *a lot of*

A. A subject beginning with *a number of* usually takes a plural verb (because *a number of* is replaceable by *some*): *A number of applicants are bilingual.* But in *Garner's Modern American Usage,* Bryan A. Garner notes that when an adjective is situated between *a* and *number,* a singular verb may be called for: *A higher number of applicants is expected this year.* A subject beginning with *the number of* usually takes a singular verb: *The number of applicants is higher this year.* But if an adjective is situated between *the* and *number,* a plural verb may be appropriate: *The greatest number of applicants are from Boston.*

- While monthly subscription rates have declined only slightly, the number of minutes offered in mobile plans have [**has**] increased significantly.

  (Matt Richtel, "$41 Billion Deal, but What's in It for Consumers?," *New York Times*, 18 Feb. 2004, p. C5)

- Murder rates for 2003 put Gary, Ind., at the top of the list in the country. Meanwhile the number of murders in Erie, a city roughly the same size, weren't [**wasn't**] even close.

  (Tim Hahn, "Murder Rate Low in Erie," *Erie Times-News*, 5 Jan. 2004, p. 1A)

B. A subject beginning with *an average of* generally takes a plural verb: *An average of thirty-five students are absent each day.* But occasionally a singular verb is required: *An average of twenty-five students per class is standard in the school district.* A subject beginning with *the average of* takes a singular verb: *The average of her five test scores is 95.* A subject consisting of *the average* always takes a singular verb: *The average is twenty-five students per class.*

C. A subject beginning with *a total of* almost always requires a plural verb: *A total of forty applicants have applied.* But occasionally a singular verb is required: *A total of fifty-one million dollars was raised during the telethon.* A subject beginning with *the total of* takes a singular verb: *The total of 342 applications received this year has set a new record.*

D. A subject beginning with *the variety of* always takes a singular verb: *The variety of course offerings is impressive.* A subject beginning with *a variety of* generally takes a plural verb: *A variety of courses are offered every semester.* (Here, *a variety of* is synonymous with *lots of.*) But occasionally a singular verb may be chosen: *A variety of courses is offered every semester.* (Here, the emphasis is on the wealth of course offerings in the aggregate.)

E. A subject beginning with *a majority of, the majority of, a minority of,* or *the minority of* preferably takes a singular verb if the object of the preposition *of* is singular, and preferably takes a plural verb if the object of the preposition *of* is plural: *A majority of the population agrees with the president. A majority of the voters agree with the president. The majority of the electorate is in favor of the referendum. The majority of the voters are in favor of the referendum.* When *majority* or *minority* is not followed by a prepositional phrase, treat the word as you would treat a collective noun (see rule 36).

- The majority of sales of self-published books occurs [**occur**] online.
  (Gayle Feldman, "Got a Book in You? More Companies Than Ever Are Willing to Get It Out," *New York Times,* 1 Mar. 2004, p. C6)

- While the more violent incidents in ancient Greek, early Roman and even Shakespearean drama (and this is true even in the bloodiest of them) happened offstage, the clear majority of such parallel incidents in numerous American films happens [**happen**] on screen, where they are recorded in almost microscopic detail.
  (Samuel Hazo, "The Sleep of Reason," *Pittsburgh Post-Gazette,* 3 July 2003, p. A13)

F. A clause whose subject presents a percentage (that is, a number followed by the word *percent,* as in *twelve percent, seventy percent,* etc.) will take a singular verb if the object in the prepositional phrase following the subject is singular, and a plural verb if the object is plural: *Sixty percent of registered voters are expected to turn out for the election. Sixty percent of the population approves of the president's performance.* If *percent* is preceded by phrasing such as *more than* or *less than,* the object in the prepositional phrase following *percent* will still determine the singularity or plurality of the verb: *Less than twenty percent of all employees are satisfied with the new medical-insurance program. More than sixty percent of our workforce approves of the changes.* If the subject is not followed by a prepositional phrase, decide which prepositional phrase is implied after the subject, and then choose the verb accordingly.

- Seventy percent is finished. (Seventy percent [of the work] is finished.)
- Seventy percent have health-care plans at work. (Seventy percent [of the employees] have health-care plans at work.)

G. A clause whose subject begins with *the percentage of* will always take a singular verb: *The percentage of high-school students who smoke cigarettes has dropped slightly.* A clause whose subject begins with *a percentage of* takes a singular verb if the object of the preposition *of* is singular and a plural verb if the object of the preposition is plural: *A lower percentage of the student population is experimenting with drugs. A lower percentage of high-school students are smoking these days.* In an inverted sentence, a subject beginning with *a percentage of* always takes a singular verb: *There is a disturbingly high percentage of middle-school students experimenting with drugs.*

When *the percentage* or *a percentage* is not followed by a prepositional phrase, *the percentage* will still require a singular verb. *A percentage* will require a singular verb if an implied prepositional phrase following *percentage* has a singular object, a plural verb if an implied prepositional phrase has a plural object: *A lower percentage [of the high-school-student population] is experimenting with drugs. A lower percentage [of high-school students] are experimenting with drugs.*

When *percentage* is not preceded by the article *a* or *the*, the singularity or plurality of the verb will be determined by the object of the preposition in the prepositional phrase following (or only implied after) *percentage: What percentage of our students are likely to attend graduate school? What percentage are unlikely to graduate? What percentage of the population is overweight? What percentage is underweight?*

H. A subject beginning with *a lot of* will take a singular verb if the object of the preposition *of* is singular, and a plural verb if the object is plural: *A lot of the donated canned goods have already been delivered to the needy. A lot of the food is likely to go to waste.*

10. Indefinite Pronouns as Subjects

An indefinite pronoun is a pronoun that lacks an antecedent and that refers to an unspecified person or thing. Indefinite pronouns fall into three categories.

A. A clause with one of the following indefinite pronouns as the subject will always require a singular verb: *another, anyone, anything, anybody, someone, something, somebody, one, nobody, no one, nothing, everybody, everything, everyone, each, either, neither, much.* (*Neither of the boys was prepared for class. Either of the restaurants sounds fine to me.*)

- Each of the 29 promotions were [was] listed in detail on a one-page photocopied timeout script that took Ms. Mandlehr two days to plan.
  (Dennis K. Berman, "Boxed Out by Ads, College Bands Press for Playing Time," *Wall Street Journal*, 6 Jan. 2004, p. A16)

- Everyone but pure Caucasians, they [the curators] imply, have [has] been excluded from this inheritance and even presented as its very opposite.
  (Ariella Budick, "Sex, Lies and Photos," *Newsday*, 21 Dec. 2003, p. D19)

- When Spin put out a list of the "50 greatest bands of all time," every one of the most important '60s groups were [was] there except the Kinks.
  (Ed Masley, "Overlooked and Underrated," *Pittsburgh Post-Gazette*, 19 May 2002, p. A&E10)

- Everything except the potato chips are [is] made on the premises and not from frozen preparations.
  (Elizabeth Downer, "The Academic's Choice," *Pittsburgh Post-Gazette*, 16 Apr. 2004, p. W36)

- ... Mr. Weinberg is certain to be asked by analysts when he and Mr. Pinault will name successors, or if their search is still ongoing. Neither have [has] commented publicly.
  (Cathy Horyn, "Sticking with London, and Himself," *New York Times*, 2 Mar. 2004, p. C18)

- Neither of the victims' names were [was] released.
  ("Two L.A. Men Fatally Stabbed in Homes," Associated Press online, 14 June 2004, paragraph 4)

- Much of contemporary women's magazines are built on chronic fakery, Ms. Blyth contends.
  (David Carr, "Lobbing a Grenade at Women's Magazines," *New York Times*, 2 Mar. 2004, p. B10)

  This erroneous sentence needs to be recast, because a prepositional phrase following the singular indefinite pronoun *much* must have a singular object. The following sentence is correct: *Much of contemporary women's-magazine journalism is built on chronic fakery.* (The sentence can also be rewritten as *Many contemporary women's magazines are built on chronic fakery, Ms. Blyth contends.*)

B. A clause with one of the following indefinite pronouns as the subject will require a plural verb: *both, many, few*. (*Both are happy. Few are neglected.*)

C. A clause with one of the following indefinite pronouns as the subject will require a singular verb if the object in the prepositional phrase following the subject is singular, and the clause will require a plural verb if the object in the prepositional phrase following the subject is plural: *all, none, some, more, any, most*. (*All of the produce is fresh. All of the apples are fresh.*)

- Some of it [the TV special], like the reflections on the early days of CNN—which used to stand, we're told, for Chicken Noodle Soup in some quarters—are [**is**] plain wonderful.

  (Dorothy Rabinowitz, "The War to Win the Vote," *Wall Street Journal*, 13 Feb. 2004, p. W1)

- Most, but not all, of the civic leadership of Pittsburgh believe [**believes**] local politics is a business far too dirty in which to participate.

  (Mike DeSantis, "Finding Our Way," *Pittsburgh Post-Gazette*, 11 July 2004, p. E2)

  Another corrective option is to substitute *leaders* for *leadership* and thus retain the plural verb.

If you want *none* to be understood as *not one*, choose a singular verb.

- None of the players was injured.

CAUTION

Be careful with *all but one* constructions. In *The Careful Writer*, Theodore M. Bernstein notes that when a noun immediately follows *all but one*, a singular verb is needed: *All but one chef was happy*. When a verb immediately follows *all but one*, a plural verb is needed: *All but one were happy*. When a prepositional phrase, rather than a noun, immediately follows *all but one*, a plural verb is needed: *All but one of the chefs were happy*.

---

11. Subjects Followed by Linking (Equational) Verbs

A linking verb agrees with its subject, not with its complement. Remember that the complement is the noun or pronoun that a linking verb equates with the subject.

In the sentences below, the subjects have been underlined and the complements italicized. Erroneous conjugations are followed by bracketed, boldfaced corrections.

- The real draw here are [**is**] the "typical Brazilian *dishes*," like superb spicy pork sausage and thick red-bean stew with a pork chop.

  (capsule review of Churrascaria Girassol, *Time Out New York*, 27 May–3 June 2004, p. 56)

- The best part of a singularly unadventuresome menu are [**is**] the small *pizzas*.

  (Robert Sietsema, "Disintegrating Gnocchi," *Village Voice*, 8–14 Sept. 2004, p. 53)

- The most intriguing discovery were [**was**] *dozens* of vials filled with white powder.

  (Dexter Filkins, "GIs Search Afghan Caves, Find Terror Material," for *New York Times*, in *Pittsburgh Post-Gazette*, 7 Apr. 2002, p. A8)

- But the only thing he has shot in the two years since he took it [hunting] up are [**is**] clay *disks*, which are ejected into the air at different angles to mimic the flight of birds.

  (Tatiana Boncompagni, "Shooting for a New Generation," *New York Times*, 9 Jan. 2004, p. D2)

- The downside of the high hopes of romantic love, of course, are [**is**] the *feelings* of depression and abandonment that come when a relationship ends.

  (Christopher F. Chabris, "Molecules of Desire," *Wall Street Journal*, 13 Feb. 2004, p. W8)

- The only indication that the old cafeteria will close permanently tonight are [is] the large "50 percent off" signs posted along the outside walls of the gift shop.

  (Paula Reed Ward, "Post House Closing Doors," *Pittsburgh Post-Gazette*, 27 June 2004, p. C4)

> **TIP:** If a sentence with a singular subject and a plural complement sounds awkward or unnatural with the grammatically correct singular verb, rewrite the sentence by positioning the complement in the subject slot and the subject in the complement slot. A plural verb will then be correct.
>
> - Her favorite part of the circus is the clowns.
> - The clowns are her favorite part of the circus.

12. Subjects Expressing Parts of a Whole in Fractions

When a subject is expressing a fractional part of a whole (such as *four-fifths of the students* or *four-fifths of the student body*), the singularity or plurality of the verb is generally determined by the singularity or plurality of the object of the preposition in the prepositional phrase following the subject: *Four-fifths of the students are in favor of the new policy. Four-fifths of the student body is in favor of the new policy.*

In the following sentence, the subject has been underlined, the object of the preposition in the prepositional phrase has been italicized, and the correct verb has been boldfaced and bracketed.

- Every day, nearly one-third of U.S. *children* aged four to 19 eats [**eat**] fast food, which likely packs on about six extra pounds per child per year and increases the risk of obesity, a study of 6,212 youngsters found.
  ("Children's Fast-Food Diet Adds Pounds, Study Says," for Associated Press, in *Wall Street Journal*, 6 Jan. 2004, p. D6)

The rigid application of this rule occasionally results in an awkward-sounding sentence. The following sentence, for example, needs the singular verb, but the result is inelegant.

- If students, who are mostly temporary residents of the city, are taken into account, literally half of the daytime population of the city are [**is**] transients in one way or another.
  (Christopher Briem, "Is Downtown Dead? Hardly," *Pittsburgh Post-Gazette*, 1 Feb. 2004, p. E3)

One solution is to rewrite the independent clause and include a different, unawkward singular verb.

- If students, who are mostly temporary residents of the city, are taken into account, literally half of the daytime population of the city consists of people who are transients in one way or another.

Another solution is to replace the verb with a verb phrase beginning with an auxiliary verb whose form is the same in the singular and in the plural. The verb phrase has been underlined.

- If students, who are mostly temporary residents of the city, are taken into account, literally half of the daytime population of the city can be classified as transients in one way or another.

When a subject expressing a fractional part of a whole is not followed by a prepositional phrase, decide which prepositional phrase is implied after the subject, and then choose the verb accordingly.

- Two-thirds are opposed to the change. (Two-thirds [of the voters] are opposed to the change.)
- Two-thirds has been completed. (Two-thirds [of the project] has been completed.)

13. Subjects Expressing Quantities and Measurements

When a subject expresses a quantity or measurement regarded as a single unit, a totality, or a lump sum, choose a singular verb. When you want to emphasize the individual elements forming a totality, choose a plural verb. The sentence *Four million dollars was stolen* emphasizes the money as a lump sum. The sentence *Millions of dollars are spent every year to prevent accidents in the workplace,* however, emphasizes millions of dollars as individual amounts of money that are pouring in from numerous sources. The sentence *Twelve ounces of Coca-Cola contains 140 calories* emphasizes twelve ounces as a single serving of soda.

- And about 500 inches of Utah's famous talcum snow fall [**falls**] here annually.

  (Christopher Solomon, "For Skiers, Is Bigger Always Better?," *New York Times,* 2 Jan. 2004, p. D4)

14. Subjects Expressing Spans of Time

If the subject is to be regarded as a single block of time, choose a singular verb. If the subject is intended to emphasize the accumulating individual units of time, such as hours or days, choose a plural verb: *Five days was too long to wait for a replacement. Five days have gone by since I've even thought about her. A child's first years are often the happiest.*

15. Subjects Expressing Distances

A singular verb is standard for such subjects: *Six miles was too far for him to walk.*

16. Subjects Expressing Arithmetical Operations

The singular verb is preferred: *Five and eight equals thirteen. Five plus eight makes thirteen. Seven times six is forty-two.*

17. Subjects Expressing the Titles of Works, or the Names of Organizations, Stores, or Corporations

The singular verb is standard for such subjects—even when the name or title is technically plural. Singular verbs are thus required for movie titles such as *Close Encounters of the Third Kind;* titles of books such as *The Elements of Style;* titles of television programs such as *Friends;* titles of plays such as *The Producers;* titles of paintings such as *The Great Bathers;* names of organizations such as People for the Ethical Treatment of Animals; names of governmental agencies such as the Centers for Disease Control and Prevention; names of department stores, specialty stores, and discount stores such as Sears, Talbots, and Big Lots; and names of corporations such as Continental Airlines and Kraft Foods.

18. Subjects Expressing the Names of Performance Groups Ending in -s

The plural verb is standard (*The Beatles are considered the most significant rock and pop group of all time*), but writers sometimes erroneously succumb to the singular.

- Albuquerque's The Shins reveals [**reveal**] hints of a band that may have been a straight-up alt-country act a decade ago.

  (Scott Mervis, review of the Shins' *Chutes Too Narrow, Pittsburgh Post-Gazette,* 14 Dec. 2003, p. Weekend27)

19. Subjects Expressing the Names of Events That Are Plural in Form

The names of events such as the Olympics and the Special Olympics can take either singular or plural verbs, as is obvious from these two headlines.

- The Olympics Are Over, but Will the Check Clear?

  (headline, John Hughes, *Christian Science Monitor* online, 27 Feb. 2002)

- U.S. Bobsledder Hopes 4th Olympics Is a Charm

  (headline, Amy Shipley, *Washington Post* online, 19 Dec. 1997)

Choose the singular verb to emphasize the event as a whole, and choose the plural verb to emphasize the event as a series of competitions.

20. Subjects Expressing Place Names That Are Plural in Form

Place names plural in form are often singular in meaning and require singular verbs: *The Great Plains, Pacific Palisades, Palm Springs, Niagara Falls, Council Bluffs.*

21. Subjects Expressing the Names of Diseases That Are Plural in Form

Nouns like *mumps, measles, AIDS,* and *delirium tremens*—which are plural in form but singular in meaning—almost always take singular verbs. But occasionally they require a plural verb: *I hope her mumps aren't contagious.*

22. Subjects Consisting of Nouns Whose Form Is Plural but Whose Meaning Is Singular

A noun denoting a course of study, a science, a field of expertise, or a realm of activity (such as *linguistics, mathematics, physics, acoustics, electronics, statistics, ethics, news, politics,* and *athletics*) requires a singular verb: *Statistics is a difficult subject. Politics is a perilous enterprise. Athletics is a big business.*

But when such a word denotes a quality, a plural verb is needed: *The acoustics of the auditorium are deplorable.*

When such a word denotes specific activity or the specific application of the science or field of expertise, a plural verb is needed: *The politics of the Psychology Department are fraught with intrigue.*

When such words denote collections of individual units, a plural verb is needed: *The statistics were baffling.* Similarly, when such words denote individual items, objects, gadgets, etc., considered in the aggregate, a plural verb is needed: *The latest electronics are disconcerting to us technophobic baby boomers.*

23. Subjects Consisting of Nouns That Are Plural in Form but That Denote Single Items

The nouns *scissors, eyeglasses, bifocals, pliers, tweezers, calipers, trousers, pants, slacks, jeans, culottes, hip-huggers, shorts, underpants, briefs, panties,* and *swimming trunks* all take plural verbs.

24. Troublesome Single-Word Subjects

Data is technically plural (the singular form is *datum*), but many writers now use a singular verb with *data* when they intend the noun to mean a body of statistics: *The data is inconclusive.* Writers continue to use a plural verb with *data* when they intend the word to mean individual statistics: *The data are still being compiled.*

Note the following troublesome single-word subjects.

- *Graffiti* is plural (the singular form is graffito) and needs a plural verb.
- *Headquarters* can take a singular verb or a plural verb. Both are correct.

- *Media* is technically plural (the singular form is *medium*), but many writers now treat *media* as singular: *The media has a liberal bias.* Many readers, however, object to the singular usage, so you are safer by treating the word as plural and choosing a plural verb.
- *Memorabilia* is plural and takes a plural verb.
- *Minutiae* is plural. (The singular form is *minutia*.)
- *Series* can be either singular or plural: *A new reality-TV series is going to debut tonight. Three new series are going to debut in October.*
- *Whereabouts* takes a plural verb in standard usage: *Her whereabouts are unknown.*

5C SUBJECT-VERB AGREEMENT: THE SUBTLETIES

25. Asyndetonic Compound Subjects

Asyndeton is the intentional omission of conjunctions between words, phrases, or clauses of equal importance. In an asyndetonic construction, a comma appears where the reader would expect to find a conjunction. Be sure to distinguish between asyndetonic compound-additive subjects and subjects followed by appositives.

Here is a sentence with an asyndetonic compound-additive subject.

- Her verbal flair, her brilliant mind dazzle the reader on every page.
     The single comma implies the conjunction *and;* the verb is therefore plural.

Here is a sentence whose subject is followed by an appositive.

- Her verbal flair, her powerful language, dazzles the reader on every page.
     The appositive (*her powerful language*) restates the subject of the sentence, and the pair of commas enclosing the appositive implies that the appositive is not essential to the sentence. The verb of the sentence agrees with the subject—not with the combination of the subject and the appositive. The verb is singular.

26. Compound Subjects Taking the Form *not only X but [also] Y*

This kind of subject arises only rarely. The verb agrees with the part of the subject closer to the verb: *Not only the teachers but the principal needs to be held accountable. Not only the principal but the teachers need to be held accountable.* (The adverb *also* could be inserted after *but* in each sentence.) It is stylistically desirable to phrase such a subject so that the plural element precedes the verb.

27. Relative-Pronoun Subjects of Adjectival Dependent Clauses

An adjectival dependent clause begins with a relative pronoun, such as *that, which, who*, or *whom*. The singularity or plurality of the verb in the adjectival dependent clause will be determined by the singularity or plurality of the antecedent of the relative pronoun—that is, the noun or pronoun to which the relative pronoun refers. If the relative pronoun serving as the subject of the clause has a singular antecedent, the verb of the dependent clause must be singular. If the relative pronoun has a plural antecedent, the verb of the dependent clause must be plural. Errors are likely to result when the relative pronoun has a compound antecedent.

In the following sentences, the adjectival dependent clauses have been underlined, the antecedents of the relative pronouns have been italicized, and the erroneous verbs are followed by bracketed, boldfaced corrections.

- It's not just the large *numbers* of readers these sites attract that is [are] so significant for the conservative cause; it's also who these readers are: younger readers.

  (Brian C. Anderson, "Liberal Media, on the Run," *Pittsburgh Post-Gazette*, 7 Dec. 2003, p. E3)

- Secreted inside [the sculpture] are Stargazer lilies, which accounts [account] for the floral scent in the otherwise empty and sterile small room.

  (Ken Johnson, "Mirrors and Minimalism, Scented with Lilies," *New York Times*, 30 Jan. 2004, p. B36)

- The *pandering* and *sadism* that passes [pass] for "reality TV" can only make one pray for fantasy.

  (Samuel G. Freedman, "New Golden Age of Radio Lures Young Listeners," *USA Today*, 29 Dec. 2003, p. 13A)

- Yet the *professionalism* and unimpeachable *taste* that marks [mark] compilations like New York Noise (dedicated to Gotham's early-eighties "no wave" moment) is [are] beginning to feel joylessly curatorial.

  (Ethan Brown, "The Glimmer Twins," *New York*, 2 Feb. 2004, p. 58)

28. Constructions in the Form *one of the Xs who/that* or *the only one of the Xs who/that*

A. In a sentence such as *Michelle is one of those employees who love to work*, one individual (Michelle) is being placed into a category of people who share a characteristic: the fact that they love to work. The adjectival dependent clause *who love to work* has as its subject the pronoun *who*, the antecedent of which is the plural noun *employees*—and thus the verb in the adjectival clause must agree in number with the antecedent of its pronominal subject. Here is another way of looking at the sentence: a single person (Michelle) is being placed into a group, and the writer is explaining what all the members of that group have in common: they all love to work. The verb of the adjectival dependent clause must encompass not only Michelle but also the other members of the group.

B. In a sentence such as *Michelle is the only one of the employees who loves to work*, Michelle is not being placed into a group of people with a characteristic in common, but instead she is being contrasted with the members of a group: The sentence is emphasizing how she is different from the other members. A singular verb is therefore necessary. (The limiting adjective *only* is a further indicator that the adjectival clause requires a singular verb; the emphasis is on Michelle as an individual. Furthermore, the antecedent of *who* in this sentence is *one*, not *employees*.)

In the following sentences, the antecedents of the pronouns *who* and *that* have been italicized. Erroneous verbs are followed by bracketed, boldfaced corrections.

- Mr. Rudnick is another one of those *jokesmiths* who keeps [**keep**] throwing punchlines against the wall to see if they stick.

  (Terry Teachout, "Queen Ludwig of Bavaria and Some Texas Teenagers," *Wall Street Journal*, 6 Feb. 2004, p. W9)

- The mad cow outbreak is one of those *events* that points [**point**] up the downsides of conservative antipathy to government regulation and liberal skittishness over every potential health hazard.

  (Walter Shapiro, "Too Little Regulation and Too Much Hysteria Feed Food Fears," *USA Today*, 26 Dec. 2003, p. 8A)

- Slowly, improbably, unwillingly, Wilco has become one of those *bands* that stands [**stand**] for something.

  (Kelefa Sanneh, "Wilco's Legend Set to Expand with Birth of 'Ghost,'" for New York Times News Service, in *Houston Chronicle* online, 22 June 2004, paragraph 1)

- In 2002 Textron offered one of those new "consumer-directed" *plans* that puts [**put**] more responsibility for financial control and health decisions onto employees.

  (Daniel Henninger, "Consumers March to the Walls of Health-Care Castle," *Wall Street Journal*, 30 Jan. 2004, p. A12)

- One of the many, many, many *things* that makes [**make**] Bill O'Reilly angry is being called a celebrity.

  (Alex Williams, "Bull Fighter," *New York*, 1 Jan. 2001, p. 58)

- Cheesecake is one of those quintessential New York *foodstuffs* that in some circles is [**are**] thought of as unsophisticated.

  (Ed Levine, "In Cheesecake City, a Quest for the Best," *New York Times*, 17 Mar. 2004, p. D1)

29. Subjects of Inverted Clauses

A. An inverted clause is a clause in which the subject follows, rather than precedes, the verb. An inverted clause is likely to have one or more phrases—such as prepositional phrases or a participial phrase—at the beginning, so make sure that you are not mistakenly regarding as the subject of the clause any noun or pronoun within those phrases. You need to find your way to the true grammatical subject of the clause.

In the following sentences, the subjects have been underlined. Erroneous verbs are followed by bracketed, boldfaced corrections.

- On the desk was [**were**] a computer, a phone, and a tape recorder.

  (Malcolm Gladwell, "Personality Plus," *New Yorker*, 20 Sept. 2004, p. 48)

- In his pocket was [**were**] a semi-automatic .22-caliber Ruger and an unopened package of earplugs.

  (Dick Polman, Raad Cawthon, and Murray Dubin, "Boys with Guns—and an Intent to Kill," *Philadelphia Inquirer*, 29 Mar. 1998, p. A20)

- Recovered from the mess was [**were**] a metallic gold belt resembling Wonder Woman's, a giant bowling pin, overflowing bags of pantyhose and socks in every shade, and at least twice as many pairs of shoes as Ivana has.

  (Marie Redding, "Making a Clean Break: Clutter Consultant Has a Chaos Theory," *New York Daily News*, 15 Mar. 1998, p. 48)

- Sitting at the far end of the loftlike room is [**are**] an Australian who wants to discuss self-esteem and a postal worker in full uniform clutching a package as though still in mid-delivery.

  (Boris Kachka, "Tricky Dicks," *New York*, 29 Sept. 2003, p. 14)

- Amid the waste was [**were**] an inexplicably dead raccoon, opossum and "possibly some rats," Milliron says.

  (Diana Nelson Jones, "One Man's Trash Is Another Man's Treasure," *Pittsburgh Post-Gazette*, 15 Apr. 2004, p. B3)

  The sentence is also weakened by faulty parallelism; see chapter 7.

- And Todd Solondz's *Welcome to the Dollhouse* was shown at the market, as was [**were**] Quentin Tarantino's Reservoir Dogs, Mina Shum's Double Happiness and Richard Linklater's Slacker.

  (Steven Rea, "400 Sneak Peeks," *Philadelphia Inquirer*, 23 Sept. 1997, p. D3)

- If the Algonquin Round Table isn't coming back, neither are [**is**] Harold Ross, William Shawn or any other patron saint of the magazine that made the Algonquin its canteen, the *New Yorker*.

  (Frank Rich, "Tina and Disney Elope," *New York Times*, 11 July 1998, p. A11)

  Here, the subject of the inverted clause is a compound-alternative subject. The singularity of the element closest to the verb (*Harold Ross*) determines the singularity of the verb.

B. Many inverted sentences begin with the expletive *there*. Do not mistake *there* for the subject; the subject will appear later in the sentence.

The subjects of the following sentences have been underlined, and erroneous verbs are followed by bracketed, boldfaced corrections.

- It's probably not impossible to get a good deal in Times Square, but there's [**there are**] just too many horror stories about bait-and-switch scams, hard sells on ghastly warranties, and various other shyster tactics to justify the risk.

  (Brendan I. Koerner, "Times Squared," *Village Voice*, 8–14 Sept. 2004, p. 16)

- And there's [**there are**] rarely so many musical opportunities to irritate people as at Christmas.

  (Teresa F. Lindeman, "Strike Up the Muzak, It's Almost Christmas," *Pittsburgh Post-Gazette*, 29 Oct. 2003, p. A8)

C. Many inverted sentences beginning with the expletive *there* have compound-additive subjects. A singular verb is perfectly acceptable in such a sentence if all of the elements in the subject are singular. (A plural verb would also be correct, but the singular verb is now more common.) A singular verb is not advisable, however, if one or more of the elements in the subject are plural.

In the following sentences, the subjects have been underlined. Inadvisable verbs are followed by bracketed, boldfaced substitutions.

- There's [**There are**] her big breasts and her deficient education, her passion for dogs and her Bill Clinton–consort fashion sense, but what else are we told about her?

  (Laura C. Moser, "Serial Adultery, Seriously: The Perils of Pretentious Pulp," *New York Observer* online, 10 Dec. 2003, paragraph 6)

- There's [**There are**] the "old demons" that have always haunted him; the "parallel lives" he alternates between (sunny on the outside, tormented on the in); the "Don't ask, Don't tell" credo he learned as a child; the determination to "drain the most out of every moment of life" that was the legacy of his father's early death; perhaps even a bit of the fright that Mr. Clinton remembers accompanying his sexual awakenings.

  (Robert Sam Anson, "Bill Tells All ... Stop Him!," *New York Observer* online, 28 June 2004, paragraph 5)

D. When an inverted sentence beginning with *there* has a compound-additive subject consisting of both singular and plural nouns, it is stylistically desirable to position a plural noun first in the series and to choose a plural verb.

> **Awkward:** There's a water fountain, bathrooms, a pay phone, even lockers for storage of sleeping bags and possessions.
>
> ("A Night in from the Cold," Steve Levin, *Pittsburgh Post-Gazette*, 11 Jan. 2004, p. A17)
>
> **Better:** There are bathrooms, a water fountain, a pay phone, even lockers for storage of sleeping bags and possessions.
>
> **Awkward:** There's no radio-size, four-minute rock here, no pop-friendly choruses, no ballads, no solos, no wayward experimentation.
>
> (Barry Walters, "Furious! Metallica Come Full Circle on the Raging 'St. Anger,'" *Rolling Stone*, 26 June 2003, p. 74)
>
> **Better:** There are no ballads here, no pop-friendly choruses, no radio-size, four-minute rock, no solos, no wayward experimentation.

30. Subjects Followed by Parenthetical or Interruptive Nounal Elements

A parenthetical or interruptive nounal element is a noun phrase that begins with the coordinating conjunction *and,* follows the subject of a clause, and is set off with commas at both ends. The punctuation removes the parenthetical element from the body of the sentence. The information presented within the parenthetical element is supplementary, rather than essential, to the sentence, and thus a truly parenthetical element does not influence the form that the verb takes in a clause.

Be sure to distinguish between a truly parenthetical element and a pseudoparenthetical element, in which a compound-additive subject has been presented with its second element set off by punctuation at both ends (to place greater stress on the second element). A clause in which the subject is followed by a pseudoparenthetical element almost always requires a plural verb.

You will need to use your judgment to determine whether the set-off element is merely supplemental to the subject (in which case the element will have no bearing on the verb of the clause) or whether the set-off element is essential to the subject—that is, part of a compound-additive subject (in which case the element will help determine the form of the verb of the clause).

Here is a sentence with a parenthetical element.

- Exercise, and plenty of it, needs to supplement any diet.
    The singularity of the subject—*exercise*—determines the singularity of the verb.

Here is a sentence with a pseudoparenthetical element.

- Her face, and her voice, are instantly recognizable.
    The verb is plural because the subject consists of both *face* and *voice*.

It is impossible to tell what the intentions of the writer of this sentence might have been.

- But suicide, and mental illness generally, are problems we virtually ignore.
    (Philip Davey, "One Suicide Too Many," *Seattle Weekly*, 14–20 Jan. 2004, p. 20)

Possible revisions include the following.

- But suicide, and mental illness generally, is a problem we virtually ignore.
- But suicide and mental illness in general are problems we virtually ignore.

The problem with pseudoparenthetical elements is that some readers will mistakenly regard them as parenthetical elements and thus sense that the verb has been misconjugated. A writer should take pains to ensure that nothing in the construction of a sentence will distract or misguide readers. It is often desirable, therefore, to replace the conjunction *and* in such elements with a multiword preposition such as *along with, as well as,* or *in addition to*. The object of the preposition will then have no bearing on the singularity or the plurality of the verb.

> **Awkward:** The power of his blues recordings, and the mystery of his largely undocumented life and death, have led blues scholars and writers to examine his life and work, hunting for the secrets of his music and influence.
> (Jim White, "On the Trail of a Blues Genius and the Music That Inspired Him," *Pittsburgh Post-Gazette*, 9 Feb. 2004, p. C4)
> **Better:** The power of his blues recordings, along with the mystery of his largely undocumented life and death, has led blues scholars and writers to examine his life and work, hunting for the secrets of his music and influence.

Another alternative is to delete the commas setting off the pseudoparenthetical element.

> **Awkward:** But in the long run, they said, an extensive overhaul of the [electronic-voting] machines, and at least a limited paper trail, are necessary.
> ("How to Hack an Election," editorial, *New York Times*, 31 Jan. 2004, p. A30)
> **Better:** But in the long run, they said, an extensive overhaul of the machines and at least a limited paper trail are necessary.

31. Subjects Followed by Contrastive Elements

A contrastive element, which will always be set off with punctuation at both ends, is treated as a parenthetical element—and thus it has no influence on the form that the verb of a clause will take. The verb agrees with the subject: *The manager, not her employees, needs to accept responsibility for what happened. It's the low tuition cost, not the research facilities, that attracts most students to the college.*

32. Singular Subjects Preceded by Two or More Adjectives Joined by *and*

A clause in which the subject consists of a singular noun preceded by two or more adjectives joined by *and* will require a plural verb if the subject is to be construed as an elliptical compound-additive subject (see rule 35). In the sentence *Modern and postmodern fiction differ in numerous ways,* the word *fiction* is implied after the word *modern;* the sentence is about two types of fiction, not one. (The sentences *Physical and emotional health are important* and *The real-life and the fictitious Christopher have a lot in common* are similarly elliptical and require plural verbs.)

But a singular verb is required whenever a singular-noun subject is preceded by two or more adjectives that are joined by the conjunction *and* and that describe a single entity.

- Stimulating and provocative fiction is difficult to write.
- Hot and muggy weather is in store for us later in the week.

33. Subjects Beginning with *many a; more than one; more than two; one or more; an X or two; one or two;* and any number of

The verb of a clause whose subject is preceded by *many a* must be singular: *Many a parent is likely to be offended by the new policy.* The verb of a clause whose subject consists of, or begins with, *more than one* must be singular: *More than one was offended. More than one parent was offended.*

The following sentence mishandles a *more than one* construction, and repairing the sentence requires more than a reconjugation of the verb.

- Yet the studies find that more than one in five Americans do [**does**] have an affair, at least once in their lives [**his or her life**].
  (Benedict Carey, "Cheating Hearts," from *Los Angeles Times,* in *Pittsburgh Post-Gazette,* 18 Nov. 2003, p. D4)

The verb of a clause whose subject consists of or begins with *more than two [or three, etc.], one or more, an X or two, one or two,* or *any number of* must be plural: *More than two parents were offended. One or more parents were offended. A parent or two are certain to be offended. One or two are likely to be offended. There are one or two parents likely to be offended. Any number of parents are likely to be offended.*

- George W. Bush and John F. Kerry might be called the two sides of the baby-boom generation, except for the inconvenient fact that this was a generation for which there was [**were**] always more than two sides.
  (David M. Shribman, "That Was Then, This Is Now," *Pittsburgh Post-Gazette,* 18 July 2004, p. E7)
  The subject *more than two sides* appears in an inverted clause.
- That way, if one or more of the conditions is [**are**] appealed and overturned in court, the overall agreement remains in force.
  (Rose Domenick, "Commissioners Set Conditions for Approval of Wal-Mart," *Pittsburgh Post-Gazette,* 21 Jan. 2004, EZ p. 2)

34. Subjects in the Form of Nominative Dependent Clauses Whose First Word Is *what*

The most thorough and sensible advice ever dispensed on the treatment of these vexatious subjects appears in *The Careful Writer,* a masterly guide to American English usage by the late Theodore M. Bernstein, a longtime editor at the *New York Times.* For the discussion that follows, we are indebted to his wise counsel.

A nominative clause is a dependent clause that functions as a noun. Nominative clauses often function as the subjects of sentences; and when those clauses begin with the pronoun *what,* opportunities for errors in subject-verb agreement arise.

There are two types of *what* clauses to worry about. In the first type, *what* is functioning as the direct object of the verb in the clause, not as the subject. When *what* is intended to mean *the thing that* or *that which,* the verb in the independent clause of the sentence will be singular: *What she needs is a clear explanation.* (In the nominative clause *What she needs, she* is the subject, *needs* is a transitive verb, and *what* is the direct object.) When *what* is intended to mean *the things that* or *those which,* the verb in the independent clause of the sentence will be plural: *What she needs are clear explanations.*

In the second type of *what* clauses, *what* is functioning as the subject. You therefore have to worry about conjugating the verb in the nominative clause as well as the verb in the independent clause of the sentence. The verb in the nominative clause of such sentences must agree in number with the verb in the independent clause. So before you can conjugate the verb in the independent clause, you have to decide whether the verb in the nominative clause needs to be singular or plural—and to arrive at that decision, you have to ask yourself whether *what* is intended to mean *the thing that* or *the things that.* If you decide that *what* means *the thing that,* choose singular verbs for both the nominative clause and the independent clause of the sentence. If you decide that *what* means *the things that,* choose plural verbs for both the nominative clause and the independent clause of the sentence.

The following sentences are correct (and in each sentence, *what* is the subject of the nominative clause).

- What is most essential is a clear explanation. (*what = the thing that*)
- What are most essential are clear explanations. (*what = the things that*)
- What is most essential is clear explanations. (*what = the thing that*)
    In this sentence, the noun *explanations* is functioning as a complement (a predicate noun); and, as you recall, the singularity or plurality of a complement does not determine the singularity or plurality of the verb. (A verb must agree with the subject of a clause, not with its complement.)

The following sentences are incorrect.

- What is most essential are clear explanations.
- What are most essential is clear explanations.

Here is another way to understand the principle: When a noun or a pronoun does not immediately follow *what* in the nominative clause, you will need to ensure that the verb in the nominative clause agrees in number with the verb in the independent clause of the sentence.

In the following sentences, however, the writers mix singular and plural interpretations of *what*.

Faulty: More vehicles have been using the turnpike in the last couple of years, but the number of troopers and the hours they work haven't changed much. What has changed are priorities and management.
("Not Just the Ticket," editorial, *Pittsburgh Post-Gazette,* 15 May 2002, p. A12)
Correct: What have changed are priorities and management.
Correct: What has changed is priorities and management.

Faulty: What really separates this band [the White Stripes] from classic-rock, in fact, are primarily issues of style and attitude.
(Ed Masley, "White Stripes Rock at Top of Their Game," *Pittsburgh Post-Gazette,* 29 Nov. 2003, p. C9)
Correct: What really separate this band from classic rock, in fact, are primarily issues of style and attitude.
Correct: What really separates this band from classic rock, in fact, is primarily issues of style and attitude.

Faulty: What comes across most vividly are the real and palpable losses suffered by the individuals and families forced to leave their homes.
(Christopher Briem, "Root Shock," *Pittsburgh Post-Gazette,* 27 June 2004, p. E4)
Correct: What come across most vividly are the real and palpable losses suffered by the individuals and families forced to leave their homes.
Correct: What comes across most vividly is the real and palpable losses suffered by the individuals and families forced to leave their homes.

Faulty: As we've watched [Michael] Jackson's combination of self-destructive and self-fetishizing impulses play out, what has been no less vividly exposed are the limitations of a given identity—even in these cosmetically transformational, "anything is possible" times.

(Daphne Merkin, "Michael on the Couch," *New York*, 8 Dec. 2003, p. 38)

Correct: ... what have been no less vividly exposed are the limitations of a given identity—even in these cosmetically transformational, "anything is possible" times.

Correct: ... what has been no less vividly exposed is the limitations of a given identity—even in these cosmetically transformational, "anything is possible" times.

35. Elliptical Subjects

The subject of a sentence is occasionally presented in elliptical form; that is, the writer omits a word or words with the expectation that the reader can mentally fill in what is missing.

Awkward: 18 Strep Deaths in Three Months Has Texas Parents Scared

(headline for Associated Press article by Eduardo Montes, in *Philadelphia Inquirer*, 7 Mar. 1998, p. A5)

Instead of filling out the elliptical construction, the writer might simply pluralize the verb.

Awkward: More women in the business helps to generate more female demand.

(Mireya Navarro, "Sex Industry Is No Longer Men's World," *New York Times*, 20 Feb. 2004, p. A14)

The writer has chosen a singular verb because the subject is to be understood as *the presence of more women in the business* or *the fact that there are more women in the business*. This kind of construction, however, is inelegant and is best avoided. Instead, write out the full construction.

Awkward: But to Mr. Kenney, one of the distinguished judges in the Westminster Kennel Club's annual judging program for dogdom supremacy, 22 Lamont Sanfords is not so difficult a proposition that he cannot choose with careful consideration a best-of-breed.

(Gene Collier, "Going to the Show Dogs," *Pittsburgh Post-Gazette*, 17 Feb. 1998, p. D1)

A phrase such as *the entry of* or *the presence of* or *the inclusion of* could be inserted before *22 Lamont Sanfords*.

36. Collective Nouns as Subjects

A collective noun is a noun that does not end in -s and that denotes a group of persons (or sometimes a group of animals or a group of things). An example is the noun *family*. The verb in a clause whose subject is a collective noun may be either singular or plural—depending on your purpose. If you want to emphasize the group as a harmonious whole, as a single unit with a common goal or purpose, choose a singular verb: *Her family is moving to Chicago.* But if you want to emphasize that the group is composed of individual members with differing opinions, motivations, or goals, choose a plural verb: *Her family are arguing about whether to move to Chicago.* Your choice of a singular or plural verb will set restrictions on (a) any subsequent verb in the sentence that also has the collective noun as its subject and (b) any pronoun in the sentence that has the collective noun as its antecedent. In the sentence *The committee is expected to announce their decision in January*, the pronoun *their* is incorrect, because its plurality clashes with the singularity of the verb *is*. The correct pronoun is therefore the singular *its*. (The writer is emphasizing the committee as a unified whole.) Your treatment of a collective noun as either singular or plural needs to be consistent throughout a sentence or a passage.

The singular interpretation of collective nouns is the prevailing interpretation in American English—so choose plural verbs and plural pronouns only in those instances when you want to emphasize the individual members of the group.

Faulty: Her family is now out of the spotlight and getting on with their lives.

(Bob Hoover, "Author Pours Clichés into Lynch Bio," *Pittsburgh Post-Gazette*, 12 Nov. 2003, p. E1)

The writer is inconsistent in his treatment of *family*. The sentence is intended to emphasize the individual members of the family, so both the verb and the pronoun should be plural.

Correct: Her family are now out of the spotlight and getting on with their lives.

Faulty: Her family was Catholic and treated like second-class citizens wherever they settled.

(Eric Schlosser, "A Grief like No Other," *Atlantic Monthly*, Sept. 1997, p. 39)

Here, too, the writer shifts from the singular interpretation of *family* to the plural. The sentence also forces the verb *was* to function simultaneously as a linking verb and as an auxiliary verb. The revision treats the collective noun plurally throughout.

Correct: Her family were Catholic and were treated like second-class citizens wherever they settled.

Faulty: One group of Peco workers has [**have**] been staying at an Alexandria Bay hotel, sleeping in sleeping bags and using flashlights to see; power was restored there only recently.

(Jeff Gammage, "Peco Crews to the Rescue," *Philadelphia Inquirer*, 14 Jan. 1998, p. A7)

The writer chose the singular verb *has* for the collective noun *group*, but the plural nouns *sleeping bags* and *flashlights* suggest that the emphasis should be on the individual members of the group.

Faulty: Having treated you at the door like social scurvy with contagious halitosis, the staff subtly changes demeanor once you're inside. They treat you like deaf cretins with learning difficulties.

(A. A. Gill, in the Aug. 2003 issue of *Vanity Fair*, cited in Frank DiGiacomo, "Grouchy Graydon Sends a Hit Man to Restaurant 66," *New York Observer* online, 28 July 2003, paragraph 16)

The writer is inconsistent with the collective noun *staff*. Either substitute *change* for *changes* in the first sentence, or begin the second sentence with *It treats*.

Faulty: For its part, the North Allegheny School District has behaved responsibly in offering pupils—many of whom may not receive adequate sex education at home—a presentation they regard [**it regards**] as balanced and unsensational.

("Sex, Faith and Videotape," editorial, *Pittsburgh Post-Gazette*, 22 Feb. 2002, p. A16)

The singular interpretation of the collective noun *North Allegheny School District* is correct, but the writer shifts to the plural interpretation in the adjectival dependent clause at the end of the sentence.

Faulty: I am encouraged by the interest that the public is taking in their health.

(Jenny L. Linnoila, "Supplements Can Be a Real Gamble," *Pittsburgh Post-Gazette*, 27 Jan. 2004, p. D2)

The public is treated both as singular and as plural.

Correct: I am encouraged by the interest that the public is taking in its health.

Correct: I am encouraged by the interest that the public are taking in their health.

Inconsistencies in the handling of collective nouns are especially common in sentences about rock bands.

Faulty: [Led] Zeppelin was labeled derivative, a hype, and every vile name anyone could possibly think of, and their [**its**] U.S. tours were scandalous, rapacious, excessive, arrogant sprees.

(Lisa Robinson, "Stairway to Excess," *Vanity Fair*, Nov. 2003, p. 360)

Faulty: A longtime favorite of the Lower East Side music scene, Luna has built a substantial following based on their [**its**] endearing, lo-fi music, which is full of references to their [**its**] downtown-Manhattan forefathers, the Velvet Underground and Television.

("Goings On About Town: Clubs," *New Yorker*, 5 Jan. 2004, p. 15)

The collective noun *couple* occasionally takes a singular verb: *The couple is planning a three-week vacation. The couple has won first place for its holiday display.* But more frequently it is regarded as plural and emphasizes the two individuals.

In the following sentence, the couple consists of two individuals who have not yet been united in a wedding ceremony, so the singular verb is both ungrammatical and illogical.

- The couple plans [**plan**] to marry in June.

  (Dave Philipps, "Jessica Lynch to Marry GI After 2-Year Romance," for *Colorado Springs Gazette*, in *Pittsburgh Post-Gazette*, 3 Nov. 2003, p. A1)

In the following examples, the emphasis should also be on the two persons.

- "The Girl Watchers Club" is an engaging read, despite a few clichés—one married couple, for instance, is [**are**] said to finish each other's sentences.

  (Brendan Miniter, review of *The Girl Watchers Club, Wall Street Journal*, 13 Feb. 2004, p. W8)

- Beneath the pope's window a couple embraces [**embrace**].

  (Dennis Roddy, "Pope's Light Remains Beacon for Those Who Love," *Pittsburgh Post-Gazette*, 24 Jan. 2004, p. D1)

All too often, the singular and plural interpretations of *couple* coexist illogically and ungrammatically in the same sentence.

- The couple has [**have**] officially broken off their engagement.

  ("Report: J. Lo, Affleck Break Off Engagement," www.nbc4.tv.com, 22 Jan. 2004, paragraph 2)

- There was a young couple in the corner [**In the corner were a young couple**], concerned only with each other and their all-consuming love, which was quite publicly displayed at times.

  ("Munch Goes to Pizza Parma," *Pittsburgh Post-Gazette*, 26 Dec. 2003, p. W33)

EXCEPTION

When an adjective following the article *the* is pressed into service as a collective noun (as in *the rich, the poor,* or *the famous*), the verb is always plural: *The rich get richer, and the poor get poorer.*

Inanimate Collective Nouns

It is now common for a plural verb to be used with an inanimate collective noun—such as *array, range, handful, plenty, crop,* and *constellation* (used figuratively of a group)—when the emphasis is on the individual items in the group: *An array of diversions, from flight-simulation computer games to scary DVDs, were available to him. A range of emotions are evident in her work. A handful of applications are promising.*

A singular verb is used, however, when a collective noun like *array* or *range* denotes a unified whole: *There is an array of paintings on display this week. There is a range of strategies that might prove useful to us.*

CHAPTER 6

OTHER ERRORS IN THE USE OF VERBS

In addition to errors in subject-verb agreement, there are four other common errors in the handling of verbs.

6A INDEFENSIBLE USE OF PASSIVE VOICE

The use of passive voice (see chapter 1) is questionable when the writer resorts to it as a means of evasion. The sentence *A bad decision was made* conveniently—and irresponsibly, one might conclude—avoids assigning blame: Who made the bad decision? Passive voice is entirely appropriate, however, when the writer does not know who performed an action, when it does not matter who performed an action, or when the emphasis belongs on the recipient of an action. You may occasionally have good reason to phrase one part of a sentence in active voice and another part in passive voice. The sentence *A number of fans of the movie complained when the soundtrack album was released without the song from the most poignant scene* legitimately shifts to the passive voice in the adverbial dependent clause, because the writer wants the spotlight on the fans and their disappointment rather than on the record company that released the soundtrack. Unintentional and unjustifiable shifts from one voice to another, however, are almost always awkward and distracting.

> **Inconsistent:** The new employees first attended an orientation session. Then a series of forms had to be filled out.
>> The first sentence is in active voice; the second is in passive voice.
> **Consistent:** The new employees first attended an orientation session. Then they filled out a series of forms.
>> Both sentences are in active voice.

6B DISTRACTING SHIFTS IN MOOD

Distracting and illogical shifts from one mood to another weaken a sentence or passage. (See chapter 1 for a discussion of the indicative, imperative, and subjunctive moods.) In the first clause of the following sentence, the subjunctive gives way to the indicative.

> **Inconsistent:** If he were to make the decision today and later was to change his mind, his family and friends might find their lives disrupted.
>
> **Consistent:** If he were to make the decision today and later were to change his mind, his family and friends might find their lives disrupted.

6C DISTRACTING SHIFTS IN TENSE

It is not uncommon for a sentence to refer to both the past and the present (*John Lennon's song "Imagine," which was released in 1971, remains popular and relevant today*), but a sentence or sequence of sentences should never shift illogically from one tense to another. (See chapter 1 for more on the tenses of verbs.)

> **Inconsistent:** In June 2005, she was transferred from a branch office to the corporate headquarters. Then she decides that she wants to change careers.
>
> **Consistent:** In June 2005, she was transferred from a branch office to the corporate headquarters. Then she decided that she wanted to change careers.

When you are recounting the events of the plot in a work of fiction or in a film, the convention is to use the present tense (often called the historical present).

> **Faulty:** The main character in the movie undergoes a series of demoralizing experiences at work and at home, but by the end, she was newly reconciled to her station in life.
>
> **Correct:** The main character in the movie undergoes a series of demoralizing experiences at work and at home, but by the end, she is newly reconciled to her station in life.

6D PROBLEMS WITH THE SEQUENCING OF TENSES

When you are writing a narrative sentence, be careful in handling the tenses so that the events or actions recounted are arranged clearly and logically along a timeline. Errors rarely arise when you are relating one event or action in the present to another event or action in the present (*I'm on my way to the kitchen when the phone rings*); all of the verbs belong in the simple present tense. Nor are errors likely to occur when you are relating one event or action in the past to another event or action taking place at the same time in the past (*As soon as I saw her, I began to wave*); all of the verbs belong in the simple past tense. The trouble is likely to start when you need to relate one event or action in the past to another event or action that occurred further back in the past.

> **Faulty:** I told him I was calling because I was sexually encroached upon twenty years ago by someone on his faculty, and I wanted to set up a confidential meeting to address it.
>
> (Naomi Wolf, "The Silent Treatment," *New York*, 1 Mar. 2004, p. 24)
>
> Here, the writer is using the past tense as the foundational tense for her narrative (she was making a phone call), but when she also uses the simple past tense to refer to an incident that occurred many years before the telephone call, she obscures the chronological relationship between the telephone call and the sexual-harassment incident. The writer needs to downshift into the past-perfect tense to relate the earlier incident.
>
> **Correct:** I told him I was calling because I had been sexually encroached upon twenty years earlier by someone on his faculty, and I wanted to set up a confidential meeting to address the matter.

The past-perfect tense, in other words, takes us back into the past before the past.

Later in the same magazine article, the writer again mismanages the sequence of tenses.

Faulty: When I described to my parents what had happened, they had gone to a friend of theirs, a scholar of Middle Eastern literature, who was close to Bloom.

(Naomi Wolf, "The Silent Treatment," *New York*, 1 Mar. 2004, p. 26)

In the introductory adverbial dependent clause (*when I described to my parents...*), the writer correctly uses the simple past tense to recount her conversation with her parents, and she correctly downshifts into the past-perfect tense in the nominative dependent clause (*what had happened*) that recounts what had occurred sometime previously. But the writer's use of the past-perfect tense in the independent clause of the sentence (*they had gone to a friend of theirs*) obscures the chronological relationship between the conversation with her parents and the course of action the parents took after the conversation: the parents sought out their friend after, not before, their conversation with their daughter. The action in the independent clause needs to be presented in the simple past tense.

Correct: When I described to my parents what had happened, they went to a friend of theirs, a scholar of Middle Eastern literature, who was close to Bloom.

Notice, also, how it might be preferable to begin the sentence with the subordinating conjunction *after* rather than with *when*, which suggests, misleadingly, that two actions occurred simultaneously.

The guiding principle for sentences recounting incidents in the past, then, is that the past-perfect tense is used to recount actions and events that occurred before the actions or events that are recounted in the simple past tense.

Faulty: I realized I forgot my password.
Correct: I realized I had forgotten my password.

Faulty: I didn't see Jennifer, who went home early.
Correct: I didn't see Jennifer, who had gone home early.

Faulty: In 1984, the runner and author James Fixx, who helped popularize the health benefits of jogging, dropped dead of a heart attack while running. . . .

("Fat Wars," editorial, *Pittsburgh Post-Gazette*, 16 Feb. 2004, p. A10)

Correct: In 1984, the runner and author James Fixx, who had helped popularize the health benefits of jogging, dropped dead of a heart attack while running. . . .

In a sentence recounting events in the past, the verb in an adverbial dependent clause that begins with the subordinating conjunction *after* does not need to be in the past-perfect tense, because the conjunction *after* sufficiently clarifies the chronological relationship between the event or action in the dependent clause and that in the independent clause.

- After we ate, we took a walk.

Following are six further guidelines to help you manage the sequence of tenses logically and correctly in your sentences and paragraphs. (You may want to review chapter 4 before reading this discussion.)

Use the present tense in a nominative dependent clause if it states an indisputable truth or presents a statement that is always regarded as true in a particular culture or true of a particular person, even if the independent clause is phrased in the past tense.

Faulty: The boy was surprised to learn that squirrels were rodents.
Correct: The boy was surprised to learn that squirrels are rodents.

Faulty: I forgot that Mother's Day was the second, not the first, Sunday in May.
Correct: I forgot that Mother's Day is the second, not the first, Sunday in May.

Faulty: He told me he was color-blind.
Correct: He told me he is color-blind.

In a sentence with two consecutive adverbial dependent clauses, the tense of the verb in the second dependent clause is determined by the tense of the verb in the first dependent clause.

Faulty: What lesson would the parents be teaching their boy if they continued to push him to practice until he cries?
Correct: What lesson would the parents be teaching their boy if they continued to push him to practice until he cried?

Avoid writing a complex sentence in which the verb phrases in both clauses take the form of *would have* followed by a past participle.

Faulty: If I would have seen her, I would have said hello.
Correct: If I had seen her, I would have said hello.

Faulty: I would have been more alert today if I would have slept longer than four hours last night.
Correct: I would have been more alert today if I had slept longer than four hours last night.

Avoid using a perfect infinitive (an infinitive in which the helping verb *have* is inserted between *to* and the stem of a verb) in a sentence that does not involve a downshift from the past into the past-before-the-past.

Faulty: He was the first boy ever to have played on the school's field-hockey team.
Correct: He was the first boy ever to play on the school's field-hockey team.

Faulty: She would have wanted to have moved to Chicago.
Correct: She would have wanted to move to Chicago.

Avoid using a perfect infinitive following a construction that includes a verb phrase such as *would have wanted, would have loved, would have liked,* or *would have preferred.*

Faulty: Jason would have preferred to have stayed home.
Correct: Jason would have preferred to stay home.

When you are shifting from the simple past tense in one sentence to the past-before-the-past in a series of sentences, use the past-perfect tense only in the first sentence of the past-before-the-past passage. The single-sentence downshift from past to past perfect will be sufficient to serve as the transition from the past to the earlier past that will be recounted in the sentences to follow. (The ensuing sentences will thus be clear of the clutter of auxiliary verbs required to form the past-perfect tense.) The paragraph below illustrates such a sequence.

- She moved to Columbus and began working for us in June 2005. She had earlier worked in Cleveland. In Cleveland she worked first at a hospital, then at a law office. For most of that time, she rented an apartment in Shaker Heights. She apparently kept to herself and had no close friends.

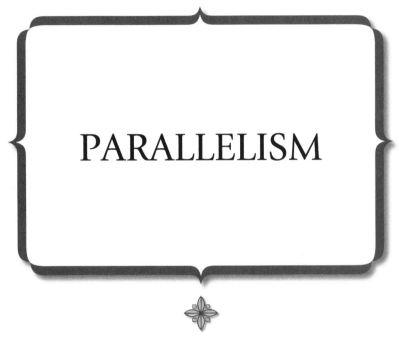

CHAPTER 7

PARALLELISM

The principle of parallelism requires that elements presented in a pair (*a and b*) and elements listed in a series (*a, b, and c*) be phrased in grammatically equivalent form. If the first element in a series is an adjectival dependent clause, for example, the other elements must also be adjectival dependent clauses.

7A BASTARD ENUMERATION

Bastard enumeration is the form of faulty parallelism exemplified by the sentence *She has visited Boston, Philadelphia, and plans to tour Washington, D.C.* In this example, *Boston* and *Philadelphia* seem to be intended as the first two elements in a series of three. The reader expects the name of a third city to follow the coordinating conjunction *and*. Instead, the reader finds a verb phrase (*plans to tour Washington, D.C.*). The reader then realizes that *Boston* and *Philadelphia*, rather than functioning as the first two elements in a series, are in fact the two direct objects of the verb *visited*, in the first of the two verb phrases that follow the subject of the sentence. The insertion of the conjunction *and* between *Boston* and *Philadelphia* will clarify the design of the sentence, whose predicate consists of two parallel verb phrases, the first of which has a compound object.

- She has visited Boston and Philadelphia, and plans to tour Washington, D.C.

Bastard enumeration, in other words, is the form of faulty parallelism in which three elements in a sentence have been misleadingly arranged and punctuated in an *a, b, and c* pattern, as if the three elements were grammatically equivalent, when in fact the sentence is presenting a pair of grammatically equivalent elements (usually two verb phrases), and embedded within one of those elements is another pair of grammatically equivalent elements (usually direct objects or complements of the verb in the first verb phrase).

The term *bastard enumeration,* which vehemently emphasizes the grammatical illegitimacy of the spurious series, was coined by H. W. Fowler and F. G. Fowler in the extraordinary book *The King's English,* first published in 1906. The Fowler brothers remarked that one cause of bastard enumeration is the superstition that the coordinating conjunction *and* should never be used more than once in a sentence. In fact, there is no restriction on the number of times *and* may appear.

Sentences afflicted with bastard enumeration can often be revised in one of four ways.

Faulty: The new software is inexpensive, user-friendly, and can be shipped to your office overnight.
Correct: The new software is inexpensive and user-friendly, and can be shipped to your office overnight.
Notice how the comma marks the boundary between the two verb phrases that constitute the compound predicate of the sentence. The deletion of the comma and the insertion of the coordinating conjunction *and* between *inexpensive* and *user-friendly* alert the reader to the fact that the adjectives form a pair.
Correct: The new software is inexpensive and user-friendly and can be shipped to your office overnight.
This revision, which omits the comma between the two parts of the compound predicate, is acceptable—but readers might initially misconstrue the sentence as one intended to present a series of three parallel elements with the conjunction *and* following both the first and the second: *She is brilliant and accomplished and unforgettable.*
Correct: The new software is inexpensive and user-friendly, and it can be shipped to your office overnight.
This revision is grammatically and punctuationally sound—but compared to the two previous revisions, it is wordy, and it requires the expansion of a simple sentence with a compound predicate into a compound sentence consisting of two independent clauses.
Correct: The new software is inexpensive, user-friendly, and easily shipped to your office overnight.
The second verb phrase in the original sentence has been reduced to an adjectival phrase, which is grammatically parallel to the first two elements in the series.

Following are more sentences weakened by bastard enumeration.

Faulty: He faces a maximum 10 years in prison, $500,000 in fines and must pay back the money he took.
(Russ Buettner, "Phone Freak Cop Admits 138G Theft," *New York Daily News,* 19 Dec. 2003, p. 38)
Correct: He faces a maximum 10 years in prison and $500,000 in fines, and must pay back the money he took.

Faulty: However, society has been slow to recognize the need for men and boys to be nurturing, sensitive and to show their feelings, characteristics associated with females.
(Monica L. Haynes, "Cracking the Gender Code," *Pittsburgh Post-Gazette,* 5 Aug. 1999, p. D1)
Correct: However, society has been slow to recognize the need for men and boys to be nurturing, sensitive, and demonstrative—characteristics associated with females.

Faulty: Mr. Schwarzenegger, 56, is still broad in the shoulders, narrow in the hips and has no visible paunch.
(Charles LeDuff, "Budget Woes to the Wind As Schwarzenegger Takes to the Road," *New York Times,* 13 Feb. 2004, p. A12)
Correct: Mr. Schwarzenegger, 56, is still broad in the shoulders and narrow in the hips, and has no visible paunch.

Faulty: Roman Abramovich—his erstwhile partner—has an $80 million house in Eaton Square, an estate in West Sussex, and owns the Chelsea football club.
(Pheobe Eaton, "How Much Is That in Rubles?" *New York,* 20 Sept. 2004, p. 30)
Correct: Roman Abramovich—his erstwhile partner—has an $80 million house in Eaton Square and an estate in West Sussex, and owns the Chelsea football club.

Correct: Roman Abramovich—his erstwhile partner—owns an $80 million house in Eaton Square, an estate in West Sussex, and the Chelsea football club.

Faulty: All clothing must have no stains, tears and all toys must be in working order.
(Marjorie Wertz, "Sale to Feature Used Children's Items," *Greensburg [PA] Tribune-Review*, 13 Apr. 2004, p. A8)
Correct: All clothing must have no stains or tears, and all toys must be in working order.

Faulty: It's [The state university is] relatively close to his hometown, less expensive than private schools, and its agriculture and life sciences program, which he wants to major in, has a stellar reputation.
(Mary Beth Marklein, "The Debate over Going to 'State,'" *USA Today*, 6 Feb. 2002, p. 1D)
Correct: It's relatively close to his hometown and less expensive than private schools, and its agriculture-and-life-sciences program, which he wants to major in, has a stellar reputation.

Faulty: He had been on WNBC's *Extra,* CNBC's *Hardball* with Chris Matthews, and found himself sitting with ABC's Bill Beutel and Roz Abrams as they covered the July 23 memorial service at the Church of St. Thomas More on Manhattan's Upper East Side.
(Andrew Goldman, "Kennedy 'Expert' C. David Heymann: Do His J.F.K. Stories Hold Up?," *New York Observer*, 2 Aug. 1999, p. 1)
Correct: He had been on WNBC's Extra and CNBC's Hardball with Chris Matthews, and found himself sitting with ABC's Bill Beutel and Roz Abrams as they covered the July 23 memorial service at the Church of St. Thomas More on Manhattan's Upper East Side.

The examples thus far have involved bastard enumerations of three elements—but bastard enumerations of four or more elements often occur as well.

Faulty: Smoking Causes Lung Cancer, Heart Disease, Emphysema, And May Complicate Pregnancy.
(surgeon general's warning on cigarette package)
Correct: Smoking Causes Lung Cancer, Heart Disease, and Emphysema, and May Complicate Pregnancy.

Faulty: Over time, this can severely impair kidney function, cause heart disease, blindness and crippling nerve damage.
(Michael Waldholz, "Researchers' Goal: Stopping Diabetes Before Kids Get It," *Wall Street Journal*, 1 Mar. 2004, p. A12)
Correct: Over time, this can severely impair kidney function and cause heart disease, blindness, and crippling nerve damage.

7B BUNGLED SERIES

A bungled series is a series in which all but one of the elements have been phrased in grammatically equivalent form. The dissimilar element needs to be recast so that it is in the same grammatical form as the other elements. (Some bungled series, as you will be sure to notice, can also be classified as bastard enumerations.)

The series in each of the following sentences is italicized; the bungled element is underlined.

Faulty: Between November 2002 and July 2003, Mr. Ptah says, he sold more than 10,000 copies *on the street, the subway and at readings* that he and Tehut-Nine had set up.
(Dinitia Smith, "A Hip-Hop Author in Search of a Publisher Finds One on the A Train," *New York Times*, 6 Jan. 2004, p. B7)
    The first and third elements are prepositional phrases; the bungled element is a noun phrase.
Correct: Between November 2002 and July 2003, Mr. Ptah says, he sold more than 10,000 copies on the street, on the subway, and at readings that he and Tehut-Nine had set up.
    The series now consists of three prepositional phrases.

Faulty: News reports can give the impression that life in the city is dominated by ways to meet an early end—*being hit by a cab, stabbed by a mugger, slipping on the ice.*
(Richard Pérez-Peña, "Following New Yorkers to a Later Grave," *New York Times*, 31 Jan. 2004, p. A13)
    The first and third elements in the series are gerund phrases; the bungled element is a participial phrase.
Correct: News reports can give the impression that life in the city is dominated by ways to meet an early end—being hit by a cab, getting stabbed by a mugger, slipping on the ice.

The series now consists of three gerund phrases.

Faulty: Its new chair *is upholstered, has a higher back,* <u>extended arms</u> *and can swivel or lock in place.*

(Keith L. Alexander, "Hotel Designers Ponder the Look, Feel of the Future," *USA Today*, 17 Mar. 1998, p. 8E)

Three of the elements in the series are verb phrases; the bungled element is a noun phrase. The bungled element is the second direct object of the transitive verb in the second verb phrase.

Correct: Its new chair is upholstered, has a higher back and extended arms, and can swivel or lock in place.

The series now consists of three verb phrases.

Faulty: Beneath the big-picture ideas are some practical ones, including *releasing Kingsbury Run from culverts and restoring its habitat;* a park linking <s>Tremont with the river's edge;</s> *and developing 26 acres on the riverfront that are owned by Zaclon Inc.*

(Tom Breckenridge, "County Unveils Plan for Cuyahoga Valley," *Cleveland Plain Dealer*, 12 Feb. 2004, p. B5)

The first and third elements in the series are gerund phrases; the bungled element is a noun phrase.

Correct: Beneath the big-picture ideas are some practical ones, including releasing Kingsbury Run from culverts and restoring its habitat; designing a park to link Tremont with the river's edge; and developing 26 acres on the riverfront that are owned by Zaclon Inc.

The series consists of three gerund phrases.

Faulty: The lowest levels [of fast-food consumption] were found in *youngsters living in the West,* <u>rural areas,</u> *Hispanics and those aged four to eight,* though more than 20% of the youngest in each of those groups reported eating fast food on any given day.

("Children's Fast-Food Diet Adds Pounds, Study Says," for Associated Press, in *Wall Street Journal*, 6 Jan. 2004, p. D6)

The series consists of four nounal elements—three noun phrases and one single-word noun. But the second, bungled element, unlike the other three elements, refers to a place, not to people.

Correct: The lowest levels were found in youngsters living in Rathe West and in rural areas, Hispanics, and those aged four to eight, though more than 20 percent of the youngest in each of those groups reported eating fast food on any given day.

Better: Hispanics, youngsters living in the West and rural areas, and children between four and eight years old were found to have the lowest levels, though more than 20 percent of the youngest in each of those groups reported eating fast food on any given day.

A series occasionally includes more than one bungled element. Such a series is out of control. The disorderly series in the following sentence has been italicized.

Faulty: The result is a bagel *that is fairly petite by today's standards, that has decent chew, excellent flavor, and manages to be dense without being leaden.*

(Ed Levine, "Was Life Better When Bagels Were Smaller?," *New York Times*, 31 Dec. 2003, p. D6)

The first two elements in the series are adjectival dependent clauses; the third element is a noun phrase; and the final element is a verb phrase.

Correct: The result is a bagel that is fairly petite by today's standards, that has decent chew and excellent flavor, and that manages to be dense without being leaden.

The series now consists of three adjectival dependent clauses.

Better (More Concise): The result is a bagel that is fairly petite by today's standards, has decent chew and excellent flavor, and manages to be dense without being leaden.

The series now consists of three verb phrases.

7C PAIRS AND SERIES WITH DETERMINERS

Be careful with the handling of determiners in a pair or series of nouns. Determiners include the articles (*a, an,* and *the*), as well as the possessive pronouns (*her, his, its,* etc.)—words, in short, that restrict the meaning of the nouns they precede.

If a determiner applies to all of the elements in a series, you have two grammatically correct options.

1. Include the determiner only once in the series—before the very first element.

- She is a talk-show host, writer, and comedian.

2. Include the determiner before each element in the series.

- She is a talk-show host, a writer, and a comedian.
    - This sentence is nonparallel: *She is a talk-show host, writer, and a comedian.*

If a single determiner does not apply to all of the elements in a series, each element must be preceded by an appropriate determiner.

Faulty: She is a talk-show host, author, and comedian.
Correct: She is a talk-show host, an author, and a comedian.

The same principle applies to pairs of nouns.

Faulty: He is an officer and gentleman.
Correct: He is an officer and a gentleman.

Corrective additions to the following sentences are bracketed and boldfaced.

- It was a pivotal moment for the then-Elizabeth Westergaard—who until that point had been an actress, [**a**] poet, and [**a**] playwright.
    (Ray Rogers, "Lizzie West: She Found Her Voice on a Subway Platform—Next Stop, Record Deal," *Interview*, Apr. 2003, p. 88)

- Vincent Gallo, a downtown New York artist active since the early eighties as a musician, [**a**] photographer, [**a**] painter, [**a**] model, [**an**] actor, and [**a**] filmmaker, has a face like a rusty hatchet (needle nose, scraggly beard), damp inky hair, and an unnerving stare.
    (David Denby, "Journeys," *New Yorker*, 13 Sept. 2004, p. 99)

    The sentence could of course be rephrased so that fewer indefinite articles are needed: *Vincent Gallo, a downtown New York artist active since the early eighties not only as a musician, photographer, painter, and model but also as an actor and a filmmaker, has a face like a rusty hatchet. . . .*

- Through Aug. 30 (the day before the one-year anniversary of Diana's death), up to 2,500 ticketed visitors a day will stream into the front gates of the 1,300-acre estate to visit the house, [**the**] grounds and a new Diana tribute museum.
    (Thomas K. Grose, "Visitors Will Mingle with Diana's Memory," *USA Today*, 30 June 1998, p. 1D)

- ... Mr. Jagger's arms, [**his**] legs, and even his magnificent lips seemed to be flying off in different directions before a sea of rapt Rolling Stones fans.
    (Frank DiGiacomo, "It's the Last Party of the Century," *New York Observer*, 13 Dec. 1999, p. 1)

- Amid the waste was an inexplicably dead raccoon, [**an**] opossum and "possibly some rats," Milliron says.
    (Diana Nelson Jones, "One Man's Trash Is Another Man's Treasure," *Pittsburgh Post-Gazette*, 15 Apr. 2004, p. B3)

    This sentence is also weakened by an error in subject-verb agreement. See rule 29A in chapter 5.

- He went on to become a deputy correction commissioner, [**the**] Juvenile Justice commissioner and the deputy police commissioner for community affairs.
    (Russ Buettner, "Phone Freak Cop Admits 138G Theft," *New York Daily News*, 19 Dec. 2003, p. 38)

7D VERTICALLY ARRANGED SERIES

The reader-friendliness of a series can be enhanced by arranging the elements vertically on the page. As in any other kind of series, the elements in a vertically arrayed series must be phrased in grammatically equivalent form. To double-check that the elements are parallel, ask yourself which word or words could be inserted at the beginning of each element to generate a grammatically complete sentence. If the same phrasing can be inserted before each item in the series, the series is parallel.

The following nonparallel lists appeared on the back covers of recent books about grammar and usage. Each list introduces prospective readers to the special features of the book. In the first example, the first three elements are verb phrases, but the final element is an adjectival phrase.

- Defines over 1000 terms, ranging from 'adjective' and 'antonym' to 'zero article' and 'zeugma'
- Covers both general and specialist vocabulary
- Shows how common errors are made and how they can be avoided
- Ideal for all those keen to improve their understanding of written and spoken English
  (from the dust jacket of the *Cassell Dictionary of English Grammar*, by James Aitchison [London: Cassell, 1996])

The final element can be transformed into a verb phrase by inserting *is* at the beginning.

- Is ideal for all those keen to improve their understanding of written and spoken English.

The phrase *The book* could now be inserted at the beginning of each element to generate a complete sentence.

In the sentences below, the first four elements are noun phrases, but the final element is a verb phrase.

- Many more examples in every chapter
- An improved, easier-to-use section on documentation
- A rewritten chapter on rights and permissions
- New material on names and terms, quotations, foreign languages
- Incorporates recent changes in style, usage, and in computer technology
  (from the dust jacket of *The Chicago Manual of Style*, fourteenth edition [Chicago: University of Chicago Press, 1993])

The final element could be revised as follows.

- Guidance on recent changes in style, usage, and in computer technology

But there is another problem with the final element: It includes an *a, b, and c* series in non-parallel form. The series *in style, usage, and in computer technology* wedges a noun between two prepositional phrases.

Inserting the preposition *in* before *usage* will resolve the problem.

- Guidance on recent changes in style, in usage, and in computer technology

A more concise revision would reduce the trio of prepositional phrases to a single prepositional phrase with three objects.

- Guidance on recent changes in style, usage, and computer technology

The phrasing *The book provides* could now be inserted at the beginning of each of the five elements to generate a complete sentence.

The next series consists of one verb phrase (the first element), one noun phrase (the second element), and three adjectival phrases.

- Covers written and spoken British and American English, across both formal and informal registers of the language
- Up-to-date and ground-breaking discussion of modern English grammar, including analysis of the scope and nature of grammar; an outline of grammar; textual patterns; words and their meanings; phonetics and intonation; and punctuation and spelling
- Uniquely innovative in its systematic use of evidence of real modern English, with examples taken from the new International Corpus of English at University College London, as well as from other American and British sources

- Lively and accessible—ideal for non-specialists as well as for students of the English language
- Written by one of the world's leading grammarians of English

(from the back cover of *The Oxford English Grammar*, by Sidney Greenbaum [Oxford and New York: Oxford University Press, 1996])

The verb phrase can easily be converted into an adjectival phrase.

- Comprehensive in its coverage of written and spoken English, across both formal and informal registers of the language

The noun phrase can be converted into an adjectival phrase by inserting *in its* between *ground-breaking* and *discussion.*

- Up-to-date and groundbreaking in its discussion of modern English grammar, including analysis of the scope and nature of grammar; an outline of grammar; textual patterns; words and their meanings; phonetics and intonation; and punctuation and spelling

The phrasing *The book provides* could now be inserted at the beginning of each element to generate a complete sentence.

7E AUXILIARY VERBS IN PAIRS AND IN SERIES

If an auxiliary verb applies to both of the main verbs in a pair or to all of the main verbs in a series, you have two grammatically correct options.

1. Include the auxiliary verb only once—before the first element in the pair or series.

- The employees have protested the new policy, written many letters to government officials, and threatened to strike.

2. Include the auxiliary verb before each element in the pair or series.

Faulty: The employees have protested the new policy, written many letters to government officials, and have threatened to strike.
   This sentence is nonparallel.
Correct: The employees have protested the new policy, have written many letters to government officials, and have threatened to strike.

The sentence below, from a mailing entitled *Year 2000 Readiness Disclosure* sent to all customers of a utility company, includes the auxiliary-verb construction *will have* before the first and the third elements but not before the second element. The inconsistency deforms the sentence.

Faulty: By the end of the year, Allegheny Power will have devoted approximately 80,000 employee hours to the Y2K-compliance project, spent as much as $20 million, and will have participated in two industry-wide Y2K drills.
   To resolve the faulty parallelism, either insert *will have* before *spent* or delete *will have* before *participated.* (The latter option will result in a more concise sentence.)
Correct: By the end of the year, Allegheny Power will have devoted approximately 80,000 employee hours to the Y2K-compliance project, will have spent as much as $20 million, and will have participated in two industry-wide Y2K drills.
Correct: By the end of the year, Allegheny Power will have devoted approximately 80,000 employee hours to the Y2K-compliance project, spent as much as $20 million, and participated in two industry-wide Y2K drills.

If an auxiliary verb is positioned at the start of only the first main verb in a series of verb phrases, each subsequent main verb needs to be conjugated to agree with the auxiliary verb. In the sentence below, the third main verb in the series of four verb phrases does not accord with the auxiliary verb *have* at the head of the series.

- In previous recessions and economic upheavals, Americans have traded in gas-guzzling cars, canceled big vacations, ate [**eaten**] out less frequently and generally moved to a more financially prudent ground.

  (Tim Jones, "Cash or Cell Phone?," for *Chicago Tribune*, in *Pittsburgh Post-Gazette*, 5 Mar. 2000, p. C3)

If an auxiliary verb positioned before the main verb in the first of a series of verb phrases applies to only some (but not all) of the main verbs in the series, the auxiliary verb must be repeated before each main verb to which it applies. In the adverbial dependent clause of the sentence below, the auxiliary verb *have* at the start of the series of three verb phrases can be carried forward to the second element but not to the third, because the third element begins with a different auxiliary verb.

> **Faulty:** We will not reveal customer information to any external organization unless we have previously informed the customer in disclosures or agreements, been authorized by the customer, or are required by law.
>
> (Citibank mailing, *Privacy Promise for Consumers*, M0999, p. 2)
>
> The quickest fix is to repeat *have* before the second element.
>
> **Correct:** We will not reveal customer information to any external organization unless we have previously informed the customer in disclosures or agreements, have been authorized by the customer, or are required by law.

A similar problem in the following sentence can be resolved by inserting the helping verb *was* at the start of the second element in the series.

> **Faulty:** The crack was first discovered in the 1940s during the Truman administration, repaired in 1989, but has now become more visible again.
>
> ("'Tomb of the Unknowns' Longtime Crack Necessitates Its Replacement," for Associated Press, in *Pittsburgh Post-Gazette*, 27 May 2003, p. A12)
>
> **Better:** The crack was first discovered in the 1940s during the Truman administration, was repaired in 1989, but has now become more visible again.

But there is a second problem with the sentence: It presents a series in the illogical *a, b, but c* form. Writers who resort to it mean *a and b but c*. The sentence above should thus be revised in one of the following ways.

> **Correct:** The crack had been discovered in the 1940s during the Truman administration and was repaired in 1989 but has now become more visible again.
>
> **Correct:** The crack had been discovered in the 1940s during the Truman administration and was repaired in 1989, but it has now become more visible again.
>
> **Correct:** The crack, which had been discovered in the 1940s during the Truman administration and was repaired in 1989, has now become more visible again.

In the following sentence, the parallelism of the five-element series in the nominative dependent clause (which begins with the subordinating conjunction *whether*) breaks down in the final element—because *it's been* can be carried forward to the second, third, and fourth elements but not to the fifth.

> **Faulty:** Both services are available to consumers and trace a vehicle's history through the vehicle identification number to find out whether it's been stolen, totaled, declared a lemon, involved in a major accident or had its odometer rolled back.
>
> (Rick Popely, "True Value: How Not to Get 'Used' When Buying, Selling a Used Car," from *Chicago Tribune*, in *Pittsburgh Post-Gazette*, 20 Oct. 2003, p. D2)

One revisional option is to repeat *been* before the second, third, and fourth elements.

> **Correct:** Both services are available to consumers and trace a vehicle's history through the vehicle-identification number to find out whether it's been stolen, been totaled, been declared a lemon, been involved in a major accident, or had its odometer rolled back.

A more concise revision, however, would group the first four elements together as a four-element series and recast the fifth element as a second nominative clause.

Correct: Both services are available to consumers and trace a vehicle's history through the vehicle-identification number to find out whether it's been stolen, totaled, declared a lemon, or involved in a major accident, or whether it's had its odometer rolled back.

If a series of verb phrases includes one or more verb phrases that include both an auxiliary verb and a main verb and one or more verb phrases that include only a finite verb (a verb functioning without the assistance of an auxiliary verb), an auxiliary verb must precede each main verb. In the following sentence, the auxiliary verb *was* at the start of the first element can be carried forward to the second element in the series but not to the third element (which requires no auxiliary verb) and not to the fourth element (which requires an auxiliary verb other than *was*).

Faulty: De Matteo was born in Queens, raised on the Upper East Side, owns a vintage clothing store and an apartment in the East Village, and is used to shooting *The Sopranos* at Silvercup Studios in Long Island City.

(Ariel Levy, "Dying Is Easy, Comedy Is Hard," *New York*, 13 Sept. 2004, p. 80)

Correct: De Matteo was born in Queens, was raised on the Upper East Side, owns a vintage-clothing store and an apartment in the East Village, and is used to shooting *The Sopranos* at Silvercup Studios in Long Island City.

Here, *was* repeats before the main verb at the start of the second element.

Better (More Concise): De Matteo was born in Queens and raised on the Upper East Side, owns a vintage-clothing store and an apartment in the East Village, and is used to shooting *The Sopranos* at Silvercup Studios in Long Island City.

The first and second elements are combined into a single compound element. The series now consists of three elements.

Be careful with compound-predicate sentences whose first auxiliary verb is fused with its subject in a contraction. If the contracted auxiliary verb is not the appropriate auxiliary verb for the other main verb or verbs in the sentence, the sentence will suffer from an imbalance.

Faulty: She's attending classes to earn a bachelor's degree and has been employed as an administrative assistant since 2003.

The contracted verb *is* has been fused with the subject—and therefore the auxiliary verb *has*, which appears in the sentence below, lacks a stand-alone subject to which it might attach itself.

Correct: She is attending classes to earn a bachelor's degree and has been employed as an administrative assistant since 2003.

In the following example, the auxiliary verb *has*, which is fused with the pronominal subject *he* in the contraction at the start of the sentence, carries forward to each of the verb phrases in the five-element series. The inclusion of *has* in the final element is thus redundant and ungrammatical.

Faulty: He's studied Kabbalah, become a dad, traveled to Africa to free Sudanese slaves, relaunched Lollapalooza, and now has reunited Jane's Addiction for its first all-new album in 13 years—that rare, nonturgid reunion album that actually fits in with the back catalogue.

("The Freak," *Vanity Fair*, Nov. 2003, from an unpaginated section)

The sentence needs to lose *has* between *now* and *reunited*.

The following sentences have been revised to eliminate problems with fused subjects.

- It's [**It has**] sold more than one and a half million copies and is published in 35 languages, but Hillary Rodham Clinton's memoir, *Living History*, is much more than a best-seller.

(Greg Sargent, "Senator Hillary Rodham Clinton: Politics," *New York*, 22–29 Dec. 2003, p. 45)

- He's already written another screenplay[,] and [he] plans to devote himself to filmmaking for the foreseeable future.

  (Diane De La Paz, "Tacoman Debuts Film at Premier Festival," [Tacoma, WA] News Tribune, 20 Jan. 2004, p. A8)

  > The sentence above could also be rewritten as: *He has already written another screenplay and plans to devote himself to filmmaking for the foreseeable future.*

In the next example, the parallelism breaks down in the five-element series presented in the adverbial dependent clause that ends the sentence.

> **Faulty:** If you're a black male between the ages of 16 and 30, there's a good chance that there's a bullet out there with your name on it if you're involved in the drug trade, unemployed, run with a gang, "steal" someone's woman or accidentally step on someone's sneaker.
>
> (Tony Norman, "Murder in Their Hearts and Guns in Their Hands," *Pittsburgh Post-Gazette*, 30 Dec. 2003, p. A9)
>
> The helping verb *are* that is contracted in *you're* at the start of the series can be carried forward to the second item in the series (the participle *unemployed*) but not to the third, fourth, and fifth items. The quickest fix is to decontract *you* and *are*, then repeat *are* before *unemployed*. The series then consists of five parallel verb phrases, as in the example below.
>
> **Correct:** ... there's a bullet out there with your name on it if you are involved in the drug trade, are unemployed, run with a gang, "steal" someone's woman, or accidentally step on someone's sneaker.

7F NONPARALLEL PAIRS

The principle of parallelism applies not only to elements arranged in a series but also to elements arranged in a pair.

> **Faulty:** If the company does not agree to changes in its advertising that the department is seeking, and to pay a fine, the department will file a lawsuit, it said.
>
> (Marian Burros, "CremaLita Chain Accused of False Advertising," *New York Times*, 31 Dec. 2003, p. D4)
>
> The introductory adverbial dependent clause mismatches a hybrid construction composed of two consecutive prepositional phrases and an adjectival dependent clause (*to changes in its advertising that the department is seeking*) with an infinitive phrase (*to pay a fine*).
>
> **Correct:** If the company does not agree to make changes in its advertising that the department is seeking and to pay a fine, the department will file a lawsuit, it said.
>
> The first construction has been converted to an infinitive phrase.
>
> **Better:** If the company does not agree to pay a fine and to make changes in its advertising that the department is seeking, the department will file a lawsuit, it said.
>
> This smoother revision reverses the sequence of the infinitive phrases.

> **Faulty:** Mr. Stern, infamous for his crude programming and who in 1995 was fined a total of $1.5 million for indecency, hasn't let the recent suspension hold him back.
>
> (Sarah McBride, "He 'Is What He Is': Advertisers Stand By Howard Stern," *Wall Street Journal*, 8 Mar. 2004, p. B11)
>
> The interruptive element that follows the subject incorrectly pairs an adjectival phrase with an adjectival dependent clause.
>
> **Correct:** Mr. Stern, who is infamous for his crude programming and who in 1995 was fined a total of $1.5 million for indecency, hasn't let the recent suspension hold him back.
>
> The interruptive element now consists of two adjectival dependent clauses.

> **Faulty:** It [a property-tax increase] too was a measure of Pittsburgh, a city desperate for cash and no real plan to solve the underlying problem of the lack of job opportunities, especially for talented young people.
>
> (Bruce Johnson and Denise Johnson, "Leadership Key to Making Pittsburgh Forward Looking," *Pittsburgh Post-Gazette*, 23 May 2004, p. C2)
>
> The nonparallel pair is in the appositive phrase *a city desperate for cash and no real plan to solve the underlying problem of the lack of job opportunities*. The noun *plan* is forced into functioning as the second object of the preposition *for*, resulting in the illogical construction *a city desperate for ... no real plan*.
>
> **Correct:** It too was a measure of Pittsburgh, a city desperate for cash and with no real plan to solve the underlying problem. ...

The preposition *with*, inserted before *no real plan*, creates an adjectival prepositional phrase parallel to the first adjectival phrase; both phrases modify *city*.

Better (More Concise): It too was a measure of Pittsburgh, a city desperate for cash and lacking any real plan to solve the underlying problem. ...

An adjectival phrase has been paired with a participial phrase, which functions adjectivally.

A common form of the nonparallel pair occurs in sentences in which the indefinite relative pronoun *that* appears at the start of a second nominative dependent clause following a verb of attribution but not at the start of the first nominative clause. Such imbalances can be corrected by inserting a parallel *that* at the beginning of the first noun clause. Parallelizing *thats* have been inserted into the following sentences.

- Most American Jewish leaders believe **[that]** they are up against huge forces around the world and that ultimately they cannot fight this fight alone.
  (Craig Horowitz, "The Return of Anti-Semitism," *New York*, 15 Dec. 2003, p. 33)

- The FDA said **[that]** it has seen no cases of inhalation anthrax in vaccinated individuals and that the vaccine was recommended "regardless of the route of exposure."
  ("Action on Anthrax," editorial, *Wall Street Journal*, 2 Jan. 2004, p. A8)

If you decide to allow the first *that* to serve for both noun clauses, be sure not to insert a comma before the coordinating conjunction that links the two clauses. Not only will such a punctuational split appear to disattribute the contents of the second noun clause from the speaker or source and, misleadingly, attribute the contents to the writer, but the split will also appear to transform the second noun clause into an independent clause (see the discussion of ambiguity in chapter 16).

Faulty: Officials said that the doctor who worked there was leaving, and finding a replacement would be too difficult.
(Paula Reed Ward, "How Snow Shoe Got a Doc," *Pittsburgh Post-Gazette*, 1 Feb. 2004, p. A1)

Correct: Officials said that the doctor who worked there was leaving and that finding a replacement would be too difficult.

In the following example, the omission of a second *that* will cause many readers to misconstrue *owners* as a second object of the preposition *with* instead of recognizing it as the subject of a second nominative dependent clause.

Faulty: Cuyahoga Falls Law Director Virgil Arrington said Wednesday that the city has tried to work with the club and owners have increased security, but problems persist, especially outside the building.
(Karen Farkas, "Cuyahoga Falls Says Boot Scoot'n Saloon Raises Ruckus, Asks Court to Shut It Down," *Cleveland Plain Dealer*, 12 Feb. 2004, p. B3)

Better: Cuyahoga Falls Law Director Virgil Arrington said Wednesday that the city has tried to work with the club and that the owners have increased security, but problems persist, especially outside the building.

But the reader might be puzzled about the source of the information in the final independent clause of the sentence. Was Arrington the source? If so, insert *that* before *problems*.

7G PAIRS WITH CORRELATIVE CONJUNCTIONS

Unlike the other conjunctions we have examined—the coordinating conjunctions (words like *and* and *but*); the subordinating conjunctions (words like *because* and *although*); and the conjunctive adverbs (words like *however* and *therefore*)—the correlative conjunctions always appear in pairs. The correlative conjunctions are *either . . . or; neither . . . nor; not only . . . but [also]; not ... but; and both ... and*. Faulty parallelism often occurs in sentences that include such conjunctions.

The phrasing following the second half of a correlative-conjunction pair must be grammatically equivalent to the phrasing following the first half of the correlative-conjunction pair. If a verb phrase follows *either,* for instance, a verb phrase must also follow *or.*

The following sentences have been revised to eliminate faulty parallelism. The parallel phrasing in the revisions has been underlined. The more concise revision is almost always the stylistically preferred revision.

Either … or and *neither … nor*

Faulty: According to network insiders, division president David Westin and other ABC executives were "disappointed and surprised" that Snyderman was either ignorant of the policy or chose to ignore it.

(Stephen Battaglio, "Reporter in Trouble," for *New York Daily News,* in *Pittsburgh Post-Gazette,* 15 Apr. 2002, p. D8)

Either is followed by an adjectival phrase; *or* is followed by a verb phrase.

Correct: According to network insiders, division president David Westin and other ABC executives were "disappointed and surprised" that Snyderman either was ignorant of the policy or chose to ignore it.

Now both halves of the correlative-conjunction pair are followed by verb phrases.

Faulty: Today one in five moviegoers is either nearing or has reached traditional retirement age—hardly the hot young demographic sought by most Hollywood producers.

(Brian McTavish, "Hollywood Sees Green in Graying Audience," for *Kansas City Star,* in *Pittsburgh Post-Gazette,* 29 Nov. 1999, p. D5)

Either is wedged between an auxiliary verb and a main verb; *nor* is followed by an auxiliary verb and a main verb.

Correct: Today one in five moviegoers either is nearing or has reached traditional retirement age—hardly the hot young demographic sought by most Hollywood producers.

Each half of the correlative-conjunction pair is now followed by an auxiliary verb and a main verb.

Faulty: In the study, people who had memorized a pair of words were later shown one of them and asked to either recall the second word or to consciously avoid thinking about it.

(Anahad O'Connor, "Theory Given on Burying of Memories," *New York Times,* 9 Jan. 2004, p. A15)

Either is sandwiched between the *to* of an infinitive and the rest of an infinitive phrase; *or* is followed by a complete infinitive phrase.

Correct: In the study, people who had memorized a pair of words were later shown one of them and asked either to recall the second word or to consciously avoid thinking about it.

Both halves of the correlative-conjunction pair are now followed by infinitive phrases.

Faulty: Usually when a comedian speaks with great seriousness about his art, he is either being totally insincere or has fallen victim to a modern cliché, the clown who's laughing on the outside and thinking on the inside.

(James Collins, "The Larry We Loved," *Time,* 1 June 1998, p. 84)

Either is followed by a participial phrase; *or* is followed by a verb phrase.

Correct: Usually when a comedian speaks with great seriousness about his art, he either is being totally insincere or has fallen victim to a modern cliché, the clown who's laughing on the outside and thinking on the inside.

Both halves of the correlative-conjunction pair are now followed by verb phrases.

Faulty: When technically limited pop artists try to emulate orchestral classics—as David Byrne did in his music to Robert Wilson's "Forest" or as Stewart Copeland did in his dreadful opera "Holy Blood and Crescent Moon"—they either turn their skeletal song inspirations over to hack classical arrangers or they ape the surface characteristics of classical music with none of its muscle and heart.

(John Rockwell, "Beyond Singles and Concept Albums, Pop Yearns for a Long Form," *New York Times,* 2 Jan. 2004, p. B3)

Either is followed by a verb phrase; *nor* is followed by an independent clause.

Correct: When technically limited pop artists try to emulate orchestral classics—as David Byrne did in his music to Robert Wilson's Forest or as Stewart Copeland did in his dreadful opera Holy Blood and Crescent

Moon—they either <u>turn their skeletal song inspirations over to hack classical arrangers</u> or <u>ape the surface characteristics of classical music with none of its muscle and heart.</u>

Each half of the correlative-conjunction pair is now followed by a verb phrase.

CAUTION

Never use a *neither ... or* construction.

> **Faulty:** He also says the agent at the rental counter neither asked him where he intended to go or told him of the restrictions.
>
> (Christopher Elliott, "Business Travel: Some Rental Cars Are Keeping Tabs on the Drivers," *New York Times*, 13 Jan. 2004, p. C6)
>
> Replace *or* with *nor*.

Not only ... but [also] and not just ... but [also]

Faulty: The children are not only pursuing bigger and better hotels but also, apparently, hipper hotels.

(Joseph Berger, "For a New Generation, Rooms to Succeed," *New York Times*, 3 Feb. 2004, p. A23)

Not only is followed by a main verb and its direct object; *but also* is followed by a noun phrase.

Correct: The children are pursuing not only <u>bigger and better hotels</u> but also, apparently, <u>hipper hotels.</u>

The two halves of the correlative-conjunction pair are each followed by a noun phrase.

Faulty: Rather than expanding the status and privileges of marriage to same-sex couples and then gradually to other kinds of caring relationships, as logic would soon require, society should find alternative ways of meeting the needs not only of same-sex couples but also interdependent friends, and dependent but unmarried kin.

(Don Browning and Elizabeth Marquardt, "A Marriage Made in History?," *New York Times*, 9 Mar. 2004, p. A27)

Not only is followed by a prepositional phrase; but also is followed by two noun phrases.

Correct: ... society should find alternative ways of meeting the needs not only <u>of same-sex couples</u> but also <u>of interdependent friends and dependent but unmarried kin.</u>

Each half of the correlative-conjunction pair is followed by a prepositional phrase.

Faulty: Tybran, a Westport, Conn., toy store, was not only frozen out of Beanie Babies shipments last year after running a special "buy five, get one free" promotion, but was unsuccessfully sued by Warner, who demanded the store change its name because it could be construed as associated with Ty Inc.

(Robert Dominguez, "Beanies' Creator an Enigma," *New York Daily News*, 21 June 1998, p. 20)

Not only has been sandwiched between a helping verb and a main verb; *but* is followed by a helping verb and a main verb.

Correct: Tybran, a Westport, Conn., toy store, not only <u>was frozen out of Beanie Babies shipments last year after running a special "buy five, get one free" promotion</u> but was <u>unsuccessfully sued by Warner.</u> . . .

Each half of the correlative-conjunction pair is now followed by a verb phrase that begins with a helping verb and a main verb.

Faulty: So the Ndebele beadwork is not only visually gripping, but also provokes thoughts about the intersection of art and history.

(Ken Johnson, "Art in Review: Ndebele," *New York Times*, 2 Jan. 2004, p. B41)

Not only is followed by an adjectival phrase; *but also* is followed by a verb phrase.

Correct: So the Ndebele beadwork not only <u>is visually gripping</u> but also <u>provokes thoughts about the intersection of art and history.</u>

Each half of the correlative-conjunction pair is followed by a verb phrase.

Faulty: Coldplay also have been labeled "the next U2," because both bands not only traffic in the kind of earnest, dramatic music that's as close to soulful as pasty guys with accents can get, but because they're fronted by men who are passionate about world affairs.

(Tracey Pepper, "Band of the Year: Coldplay," *Spin*, Jan. 2004, p. 58)

Not only is followed by a verb phrase; *but* is followed by an adverbial dependent clause.

Correct: Coldplay have also been labeled "the next U2," because both bands not only ~~traffic in the kind of earnest, dramatic music that's as close to soulful as pasty guys with accents can get~~ but ~~are fronted by men who are passionate about world affairs.~~

Each half of the correlative-conjunction pair is followed by a verb phrase.

Faulty: Linda Tripp now portrays her friend Lucianne Goldberg as a master puppeteer who not only urged Tripp to turn over her tapes of Monica Lewinsky to Kenneth Starr, the independent counsel, but who told Tripp to reveal Lewinsky's affair with President Clinton to lawyers for Paula Jones.

(Elisabeth Bumiller, "Goldberg Proud of Setting Off Lewinsky Affair," for *New York Times*, in *Pittsburgh Post-Gazette*, 13 Feb. 1999, p. A11)

Not only is followed by a verb phrase; *but* is followed by an adjectival dependent clause.

Correct: Linda Tripp now portrays her friend Lucianne Goldberg as a master puppeteer who not only ~~urged Tripp to turn over her tapes of Monica Lewinsky to Kenneth Starr, the independent counsel,~~ but [also] ~~told Tripp to reveal Lewinsky's affair with President Clinton to lawyers for Paula Jones.~~

Each half of the correlative-conjunction pair is followed by a verb phrase; *also* was added after *but* to smooth out the phrasing.

Faulty: The net effect of her [*Star* editor Bonnie Fuller's] tenure so far has been to reinforce the idea that not only is your average celebrity "just like us" (to use Bonnie's signature *US Weekly*–era phrase), but that he or she is badly in need of an intervention.

(Simon Dumenco, *New York*, 8 Dec. 2003, p. 37)

Not only is wedged between a relative pronoun that marks the beginning of an adjectival dependent clause and the rest of the contents of the adjectival dependent clause, which are presented in inverted form; *but* is followed by an entire adjectival dependent clause.

Correct: The net effect of her tenure so far has been to reinforce the idea that not only ~~is your average celebrity "just like us" (to use Bonnie's signature US Weekly–era phrase)~~ but ~~he or she is badly in need of an intervention.~~

Both halves of the correlative-conjunction pair are followed by clauses, the first in inverted form.

Faulty: Though Richard Strauss's "Metamorphosen for 23 Strings," which here received a cogent and unsentimental reading, was his response to the Allied bombings of Dresden and Weimar during World War II, it's tempting to hear this ruminative music as not just a lamentation for humanity but also as an old man's apologia for his obliviousness to the realities of the Nazi era.

(Anthony Tommasini, "Spoken Words Help Melody Face the Unspeakable," *New York Times*, 2 Mar. 2004, p. B5)

Not just is followed by a noun phrase; *but also* is followed by a prepositional phrase.

Correct: ... it's tempting to hear this ruminative music not just ~~as a lamentation for humanity~~ but also ~~as an old man's apologia for his obliviousness to the realities of the Nazi era.~~

Both halves of the correlative-conjunction pair are followed by prepositional phrases.

Faulty: Americans need to recognize that we are facing not just a threat to our environment but to our values, and to our democracy.

(Robert F. Kennedy Jr., "Crimes Against Nature," *Rolling Stone*, 11 Dec. 2003, p. 194)

Not just is followed by a noun phrase; *but* is followed by a pair of prepositional phrases.

Correct: Americans need to recognize that we are facing a threat not just ~~to our environment~~ but ~~to our values, and to our democracy.~~

Both halves of the correlative-conjunction pair are followed by prepositional phrases. The comma, which had been inserted between *values* and *and* for a dramatic pause, might be replaced by a dash.

Not ... but

Faulty: A friend sends Frances on a trip to Tuscany, where she falls in love not with a guy but an old villa, which she buys on impulse.

(Peter M. Nichols, "New DVD's: Making a Relaxed, Low-Key Film in Madcap Tokyo," *New York Times*, 3 Feb. 2004, p. B8)

Not is followed by a prepositional phrase; *but* is followed by a noun phrase.

Correct: A friend sends Frances on a trip to Tuscany, where she falls in love ~~not with a guy~~ but ~~with an old villa,~~ which she buys on impulse.

Each half of the correlative-conjunction pair is followed by a prepositional phrase.

Faulty: Each week, one aspirant is eliminated—not voted off by his rivals, as is the case on other shows, but by ~~Mr. Trump~~, who presses the losers to turn on their weakest link before delivering judgment ("You're fired!").

(Alessandra Stanley, "Contestants, Meet the King of the Jungle," *New York Times*, 8 Jan. 2004, p. B1)

Not is followed by a participial phrase; *but* is followed by a prepositional phrase.

Correct: Each week, one aspirant is eliminated—voted off not ~~by his rivals~~, as is the case on other shows, but by Mr. Trump, who presses the losers to turn on their weakest link before delivering judgment ("You're fired!").

Each half of the correlative-conjunction pair is followed by a prepositional phrase.

Faulty: The largely Christian Arab quarter between Court and Clinton Streets has shrunk, not because of rising rents but because the shopkeepers' sons and daughters are spurning the long hours of a grocery for the longer hours of corporate law.

(Joseph Berger, "Brooklyn's Mile-Long Makeover," *New York Times*, 20 Mar. 2004, p. A20)

Not is followed by an adverbial phrase; *but* is followed by an adverbial dependent clause.

Correct: The largely Christian Arab quarter between Court and Clinton streets has shrunk, not ~~because rents are rising~~ but ~~because the shopkeepers' sons and daughters are spurning the long hours of a grocery for the longer hours of corporate law~~.

Each half of the correlative-conjunction pair is followed by an adverbial dependent clause.

Both ... and

Faulty: Airports are putting on the exhibits both to entertain travelers and showcase local artists.

(Sharon McDonnell, "Art Exhibits Help Make Time Fly Between Flights," *New York Times*, 20 Dec. 2003, p. C6)

Both is followed by an infinitive phrase; *and* is followed by a verb phrase.

Correct: Airports are putting on the exhibits both ~~to entertain travelers~~ and ~~to showcase local artists~~.

Both halves of the correlative-conjunction pair are followed by infinitive phrases.

Faulty: Ms. Blyth said she had written "Spin Sisters" both as a corrective and a penance.

(David Carr, "Lobbing a Grenade at Women's Magazines," *New York Times*, 2 Mar. 2004, p. B10)

Both is followed by a prepositional phrase; *and* is followed by a noun phrase.

Correct: Ms. Blyth said she had written "Spin Sisters" both ~~as a corrective~~ and ~~as a penance~~.

Each half of the correlative-conjunction pair is followed by a prepositional phrase.

Correct and More Concise: Ms. Blyth said she had written "Spin Sisters" as both ~~a corrective~~ and ~~a penance~~.

Each half of the correlative-conjunction pair is followed by a noun phrase.

Faulty: Liquid neon works, and it is much less expensive than liquid helium, both in the cost of materials and the cost of maintaining its temperature.

(Winn L. Rosch, "Superconducting Discovery May Have a Huge Impact," *Cleveland Plain Dealer*, 12 Feb. 2004, p. C2)

Both is followed by a prepositional phrase; and is followed by a noun phrase.

Correct: Liquid neon works, and it is much less expensive than liquid helium, both ~~in the cost of materials~~ and ~~in the cost of maintaining its temperature~~.

Each half of the correlative-conjunction pair is followed by a prepositional phrase.

Better (More Concise): Liquid neon works, and it is much less expensive than liquid helium, in both ~~the cost of materials~~ and ~~the cost of maintaining its temperature~~.

Each half of the correlative-conjunction pair is followed by a noun phrase.

7H | MISCELLANEOUS CONSTRUCTIONS

Less X than Y; more X than Y; X as well as Y

In such constructions, the phrasing following *less* must be grammatically equivalent to the phrasing following *than;* the phrasing following *more* must be grammatically equivalent to the phrasing following *than;* and the phrasing following *as well as* must be grammatically equivalent to the phrasing preceding it.

Faulty: She was interested more in the theory than the practical applications of it.
A prepositional phrase follows *more;* a noun phrase follows *than.*
Correct: She was interested more in the theory than in the practical applications of it.
Both *more* and *than* are followed by prepositional phrases.

Faulty: Mr. Starr's involvement now owes less to his own initiative than being the recipient of information that could not be ignored.
("Shooting Starr," editorial, *Pittsburgh Post-Gazette*, 27 Jan. 1998, p. A10)
Correct: Mr. Starr's involvement now owes less to his own initiative than to his having been the recipient of information that could not be ignored.

Faulty: And the impact of the war is felt more in some places than others.
(Leroy Sievers and the *Nightline* staff, "*Nightline* Daily E-Mail," 23 June 2004, paragraph 3)
Correct: And the impact of the war is felt more in some places than in others.

X rather than Y

The phrasing that follows *rather than* should be grammatically equivalent to the phrasing that precedes it. (In the following examples, *than* is a subordinating conjunction, preceded by the adverb *rather.*)

Faulty: Investigate your alternatives rather than acting rashly.
Investigate your alternatives is an independent clause with *you* as the implied subject; *acting rashly* is a gerund phrase.
Correct: Investigate your alternatives rather than act rashly.

Faulty: Ms. Barb Wallis-Smith said she also tried to help mothers and teachers accept and interpret the rowdiness often inherent in boys' play rather than trying to quash it.
(Carey Goldberg, "After Girls Get the Attention, Focus Shifts to Boys' Woes," *New York Times*, 23 Apr. 1998, p. A1)
Correct: Ms. Barb Wallis-Smith said she also tried to help mothers and teachers accept and interpret the rowdiness often inherent in boys' play rather than try to quash it.

As much X as Y; not so much X as Y

The phrasing that follows *as* must be grammatically equivalent to the phrasing that follows *as much* or *not so much.*

Faulty: More than any of the other wives, Mrs. Kerry's campaign commentary tends to focus at least as much on her own opinions as those of her husband.
(Nancy Keates, "First Wives Club," *Wall Street Journal*, 30 Jan. 2004, p. W7)
Correct: More than that of any of the other wives, Mrs. Kerry's campaign commentary tends to focus at least as much on her own opinions as on those of her husband.
The original version of the sentence was also weakened by a faulty comparison; see chapter 13.

Faulty: She is not so much a thinker as she is a believer.
Correct: She is not so much a thinker as a believer.

CHAPTER 8

ERRORS IN MODIFICATION: MISPLACED, DANGLING, AND AMBIGUOUS MODIFIERS

A modifier is a word, a phrase, or a dependent clause functioning either as an adjective or as an adverb. Adjectives describe or limit the meaning of nouns and pronouns; adverbs modify verbs, adjectives, and other adverbs. Errors in the handling of modifiers result when writers do not position modifiers directly before or after the words they are intended to modify; when writers carelessly omit from their sentences the words that modifiers are intended to modify; and when writers position modifiers so carelessly that the sentences in which they appear are susceptible to more than one interpretation.

8A MISPLACED MODIFIERS

A misplaced modifier is a word, phrase, or dependent clause that has not been positioned directly before or after the word it is intended to modify. That is, the modifier has not been inserted in the appropriate position in the sentence. The modifier ends up modifying a different word in the sentence (the word directly preceding or following the modifier), and the result is a sentence that does not communicate the meaning the writer wanted to express. A sentence weakened by a misplaced modifier has only one meaning (the sentence is not ambiguous), but the meaning is not the one intended by the writer. To correct a sentence with a misplaced modifier, you can remove the modifier from its inappropriate position and reinsert it where it belongs, or you can recast the entire sentence.

Some sentences afflicted with misplaced modifiers are unintentionally humorous, such as the following (from a college student's essay): *The cohabitation policy states that students cannot visit the dormitories of students that are of a different gender after one o'clock in the morning.* But most sentences weakened by misplaced modifiers are not silly—just shoddy.

In the following sentences, the misplaced modifiers have been underlined.

Faulty: Great news! Now, every morning you can find more than great food and great value at McDonald's. Conveniently located in a bright yellow and red box you'll also find the *Pittsburgh Post-Gazette*.
(McDonald's trayliner, Sept. 1997)

You, the reader, are not in a box. The participial phrase *conveniently located in a bright yellow and red box* should be modifying the *Pittsburgh Post-Gazette*, not you.

Correct: Now, every morning you can find more than great food and great value at McDonald's. You'll also find the *Pittsburgh Post-Gazette*, conveniently located in a bright yellow and red box.

Faulty: Armstrong County District Attorney Scott Andreassi said authorities also found an incendiary device inside the trailer that was attached to an electronic timer that plugged into a wall.
(Paula Reed Ward, "Suspect Sought in Slaying of Three," *Pittsburgh Post-Gazette*, 15 Jan. 2004, p. A14)

The sentence declares that a trailer was attached to a timer.

Correct: Armstrong County District Attorney Scott Andreassi said authorities searching the trailer also found an incendiary device that was attached to an electronic timer plugged into a wall.

Faulty: No matter how formulaic and dippy, few can forget their favorite teen movies.
(Lionel Beehner, "Theater: Funny Summer," *New York Press Summer Guide*, 26 May–1 June 2004, p. 82)

The writer wants to tell us that the *movies*, not *few* [*people*], are *formulaic and dippy*, but the introductory phrase is modifying the indefinite pronoun *few*.

Correct: Few can forget their favorite teen movies, no matter how formulaic or dippy.

Faulty: Two new drugs are on the horizon that can help balding men grow more hair.
(unbylined "Health Brief," *Pittsburgh Post-Gazette*, 9 Dec. 1997, p. G1)

Regardless of what the sentence declares, the horizon lacks any hair-restoring powers. The adjectival dependent clause *that can help balding men grow more hair* has been mispositioned.

Correct: On the horizon are two new drugs that can help balding men grow more hair.

Correct: Two new drugs that can help balding men grow more hair are on the horizon.

Faulty: I dump the publications I've lugged home on the dining-room table.
(E. J. Kahn, Jr., *Year of Change* [New York: Viking, 1988], p. 121)

The sentence tells us, misleadingly, that the dining-room table was the conveyance by which the publications have been brought home.

Correct: I let the publications I've lugged home fall onto the dining-room table.

Correct: The publications I've lugged home get dumped onto the dining-room table.

Faulty: Donald Runnicles, the conductor, chose compositions written in response to cataclysmic events, all vibrantly performed.
(Anthony Tommasini, "Spoken Words Help Melody Face the Unspeakable," *New York Times*, 2 Mar. 2004, p. B5)

The phrase *all vibrantly performed* is modifying *events*.

Correct: Donald Runnicles, the conductor, chose compositions that had been written in response to cataclysmic events, and all were vibrantly performed.

Faulty: Normally, authors say where they work on the dust jackets of their books.
(David E. Rosenbaum, "Senate Staff Member's Book Is Restricted by Ethics Panel," *New York Times*, 5 Mar. 2004, p. A13)

The sentence seems to be telling us that authors are usually forthcoming about where they compose the sentences that appear in the dust-jacket biographical notes that accompany their books.

Correct: A dust-jacket biographical note usually mentions where the author works.

Faulty: In fact, the challenge of the Republicans' four-day party for Commissioner Ray Kelly is its almost unimaginable complexity.
(Craig Horowitz, "How to Care for an Angry Mob," *New York*, 17 May 2004, p. 22)

This sentence, from an article about preparations for the 2004 Republican National Convention, misleadingly declares that the *four-day party* (the convention) is in honor of the police commissioner. The adjectival prepositional phrase *for Commissioner Ray Kelly* is modifying *party* rather than *challenge*.

Correct: For Commissioner Ray Kelly, in fact, the challenge of the Republicans' four-day party is its almost unimaginable complexity.

Faulty: Rite Aid says it reminds patients who take medication for chronic conditions to refill prescriptions as a public service, says spokeswoman Sarah Datz.

(Julie Appleby, "File Safe?," *USA Today*, 23 Mar. 2000, p. 2A)

> The sentence tells us that patients are performing a public service by refilling their prescriptions. The prepositional phrase *as a public service*, functioning as an adverb, is modifying the infinitive phrase *to refill prescriptions*.

Correct: As a public service, Rite Aid reminds patients taking medication for a chronic condition that they should have their prescriptions refilled, says spokeswoman Sarah Datz.

Faulty: Sapida became aware of how many teen-age girls were at risk for AIDS/HIV through her work as a professional fund-raiser with schools in the eastern suburbs.

(M. J. Place, "Group's Founder Aims AIDS Message at Girls," *Pittsburgh Post-Gazette*, 21 Jan. 1998, p. B3)

> Contrary to the writer's assertion, it was not Sapida's fund-raising work that put the girls at risk. The adverbial phrase *through her work as a professional fund-raiser with schools* in the eastern suburbs is modifying the verb phrase were at risk for AIDS/HIV.

Correct: Through her work as a professional fund-raiser with schools in the eastern suburbs, Sapida became aware of how many teen-age girls were at risk for AIDS/HIV.

Faulty: As one of Hollywood's few geniuses, the sickening trajectory of his life has an all-too-familiar arc— Buster Keaton comes to mind, and Orson Welles, who like Brando swelled into a cartoon of himself.

(Peter Rainer, "Different Drummer," *New York*, 19 July 2004, p. 50)

> The actor under discussion, not the *trajectory of his life*, was *one of Hollywood's few geniuses*.

Correct: The sickening trajectory of his life as one of Hollywood's few geniuses has an all-too-familiar arc ...

Faulty: Blacks seldom publicly concede that some of the dysfunction suffered by the black underclass is self-inflicted for fear of giving aid and comfort to bigotry.

(Leonard Pitts Jr., "Cosby's Hard Words," *Pittsburgh Post-Gazette*, 27 May 2004, p. A15)

> The adverbial phrase *for fear of giving aid and comfort to bigotry* is modifying the verb phrase *is self-inflicted* rather than the verb *concede*. The result is that the sentence misleadingly states that the reason the dysfunction is self-inflicted is the fear of giving aid and comfort to bigotry.

Correct: For fear of giving aid and comfort to bigotry, blacks seldom publicly concede that some of the dys-function suffered by the black underclass is self-inflicted.

Faulty: New York's highest court ruled last year that Albany had failed to provide the city's public school children with a sound, basic education in violation of the state Constitution.

("The Schools Need HOW Much?," editorial, *New York Daily News*, 19 Dec. 2003, p. 60)

> *Albany*, not the *basic education*, was in violation.

Correct: New York's highest court ruled last year that Albany, in violation of the state Constitution, had failed to provide the city's public school children with a sound, basic education.

Better: New York's highest court ruled last year that Albany violated the state Constitution by failing to pro-vide the city's public school children with a sound, basic education.

Faulty: Long Island drudge Joel (a subdued Jim Carrey) skips work and heads to the beach at Montauk on Valentine's Day where he meets the punkishly extroverted Clementine (Kate Winslet). ...

(Graham Fuller, "Shots in the Dark," *Interview*, Apr. 2004, p. 100)

> The *beach*, not *Valentine's Day*, is the place where he meets the woman.

Correct: ... Joel (a subdued Jim Carrey) skips work on Valentine's Day and heads to the beach at Montauk, where he meets the punkishly extroverted Clementine. . . .

Faulty: To the statistically minded or just plain morbid, the report is a treasure, 67 pages of revealing, quirky and sometimes startling numbers about how New Yorkers live and, mostly, how they die, broken down by cause, age, sex, race, borough and even neighborhood.

(Richard Pérez-Peña, "Following New Yorkers to a Later Grave," *New York Times*, 31 Jan. 2004, p. A13)

The statistics, not the New Yorkers, have been broken down by cause, age, sex, etc.

Correct: To the statistically minded or just plain morbid, the report is a treasure: 67 pages of revealing, quirky, and sometimes startling numbers—broken down by cause of death, age, sex, race, borough, and even neighborhood—about how New Yorkers live and, mostly, how they die.

Punctuation can occasionally come to the rescue of a sentence with a misplaced modifier.

> **Faulty:** But he had just arrived at the Seventh Avenue restaurant not far from his Chelsea home that he had chosen for our meeting.
>
> (Michael Bracken, "The Accidental Actor," *Newsday*, 21 Dec. 2003, p. D27)
>
> The restrictive adjectival dependent clause *that he had chosen for our meeting* is erroneously modifying *home*. But you can set off the phrase *not far from his Chelsea home* with a pair of commas. The commas will detach the phrase from the main body of the sentence.
>
> **Correct:** But he had just arrived at the Seventh Avenue restaurant, not far from his Chelsea home, that he had chosen for our meeting.

Some misplaced modifiers are unlikely to cause misreading but result in untidy sentences just the same.

> **Awkward:** In fine print, they [the signs] say lots of items inside are not subject to the lower prices, ~~including CDs, DVDs and some candy~~.
>
> (Paula Reed Ward, "Post House Closing Doors," *Pittsburgh Post-Gazette*, 27 June 2004, p. C4)
>
> The participial phrase should be modifying *items inside*, not *prices*.
>
> **Better:** In fine print, they say lots of items inside, including CDs, DVDs, and some candy, are not subject to the lower prices.
>
> **Awkward:** There's a man in the back seat in a suit ~~with a plate of beef on a silver tray~~.
>
> (Malcolm Gladwell, "The Ketchup Conundrum," *New Yorker*, 6 Sept. 2004, p. 129)
>
> Five prepositional phrases have been set out in a row, and the clumsy result is that the plate of beef seems to belong to the suit and not to the man.
>
> **Better:** In the back seat, a man in a suit has a plate of beef on a silver tray.
>
> **Better:** In the back seat, a man in a suit is holding a silver tray with a plate of beef on it.

Special Cases

All ... not *Constructions*

Avoid writing sentences such as *All athletes do not use steroids*—unless the intended meaning is *No athletes use steroids*. If the intended meaning is that at least some athletes do not use steroids, the phrasing should be *Not all athletes use steroids*. In the original sentence, then, the adverb *not* is a misplaced modifier: It should be modifying *all*, not *use*. TCI, a cable-TV company, notified subscribers in May 1998 that *all services may not be available in all areas*. The sentence declares, in effect, that no services may be available anywhere. The intended meaning? *Not all services may be available in all areas.*

> **Faulty:** Believe it or not, everyone in America does not use Medicare.
>
> (Daniel Henninger, "Consumers March to the Walls of Health-Care Castle," *Wall Street Journal*, 30 Jan. 2004, p. A12)
>
> **Correct:** Believe it or not, not everyone in America uses Medicare.
>
> **Faulty:** All of the WMD [Weapons of Mass Destruction] dominoes haven't fallen yet, but the ground underneath them gets shakier all the time.
>
> ("More WMD Dominoes," editorial, *Wall Street Journal*, 3 Feb. 2004, p. A14)
>
> **Correct:** Not all of the WMD dominoes have fallen yet, but the ground underneath them gets shakier all the time.

Faulty: All sex is not sexual harassment.

(Catharine A. MacKinnon, letter to the editor, *New Yorker*, 23 Feb.–2 Mar. 1998, p. 28)

Correct: Not all sex is sexual harassment.

Only, merely, just, *and Similar One-Word Modifiers*

There are two schools of thought about where the word *only* (as well as the words *merely* and *just* and similar modifiers) should be positioned in a sentence.

The traditional approach requires that the writer position *only* (or any similar modifier) directly before the word it is intended to modify, as in the sentence *I have only five dollars to spare.* (Here, *only* modifies *five;* the positioning of *only* emphasizes the limited financial resources of the writer.) This approach is favored in academic writing—and it ensures that a sentence will be precise, logical, and unambiguous. The disadvantage of this approach is that the sentence may strike some readers as fussy, pretentious, and stiffly formal.

The placement of the adverb *practically* in this sentence violates the traditional approach.

- There may be just as many gay bars and clubs as there are Gap stores in New York, but you can practically count all the lesbian establishments on one hand, with the effect that everybody is somebody's ex-girlfriend, former tryst, or conquest.

(Kera Bolonik, "Not Your Mother's Lesbians," *New York*, 12 Jan. 2004, p. 21)

The traditional approach would require that *practically* be positioned after *on.*

The informal, idiomatic approach involves placing *only* (or any similar modifier) directly before the verb (or between an auxiliary verb and a main verb), as in the sentence *I only have five dollars to spare.* This approach is sometimes favored in the world of commercial publishing—especially in magazines and books aiming for a casual, conversational tone. The resulting sentences are natural-sounding and are representative of the patterns and rhythms of ordinary speech. There are, however, two disadvantages to this approach. First, many readers have been taught that it is wrong to position the modifier anywhere in a sentence other than directly before the word it is intended to modify. The idiomatic positioning can thus be a distraction—many readers will think that you have committed an error. The second, more serious disadvantage of this approach is that it can lead to ambiguity. Examine the sentence *I only talked to three of the applicants.* Is the sentence intended to express the limited nature of the writer's interaction with the three applicants (that is, the writer talked to them but did not hire them, did not invite them to dinner, etc.), or is the sentence intended to emphasize the limited number of the applicants the writer talked to? The reader will be confused. Here is another example: *I only think I know one of the applicants.* Does the sentence mean *I am not fully certain that I know one of the applicants,* or does it mean *I think I know only one of the applicants?* The alert reader cannot possibly know which of the two meanings is the one intended by the writer. Whenever ambiguity might result, therefore, prefer the conventional placement of *only.*

The following sentences illustrate the informal, idiomatic positioning of *only.* (In each example, *only* has been inserted, boldfaced and bracketed, where traditional usage would demand.)

- My garage only has room for **[only]** one old car, so if I buy a car, I have to sell a car.

(Dana White, "My Life, My '58 Lincoln," *New York Times*, 30 Jan. 2004, p. D9)

- I return despite waiters who only fill the water glass **[only]** halfway.

(Julia Gorin, "What Would Eloise Do?," *New York Post*, 11 Jan. 2004, p. 61)

- Even a million-selling record would only net Jackson [only] $3 million—barely enough to cover living expenses for three months.

  (Tracy Connor, "Jacko May Go Broke-o," *New York Daily News*, 25 Apr. 2004, p. 8)

- When it comes to her age, she only has [only] herself to blame for some misinformation.

  (John Soeder, "The Gray Area," *Cleveland Plain Dealer*, 6 Jan. 2004, p. E4)

- The basic version, however, only works [only] with Windows PC's that have a composite video or S-video connector.

  (Larry Magid, "Plays Well with Others: The Video Sender," *New York Times*, 29 Jan. 2004, p. E8)

- Few people heard the recording "Jimmie Dale and the Flatlanders" when it was originally released in 1973, partly because it was only available [only] on eight-track tape.

  (Neil Strauss, "Getting It Right the First Time," *New York Times*, 2 Feb. 2004, p. B3)

In the following example, the idiomatic positioning of *only* results in ambiguity.

- Only use bleach on white or colorsafe fabrics.

  (Stephanie Dunnewind, "How to Keep Kids' Clothes Stain-free," *Seattle Times*, 17 Jan. 2004, p. E8)

The writer most likely intends the sentence to mean *Use bleach on only white or colorsafe fabrics*. But anyone could initially misinterpret the sentence as meaning *Use no cleaning product other than bleach on white or colorsafe fabrics*. The conventional placement of the modifier (after the preposition *on*) would therefore improve the readability of the sentence.

> **Confusing:** Those changes were only instituted in January, in response to the NRC's latest concerns.
>
> (John Mangels and John Funk, "FirstEnergy to Ask Again for OK to Start Davis-Besse," *Cleveland Plain Dealer*, 12 Feb. 2004, p. C3)
>
> A reader could interpret this sentence as meaning that the changes were only instituted and not, for instance, enforced.
>
> **Clear:** Those changes were instituted only in January, in response to the NRC's latest concerns.

As Theodore M. Bernstein notes in *The Careful Writer,* it is to the reader's benefit for a writer to use the informal, idiomatic positioning of *only* in a sentence such as *I will only go to the concert if I don't have to work Friday night*. The placement of *only* between the helping verb and the main verb ensures that the reader will learn very early in the sentence that it is not absolutely certain that the writer will be attending the concert. A sentence with the traditional placement of *only*—*I will go to the concert only if I don't have to work Friday night*—postpones the reader's realization that it is not absolutely certain that the writer will be attending the concert.

Following are more examples of sentences in which the early, idiomatic positioning of the modifier alerts the reader to the fact that a restriction will be placed on the scope of the main idea of the sentence (in each example, *only* has been inserted, boldfaced and bracketed, where traditional usage would demand).

- Minors can only go to a business with a liquor license [only] if they are accompanied by a parent or if 70 percent of the business's combined food and liquor sales are from food, said Sam Yurich, a supervisor with the state police Bureau of Liquor Control Enforcement.

  (Cristina Rouvalis, "Horrors! Picture Show's Run at Beehive Is Over," *Pittsburgh Post-Gazette*, 13 Aug. 1999, p. B3)

- I played a role in the Korean experiment, but due in part to the laws in the state of Michigan I was only able to help them validate their results [only] after the cloning procedure was performed.

  (Jose Cibelli, "Wake Up America," *Wall Street Journal*, 1 Mar. 2004, p. A16)

- An apartment can only be rent-controlled [only] if it is in a building constructed before 1947 and if its current tenant (or his family) has occupied it since 1971.

  (Mariah L. Sachs, "Unstable and Out of Control," *New York Times*, 13 Jan. 2004, p. A27)

- But because the military has a limited number of satellite decoders, live broadcasts of the game could only be watched by off-duty troops at [only] a few locations, like mess halls and operations centers.
  (Ian Austen, "Catching the Big Game by Satellite Feed in Iraq," *New York Times*, 29 Jan. 2004, p. E6)

- Since his gun turned out to be a toy, Sinclair is only being charged [only] with menacing, harassment and being unable to think outside the box.
  ("Crime Blotter: Missing the Boat," *New York Press*, 17–23 Dec. 2003, p. 4)

Writers and editors should know how to position *only* conventionally, and they should also know when it is desirable—or at least justifiable—to depart from the conventional placement.

8B DANGLING MODIFIERS

A dangling modifier is a descriptive phrase—most often found at the beginning of a sentence—that is logically incompatible not only with the noun or pronoun that immediately follows it but also with any other noun or pronoun in the sentence. That is, the noun or pronoun that the phrase is intended to modify does not appear anywhere within the sentence, and the result is an incoherent, illogical statement. In the publishing world, a dangling modifier is often called a floater, because it hovers about a sentence without any noun or pronoun to which it might securely attach itself.

Most dangling modifiers are participial phrases. In the sentence *Walking into the club, the noise was louder than usual,* the participial phrase *walking into the club* needs to modify a noun designating the person or persons who walked into the club and noticed that the noise was louder than usual—but no human beings are explicitly mentioned in the sentence. The modifier *walking into the club* is said to be dangling because it is literally hanging loose: there is nothing in the sentence to which the modifier might fasten itself stably and logically. So the participial phrase hooks itself up, precariously, with the only available noun in the independent clause (*noise*)—and the result is a sentence claiming, absurdly and preposterously, that the noise walked into the club. Sentences with dangling modifiers make assertions that are contrary to reality as we know it.

Like a sentence weakened by a misplaced modifier, a sentence with a dangling modifier usually has only one meaning (the sentence is not ambiguous), but that meaning is not the one intended by the writer. Unlike a sentence afflicted with a misplaced modifier, however, a sentence weakened by a dangling modifier cannot be corrected merely by repositioning the modifier; a sentence with a dangling modifier does not include all of the components necessary for a logically sound and grammatically correct sentence. Something is missing—namely, the noun or pronoun that the modifier is intended to modify. Correcting such a sentence requires rewriting part of the sentence and adding the missing component.

There are two easy ways to revise a sentence weakened by a dangling modifier.

1. Convert the dangling modifier into an adverbial dependent clause but leave the independent clause unchanged.

   - As I walked into the club, the noise was louder than usual.
     There is now a human being explicitly present in the sentence—someone who walked into the club and noticed that the noise was louder than usual.

2. Retain the introductory modifier exactly as it was phrased in the original sentence, but rephrase the independent clause of the sentence so that it begins with a subject logically compatible with the modifier.

- Walking into the club, I noticed that the noise was louder than usual.
   Now we know who it was who walked into the club.

Dangling Participial Phrases at the Beginning of Sentences

The following sentences are weakened by dangling present-participial phrases, along with suggested revisions:

Faulty: Campaigning in 1960 as a vessel of "vigor," his health often forced him to spend about half of the day in bed.

(George F. Will, "JFK: A Man in a Hurry," for *Washington Post*, in *Pittsburgh Post-Gazette*, 24 Nov. 2003, p. A15)

The sentence claims that Kennedy's health campaigned in 1960.

Correct: Although in 1960 Kennedy campaigned as a vessel of "vigor," his health often forced him to spend about half of the day in bed.

Correct: Campaigning in 1960 as a vessel of "vigor," Kennedy was in such poor health that he was often forced to spend about half of the day in bed.

Faulty: Growing up in the Adirondacks, summer always meant working long hours, scraping together change to afford things like concert tickets and guitar gear and dreading Labor Day, when those annoying back-to-school ads returned.

(Lionel Beehner, "Theater: Funny Summer," *New York Press Summer Guide*, 26 May–1 June 2004, p. 82)

The sentence declares that summer grew up in the Adirondacks.

Correct: When I was growing up in the Adirondacks, summer always meant working long hours, scraping together change to afford things like concert tickets and guitar gear, and dreading Labor Day, when those annoying back-to-school ads returned.

Faulty: Watching Conor Oberst it's almost impossible to keep the words "new" and "Dylan" out of your head.

(Scott Mervis, "Conor Oberst/Jim James/M. Ward," *Pittsburgh Post-Gazette*, 24 Feb. 2004, p. D5)

According to the sentence, it watched Conor Oberst perform.

Correct: While you're watching Conor Oberst, it's almost impossible to keep the words "new" and "Dylan" out of your head.

Correct: Watching Conor Oberst, you find it almost impossible to keep the words "new" and "Dylan" out of your head.

Rephrasing the dangling modifier as an adverbial dependent clause or recasting the independent clause is not the only way to correct a sentence with a dangling modifier. Sometimes it is better to rewrite the entire sentence.

Faulty: But looking closer, our carrot chips were noticeably thinner through the middle and thicker on the ends. . . .

(Lisa Kalis, "Slicers on the Cutting Edge," *Wall Street Journal*, 13 Feb. 2004, p. W4)

Correct: But a closer look revealed that our carrot chips were noticeably thinner through the middle and thicker on the ends. . . .

Faulty: Taking both games into account, there are more than 70 playable characters (complete with new power moves) and 10 game modes.

(Damon P. Sims, "Game Patrol," *Cleveland Plain Dealer*, 12 Feb. 2004, p. F7)

Correct: The two games together involve more than 70 playable characters (complete with new power moves) and 10 game modes.

PRESENT-PARTICIPIAL PHRASES AND CLEAR CHRONOLOGY

Make sure that a present-participial phrase does not mislead the reader about the chronology of events recounted in a sentence. Do not use a present-participial phrase to express an action that occurred before or after the action expressed by the verb in the independent clause of a sentence. A present-participial phrase is used correctly when the action it recounts occurred simultaneously with the action recounted in the independent clause. The following sentences misleadingly imply that two actions occurred simultaneously, when in fact one preceded the other.

> **Faulty:** He exited the [bed]room, scrounging up some trash bags in the kitchen.
> (David Amsden, "The Siege of Fulton Avenue," *New York*, 14 June 2004, p. 166)
> **Correct:** He exited the room, then scrounged up some trash bags in the kitchen.
> **Correct:** After exiting the room, he scrounged up some trash bags in the kitchen.

> **Faulty:** He himself was born in India, in 1811, leaving at the age of five. ...
> (Anthony Lane, "Power Plays," *New Yorker*, 6 Sept. 2004, p. 170)
> **Correct:** He himself was born in India, in 1811, and left at the age of five. . . .

> **Faulty:** Dividing her childhood between Paris, New York, and L.A. with her actress mother and photographer father, Davalos struck out on her own at 17 and headed to New York City.
> (Henry Cabot Beck, "Alex Davalos," *Interview*, July 2004, p. 34)
> **Correct:** After dividing her childhood between Paris, New York, and L.A. with her actress mother and photographer father, Davalos struck out on her own at 17 and headed to New York City.
> The sentence, however, is also weakened by two false-restrictive elements; see rule 33F of Chapter 18.

Like present-participial phrases, past-participial phrases are often left to dangle at the beginning of sentences.

> **Faulty:** Best known for playing a schizophrenic's imagined companion in *A Beautiful Mind* (2001), Paul Bettany's current hot streak is anything but illusory.
> (Stellan Skarsgård, "Paul Bettany: After Playing a Specter in *A Beautiful Mind*, This Actor Keeps On Delivering Haunting Performances," *Interview*, Dec./Jan. 2004, p. 118)
> The sentence tells us that a *hot streak* is known for playing a particular role.
> **Correct:** Although Paul Bettany is best known for playing a schizophrenic's imagined companion in *A Beautiful Mind* (2001), his current hot streak is anything but illusory.
> **Correct:** Best known for playing a schizophrenic's imagined companion in *A Beautiful Mind* (2001), Paul Bettany is enjoying a hot streak that is anything but illusory.

> **Faulty:** Dressed in a white Kangol newsboy's hat, a white double-breasted jacket with dark piping, orange pants and a sheen of sweat, Mr. Jagger's arms, legs and even his magnificent lips seemed to be flying off in different directions before a sea of rapt Rolling Stones fans.
> (Frank DiGiacomo, "It's the Last Party of the Century," *New York Observer*, 13 Dec. 1999, p. 1)
> The sentence would have us believe that Jagger's limbs and lips were wearing a hat, a jacket, a pair of pants, and a glaze of perspiration.
> **Correct:** Dressed in a white Kangol newsboy's hat, a white double-breasted jacket with dark piping, orange pants, and a sheen of sweat, Mr. Jagger let his arms, his legs, and even his magnificent lips fly off in seemingly different directions before a sea of rapt Rolling Stones fans.

> **Faulty:** Endowed with a brilliant, curious mind that led him to apply techniques of scientific observation to every phenomenon of the natural world, and to develop insights and inventions without precedent in his time, his research remained unknown to his contemporaries, and his discoveries were left to be rediscovered, independently, by scientists of the seventeenth and eighteenth centuries.

(Juergen Schulz, "Leonardo da Vinci," in *Atlantic Brief Lives* [Boston: Little, Brown, 1971], pp. 454–455)

The sentence asks us to accept that *research*, rather than the researcher, was *endowed with a brilliant, curious mind.*

Correct: Although Leonardo da Vinci was endowed with a brilliant, curious mind that led him to apply techniques of scientific observation to every phenomenon of the natural world and to develop insights and inventions without precedent in his time, his research remained unknown to his contemporaries, and his discoveries were left to be rediscovered, independently, by scientists of the seventeenth and eighteenth centuries.

Faulty: Lauded by reviewers and art-house audiences alike, *Lost in Translation*'s failure to cross over to mainstream audiences may repeat itself within the Academy.

(Anne Thompson, "Off to the Races," *New York*, 8 Dec. 2003, p. 32)

The sentence tells us that the movie's *failure*, not the movie itself, was lauded.

Correct: Although *Lost in Translation* was lauded by reviewers and art-house audiences alike, its failure to cross over to mainstream audiences may repeat itself within the Academy.

Occasionally, one dangling participial phrase will be immediately followed by another.

Faulty: Standing here in the epicenter of pre-Christmasism, laden with shopping bags of merchandise that proved my worth both as a provider and as a conspicuous consumer, a nagging thought rooted in the dim past intrudes: Is this the way I want to spend my leisure time?

(William Safire, "Musings on Mall Madness," for *New York Times*, in *Pittsburgh Post-Gazette*, 30 Nov. 1999, p. A21)

A *thought*, we are told, is standing and holding bagfuls of holiday presents.

Correct: Standing here in the epicenter of pre-Christmasism, laden with shopping bags of merchandise that prove my worth both as a provider and as a conspicuous consumer, I am visited by a nagging thought rooted in the dim past: Is this the way I want to spend my leisure time?

CAUTION

An introductory phrase (such as a participial phrase) that is not immediately followed by a noun or pronoun with which it is logically compatible is not necessarily a dangling modifier. Later in the sentence, there may well be a noun or a pronoun that the introductory element is intended to modify—in which case the modifier is not dangling but merely misplaced.

Faulty: Given direction, tolerance and, yes, even a little parental love, life might have turned out differently for this gifted and dedicated person.

(Bob Hoover, "Love Might Have Made the Difference Between Loser and Genius," *Pittsburgh Post-Gazette*, 22 Feb. 2004, p. E5)

Correct: Given direction, tolerance, and, yes, even a little parental love, this gifted and dedicated person might have turned out differently.

Dangling Prepositional Phrases

Not all dangling modifiers take the form of participial phrases. A prepositional phrase can also dangle, as in the sentence *At the age of five, my grandmother died.* (The writer obviously meant *When I was five, my grandmother died.*)

Faulty: By giving to United Way, your dollars get tangible results.

(*Living Proof: Your Gift Makes a Difference*, United Way of Southwestern Pennsylvania brochure, C2, 1999)

Correct: When you give to United Way, your dollars get tangible results.

Correct: By giving to United Way, you can be sure that your dollars will get tangible results.

Faulty: As a writer and producer on acclaimed television shows *My So-Called Life* and *Once and Again*, and as the filmmaker behind *Glory* and *Legends of the Fall*, [Edward] Zwick's work has often been distinguished by intelligent characters yearning for a satisfaction that seems beyond their grasp.

(Andrew Johnson, "Civil War: In *The Last Samurai*, Edward Zwick Introduces an American Soldier to the Far East," *Time Out New York*, 4–11 Dec. 2003, p. 89)

The sentence professes that a man's *work*, rather than the man himself, was a writer, producer, and filmmaker.

Correct: As a writer and producer on the acclaimed television shows *My So-Called Life* and *Once and Again*, and as the filmmaker behind *Glory* and *Legends of the Fall*, Zwick has often created work distinguished by intelligent characters yearning for a satisfaction that seems beyond their grasp.

Faulty: Upon hearing that Alanis Morissette was releasing an album from the tired forum of "MTV Unplugged," my first thought was "Why?"

(Tracy Collins, "Recordings," *Pittsburgh Post-Gazette*, 12 Dec. 1999, A&E p. 2)

A *thought* has been endowed with a sense of hearing.

Correct: When I heard that Alanis Morissette was releasing an album from the tired forum of "MTV Unplugged," my first thought was "Why?"

Dangling Adjectival Phrases

Some danglers are nonparticipial adjectival phrases.

Faulty: Capable of great tenderness (especially to his daughter, Wylie), his ability to understand the inner life of his female characters was admired by such writers as Dorothy Parker (his lifelong champion) and Fran Lebowitz.

(Andre Bernard, "A Writer Writes a Writer's Life: Awful O'Hara in Human Scale," *New York Observer* online, 25 Aug. 2003, paragraph 1)

The sentence contends that a man's *ability* is *capable of great tenderness*.

Correct: Capable of great tenderness (especially to his daughter, Wylie), O'Hara was admired by such writers as Dorothy Parker (his lifelong champion) and Fran Lebowitz for his ability to understand the inner life of his female characters.

Correct: O'Hara was capable of great tenderness (especially to his daughter, Wylie), and his ability to understand the inner life of his female characters was admired by such writers as Dorothy Parker (his lifelong champion) and Fran Lebowitz.

Faulty: Chockablock with top-notch effects and acid-tinged teen angst, fans of the first film might experience yet another "best movie ever!" moment.

(Henry Cabot Beck, preview of *Spider-Man 2*, *Interview*, July 2004, p. 38)

The sentence proposes that fans, rather than a sequel, are *chockablock* with special effects and angst.

Correct: Because the sequel is chockablock with top-notch effects and acid-tinged teen angst, fans of the first film might experience yet another "best movie ever!" moment.

Faulty: Blind for 43 Years, Man's Restored Sight Taxes Brain Process

(headline for Associated Press article by Andrew Bridges, in *Pittsburgh Post-Gazette*, 25 Aug. 2003, p. A3)

The headline asserts that a man's restored sight, rather than the man himself, had been blind.

Correct: Blind Man's Sight, Restored After 43 Years, Taxes Brain Process

Midsentence and Sentence-Ending Dangling Modifiers

Not every dangling modifier appears at the beginning of a sentence. In the following sentence, the dangling modifier (the phrase *just while standing*) appears between the subordinating conjunction and the subject of the adverbial dependent clause ending the complex sentence.

Faulty: The lower back, otherwise known as the lumbar spine, is particularly vulnerable because, just while standing, it supports approximately 100 pounds of pressure.

(Highmark Blue Cross Blue Shield, "Back in Action! Finding Relief from Chronic Back Pain," *Looking Healthward*, fall 1999, p.1)

The lower back, the sentence tells us, is capable of standing on its own.

Correct: The lower back, otherwise known as the lumbar spine, is particularly vulnerable because, even when you're just standing, it supports approximately 100 pounds of pressure.

The next example is also weakened by a dangling interruptive element.

Faulty: Inside McCormick Place, while bumping into hundreds of people cramming aisles lined with displays of books and authors, it's easy to forget that there's a real world outside.

(Bob Hoover, "Bill Clinton, Author, Hasn't Lost His Touch as a Speaker," *Pittsburgh Post-Gazette*, 13 June 2004, p. E5)

Correct: Inside McCormick Place, while bumping into hundreds of people cramming aisles lined with displays of books and authors, you can easily forget that there's a real world outside.

A dangling modifier occasionally appears at the very end of a sentence. In the following examples, the italicized participial phrases are the dangling elements.

Faulty: There's always been a pronounced streak of sadomasochism and martyrdom running through [Mel] Gibson's movies, *both as an actor and as a filmmaker.*

(David Ansen, "So What's the Good News?," *Newsweek*, 1 Mar. 2004, p. 60)

Correct: There's always been a pronounced streak of sadomasochism and martyrdom running through Mel Gibson's acting and filmmaking.

Faulty: One man got shot rather than hand over his Nokia, *suggesting that New Yorkers may be a little too attached to their cell phones.*

(subheadline for Elizabeth Spiers, "Tough Call," *New York*, 26 Apr. 2004, p. 13)

The incident, not the man, suggests the pervasiveness of the trend.

Correct: New Yorkers may be a little too attached to their cell phones. One man got shot rather than hand over his Nokia.

Faulty: A few short moments later, the 10-year-old Cara was in front of a heart-shaped mirror having her hair and eyes done, *topped off with a glam bit of glitter lipstick and a spritz of glitter hairspray to make her into the perfect Party Pop Princess.*

(Teresa F. Lindeman, "Clubbing (Tweener Style)," *Pittsburgh Post-Gazette*, 16 Apr. 2004, p. C1)

Contrary to what the sentence would have us believe, it was the makeover, not the girl, that was *topped off.*

Correct: A few moments later, 10-year-old Cara was in front of a heart-shaped mirror having her hair and eyes done, then getting glammed up with glitter lipstick and spritzed with glitter hairspray to make her into the perfect Party Pop Princess.

Dangling Appositives

Not all dangling elements in sentences function as modifiers. An appositive, for instance, can also dangle. (Remember that an appositive is a noun or a noun phrase that provides additional information about a preceding or following noun or pronoun.) In the following sentence, the appositive *a loyal employee* is dangling.

Faulty: A loyal employee, her attendance record is exceptional.
Correct: A loyal employee, she has an exceptional attendance record.

Following are further examples of sentences with dangling appositives.

Faulty: A visiting professor at the MIT Media Lab, her studies challenge the cognitive-science dogma that only humans are capable of sophisticated language and consciousness.

(Sharon Begley, "Scientists Who Give Their Minds to Study, Can Give Names, Too," *Wall Street Journal*, 2 Jan. 2004, p. B1)

The sentence declares that *studies* were a visiting professor.

Correct: A visiting professor at the MIT Media Lab, she conducts research challenging the cognitive-science dogma that only humans are capable of sophisticated language and consciousness.

Faulty: Nobody epitomized the maddeningly fickle nature of pop better than Mariah Carey. A best-selling singer in the 1990s, her latest release, Glitter, bombed.

(David Lieberman, "Musicmakers Lure Grown-Ups," *USA Today*, 18 Feb. 2002, p. 2B)

The sentence tells us that an album is a singer.

Correct: Though she was a best-selling singer in the 1990s, her latest release, Glitter, bombed.

Faulty: A natural born radical, my house already had coed bathrooms.

(Ellen Goodman, "Ironies of the Equal Rights Battle," *Boston Globe* online, 14 Dec. 2003, paragraph 4)

The sentence claims that a house was a radical.

Correct: Because I was a natural-born radical, my house already had coed bathrooms.

Correct: A natural-born radical, I already had coed bathrooms in my house.

UNDERSTANDING *CONSIDERING* AND *CONCERNING*

The English language continues to evolve, and a limited number of participles (verbal adjectives) have begun to function as prepositions in some contexts. Among these participles are *considering* and *concerning*.

In a sentence such as *Considering the increasing number of problems with the outdated software, the best solution is to install the newest version of the software*, the word *considering* is not functioning as a participle describing a noun but instead is functioning in the manner of a preposition (*considering* could be replaced by *as for* or *on the matter of*). Therefore, the phrase *considering the increasing number of problems with the outdated software* is not a dangling modifier; the reader is not waiting, futilely, for the writer to reveal who is doing the considering. Similarly, in the sentence *Speaking of good movies, Ghost World is brilliant and moving*, the phrase *speaking of* is functioning as a preposition (the opening phrase is the equivalent of *on the subject of good movies*), and thus *speaking of good movies* is not a dangling modifier. Furthermore, when a TV weatherperson says, "*Looking ahead to the weekend, Saturday promises to be sunny and pleasant*," the phrase *looking ahead to the weekend* is functioning not as a participial phrase but as a prepositional phrase— and thus is not dangling. (You may, of course, still choose to avoid any such construction.)

Be careful to distinguish between, on the one hand, the vast number of participles that function only adjectivally and, on the other hand, the very small number of participles that have acquired prepositional force in some sentences. When in doubt about the current standing of a particular word, take a trip to a good up-to-date dictionary. The fourth edition of *Webster's New World College Dictionary*, for instance, classifies *considering* and *concerning* as prepositions.

8C AMBIGUOUS MODIFIERS

An ambiguous modifier is a modifier whose careless positioning in a sentence gives the sentence more than one meaning, thus pitching the reader into confusion. The sentence *The girl who attacked her classmate repeatedly apologized for her actions* suggests two conflicting interpretations: Either the girl repeatedly attacked her classmate, or she apologized repeatedly for her actions. An ambiguous modifier never appears at the beginning or at the end of a sentence; it always appears somewhere in the middle, and, like the adverb *repeatedly* in the example above, it reaches both backward and forward for something to modify. Unlike sentences with misplaced or dangling modifiers, therefore, a sentence with an ambiguous modifier is always susceptible to more than one interpretation. Furthermore, although misplaced and dangling modifiers are very common, ambiguous modifiers occur only rarely, and even when they do, a reader sometimes has to misinterpret a sentence willfully and dramatically to find an alternative meaning. The surgeon general's cigarette-package warning *Quitting Smoking Now Greatly Reduces Serious Risks to Your Health*, for instance, could elicit the rejoinder "You mean it didn't always reduce the risks?" It is therefore best to phrase a sentence so that finicky readers intent on discerning ambiguities will not find even the trace of an alternative meaning.

Similarly, a reader of the following sentence might perversely construe the adverb *precisely* as modifying both what follows it as well as what precedes it.

> **Ambiguous:** Census officials said numbers [population statistics] don't add up precisely because the "statistical modeling" in their calculations don't [sic] account for all factors.
>
> (Judy Packer-Tursman, "Migration Leaves Metro Population Behind," *Pittsburgh Post-Gazette*, 18 Mar. 1998, p. B2)
>
> **Clear:** According to census officials, the reason the numbers don't add up is that the "statistical modeling" in their calculations doesn't account for all factors.

> **Ambiguous:** She doesn't remember every dream, of course, but those that she does recall frequently have similar themes and images.
>
> (Virginia Linn, "10 Years of Dreams Recorded in Vivid Watercolors and Words," *Pittsburgh Post-Gazette*, 7 Dec. 2003, p. A17)
>
> *Frequently* is simultaneously modifying *recall* and *have*. Most likely, the writer wants *frequently* to modify *have*.
>
> **Clear:** She doesn't remember every dream, of course, but frequently those that she does recall have similar themes and images.
>
> **Clear:** She doesn't remember every dream, of course, but those that she does recall have recurrent themes and images.
>
> **Clear:** She doesn't remember every dream, of course, but the recallable ones frequently have similar themes and images.

> **Ambiguous:** It went so right for Annie Lennox on Saturday night that when she sat down for a piano version of "Here Comes the Rain Again," as if on cue, it started to rain.
>
> (Scott Mervis, "Lennox, PNME, Keb' Mo', Dance Ensemble Give Fine Shows," *Pittsburgh Post-Gazette*, 13 July 2004, p. D4)
>
> The adverbial phrase *as if on cue* reaches back to the phrasal verb *sat down* and also forward to *started to rain*.
>
> **Clear:** Everything went so right for Annie Lennox on Saturday night that when she sat down for a piano version of "Here Comes the Rain Again," it started to rain, as if on cue.

CHAPTER 9

OTHER ERRORS IN MODIFICATION

In addition to misplaced modifiers, dangling modifiers, and ambiguous modifiers, there are seven types of errors in modification that can undermine the logic and precision of your sentences.

9A ERRORS IN THE USE OF COMPARATIVES AND SUPERLATIVES

1. When you are comparing only two persons or things, use comparative adjectives (adjectives ending in *-er*) or phrases consisting of *more* or *less* followed by an adjective: *She is the stronger of the twins. She is the more accomplished of the twins.* When you are comparing three or more persons or things and are declaring that one of them possesses the highest or lowest degree of a particular quality, use superlative adjectives (adjectives ending in *-est*) or phrases consisting of *most* or *least* followed by an adjective: *Mandy is the strongest of the triplets. Ursula is the most courageous of the volunteers.* (Remember, however, that some adjectives form their single-word comparative and superlative forms in irregular ways—for example, *good, better, best; bad, worse, worst.*)

A common error is the use of superlatives when comparatives are called for.

> **Faulty:** Ellen is the best of the two new employees. Ellen is the most qualified of the two.
> **Correct:** Ellen is the better of the two new employees. Ellen is the more qualified of the two.

> **Faulty:** Of the two organizations, ours is the largest and most diverse.
> **Correct:** Of the two organizations, ours is the larger and more diverse.

Faulty: If one subject is plural and one is singular, make the verb agree with the subject closest to the verb.

(Joanne Feierman, *ActionGrammar* [New York: Fireside, 1995], p. 141)

Correct: If one subject is plural and one is singular, make the verb agree with the subject closer to the verb.

Faulty: Prince Charles took his youngest son Harry to a rehabilitation clinic to show him the dangers of drug and alcohol abuse, after the young prince admitted having smoked marijuana and getting drunk when he was 16, a Sunday newspaper reported.

("World Briefs: Prince Harry and Drugs," *Pittsburgh Post-Gazette*, 13 Jan. 2002, p. A8)

Correct: Prince Charles took his younger son, Harry, to a rehabilitation clinic. ...

The reason why the two commas need to be inserted is discussed in rule 33A of Chapter 18.

2. When a pair or a series of adjectival elements includes (a) at least one single-word adjective in the *-er* comparative form or in the *-est* superlative form and (b) at least one two-word adjectival phrase in the **more [or less] + adjective** comparative form or in the **most [or least] + adjective** superlative form, the single-word adjectives must precede the two-word adjectival phrases.

Faulty: Marcie is more coordinated and taller than Heather.

The adverb *more* is carried forward to the comparative adjective *taller*, resulting in the redundancy of *more taller*.

Correct: Marcie is taller and more coordinated than Heather.

Faulty: The more familiar and stronger of the two [musicals] is "Gypsy," a staple since 1960.

(Christopher Rawson, "Women Make 'Gypsy' and 'Nine' Sparkle," *Pittsburgh Post-Gazette*, 31 July 2003, p. D1)

Correct: The stronger and more familiar of the two is Gypsy, a staple since 1960.

Faulty: All these books are predicated on the idea that computers are more difficult and harder to understand than most things in life.

(Michael Newman, "Dummies May Not Be So Stupid After All," *Pittsburgh Post-Gazette* online, 5 Apr. 1998, paragraph 5)

Correct: All these books are predicated on the idea that computers are harder to understand and more difficult than most other things in life.

Faulty: The activity also makes clear a fact that most scientists keep trying to underscore, that the best, most exciting and cheapest science involves unmanned spacecraft.

(Lawrence M. Krauss, "In Search for Life on Mars, Machines Can Boldly Go Where Humans Can't," *New York Times*, 6 Jan. 2004, p. D2)

Correct: The activity also makes clear a fact that most scientists keep trying to underscore—that the best, most exciting, and least expensive science involves unmanned spacecraft.

CAUTION

Do not treat an absolute adjective as if it were a comparative or superlative adjective. That is, avoid using adverbs of degree (*least, less, more,* and *most*), as well as adverbs like *very*, before absolute adjectives, which include *unique, perfect, equal,* and *final.* An adjective is considered to be absolute if it describes a quality that is either possessed or not possessed by someone or something. Something might be unique, for instance, or it might not be; but there is no in-between—there are no gradations of uniqueness.

9B ADVERBS FORCED TO SERVE AS PREDICATE ADJECTIVES (SUBJECTIVE COMPLEMENTS)

Do not force an adverb to do the work of a predicate adjective (or subjective complement). Use adverbs to modify verbs; do not use adverbs as complements of linking (equational) verbs. Be especially careful with verbs such as *taste, smell, feel,* and *hear* (which can function transitively, intransitively, and equationally) and with *look* and *appear* (which can function intransitively and equationally). When such a verb is functioning equationally—that is, when it is equating the subject with a predicate adjective serving as the complement—make sure that an adjective, not an adverb, follows it. When the verb is expressing an action, choose an adverb, not an adjective, to modify the verb.

- The punch tasted bad.
    Tasted is a linking verb; *bad* is a predicate adjective.
- The flowers smelled fresh.
    Smelled is a linking verb; *fresh* is a predicate adjective.
- The girl looked angry.
    Looked is a linking verb, and *angry* is a predicate adjective; the sentence means the girl was angry.
- The girl looked angrily at her brother.
    Looked is an intransitive verb, and *angrily* is an adverb; the sentence means the girl looked at her brother in an angry way.

Among other verbs that sometimes function equationally are *arrive* (*they arrived happy*), *grow* (*she grew sullen*), *keep* (*he kept quiet*), *prove* (*the advice proved useless*), *remain* (*she remains upbeat*), *sound* (*he sounded sad*), *stay* (*she stayed happy*), *turn* (*things turned ugly*), and *wear* (*my patience was wearing thin*). The sentences *He stayed happy* and *He stayed happily* have completely different meanings: The former (in which *stayed* is a linking verb) means he continued to be happy, and the latter (in which *stayed* is an intransitive verb) means that he was happy about staying. (This topic is discussed in more detail in Chapter 2.)

9C ADJECTIVES FORCED TO SERVE AS ADVERBS

Do not force an adjective to do the work of an adverb. The adjective *real* is often pressed into service as an adverb, and the result is an ungrammatical sentence.

Faulty: The food was real good.
    Real is an adjective. An adverb is needed to modify *good*.
Correct: The food was really good.
    Really is an adverb modifying an adjective.

9D PROBLEMS WITH THE POSITIONING OF ADVERBS

When a single-word adverb (rather than an adverbial phrase) is modifying a verb phrase composed of a helping verb and a main verb, the natural and stylistically desirable position for the adverb is between the helping verb and the main verb. (Do not, however, wedge an adverbial phrase between a helping verb and a main verb—unless the result sounds natural, as in *We've only just begun.*) If more than one helping verb precedes the main verb, experiment with positioning the adverb after each helping verb until you decide which resulting phrase sounds natural.

Awkward: The scandal *already* has forced several executives to resign.
Better: The scandal has already forced several executives to resign.

Awkward: Entrance requirements *gradually* will be raised.
Better: Entrance requirements will gradually be raised.

Awkward: The case may have been *finally* cracked.
Better: The case may have finally been cracked.

Awkward: Evans-Freke thinks his team *eventually* can shrink the drug-design process to seven years and, in the process, rake in profits from drug successes sooner and save millions of research dollars aimed at drugs doomed to fail. To do so, Sugen and about 2,000 other biotech firms in this northern California biotech belt and elsewhere *increasingly* are supplementing the costly trial-and-error work of test tubes and tissue samples with high-speed computer analysis and genetic advances.

(Doug Levy, "Computing Cures Database May Put Drugs on Shelves Years Faster," *USA Today*, 17 Mar. 1998, p. 1B)

Better: Evans-Freke thinks his team can *eventually* shrink the drug-design process. ... To do so, Sugen and about 2,000 other biotech firms in this northern-California biotech belt and elsewhere are *increasingly* supplementing the costly trial-and-error work. . . .

Awkward: They could, under Arkansas law, walk to the nearest pawnshop or firearm store and buy a gun.

(Rick Bragg, "Jonesboro Dazed by Its Darkest Day," *New York Times*, 18 Apr. 1998, p. A7)

Better: Under Arkansas law, they could walk to the nearest pawnshop or firearm store and buy a gun.

Awkward: But inside, Colfax Elementary School has, for the past half-decade, been anything but an oasis of learning.

(Mackenzie Carpenter, "New Principal Hopes to Avert Showdown over School's Future," *Pittsburgh Post-Gazette* online, 20 July 1998, paragraph 2)

Better: But, for the past half decade, Colfax Elementary School has been anything but an oasis of learning.

9E PROBLEMS WITH THE REACH OF MODIFIERS

When the first element in a pair or in a series is preceded by a modifier intended to modify only that one element, there is always the chance that a reader will mistakenly infer that the modifier is intended to be carried forward to the other element or elements in the pair or series as well. The result is that the reader may initially misconstrue the meaning of the sentence.

Awkward: Thomas demanded that Wendy's burgers never be frozen and be sold made-to-order.

(Bruce Horovitz and Theresa Howard, "Wendy's Loses Its Legend," *USA Today*, 9 Jan. 2002, p. 2B)

Readers might mistakenly carry the adverb *never* forward to the second element in the pair and thus read the second element as *never be sold made-to-order*.

Better: Thomas demanded that Wendy's burgers never be frozen and always be sold made-to-order.

Awkward: But by the late 1990s, patrons were complaining that it [the auditorium] had too few restrooms, narrow aisles and cramped seats, some with dismal views.

(Micheline Maynard, "Michigan's Gem of an Auditorium Glitters Again," *New York Times*, 8 Jan. 2004, p. B5)

Readers might mistakenly carry *too few* forward to the other two elements in the series.

Better: But by the late 1990s, patrons were complaining that it had narrow aisles, cramped seats (some with dismal views), and too few restrooms.

Awkward: So they are either on a diet where they deprive themselves of different foods and are chronically hungry, or they are not dieting and going hog-wild eating as much as they want of whatever they want.

(Nanci Hellmich, "Today's Kids Are Helping Themselves," *USA Today*, 20 Nov. 2003, p. 2D)

In the second independent clause, readers might initially carry *not* forward to *going hog-wild*.

Better: So they are either on a diet where they deprive themselves of different foods and are chronically hungry, or they are not dieting and are going hog-wild eating as much as they want of whatever they want.

9F INDEFENSIBLE SPLIT INFINITIVES

The superstition that the two parts of an infinitive (the particle *to* and the stem of the verb) must never be split by a single-word adverb sometimes stands in the way of graceful, idiomatic phrasing. Although it is true that most split infinitives are clumsy, inelegant, and amateurish, a writer once in a very great while seems to have no choice but to split an infinitive. Keeping the infinitive together will result in an awkward or ambiguous sentence, and if the sentence cannot be satisfactorily rephrased without the infinitive, go ahead and split the infinitive—but be aware that by doing so you will disappoint or exasperate those readers who naively persist in the notion that every split infinitive is an atrocity. In short, do not resort to splitting an infinitive until you have exhausted all of your other options.

Many split infinitives are indefensible. In the following examples, the adverbs splitting the infinitives can easily be repositioned, or the sentences can easily be rephrased to avoid the splits.

Indefensible: I advise parents to not tolerate blatant misbehavior.
(John Rosemond, "What to Do If Your Daughter Becomes a Witch," *Pittsburgh Post-Gazette*, 4 Nov. 2003, p. D5)
Rephrased: I advise parents not to tolerate blatant misbehavior.

Indefensible: And though few are expecting Mr. Eisner to immediately lose his job, it appears unlikely that Mr. Eisner can emerge from this battle without at least seeing his power curbed.
(Bruce Orwall and Joann S. Lublin, "For Disney's Eisner, Years of Corporate Sparring Catch Up," *Wall Street Journal*, 1 Mar. 2004, p. A1)
Rephrased: And though few are expecting Mr. Eisner to lose his job immediately. . . .

Indefensible: Their argument is that there's no way to completely eliminate food risk.
(Bill Radke, "Answers Sure to Make You Feel Better About What You're Eating," *Seattle Post-Intelligencer*, 17 Jan. 2004, p. B5)
Rephrased: Their argument is that there's no way to eliminate food risk completely.

Indefensible: Foes [of bankruptcy-law reform], mainly those who work in the courts, view the pending legislation as overkill, and criticize it for failing to target the real problem: overzealous credit card issuers that entice people to habitually overspend.
(Patricia Sabatini, "Fresh Start or Fool's Paradise?," *Pittsburgh Post-Gazette* online, 19 July 1998, paragraph 3)
Rephrased: ... overzealous credit-card issuers that entice people to overspend habitually.
Rephrased: ... overzealous credit-card issuers that lure people into habitual overspending.

Indefensible: Fashion designers this season may have been able to inadvertently achieve the kind of focus on good living that doctors and nutritionists could never get from their fashionista patients.
(Tony Moxham, "Exercising Fashion Options," *Interview*, Apr. 2003, p. 94)
Rephrased: Fashion designers this season may have inadvertently achieved the kind of focus on good living that doctors and nutritionists could never get from their fashionista patients.

In the following examples, the split infinitives might be defended, because in each instance, the adverb splitting the infinitive cannot easily be repositioned elsewhere in the sentence. Yet each sentence can be rephrased to avoid the split.

Defensible: She tries to promptly answer every e-mail she receives at work.
Rephrased: She tries to be prompt in answering every e-mail she receives at work.

Defensible: The secret to their buzz lies in their ability to effortlessly cadge the best elements from various genres and twist them into a sound all their own.
(Matt Diehl, "A Guided Tour Through the Rock Maze of New Bands in 2003," *Interview*, May 2003, p. 46)
Rephrased: The secret to their buzz lies in how effortlessly they cadge the best elements from various genres and twist them into a sound all their own.

Defensible: The copper wire enables IBM to vastly increase the number of transistors on a computer chip, thus boosting performance by about 40 percent, IBM said.
(Bob Fernandez, "IBM Lays Claim to Advance in Microchips," *Philadelphia Inquirer*, 23 Sept. 1997, p. A10)
Rephrased: Using copper wire, IBM has vastly increased the number of transistors on a computer chip. . . .

Defensible: Its [the restaurant's] heyday, however, was more than a decade ago, and its owner, Michael Weinstein, president of Ark Restaurants, cited the decline in expense-account business and the restaurant's inability to successfully modernize the cuisine of Andre Soltner, the former chef and owner.
(Glenn Collins and William Yardley, "A Day to Cry in Your Médoc: Venerable Restaurants Closing," *New York Times*, 13 Feb. 2004, p. A26)
Rephrased: ... Michael Weinstein ... cited the decline in expense-account business and the restaurant's unsuccessful efforts to modernize the cuisine of Andre Soltner, the former chef and owner.

Defensible: The city and the state are to officially open a bike route today through Point State Park, where bicycling and all manner of other wheeled recreation have been outlawed since the park was dedicated in 1974.

(Bob Batz Jr., "Cyclists Can Now Pedal on Point," *Pittsburgh Post-Gazette* online, 24 July 1998, paragraph 4)

Rephrased: The city and the state will officially open a bike route today. . . .

Defensible: The idea is to better align school curricula with the needs of employers concerned about whether they will have an adequate supply of trained workers.

(Jim McKay, "Skill Levels for Students Studied," *Pittsburgh Post-Gazette* online, 2 Apr. 1998, paragraph 4)

Rephrased: The idea is to achieve a better alignment of school curricula with the needs of employers. . . .
Rephrased: The idea is to align school curricula more effectively with the needs of employers. . . .

When the modifier splitting the infinitive consists of more than one word, the split is sometimes defensible. Yet the sentence can almost always be rephrased without an infinitive.

Defensible: The number of lawsuits is expected to more than triple in 2006.
Rephrased: More than three times as many lawsuits are expected in 2006.

Defensible: She refused to so much as show up for her daughter's performance.
Rephrased: She would not even show up for her daughter's performance.

When attempts to avoid splitting an infinitive result in especially ungraceful phrasing, either split the infinitive or rephrase the sentence.

Awkwardly Unsplit: He is disputing his credit card charge and is considering suing Payless, contending that, among other things, it failed adequately to disclose the tracking device and violated his right to privacy.

(Christopher Elliott, "Business Travel: Some Rental Cars Are Keeping Tabs on the Drivers," *New York Times*, 13 Jan. 2004, p. C6)

Split: . . . it failed to adequately disclose the tracking device. . . .
Rephrased: He is disputing his credit-card charge and is considering suing Payless, contending that, among other things, it did not adequately disclose the tracking device and violated his right to privacy.

Awkwardly Unsplit: The new technology will enable us better to compete with our rivals.
Split: The new technology will enable us to better compete with our rivals.
Rephrased: The new technology will enable us to be more competitive with our rivals.
Rephrased: With the new technology, we can better compete with our rivals.

Awkwardly Unsplit: Off the record, the university's attorney told me they wanted quietly to push him out.

(Naomi Wolf, "The Silent Treatment," *New York*, 1 Mar. 2004, p. 27)

Split: Off the record, the university's attorney told me they wanted to quietly push him out.
Rephrased: Off the record, the university's attorney told me they wanted to push him out quietly.

Sometimes the infinitive-splitting adverb may even be disposable:

Awkwardly Unsplit: The proposal, which would have to be approved by the Board of Supervisors, could make San Francisco the first city in the world actively to provide marijuana to its [ailing] citizens.

(Zachary Coile, "Hallinan: Let the City Pass Out Pot If Clubs Close," *San Francisco Examiner*, 15 Mar. 1998, p. A1)

Rephrased: The proposal, which would have to be approved by the Board of Supervisors, could make San Francisco the first city in the world to provide marijuana to its citizens.

TIP: The advice that infinitives not be split applies only to infinitives consisting of *to* and the stem of a verb. But some infinitives consist of three elements: *to*, an auxiliary verb, and a participle. An example is the present-perfect infinitive *to have disappeared*. It is perfectly acceptable to split such infinitives: *The money seems to have slowly disappeared.*

9G MISUSE OF FLAT ADVERBS

When an adverb is available both in a form with *-ly* at its end and in a form without *-ly* (such as *slowly* and *slow*; *quickly* and *quick*; *fairly* and *fair*; *loudly* and *loud*; *roughly* and *rough*) and both forms express exactly the same meaning, confine the use of the shorter form—known as a flat adverb—to short sentences, especially those expressing a command: *go slow*; *get rich quick*; *play fair*; *don't talk so loud*; *don't play so rough*. (This topic is covered more fully in Chapter 2.)

Faulty: The students were cautioned to proceed slow through the corridors of the museum.

Correct: The students were cautioned to proceed slowly through the corridors of the museum.

CHAPTER 10

PERSONAL PRONOUNS

The misuse of personal pronouns is rare in newspapers, magazines, and books. Errors in the use of personal pronouns are very common, however, in conversation and in e-mails, letters, memos, diaries, and journals.

Direct quotations that are included in articles in newspapers and magazines sometimes reveal the kinds of personal-pronoun errors that are widespread in casual speech.

- Mr. Moss said, "My conversations with Howell are between he [**him**] and I [**me**]."
  (Gabriel Snyder, "Off the Record," *New York Observer*, 4 Mar. 2002, p. 6)

The rules governing the correct use of personal pronouns are easy enough to learn. *I, we, you, he, she,* and *they* are subjective personal pronouns, as are *who* and *whoever. Me, us, you, him, her,* and *them* are objective personal pronouns, as are *whom* and *whomever.* (The pronoun *you* does not change form from the subjective to the objective, so you don't have to worry about it.)

10A THE SIX USES OF SUBJECTIVE PRONOUNS

Subjective pronouns (*I, we, she, he,* and *they*) are used:

1. As subjects of explicit verbs.

- She and I go to yard sales every Saturday.
- Stephen and she are in love.
- Margot and he are dieting again.

2. As subjects of implied verbs in elliptical (incomplete) adverbial dependent clauses.

- She is taller than I.
  - *Than I* is an elliptical version of the adverbial dependent clause *than I am*.
- She is as qualified as I.
  - *As I* is an elliptical version of the adverbial dependent clause *as I am*.
- She loves her cat more than I.
  - *Than I* is an elliptical version of the adverbial dependent clause *than I do* or *than I love her cat*.

TIP: When you are trying to determine whether a subjective pronoun or an objective pronoun is needed after *as* or *than* in an elliptical adverbial dependent clause, mentally add the necessary word or words to fill out the clause, and the appropriate pronominal choice will instantly be obvious.

- He is not as enthusiastic as *[she/her]*.
  - He is not as enthusiastic as *she* is.

---

3. In appositives following the subjects of clauses.

- The Morrisons—both he and she—have been invited.
- The three new employees—Janice, Fianelle, and I—attended an orientation session this afternoon.

4. Before appositives that are part of the subjects of clauses.

- We employees are pleased with the new policy.

5. As predicate pronouns (complements of linking verbs) in semiformal and formal contexts.

- It was I on the phone.
- It was I who called.
- It might have been she who left the message.
- The winners are he and I.
- It was they who objected to the proposal.
- Lianne finally admitted that the person who ate the last piece of chocolate was she.
- Are you certain that the contestants were they?

6. As predicate pronouns (complements) following the linking-verb infinitive *to be* in infinitive phrases.

- The manager seemed to be she.
  - *To be she* is an infinitive phrase. Remember that an infinitive phrase has no subject; that is, there is no noun or pronoun immediately preceding the infinitive.

10B THE SEVEN USES OF OBJECTIVE PRONOUNS

Objective pronouns (*me, us, her, him,* and *them*) are used:

1. As objects of transitive verbs and verbals.

- He invited Jodie and me.
  - *Jodie* and *me* are direct objects.
- Larry will be calling her and me tomorrow.
  - *Her* and *me* are direct objects.
- She gave him and me some advice.

Him and *me* are indirect objects.

- The woman marrying him is a physicist.
  Him is the object of a participle.

- I thanked Greta for helping them.
  Them is the object of a gerund.

- I did not want to disappoint her.
  Her is the object of an infinitive.

2. As objects of prepositions.

- The disagreement was between her and me.
- Russell gave gifts to him and her.

3. In appositives following objects.

- We invited the Morrisons—both him and her.
- Let's you and me take a walk.
  The pronoun to which *you* and *me* are in apposition is the objective pronoun *us*, which has been contracted and fused with the verb *let*.

4. Before appositives serving as objects.

- The new policy is fair to us employees.
- She praised us volunteers.

5. As predicate pronouns (complements of linking verbs) in a casual, informal context—unless an adjectival dependent clause follows the pronoun. *It was me on the phone. It was her at the door.*

  Faulty: It was me who called.
  Correct: It was I who called.

  Faulty: It was them who questioned our motives.
  Correct: It was they who questioned our motives.

6. As direct objects of implied subject-verb constructions in elliptical (incomplete) adverbial dependent clauses.

- She loves her cat more than me.
  Than me is an elliptical version of the adverbial clause *than she loves me*.

7. As predicate pronouns (complements) following the linking-verb infinitive *to be* in infinitive clauses.

- We thought the manager to be her.
  The manager to be her is an infinitive clause whose subject is *manager*. The infinitive clause is a dependent clause serving nominatively as the direct object of *thought*, the predicate verb of the independent clause of the sentence. The subject of an infinitive clause is always in the objective form, so a predicate pronoun (complement) in such a clause needs to be in the same form as the pronoun with which it is being equated by the linking-verb infinitive.

TIP: To determine which pronoun belongs in a compound subject or in a compound object, remove half of the compound subject or compound object—and then the correct pronominal choice should become obvious.

- My cousin and [*he/him*] will be coming for a visit.

> *He* will be coming for a visit.
> - I invited Leon and [*she/her*].
>   I invited her.

10C *WHO* AND *WHOM*; *WHOEVER* AND *WHOMEVER*

Everybody understands that *whom*, not *who*, belongs in the expression *to whom it may concern*, but elsewhere, in nominative dependent clauses (which function like nouns and are discussed in chapter 4) and in adjectival dependent clauses (which function like adjectives and are discussed in chapter 4), writers often choose *whom* or *whomever* when *who* or *whoever* is correct, and they choose *who* or *whoever* when *whom* or *whomever* is correct.

Who and *whoever* are subjective pronouns: They function as subjects and as complements. *Whom* and *whomever* are objective pronouns: They function as objects of verbs, as objects of gerunds and participles, and as objects of prepositions. We will discuss two methods by which you can ensure that you are choosing the correct pronoun. The first method requires only an elementary knowledge of grammar; the second method requires a more sophisticated knowledge.

The easy method to determine whether *who* (or *whoever*) or *whom* (or *whomever*) is the appropriate pronoun in a dependent clause consists of three simple steps.

1. Partition off the dependent clause in which the pronoun appears.

2. Ask yourself whether the pronoun in the dependent clause could be replaced by a subjective pronoun (such as *he*, *she*, or *they*) or by an objective pronoun (such as *him*, *her*, or *them*). You may first have to rearrange the words in the clause so that they appear in the order one expects to find in a declarative sentence (with the subject preceding the verb).

3. If a subjective pronoun fits in the clause, you want the subjective pronoun *who* (or *whoever*). If an objective pronoun fits in the clause, you want the objective pronoun *whom* (or *whomever*).

Using the more sophisticated method to determine which pronoun belongs in the clause, you again have to isolate the dependent clause in which the pronoun appears, and then you have to ask yourself how the pronoun is functioning within the clause. If the pronoun is serving as a subject or a complement, you need the subjective pronoun *who* (or *whoever*). If the pronoun is serving as an object (such as the direct object of a transitive verb or the object of a preposition), you need the objective pronoun *whom* (or *whomever*).

- Caesar's Palace has set the bar high for [*whoever/whomever*] follows.
  (Bruce Keidan, "Celine Dion's Megadeal Heralds the Future of Las Vegas Entertainment," *Pittsburgh Post-Gazette*, 20 July 2003, A&E p. 8)

Using the easy method, we isolate the dependent clause—[*whoever/whomever*] *follows*—and realize that *he* or *she* could be substituted for the bracketed pronouns. The subject pronoun *whoever* is thus the correct choice.

Using the more sophisticated method, we recognize that the pronoun is serving as the subjective of a nominative dependent clause that is functioning as the object of the preposition *for*. The subjective pronoun *whoever* is therefore the correct choice. (The writer of the sentence incorrectly chose *whomever*—perhaps because he was regarding *whomever* as the object of the preposition *for*. But the object of the preposition *for* is the entire nominative dependent clause *whoever follows,* in which *whoever* is serving as the subject.)

- Nevertheless, some foreign airlines have taken issue with air marshals, [*who/whom*] they liken to American cowboys.

  ("The Air Marshals Plan: Not-So-Friendly Skies," editorial, *Greensburg (PA) Tribune-Review*, 12 Jan. 2004, p. A6)

Method 1: The dependent clause in which the pronoun appears is [*who/whom*] *they liken to American cowboys*. The clause can be rearranged to read *they liken* [*who/whom*] *to American cowboys*. The objective pronoun *them* can be substituted for the bracketed pronouns. The correct pronoun is the objective *whom*.

Method 2: The dependent clause within which the pronoun appears is an adjectival clause modifying *air marshals*. Within the clause, *whom* is the direct object of the verb *liken*. The clause therefore requires the objective pronoun *whom*.

- She dates [*whoever/whomever*] she feels like dating. ...

  (Ariel Levy, "Where the Bois Are," *New York*, 12 Jan. 2004, p. 26)

Method 1: The dependent clause in which the pronoun appears is [*whoever/ whomever*] *she feels like dating*. The clause can be rearranged to read *she feels like dating* [*whoever/whomever*]. The objective pronoun *her* can be substituted for the bracketed pronouns. The correct pronoun is the objective *whomever*.

Method 2: The dependent clause within which the pronoun appears is a nominative clause functioning as the direct object of *dates*. Within the clause, *whomever* is the object of the gerund *dating*. The objective pronoun *whomever* is required.

- Simply by deciding what kind of clothes he [Michael Jackson] wanted to wear, he could decide [*who/whom*] he wanted to be.

  (Daphne Merkin, "Michael on the Couch," *New York*, 8 Dec. 2003, p. 38)

Method 1: The dependent clause in which the pronoun appears is [*who/whom*] *he wanted to be*. The clause can be rearranged to read *he wanted to be* [*who/whom*]. The subjective pronoun *he* could be substituted for the bracketed pronouns. The correct pronoun is the subjective *who*.

Method 2: The dependent clause in which the pronoun appears is a nominative clause functioning as the direct object of *decide*. Within the clause, the pronoun serves as the complement of the linking-verb infinitive *to be*. The subjective pronoun *who* is required.

- Now a PBS documentary, "Judy Garland: By Myself," part of the "American Masters" series, is using portions of the tapes to explore this troubled and extraordinary performer [*who/whom*] Tony Bennett calls "the greatest singer of the century."

  (Bernard Weinraub, "Garland's Midnight Blues, Recalled in a TV Portrait," *New York Times*, 24 Feb. 2004, p. B1)

Method 1: The dependent clause in which the pronoun appears is [*who/whom*] *Tony Bennett calls "the greatest singer of the century."* The clause can be rearranged to read *Tony Bennett calls* [*who/whom*] *"the greatest singer of the century."* The objective pronoun *her* could be substituted for the bracketed pronouns. The correct pronoun is the objective *whom*.

Method 2: The dependent clause in which the pronoun appears is an adjectival clause modifying the noun *performer*. Within the clause, the pronoun serves as the direct object of *calls*. (The noun phrase *the greatest singer of the century* functions as an object complement.) The objective pronoun *whom* is required.

- You can search for long-lost pals or see [*who/whom*] exes may be hooking up with.
  (John Sellers, "Can We Still Be Friendsters?," *Spin*, Nov. 2003, p. 104)

Method 1: The dependent clause in which the pronoun appears is [*who/whom*] *exes may be hooking up with*. The clause can be rearranged to read *exes may be hooking up with* [*who/whom*]. The objective pronoun *them* can be substituted for the bracketed pronouns. The correct pronoun is the objective *whom*.

Method 2: The dependent clause within which the pronoun appears is a nominative dependent clause functioning as the direct object of the transitive verb *see*. Within the clause, *whom* is the object of the preposition *with*.

- But in the contemporary young gay women's world, what you like and what you do and [*who/whom*] you do it with are [*who/whom*] you are.
  (Ariel Levy, "Where the Bois Are," *New York*, 12 Jan. 2004, p. 25)

This sentence is more complicated than the previous examples, because it includes two dependent clauses that require the writer to make a choice between *who* and *whom*. The writer mis-chose in the first dependent clause but chose correctly in the second dependent clause.

Method 1: The first dependent clause in which the pronoun appears is [*who/whom*] *you do it with*. The clause can be rearranged to read *you do it with* [*who/whom*]. The objective pronoun *her* can be substituted for the bracketed pronouns. The correct pronoun is the objective *whom*. The second dependent clause in which the pronoun appears is [*who/whom*] *you are*. The clause can be rearranged to read *you are* [*who/whom*]. The subjective pronoun *she* can be substituted for the bracketed pronouns. The writer thus correctly chose the subjective pronoun *who*.

Method 2: The first dependent clause in which the pronoun appears is the nominative clause [*who/whom*] *you do it with*, and it functions as one of three elements in the compound-additive subject of the sentence. Within the clause, the pronoun is serving as the object of the preposition *with*. The writer should have thus chosen the objective pronoun *whom*. The second dependent clause in which the pronoun appears—[*who/whom*] *you are*—is also a nominative clause, but it is serving as the complement of the linking verb *are* in the independent clause of the sentence. Within the dependent clause, *who* is the complement of the linking verb *are*. A pronoun serving as a complement needs to be a subjective pronoun, so the correct choice is *who*.

- Igby is determined not to go down like his dad. That means declaring war on his dysfunctional mother, Mimi (Susan Sarandon), an acid-tongued pill popper who ships him off to a Midwestern military school, where cadets beat him with broomsticks, and on his brother Oliver (Ryan Phillippe), a young Republican [*who/whom*] Igby claims is majoring in fascism at Columbia.
  (Peter Travers, "Hot Culkin: Kieran," review of *Igby Goes Down*, *Rolling Stone*, 3 Oct. 2002, p. 111)

Method 1: The dependent clause in which the pronoun appears is [*who/whom*] *Igby claims is majoring in fascism at Columbia*. The clause can be rearranged to read *Igby claims* [*who/whom*] *is majoring in fascism at Columbia*. The subjective pronoun *he* can be substituted for the bracketed pronouns. The writer thus should have chosen the subjective pronoun *who*.

Method 2: The dependent clause in which the pronoun appears is an adjectival clause modifying *Republican*. Within the clause, there is an embedded nominative clause—*that* [*who/whom*] *is* *majoring in fascism at Columbia*—serving as the direct object of *claims*. In the nominative clause, the relative pronoun *that* is only implied, and the subject slot obviously needs to be filled by a subjective pronoun. The subjective pronoun *who* is therefore the appropriate choice.

In each of the following sentences, as in the example immediately above, the adjectival dependent clause is structurally intricate, because embedded within it is another clause. The embedded clause consists of a subject and a transitive verb, followed by the implicit indefinite relative pronoun *that*. (The direct object of the verb in the embedded clause is a nominative dependent clause whose contents are all of the remaining words in the adjectival dependent clause.) It's advisable to ignore the embedded clause entirely, because it cannot help you determine whether the subjective pronoun or the objective pronoun is the correct choice for the hosting clause. The embedded clause can easily distract you from making the appropriate pronominal choice. In each of the sentences below, the embedded clause has been italicized, and the correct pronoun for the adjectival clause has been bracketed and boldfaced. Each sentence is followed by a brief explanation of how the correct pronoun is functioning within its dependent clause.

- At the time, Theresa is a little girl whom [**who**] *everyone believes* is blessed.
  (Harry Kloman, "Manna from Heaven," *Pittsburgh City Paper*, 17 Sept.–24 Sept. 2003, p. 61)
  Who is the subject of the clause whose predicate is *blessed*.

- Mr. Melillo stoutly defended his 2003 program—even Mr. Maxwell, whom [**who**] *he conceded* did not enjoy a success with the public, but who would have been better served, he argued, by a more intimate, 300-seat theater.
  (John Rockwell, "Critic's Notebook: A Festival Not Resting on Its Laurels," *New York Times*, 31 Dec. 2003, p. B12)
  Who is the subject of the clause whose predicate begins with the verb phrase *did not enjoy*.

- ... she was coincidentally seated in a restaurant next to a colleague whom [**who**] *she knew* had hated the book.
  (Sara Nelson, "The Amazon Epidemic: Writers Addicted to Rankings," *New York Observer* online, 8 Mar. 2004, paragraph 3)
  Who is the subject of the clause whose predicate begins with the verb phrase *had hated*.

In each of the examples thus far, the embedded clause has consisted of only two words: a noun or pronoun and a transitive verb. In the next three examples, however, the embedded clauses grow progressively longer.

- When Mr. Broomfield looks back on Wuornos, whom [**who**] *he "always believed* was psychotic," he remembers her eyes.
  (Nancy Ramsey, "Portraits of a Social Outcast Turned Serial Killer," *New York Times*, 30 Dec. 2003, p. B5)
  Who is the subject of the clause whose predicate begins with the verb *was*.

- That's the number [10 million] of noncitizens, give or take a couple million, whom [**who**] the *Department of Homeland Security estimates* live illegally in the United States.
  ("A Sharper Eye," editorial, *Cleveland Plain Dealer*, 6 Jan. 2004, p. B8)
  Who is the subject of the clause whose predicate begins with the verb *live*.

- Leonard Muhammad, a man whom [**who**] *friends, employees and business associates of Michael Jackson say* is running many of the pop star's affairs, has a history of failed businesses, fraud allegations and unpaid tax bills behind him.
  (Sharon Waxman, "Questions Shadow New Jackson Adviser," *New York Times*, 3 Jan. 2004, p. A13)
  Who is the subject of the clause whose predicate begins with the verb phrase *is running*.

You have probably noticed that the subjective pronoun *who* is always the correct pronoun for an adjectival dependent clause that has another clause embedded within it.

10D COMPOUND PERSONAL PRONOUNS

The compound personal pronouns—*myself, ourselves, yourself, yourselves, himself, herself,* and *themselves*—have only two legitimate uses. The first legitimate use is known as the intensive or emphatic use. Use a compound personal pronoun after a noun or another pronoun to place more emphasis on the noun or pronoun.

- The manager herself should inform her employees of the new safety guidelines.
- I myself am impressed with your work.

The second legitimate use is known as the reflexive use. Use a compound personal pronoun as the direct object of a verb, as the indirect object of a verb, as the object of a verbal, or as the object of a preposition when both the subject of the clause and the object refer to the same person.

- I hurt myself when I don't get enough sleep.
- I gave myself two hours to finish the job.
- I need to push myself harder.
- She needs to be herself.
- I need to be by myself.

Many speakers and writers, unfortunately, are increasingly resorting to a compound personal pronoun when they cannot decide whether a subjective or an objective personal pronoun is the correct pronoun for a sentence. Compound personal pronouns, however, should never be used as alternatives to personal pronouns. Boldfaced, bracketed corrections have been inserted into the following sentences.

- *PGR2* [*Project Gotham Racing 2*] is an extremely robust game, with more than 100 different cars to choose from, but it never really gets overwhelming, even for simple folk like myself [**me**].
  (Ryan Baxter, "Gaming," *New York Press*, 17–23 Dec. 2003, p. 36)
- There have been scores of tributes to the late editor in the past week, the vast majority written by men and women far more eloquent on the subject than myself [**I**].
  (Russ Smith, "Who Was Robert Bartley?," *New York Press*, 17–23 Dec. 2003, p. 23)

> **TIP:** Sometimes a personal pronoun is perfectly acceptable in a prepositional phrase even when the subject of the clause and the object of the preposition refer to the same person. Both of the following sentences are correct:
>
> - I ended up with red paint all over myself.
> - I ended up with red paint all over me.

10E POSSESSIVE PRONOUNS

The possessive personal pronouns are *my, mine, our, ours, your, yours, his, her, hers, their,* and *theirs. My, our, your, his, her,* and *their* are used adjectivally (*my eccentricities; your problems; his issues*). *Mine, ours, yours, his, hers,* and *theirs* are used as subjects (*Yours is better than Mike's*), as objects (*I prefer mine to yours*), and as complements (*The suggestion was hers*). Note that none of the possessive pronouns include apostrophes.

A common error is the use of an objective personal pronoun before a gerund. A pronoun preceding a gerund should be in possessive form.

Faulty: She is tired of me being late.
Correct: She is tired of my being late.

Faulty: I was impressed by him taking initiative for once.
Correct: I was impressed by his taking initiative for once.

Similarly, a noun preceding a gerund should be in possessive form.

Faulty: The affair resulted in Welch divorcing his second wife, Jane, and Wetlaufer, a divorced mother of four, losing her job.

(Thomas Hinton and Dan Kadison, "Power Marriage," *New York Post*, 25 Apr. 2004, p. 11)

The error in the first half of the sentence is easily corrected (*The affair resulted in Welch's divorcing his second wife, Jane*). In the second half of the sentence, however, the conversion of *Wetlaufer* to *Wetlaufer's* will leave a possessive noun preceding a nonpossessive appositive; the result is a different kind of error (see Chapter 21). A better remedy is to recast the sentence.

Correct: As a result of the affair, Welch divorced his second wife, Jane, and Wetlaufer, a divorced mother of four, lost her job.

TIP: Do not confuse gerunds with participles. In the following examples, objective pronouns, not possessive pronouns, precede the words ending in -*ing*—because the words ending in -*ing* are functioning as participles, not as gerunds.

- She couldn't see me waving.
- I saw him stealing the candy bar.
- She didn't want him dating her daughter.

In these sentences, the objective pronouns are emphasizing the performers of the actions expressed by the participles. In a sentence in which a pronoun precedes a gerund, however, the emphasis is on the action and not on the performer of the action.

- I don't like him driving.
    The emphasis is on the person. *Driving* is a participle.

- I don't like his driving.
    The emphasis is on the action. *Driving* is a gerund.

Similarly, a noun preceding a participle should not be in possessive form.

- I saw Hannah jumping on the trampoline.

Boldfaced, bracketed corrections have been inserted into the following sentences.

- The odds of him [**his**] getting another deal like the $65 million contract he signed with Sony in 1991 are slimmer than his chances of being nominated father of the year.
    (Tracy Connor, "Jacko May Go Broke-o," *New York Daily News*, 25 Apr. 2004, p. 8)

- The big deal is that the cellular phone has completely changed the way we behave in public and, even more, completely blurred the line between the public sphere and the private without us [**our**] even realizing it, with wide-reaching implications for how we treat each other—and ourselves.
    (Anne Taylor Fleming, "The Tyranny of the Cell Phone," for *Los Angeles Times*, in *Pittsburgh Post-Gazette*, 15 Aug. 1999, p. E1)

- My mother doesn't approve of me [**my**] living in New York and working for *Vogue*.
    ("The Digested Read: *Bergdorf Blondes* by Plum Sykes," *Guardian* online, 26 Apr. 2004, paragraph 3)

- Parents [**Parents'**] criticizing—or condescending to—other parents over what they feed their kids has become a serious fault line in the preschool and elementary-school set.
    (Sarah Bernard, "Baby Fat," *New York*, 23 Feb. 2004, p. 27)

- If you read the Nov. 17 *New York Times* story about Time Warner [**Time Warner's**] pondering whether to refinance or buy out the Maverick label, as well as the value of the stock options that the Material Girl holds, you might say that a denouement to the Madonna era is close at hand.

  (Frank DiGiacomo, "Fools for Scandal," *New York Observer* online, 24 Nov. 2003, paragraph 31)

- So much of what we've had to report in the past few years has been distressing—the city [**city's**] tumbling toward bankruptcy, the death of a national icon like our own Fred Rogers, the Penguins [**Penguins'**] finishing in last place and still not managing to get the top draft choice.

  (David M. Shribman, "Why Newspapers Bring You Some Bad News," *Pittsburgh Post-Gazette*, 2 May 2004, p. E3)

- Indeed, in a town where something like J-Lo's breakup with Ben Affleck can be phone fodder for days, the prospect of Disney boss Michael Eisner [**Eisner's**] getting his comeuppance will easily occupy the industry at least into the Oscars.

  (John Lippman, "Mouse-Hunt Jitters," *Wall Street Journal*, 13 Feb. 2004, p. W1)

10F PRONOMINAL POINT OF VIEW

Pronominal point of view is the term that denotes the vantage point from which a writer is engaging his or her subject matter. A writer must choose one point of view from among three alternatives—first person, second person, and third person—and then use it consistently throughout a piece of writing.

The first-person point of view is that of the writer and makes use of the personal pronouns *I* and *me* (singular) or *we* and *us* (plural). Despite what you may have learned elsewhere about the use of such pronouns, they are entirely appropriate when you are writing about your life and your experiences—whether in an essay or in letters, e-mails, journal entries, and diary entries.

The second-person point of view is that of the person or persons being addressed—that is, your readers. This point of view makes use of the personal pronouns *you* and *your* for both the singular and the plural. Although you may have been taught never to use the pronoun *you* in your writing, its use is not only correct but also desirable when your purpose in writing is to provide advice, suggestions, or instructions on how the reader should go about performing a process or completing a task.

The third-person point of view is that of the person or persons about whom you are writing. This point of view makes use of the personal pronouns *he, him, she,* and *her* (singular forms) and *they* and *them* (plural forms), as well as the singular indefinite pronouns *one, everyone, everybody, someone,* and *somebody*. This is the most formal and objective point of view, and it is preferred for formal writing in the academic and professional worlds.

When you are writing about an unspecified but representative person, use *one* (or its variants) in formal contexts and *you* in semiformal and informal contexts.

Do not shift from one point of view to another. In the following sentence, the writer shifts illogically from the first-person plural to the second person.

Faulty: Once or twice a year if we're lucky, a movie comes along that bears no resemblance to anything you've ever seen before.

(Ron Weiskind, "As Strange As It Gets," *Pittsburgh Post-Gazette*, 5 Nov. 1999, p. W26)

Correct: Once or twice a year if we're lucky, a movie comes along that bears no resemblance to anything we've ever seen before.

This is the consistent handling of first-person-plural point of view.

Correct: Once or twice a year if you're lucky, a movie comes along that bears no resemblance to anything you've ever seen before.

This is the consistent handling of second-person point of view.

In the next example—which appeared in the description of a course called On Your Own, offered by a high school in western Pennsylvania—the point of view shifts not once but twice.

Faulty: This course is designed to help the student in coping with the reality of being on your own once they have left home.

The third-person-singular point of view, established by the noun *student*, is violated by the shift to the second-person point of view (*your*) and then to the third-person-plural point of view (*they*).

Correct: This course is designed to help students cope with the reality of being on their own once they have left home.

This is the consistent handling of third-person-plural point of view.

Correct: This course is designed to help you cope with the reality of being on your own once you have left home.

This is the consistent handling of second-person point of view.

In the following example, the writer shifts from the third-person point of view in the first sentence to the second-person point of view in the second sentence.

Faulty: Someone who stands on one of the glass-paved walkways threaded through Grand Central Terminal's magnificent arched windows has a view unique in the world. Up there, suspended between the blue vault of heaven disguised as a ceiling and the array of humanity scurrying about 40 feet below, you can look back 95 years and well into the future.

("Putting the Grand in Grand Central," *New York Daily News*, 22 Mar. 1998, p. 48)

Correct: Stand on one of the glass-paved walkways threaded through Grand Central Terminal's magnificent arched windows, and you have a view unique in the world. Up there, suspended between the blue vault of heaven disguised as a ceiling and the array of humanity scurrying about 40 feet below, you can look back 95 years and well into the future.

This is the consistent handling of second-person point of view.

Correct: Someone who stands on one of the glass-paved walkways threaded through Grand Central Terminal's magnificent arched windows has a view unique in the world. Up there, suspended between the blue vault of heaven disguised as a ceiling and the array of humanity scurrying about 40 feet below, he or she can look back 95 years and well into the future.

This is the consistent handling of third-person singular point of view.

CHAPTER 11

AGREEMENT OF PRONOUNS AND THEIR ANTECEDENTS

A pronoun must agree in number with its antecedent—the noun or noun equivalent to which the pronoun refers. If the antecedent is singular, the pronoun must be singular; and if the antecedent is plural, the pronoun must be plural. The rule could not be simpler—yet it is violated so often, both in speech and in writing, that many listeners and readers do not even seem to recognize that anything is wrong with sentences in which the violations appear.

Faulty: Whenever I see someone trying to sneak through that illegal 11th item in the Express Lane, I just feel like busting them over the head with my half-pound filet of Chilean sea bass.
(David Grimes, "Rage Is All the Rage These Days," *Pittsburgh Post-Gazette*, 28 Dec. 2003, p. C2)

Faulty: It's amazing how hysterical everyone becomes when they're involved with a Broadway musical.
(John Heilpern, "Rosie and Boy's Big Identity Crisis," *New York Observer* online, 24 Nov. 2003, paragraph 1)

Faulty: These days, it's tough to find anybody who doesn't think they're a dork.
(Ian R. Williams, "Twilight of the Dorks?," Salon.com, 29 Oct. 2003, paragraph 9)

Faulty: Each tester, according to protocol, took the fries one by one, dipped them into the cup—all the way, right to the bottom—bit off the portion covered in ketchup, and then contemplated the evidence of their senses.
(Malcolm Gladwell, "The Ketchup Conundrum," *New Yorker*, 6 Sept. 2004, p. 135)

Faulty: Every working writer has a trunkful of humiliating stories about their first attempts to get published, so here's one of mine.
(Paul Collins, "This Genteel Racket," *Village Voice* online, 6 July 2004, paragraph 1)

In each of the five examples, a plural pronoun (*they, them,* or *their*) refers back to a singular antecedent—either a singular indefinite pronoun (*someone, everyone, anybody*) or a singular noun (*tester, writer*). The sentences are thus not only ungrammatical but also illogical. Using a plural pronoun to refer back to a singular antecedent is not unlike declaring that one equals more than one—a declaration that no commonsensical person would accept as true.

Why then are such errors so common? The primary reason is that as rich as the English language is, it lacks something that would make our communication a lot less burdensome. Our language lacks a gender-neutral, third-person-singular pronoun—a single word whose meaning would be *he or she*. Many speakers and writers attempt to compensate for this lack (and thereby encompass persons of both genders) by using *they, them, their*, or *themselves* even when the antecedent of the pronoun is singular. But many reasonable people do not accept this usage, because it is patently illogical and contrary to common sense.

11A THIRD-PERSON-PLURAL PRONOUNS AND SINGULAR ANTECEDENTS

There are five methods by which you can easily correct the kind of error exhibited in the sentences presented above. Before we discuss the methods, however, bear in mind that there *are* some legitimate reasons for violating the principle that the plural pronouns *they, them, their*, and *themselves* should not be used with singular antecedents. You can violate the principle in dialogue, in quotations of casual speech, and in other sentences in which you are intentionally aiming for a very informal, conversational style. In all other instances, however, you need to preserve the distinction between singularity and plurality—because the distinction strengthens the precision of your sentences.

Faulty: If everyone who slept eight [sic] hours a night instead slept six-and-a-half hours, they would gain an extra eight [sic] hours each week for work or play.

(Michael Woods, "Sleeping Your Life Away? Maybe," *Pittsburgh Post-Gazette*, 23 Feb. 2004, p. A9)

Method 1: Replace the plural pronoun with *he or she, him or her,* or *his or her*.

Correct: If everyone who slept eight hours a night instead slept six and a half hours, he or she would gain an extra ten and a half hours each week for work or play.

The use of *he or she, him or her,* and *his or her* is inclusive and nonsexist (it excludes neither gender) and thus is politically correct. But it is also wordy. The frequent use of the doubled pronouns in a paragraph or in a passage is stylistically inelegant, because it clutters the page. (The alternative forms *s/he, he/she, she/he, him/her,* and *his/her* are even more distracting; they are also considered unprofessional.)

Method 2: Pluralize the antecedent and retain the plural pronoun.

Correct: If people who slept eight hours a night instead slept six and a half hours, they would gain an extra ten and a half hours each week for work or play.

Method 3: Rewrite the sentence, eliminating the personal pronoun.

Correct: People who slept six and a half hours a night instead of eight hours would gain an extra ten and a half hours each week for work or play.

Method 4: Rewrite the sentence, using the second-person pronoun *you* (in contexts in which it is not inappropriate to address the reader directly).

Correct: If you slept six and a half hours a night instead of eight hours, you would gain an extra ten and a half hours each week for work or play.

Method 5: Use either *he* or *she* consistently throughout a paragraph or a passage—and do so without apologizing for your choice.

> **Correct:** If everyone who slept eight hours a night instead slept six and a half hours, he would gain an extra ten and a half hours each week for work or play.
>> Until the mid-nineteen-sixties, American schoolchildren had long been taught that *he* could be used to encompass persons of both sexes.
>
> **Correct:** If everyone who slept eight hours a night instead slept six and a half hours, she would gain an extra ten and a half hours each week for work or play.

The fifth option is limited to passages in which the gender of the persons being written about is not relevant.

In *Dictionaries: The Art and Craft of Lexicography*, Sidney I. Landau observes that "the cumulative effect of the iteration of masculine pronouns obliterates the female from one's consciousness," and he recommends "that men use the masculine pronoun for neutral use, because they naturally identify with the masculine gender, and that women use feminine pronouns for the analogous reason." His proposal makes much sense, and more and more writers have begun using pronouns in the way Landau recommends. Whether you are female or male, however, what matters most is that you be consistent in your handling of third-person pronouns referring to a representative but unspecified person. The writer of the following sentence shifts from the inclusive *his/her* to the exclusive *him*.

> · If someone lies about his/her background on a biography at one school, it almost surely will follow him [**him or her**] to the next.
>
> (Ray Fittipaldo, "False Biographies Place Coaches, Schools at High Risk," *Pittsburgh Post-Gazette*, 29 June 2002, p. B2)

Another problem to avoid is the alternating use of *he* and *she* throughout a passage. That is, do not use *he* in one sentence, *she* in a second, *he* in a third, and so on, when you are writing about a representative person. Such pronominal gender-bending will distract the alert reader. In the following excerpt, for instance, the leader seems to have undergone a sex-change operation between the second and third sentences.

> · Further, a leader's intelligence has to have a strong emotional component. He has to have high levels of self-awareness, maturity and self-control. She must be able to withstand the heat, handle setbacks and, when those lucky moments arise, enjoy success with equal parts of joy and humility.
>
> (Jack Welch, "Four E's [a Jolly Good Fellow]," *Wall Street Journal*, 23 Jan. 2004, p. A14)

Inconsistencies in Number Throughout a Sentence

Whichever of the five methods you use to ensure that pronouns agree with their antecedents, be sure to be consistent in number throughout an entire sentence or passage. Writers often lose track of their choices, as the following sentences illustrate. (Corrections have been boldfaced and bracketed.)

> · There must be someone out there who hates his or her life so much that they [**he or she**] can't stand the thought of other people drawing breath unassisted by a hospital ventilator.
>
> (Tony Norman, "Murder in Their Hearts and Guns in Their Hands," *Pittsburgh Post-Gazette*, 30 Dec. 2003, p. A9)
>
> · Then, while waiting in the [airport] boarding area, I call someone I love to remind him that I do and to reassure myself that they love [**he loves**] me back.
>
> (Susan Spano, "Make a List, Check It Twice Before You Leave on Vacation," from *Los Angeles Times*, in *Pittsburgh Post-Gazette*, 28 Dec. 2003, p. G3)

- In the Oakland County school district in Michigan, for example, one report said one of every four high school seniors said he or she had been physically threatened. One of 11 said they [he or she] personally had taken guns or knives to school.

  (Ann McFeatters, "A Deadly Problem That Defies Logic and Solution," *Pittsburgh Post-Gazette*, 21 Apr. 1999, p. A15)

11B AGREEMENT AND COLLECTIVE NOUNS

A collective noun is a noun that denotes a group of people and that does not end in *-s*. Such a noun can be construed as either singular or plural. Choose the singular interpretation of the collective noun when you want to emphasize the group as a unified whole, and choose the plural interpretation when you want to emphasize the group as a collection of individuals.

Your interpretation will determine the singularity or plurality of (a) the verb (or verbs) in the clause with the collective noun as the subject, (b) any other verbs in the sentence with the collective noun as their subject, and (c) any pronouns whose antecedent is the collective noun. Your interpretation of the collective noun as either singular or plural must be consistent throughout each sentence. In fact, the entire passage in which the group named by the collective noun is under discussion should be consistent in its treatment of the collective noun—unless there is a justifiable reason for shifting from a singular interpretation to a plural interpretation (or vice versa).

Errors violating this principle are especially common in sentences about rock groups. In each of the following examples, the singular interpretation is preferred, but the writers mix singular verbs with plural pronouns. Corrections have been boldfaced and bracketed.

- This unsmiling Boston band [Godsmack], named after a song by the nineties grunge-metalheads Alice in Chains, pounds out angst-filled guitar rock, but without the tunefulness that made their [its] Seattle heroes memorable.

  ("Clubs," *New Yorker*, 17 Nov. 2003, p. 32)

- Like Billy Joel before them [it], the Pleased is in a New York state of mind.

  (Leah Greenblatt, review of The Pleased's *Don't Make Things, Time Out New York*, 1–8 Jan. 2004, p. 99)

- Radiohead recorded their [its] third album [OK Computer] in the mansion of actress Jane Seymour while she was filming *Dr. Quinn, Medicine Woman*. *OK* is where the band began pulling at its sound like taffy, seeing what happened, not worrying if it was still "rock."

  ("The 500 Greatest Albums of All Time," *Rolling Stone*, 11 Dec. 2003, p. 134)

- The feminist band Le Tigre has a song on their [its] debut album called "What's Ya Take on Cassavettes [*sic*]?"

  (Emily Barton, "Short Friction," *Bookforum*, spring 2004, p. 48)

- By the time their [its] fifth album was released, Kiss was the most popular band in America, with sold-out stadium tours and eventually its own pinball machines, makeup line and a TV movie.

  ("The 500 Greatest Albums of All Time," *Rolling Stone*, 11 Dec. 2003, p. 178)

- After 1999's self-parody "Dark Side of the Spoon," Ministry looked ready for the scrap heap, having been sold for parts to the acts they [it] had influenced. But with its ninth studio album, the quintessential industrial-metal act returns to eat its young—and pays homage to its forefathers.

  (Robert Cherry, review of Ministry's *Animositisomina, Rolling Stone*, 6 Mar. 2003, p. 68)

The singular interpretation of collective nouns tends to prevail in American English. The writer of the following sentence, however, seems to want to emphasize the individual members of the band as songwriters, so the verb in the second independent clause should be plural.

- The sound is more rock-oriented and vibrant, and the band has [**have**] actually learned to write songs—and not just because they collaborated with Itaal Shur, co-author of Santana's "Smooth."

  (Jem Aswad, "Kinky Kronicles," *Village Voice*, 17-23 Dec. 2003, p. 94)

The plural interpretation is also appropriate to the following:

- Famously featuring the actor Jason Schwartzman (best known for his role as Max Fischer in "Rushmore") on drums, Phantom Planet is [**are**] an indie-pop combo from Los Angeles. They clear the hurdle of having a movie star in their ranks (see Keanu Reeve's Dogstar for a worst-case scenario) with a promising knack for memorable, sunny pop melodies.

  ("Clubs," *New Yorker*, 17 Nov. 2003, p. 32)

In the following sentences, the writers are inconsistent in their treatment of the collective nouns *generation, family, unit,* and *staff* (corrections have been bracketed and boldfaced).

- Perhaps because they are children of the technological age, a generation of younger designers seems [**seem**] particularly skilled at translating the subtler dimensions of sexual expression.

  (Ginia Bellafante, "From Young Designers, Sense and Sensuality," *New York Times*, 13 Feb. 2004, p. A25)

- Now the family has [**have**] enrolled their two other children in studies that someday may help produce a treatment to prevent juvenile onset, or type 1, diabetes.

  (Michael Waldholz, "Researchers' Goal: Stopping Diabetes Before Kids Get It," *Wall Street Journal*, 1 Mar. 2004, p. A1)

  A more appropriate subject for the sentence would be *parents: Now the parents have enrolled their two other children in studies that someday may help produce a treatment to prevent juvenile onset, or type 1, diabetes.*

- Over the years, the unit has [**have**] come to be called the most hated unit in the army, because they are so good at playing the enemy.

  (Leroy Sievers and the *Nightline* staff, "*Nightline* Daily E-Mail," 23 June 2004, paragraph 2)

- The staff is [**are**] accommodating—when they had only a half-serving left of a side dish we'd ordered, they brought us an extra that we hadn't—and generous, dishing up seconds upon request.

  (Angelique Bamberg and Jason Roth, "Quiet Storm Tuesday Night Supper Club," *Pittsburgh City Paper*, 25 Feb.–3 Mar. 2004, p. 46)

- An army of women's rights activists—up to three quarters of a million strong—was [**were**] headed for Washington today for their first major rally in the capital in a dozen years, organizers said.

  (Aly Sujo, "Pro-abort Activists Flood D.C.," *New York Post*, 25 Apr. 2004, p. 17)

  The plural interpretation should prevail here, for the noun *army* is used figuratively, and, as the context makes clear, the protesters streamed in from all over, and they represented many organizations.

The trouble with the next example is not remedied as easily.

- When Gen Y thinks about health care[,] it isn't Medicare and prescription drugs or the high cost of insurance, it's getting any insurance. When they think [**it thinks**] about the economy, it isn't 401(k)s and tax cuts, it's getting jobs and paying student loans.

  (Ellen Goodman, "Citizens or Cynics?" *Pittsburgh Post-Gazette*, 19 Nov. 2003, p. A21)

  The revision leads to an awkward profusion of its. In sentences such as these, it is helpful to insert the phrase *the members of* before the collective noun and then pluralize the verbs as well as the pronouns: *When the members of Gen Y think about health care. ... When they think about the economy. ...*

As we saw in chapter 5, the collective noun *couple* is generally construed in the plural sense; this usage emphasizes the two individuals of which the couple is composed. When you choose the plural interpretation for clauses in which *couple* is the subject, be sure that both the verbs and the pronouns are plural. In the following sentences, the writers correctly chose plural pronouns but incorrectly chose singular verbs.

- The couple still lives [**live**] in the same house, surrounded by trees and well-tended gardens and happy memories that held them there, despite their tragedy.

  (Cindi Lash, "30 Years After Girl's Murder, Memories Still Raw," *Pittsburgh Post-Gazette*, 12 Oct. 2003, p. A20)

- When her car breaks down, an older couple invites [**invite**] her to ride in their RV, and teaches [**teach**] her a few roadside tricks.

  (Scott Lyle Cohen, "Emily Grace," *Interview*, Nov. 2003, p. 36)

11C PRONOUNS REFERRING TO THINGS

We have thus far been looking only at pronouns whose antecedents are either nouns or indefinite pronouns that refer to people. But errors in the agreement of pronouns and their antecedents also occur when the antecedent is an indefinite pronoun referring to a thing or is a noun naming a thing. In the following examples, the antecedents have been italicized, and corrections have been bracketed and boldfaced.

- Outrageously luxurious multimillion-dollar resorts line the coast with imposing facades, *each* trying to one-up their [**its**] neighbor in style and chic.

  (Julia Chaplin, "Making a Splash at Cabo San Lucas," *New York Times*, 30 Jan. 2004, p. D7)

- Mr. Bush did not mention the *commercials* during a stop in Bakersfield, Calif., to talk about the economy. Nor did he bring it [**them**] up at a fund-raiser here. ...

  (Richard W. Stevenson and Jim Rutenberg, "Bush Campaigns amid a Furor over Ads," *New York Times*, 5 Mar. 2004, p. A11)

- Sale of the naming *rights* to a building—or giving it [**them**] to a corporation in return for a pledge of support—has become increasingly common, not only in professional sports but in college athletics too.

  (Bill Schackner, "For Sale: Pitt Center Name," *Pittsburgh Post-Gazette*, 22 Jan. 1998, p. A9)

- Employers, beware. A new technology is gaining popularity in the United States that poses a threat to your company. The technology is the *camera cell phone*. If you think they are [**it is**] not a business concern, think again.

  (James B. Brown and Kimberly A. Craver, "Can You See Me Now?," *Pittsburgh Post-Gazette*, 24 Feb. 2004, p. C2)

- We see homemade *bombs* going off almost every day in Iraq, killing and wounding American soldiers. Where is [**are**] all that [**those**] coming from?

  (Leroy Sievers and the *Nightline* staff, "*Nightline* Daily E-Mail," 13 Sept. 2003, paragraph 4)

- Burger King took out a full-page advertisement in *USA Today* last week to tout its unlikely new product, showing a giant *Whopper* with dotted lines marking the outlines of where a bun would normally be. The Miami-based chain is selling them [**it or the bunless Whopper**] in plastic salad bowls [**in a plastic salad bowl**], with knife and fork, after reporting an increasing number of such requests over the past year.

  (Dave Carpenter, "Hold the Pickles, Hold the Bun?," for Associated Press, in *Pittsburgh Post-Gazette*, 23 Jan. 2004, p. B14)

Sometimes the best solution is to recast a sentence or passage entirely.

> **Faulty:** Scripting a series finale is never easy and they rarely satisfy, as the producers of "Friends," "Frasier" and "Angel" are likely to discover in May.
>
> (Rob Owen, "Rating 'Sex,'" *Pittsburgh Post-Gazette*, 26 Feb. 2004, p. B10)
>
> **Correct:** A series finale is never easy to script, and it's rarely satisfying, as the producers of *Friends*, *Frasier*, and *Angel* are likely to discover in May.

In the next example, the writer is inconsistent in the handling of the indefinite-pronoun antecedent *none*, treating it first singularly (with the singular verb *loses* and the singular pronoun *its*), then shifting to the plural pronoun *their*.

> **Faulty:** None of the songs loses its emotion, despite losing their musical explosiveness in the unplugged format.
>
> (Tracy Collins, review of Alanis Morissette's *MTV Unplugged*, *Pittsburgh Post-Gazette*, 12 Dec. 1999, A&E p. 2)
>
> **Correct:** None of the songs loses its emotion, despite losing its musical explosiveness in the unplugged format.
> **Correct:** None of the songs lose their emotion, despite losing their musical explosiveness in the unplugged format.

11D ANTECEDENTS EXPRESSING THE NAMES OF BUSINESSES

A pronoun whose antecedent is the name of a business should be singular. In the following examples, corrections have been bracketed and boldfaced.

- Footlight [Records] specializes in Broadway and movie soundtracks, and they have [**it has**] huge collections (on CD and vinyl) of big-band and easy-listening albums. Also, it's the best place in the city to find those vintage Richard Pryor or Bob Newhart comedy records you grew up with.
  ("Breaking the Chains," *New York Post*, 20 Dec. 2003, p. 27)

- *Princess Cruise Lines* will be charting new waters this fall when it launches their [**its**] most ambitious Caribbean season ever.
  ("Follow the Sun on Princess Cruises," *AAA Motorist*, Westmoreland [PA] Region, Jan. 2004, p. 1)

The five principles of pronoun-antecedent agreement discussed below apply equally to pronouns whose antecedents refer to people and to pronouns whose antecedents refer to things.

11E PRONOUNS WITH COMPOUND-ADDITIVE ANTECEDENTS

Compound-additive antecedents (which take the form of *A and B*) generally require plural pronouns.

- The manager and the assistant manager must submit their weekly reports no later than three o'clock on Friday afternoon.

There is one exception: if the compound-additive antecedent is preceded by *each* or *every*, the pronoun will be singular.

- Each manager and administrative assistant must submit his or her weekly report no later than three o'clock on Friday afternoon.

11F PRONOUNS WITH COMPOUND-ALTERNATIVE ANTECEDENTS

A compound-alternative antecedent takes the form *A or B, A nor B, either A or B,* or *neither A nor B*. A pronoun with a compound-alternative antecedent must agree in number with the *B* element—that is, the element of the compound antecedent that is closer to the pronoun.

- When the Kansas board of education removed evolution from the science curriculum testing to make way for creationism, neither Gore nor Bush could bring themselves [**himself**] to utter a word in defense of scientific truth.
  (Maureen Dowd, "Playing the Jesus Card," for *New York Times*, in *Pittsburgh Post-Gazette*, 16 Dec. 1999, p. A31)
    The compound-alternative antecedent is *neither Gore nor Bush,* so the singularity of *Bush* determines the singularity of the pronoun.

- If you offered them some fresh pineapple or stir-fried snow peas, many would refuse to even try it [**them**], yet these are wonderfully tasty foods, she says.
  (Nanci Hellmich, "Today's Kids Are Helping Themselves," *USA Today,* 20 Nov. 2003, p. 2D)
    The compound-alternative antecedent is *fresh pineapple or stir-fried snow peas.* Because *stir-fried snow peas* is the *B* element, its plurality determines the plurality of the pronoun.

The following sentences are correct.

- Neither Heather nor her sisters needed help with filling out their tax returns.
- Neither Heather nor Ellen needed help with filling out her tax return.

- Either the parents or the children will need to change their plans.
- Either Marcie or Patti is going to take her vacation a week early.
- Did Lewis or Reed lose his temper?
- Neither my son nor my daughters are happy about their SAT scores.

11G PRONOUNS WITH ANTECEDENTS IN *NOT ONLY … BUT ALSO* CONSTRUCTIONS

The pronoun whose antecedent appears in a *not only … but also* construction must agree in number with the noun or pronoun following *but also*.

- Not only the teacher but also her students had trouble with their new computers.

If a *not only … but also* construction includes both a singular element and a plural element, it is stylistically desirable to position the plural element after *but also*.

> **Awkward:** Although not only the textbooks but also the instructor's manual had been misplaced, it was later found in a storeroom.
>
> **Better:** Although not only the instructor's manual but also the textbooks had been misplaced, they were later found in a storeroom.

11H DEMONSTRATIVE PRONOUNS

The demonstrative pronouns *this* and *that* refer back to singular antecedents; the demonstrative pronouns *these* and *those* refer back to plural antecedents. A bracketed, boldfaced correction has been inserted into the following excerpt.

- The monster cleanup [of Times Square following New Year's Eve] was handled by 66 city workers, 54 of whom worked from 11 P.M. Wednesday night until 7 A.M. yesterday and another dozen of whom worked from 6 A.M. to 2 P.M. Of that [**those**], 24 workers swept up with hand brooms (manual litter patrol) and two others used backpack-style leaf blowers.

  (Colin Moynihan and Corey Kilgannon, "How Wild Was the Party? Ask an Army of Sweepers Who Measure Confetti by the Ton," *New York Times*, 2 Jan. 2004, p. A16)

11I PRONOUNS WITH SINGULAR INDEFINITE-PRONOUN ANTECEDENTS

As we saw at the outset of this chapter, many of the most common errors in the agreement of pronouns and their antecedents appear in sentences with singular indefinite pronouns as the antecedents. Only a singular pronoun may be used with a singular indefinite-pronoun antecedent. The singular indefinite pronouns, as you recall, are *anyone, anything, anybody, someone, somebody, something, one, nobody, no one, nothing, everybody, everything, everyone, another, each, either,* and *neither*.

- Each of the employees was happy about his or her raise.
- Neither of the waitresses said she could work on Friday night.
- Everyone was pleased with his or her performance review.
- Each of the proposals has its drawbacks.
- Neither of the cities has lost more than five percent of its population in the past decade.

11J PRONOUNS IN ADJECTIVAL DEPENDENT CLAUSES AND IN INFINITIVE CLAUSES

As we saw in rule 28 of chapter 5, writers often choose the wrong verb for the adjectival dependent clause of a sentence such as *She is one of the employees who arrive early almost every day*. To choose the correct verb, a writer must recognize that *employees,* not *one,* is the antecedent of *who,* which is functioning as the subject of the verb in the dependent clause. The ability to recognize the antecedent of the pronoun serving as the subject of an adjectival dependent clause will also prevent errors in pronoun-antecedent agreement.

Faulty: Hal Sirowitz is one of those rare New York writers who is willing—eager, in fact—to identify himself with the borough of Queens.

(Robert F. Worth, "Ah, Poetic Injustice! Seeking a Laureate, Queens Goes Blank," *New York Times,* 17 Mar. 2004, p. A1)

The antecedent of the pronoun *who,* which serves as the subject of the adjectival dependent clause, is the plural noun *writers.* The second appearance of the singular verb *is,* therefore, is incorrect, and so is the singular pronoun *himself.*

Correct: Hal Sirowitz is one of those rare New York writers who are willing—eager, in fact—to identify themselves with the borough of Queens.

Similar errors occur in sentences with infinitive clauses.

Faulty: CBS News legend Dan Rather was one of the few people to get his hands on an advance copy of the hotly awaited and tightly guarded 975-page memoir My Life, by former President Bill Clinton.

(Joe Hagan, "Rather Digs Clinton's Life ... Reagan's Funeral Director," *New York Observer* online, 28 June 2004, paragraph 1)-

The writer could have avoided the error in pronoun-antecedent agreement by recognizing that the sentence is placing one person (*Dan Rather*) into a category (*few people*) and then declaring something about all of the people in that group—namely that the people in the group got their hands on advance copies. The antecedent of the possessive pronoun is *people,* not *one.*

Correct: CBS News legend Dan Rather was one of the few people to get their hands on advance copies of the hotly awaited and tightly guarded 975-page memoir *My Life,* by former President Bill Clinton.

CHAPTER 12

REFERENCES OF PRONOUNS

With the exceptions of the first-person personal pronouns (*I, me, we, us*), the second-person personal pronoun (*you*), and the indefinite pronouns (such as *anybody, everybody, none,* and *some*), every pronoun must have an antecedent—a noun (or noun equivalent) to which the pronoun clearly, unmistakably, refers. Verbs, adjectives, and adverbs—as well as phrases functioning as verbs, adjectives, or adverbs, and dependent clauses functioning as adjectives or adverbs—cannot serve as antecedents.

12A PRONOUNS AND EXPLICIT ANTECEDENTS

Make sure that every pronoun has an explicit antecedent. A sentence in which a pronoun lacks a clear and explicit antecedent suffers from an error in pronoun reference.

Faulty: Breathe in through your nose, hold it for a few seconds, then breathe out through your mouth.
(Debbie Cafazzo, "Ten Steps Toward Tranquility," *Tacoma [WA] News Tribune*, 20 Jan. 2004, p. D1)

> The writer obviously wants *it* to mean *your breath*, but the noun *breath* does not appear earlier (or anywhere else) in the sentence. The verb *breathe* cannot serve as the antecedent of *it*. The only noun to which *it* could conceivably refer is *nose*, but the writer certainly does not want the reader to hold her nose for a few seconds.

Correct: Breathe in through your nose, hold your breath for a few seconds, then breathe out through your mouth.

Faulty: Times have changed, and you'd probably be foolish to hitchhike and even more foolish to pick up one, but for decades hitchhiking was how college students and members of the armed services got around.
(Dale McFeatters, "I Got Around," *Pittsburgh Post-Gazette*, 4 Dec. 2003, p. B2)

The antecedent of *one* is submerged, and only implied, in the infinitive *to hitchhike*, which is functioning adverbially.

Correct: Times have changed, and you'd probably be foolish to hitch a ride and even more foolish to pick up a hitchhiker, but for decades college students and members of the armed services got around by thumbing their way.

12B AVOIDING AMBIGUOUS ANTECEDENTS

Make sure that the antecedent of a pronoun is not ambiguous. That is, make sure that there is only one noun to which the pronoun refers.

Ambiguous: Marcie told Lianne that she needs to lower her expectations.
    Who needs to lower her expectations—Marcie or Lianne? If it's Marcie, the first two revisions will solve the ambiguity. If it's Lianne, the last two revisions will do the trick.
Clear: Marcie confided in Lianne that she needs to lower her expectations.
Clear: Marcie told Lianne, "I need to lower my expectations."
Clear: Marcie recommended that Lianne lower her expectations.
Clear: Marcie told Lianne, "You need to lower your expectations."

Here's another example.

Ambiguous: Joey e-mailed Matt every day while he was on his honeymoon.
    Who was on the honeymoon—Joey or Matt?
Clear: While Joey was on his honeymoon, he e-mailed Matt every day.
Clear: While Matt was on his honeymoon, Joey e-mailed him every day.

12C AVOIDING VAGUE ANTECEDENTS

Avoid using the pronouns *they* and *it* with unspecified, indefinite antecedents.

Faulty: Here at work they expect us to show initiative.
Correct: Here at work the managers expect us to show initiative.
Correct: Here at work we're expected to show initiative.

Faulty: In the owner's manual it emphasizes that you should have the oil changed every three thousand miles.
Correct: The owner's manual emphasizes that you should have the oil changed every three thousand miles.

12D AVOIDING REMOTE ANTECEDENTS

Make sure that the antecedent of a pronoun appears in the same sentence as the pronoun or in the sentence immediately preceding the pronoun. In the following three-sentence excerpt, the pronoun *they*, serving as the subject of the third sentence, is remote from its antecedent (*mussels*), which appears in the first sentence.

Faulty: Nicknamed "the poor man's oyster," mussels are bite-sized, and come in their own single-serving "dish." The flesh is meaty and a little sweet. They do not taste like chicken.
    (Marlene Parrish, "Mussels: This Fast-Food Mollusk Flexes Its Dietary Muscle—And It's Yummy to Boot," *Pittsburgh Post-Gazette*, 8 Jan.1998, p. D1)
Correct: Mussels do not taste like chicken.
Correct: It does not taste like chicken.
    The singular pronoun *it* has *flesh* as its antecedent.

12E AVOIDING IDENTICAL PRONOUNS WITH DIFFERENT ANTECEDENTS

Confusion often arises when two or more pronouns in a sequence are identical in point of view and in number but do not share the same antecedent. If, for instance, two or more third-person-plural pronouns appear in a row, make sure that their antecedent is the same plural noun. In the following passage, the plural pronoun *them* has *hallways* as its antecedent, but the two *they*s have *people*, not *hallways*, as their antecedent.

Confusing: So people line the hallways, two and three deep, making them auxiliary waiting rooms. They slouch in corners. They slump on the floor.

(Barbara White Stack, "The Empty Bench—A Child Waits," *Pittsburgh Post-Gazette*, 16 Feb. 1998, p. A8)

Clear: So people line the hallways, two and three deep, making them auxiliary waiting rooms. Children and their parents slouch in corners. They slump on the floor.

TIP: Sometimes a writer deliberately withholds the antecedent of a pronoun to create suspense or arouse curiosity, as in the following paragraph.

- They are often more popular than presidents. They earn more in a year than many seasoned CEOs earn in a decade. Their breakups and breakdowns are beamed onto every television screen. Even so, pop stars often have a very short shelf life.

12F AVOIDING THE CASUAL *THIS* AND *THESE*

In formal and semiformal writing, avoid the loose, antecedentless use of the demonstrative adjectival pronouns *this* and *these*. Substitute the indefinite article *a* or *an* for *this;* substitute the indefinite pronoun *some* for *these*.

Faulty: I saw this really great movie last night.
Correct: I saw a really great movie last night.

Faulty: I have this friend who works as a bouncer.
Correct: I have a friend who works as a bouncer.

Faulty: We saw these strange people at the mall.
Correct: We saw some strange people at the mall.

12G AVOIDING *THIS, THAT,* AND *IT* AS ANTECEDENTLESS SUBJECTS

Avoid beginning a clause or a sentence with the demonstrative pronoun *this*, the demonstrative pronoun *that*, or the pronoun *it* as the subject—unless the antecedent of the pronoun (in the previous clause or sentence) will be instantly clear to the reader. If the antecedent is not both explicit and unmistakable, the reader will have to strain in order to discern what *that, this,* or *it* refers *to*, and the reader's time will have been wasted.

Antecedentless *this*

The easiest way to correct the pronoun-reference error in a sentence whose subject is an antecedentless *this* is (a) to transform the demonstrative pronoun *this* into the demonstrative adjective *this* and (b) to insert, following the adjectival *this*, a noun or a noun phrase that explicitly identifies what was only implied as the antecedent of the demonstrative pronoun *this*.

Faulty: The company's employees are expected to enroll in two all-day business-writing seminars next month. This has provoked considerable resentment.

What has provoked considerable resentment? *This* lacks an explicit antecedent. Remember that an antecedent must be a noun, a noun phrase, or a noun clause—and the antecedent must agree in number with the pronoun that refers to it. A singular pronoun, such as *this*, needs a singular antecedent. If the writer intended *seminars* to serve as the antecedent, the beginning of the second sentence would have to be rephrased as *these have*. More likely, though, the writer had in mind as the antecedent of *this* the entire idea expressed in the first sentence. An independent clause, however, cannot serve as the antecedent of a pronoun—except in a couple of special cases that will be discussed later in this chapter.

Correct: The company's employees are expected to enroll in two all-day business-writing seminars next month. This requirement has provoked considerable resentment.

Sometimes the demonstrative pronoun *this* is ambiguous.

Faulty: The employees learned last week that they are expected to enroll in an all-day business-writing seminar next month. This has provoked considerable resentment.

In the second sentence, the demonstrative pronoun *this* could have as its antecedent either the noun *seminar* or the nominative dependent clause *that they are expected to enroll in an all-day business-writing seminar next month*. If the former interpretation is the desired one, expand the subject of the second sentence into *this class* (or *this seminar*). If the latter interpretation is the desired one, expand the subject into *this requirement* or a phrase equivalent in meaning.

Correct: The employees learned last week that they are expected to enroll in an all-day business-writing seminar next month. This class has provoked considerable resentment.

Correct: The employees learned last week that they are expected to enroll in an all-day business-writing seminar next month. This requirement has provoked considerable resentment.

Faulty: The mission of Citibank and of all Citigroup affiliates is to help you meet your personal financial goals by providing you with the right products and services at the right time. To accomplish this—and to help us anticipate your needs—the bank may share information about you with other Citigroup affiliates on a confidential basis. This allows us to understand your financial needs better.
(Citibank mailing, *Privacy Promise for Consumers*, M0999, p. 3)

The antecedent of *this* in sentence two, in which *this* is functioning as the object of an infinitive, is explicit and unambiguous (the antecedent is the infinitive phrase *to help you meet your personal financial goals by providing you with the right products and services at the right time*); but the pronoun *this* functioning as the subject of the third sentence lacks an explicit antecedent. What exactly is it that *allows us to understand your financial needs better*?

Correct: This exchange of information enables us to understand your financial needs better.

Faulty: Eleven of the 34 remains had shattered or missing skulls and chopped skeletons. This may have been done right after death, "to render protection from mysterious spells believed to emanate from the deceased," Dr. Fedorova said in a report. . . .
(Charles Q. Choi, "At Trading Crossroads, Permafrost Yields Siberian Secrets," *New York Times*, 6 Jan. 2004, p. D3)

Correct: This mangling and mutilation may have been done right after death. . . .

Correct: The bodies may have been mangled and mutilated right after death. . . .

Faulty: Sullivan's variety shows have too often been hacked up for highlight presentations from Sofa. By presenting the entire telecasts of shows with the Beatles, this provides important context, showing where the Fab Four stood among the day's entertainers.
(R. D. Heldenfels, "TV Shows on DVD Are No Longer Just for Cultists," *Pittsburgh Post-Gazette*, 2 Jan. 2004, p. W29)

Instead of inserting a clarifying noun after *this* in the independent clause of the second sentence, you can streamline the sentence by eliminating the preposition *by*, allowing the gerund phrase *presenting the entire telecasts of shows with the Beatles* to serve as the subject, and deleting the comma following *Beatles*.

Correct: Presenting the entire telecasts of shows with the Beatles provides important context, showing where the Fab Four stood among the day's entertainers.

Antecedentless *that*

Clauses or sentences beginning with an antecedentless *that* can be revised (a) by converting the pronoun *that* into the pronominal adjective *that* and inserting a noun or a noun phrase after *that,* (b) by replacing *that* with a noun or a noun phrase, or (c) by recasting the sentence or its predecessor so that the pronoun *that* will have an explicit antecedent.

> **Faulty:** The General Accounting Office warned in 2002 that the nation's food supply was quite vulnerable to mad-cow disease, given that bans on feeding infected mad-cow tissue to other animals was [sic] not being enforced by the Food and Drug Administration. That does not inspire confidence.
> (Phillip Morris, "Cow Consumers Have a Right to Get Mad, Too," *Cleveland Plain Dealer,* 6 Jan. 2004, p. B9)
> **Correct:** That admission does not inspire confidence.

TIP: Many editors would accept the use of *that* or *this* as a subject whose implicit antecedent is the entire sentence preceding the sentence that begins with *that* or *this*—but only if (a) the preceding sentence is a very short simple sentence (remember that a simple sentence is a sentence consisting of only one independent clause and no dependent clauses) and (b) the preceding sentence does not include any noun or noun phrase that might be misconstrued as the antecedent of the pronoun *that* or *this.*

> **Faulty:** Flu season is here. That means it's time for a flu shot.
> (Highmark Blue Cross Blue Shield, "Flu Shot Time Again!," *Looking Healthward,* fall 1999, p. 1)
> The implied antecedent of *that* is the entirety of the previous sentence— a sentence brief enough to serve as an antecedent. (Few readers would fail to grasp the antecedent of *that.*) Nevertheless, the pronoun *that* could be edited out of the second sentence.
> **Correct:** Flu season is here. So it's time for your flu shot.
> **Correct:** Flu season is here—time for your flu shot.

> **Faulty:** If she has shapely legs, she should wear skirts and pants with funky patterns. That, too, will draw the eye away from the bustline.
> (Diane D., "Dear Abby," Cleveland Plain Dealer, 12 Feb. 2004, p. F8)
> Instead of searching for a noun to insert after the demonstrative pronoun at the start of the second sentence, you might find it easier to rewrite the first sentence so that the pronoun will have an explicit antecedent.
> **Correct:** If she has shapely legs, she should consider wearing skirts and pants with funky patterns. That, too, will draw the eye away from the bustline.
> The gerund phrase *wearing skirts and pants with funky patterns* functions as a noun—and thus can serve as the antecedent of *that.*
> **Correct:** If she has shapely legs, she should wear skirts and pants with funky patterns. Those, too, will draw the eye away from the bustline.
> *Those,* the demonstrative pronoun at the start of the second sentence, is plural and has *skirts and pants* as its compound antecedent.

> **Faulty:** Storms, traffic accidents, and other unforeseen problems can disrupt your electric service at any time. If that happens, it helps to be prepared.
> (Allegheny Power, *Allegheny Customer,* vol. 5, 1999, p. 2)
> The entire adverbial dependent clause of the second sentence is disposable.
> **Correct:** Storms, traffic accidents, and other unforeseen problems can disrupt your electric service at any time. It helps to be prepared.

Antecedentless *it*

Whenever the pronoun *it* serves as the subject of a clause or a sentence, *it* must have an explicit, unmistakable antecedent.

- Be sure to memorize your employee-identification number. It needs to be included on many forms you will be submitting each week.

When the pronoun *it* lacks an explicit antecedent, replace *it* with a noun or a noun phrase that explicitly names what *it* was only implicitly referring to, or recast the sentence entirely.

> **Faulty:** Drafts of documents for which you are soliciting comments should be triple-spaced throughout. It makes editing easier.
>
> (Kenneth Roman and Joel Raphaelson, *Writing That Works* [New York: HarperPaperbacks, 1992], p. 134)
>
> **Correct:** Drafts of documents for which you are soliciting comments should be triple-spaced throughout. The extra space between lines makes editing easier.
>
> **Correct:** Drafts of documents for which you are soliciting comments should be triple-spaced throughout to make editing easier.

> **Faulty:** In his 60s, Harold works out with light weights, uses the treadmill and stationary bike and participates in aerobics. It gets him up and out of the house, and, says Harold, "this fitness class allows me to maintain my quality of life."
>
> (*Living Proof: Your Gift Makes a Difference*, United Way of Southwestern Pennsylvania brochure, C-2, 1999)
>
> **Correct:** The routine gets him up and out of the house. . . .

12H AVOIDING *THIS, THAT,* AND *IT* AS ANTECEDENTLESS OBJECTS

This, that, and *it* cause trouble not only when they appear without antecedents at the beginning of sentences and clauses, but also when they are forced to serve without antecedents as the objects of prepositions, of transitive verbs, and of verbals (participles, gerunds, and infinitives). In the following examples, the antecedentless pronouns have been italicized and are functioning as direct objects.

> **Faulty:** His [Peter Biskind's] new book is an even bouncier ride. It's thick with typos, longueurs and woefully misplaced commas; it feels as if it were written at great speed and edited at even greater speed. But Mr. Biskind's voice is so amiable and incisive that you shrug this off and hang on for the briskly guided tour.
>
> (Dwight Garner, "The Cowboys Who Took On the Indies," *New York Times*, 14 Jan. 2004, p. B1)
>
> **Correct:** But Mr. Biskind's voice is so amiable and incisive that you shrug off this slapdashery and hang on for the briskly guided tour.
>
> *This* has been converted to a pronominal adjective, followed by a clarifying noun.

> **Faulty:** Minute Maid Heart Wise Orange Juice contains plant sterols, a natural component of plants professed to have cholesterol-lowering properties. Sterols do that by blocking the absorption of cholesterol in the small intestine.
>
> (Bonnie Tandy Leblang and Carolyn Wyman, "Minute Maid Juices Up on Sterols for the Heart," *Pittsburgh Post-Gazette*, 29 Jan. 2004, p. B5)
>
> **Correct:** Minute Maid Heart Wise Orange Juice contains plant sterols, a natural component of plants professed to have cholesterol-lowering properties. Sterols block the absorption of cholesterol in the small intestine.

12I AVOIDING THE EXPLETIVE *IT* IN PROXIMITY TO THE PRONOUN *IT*

Avoid writing sentences in which the expletive *it* appears within the vicinity of the pronoun *it*. The expletive *it* is not a pronoun: It has no antecedent and instead serves merely as a structural support in a sentence. (The expletive *it* appears in sentences such as *It is raining* and *It is difficult to find a parking space.*) In the sentence *Buying automobile insurance is no different from making any other purchase; it pays to compare,* the *it* appearing at the start of the second independent clause does not refer to anything: It is not a pronoun. (The second clause could be rephrased as *comparing prices pays off.*) But whenever *it* is serving as a pronoun, as in the independent clause of the sentence you are now reading, it must have an explicit antecedent.

A sentence including both the expletive *it* and one or more uses of the pronominal *it* can easily confuse or distract the reader.

Confusing: The new sitcom in the 8:30 time slot on Thursday nights is a dud. It is neither well written nor capably acted, and it is hard to imagine how network executives thought that it would appeal to young viewers.

> In the second sentence, *it* appears first as a pronoun (whose antecedent is *sitcom*), then as an expletive (in *it is hard to imagine*), and finally as a pronoun again (with the antecedent *sitcom*). By the time readers reach the second *it* of the sentence, they are likely to think *it* is another stand-in for the antecedent *sitcom*, but a few words later, they will experience a mild but unnecessary (and preventable) jolt.

Clear: The series is neither well written nor capably acted, and it is hard to imagine how network executives thought that such an uninspired program would appeal to young viewers.

Clear: It is neither well written nor capably acted, and one wonders how network executives could have thought that it would appeal to young viewers.

Confusing: When Madonna, for example, got buff in training for an album tour or when Angela Bassett muscled up to play Tina Turner in "What's Love Got to Do with It?," it was worth wondering how they did it.

(Lisa Lytle Liddane, "As Sold by the Stars!," for *Orange County Register*, in *Pittsburgh Post-Gazette*, 12 Oct. 1999, p. G2)

Clear: When Madonna, for example, got buff in training for an album tour or when Angela Bassett muscled up to play Tina Turner in What's Love Got to Do with It?, it was worth wondering how they achieved such results.

TIP: Avoid two uses of the expletive *it* in one sentence.

> **Confusing:** Dusk approached, and as it grew colder it occurred to us that we could possibly die.
>
> (David Sedaris, "Let It Snow," *New Yorker*, 22–29 Dec. 2003, p. 84)
>
> **Clear:** Dusk approached, and as we got colder it occurred to us that we could possibly die.

The Use of the Pronoun *it* More Than Once in a Single Sentence

Avoid writing a sentence in which the pronoun *it* is used more than once and has a different antecedent (either explicit or, even worse, only implicit) each time it appears. Do not force your readers to play a game of Find the Antecedent.

Confusing: Terrorism is a difficult subject to discuss with young children. When children are introduced to it, it must be in an unthreatening, reassuring manner.

> The first *it* in the second sentence clearly has *terrorism* as its antecedent, but the second *it* not only does not refer to *terrorism* but lacks any explicit antecedent.

Clear: Terrorism is a difficult subject to discuss with young children. They should be introduced to it in an unthreatening, reassuring manner.

Confusing: While technology is changing the nature of second-home ownership, it is not entirely transforming it.

(Marek Fuchs, "Forget a Key Under the Mat; The E-Caretaker Is Watching," *New York Times*, 9 Jan. 2004, p. D5)

Clear: Technology is changing the nature of second-home ownership but not entirely transforming it.

12J AVOIDING OBJECTS OF PREPOSITIONS AS ANTECEDENTS

Make sure that the noun or noun equivalent serving as the antecedent of a pronoun is functioning as a major structural element in the sentence. The antecedent should ideally be functioning as the subject of a clause, as the object of a transitive verb or verbal, or as the complement of a linking verb. Objects of prepositions do not make strong antecedents.

Faulty: Suddenly, the very passage of time—the nearly three years that have passed since 9/11—has become a fact to be wondered at, factored in, as we finally confront the question of how long our immunity from a repetition will last, as well as whether it can be prevented, and how things will change if it does happen.

(Ron Rosenbaum, "Did 'Threat Fatigue' Lull Us into Denial of Another 9/11?," *New York Observer* online, 26 July 2004, paragraph 1)

The first *it* (in the nominative dependent clause *whether it can be prevented*) is intended to have *repetition* as its antecedent, but *repetition* occupies a grammatically insignificant position: It's tucked away in a prepositional phrase in the nominative dependent clause *how long our immunity from a repetition will last*, whose subject, *immunity*, is much more eligible to serve as an antecedent.

Correct: ... as we finally confront the question of how long our immunity from a repetition will last, as well as whether another attack can be prevented, and how things will change if it does happen.

TIP: A pronoun cannot have as its antecedent a noun understood in a sense different from the sense in which the noun is used in the sentence.

Faulty: Some of it [the program], like the reflections on the early days of CNN—which used to stand, we're told, for Chicken Noodle Soup in some quarters—are [sic] plain wonderful.

(Dorothy Rabinowitz, "The War to Win the Vote," *Wall Street Journal*, 13 Feb. 2004, p. W1)

The antecedent of *which* is meant to be *CNN* understood as merely a combination of letters—but that is not the way *CNN* is used, and understood, in the sentence. *CNN* appears in the sentence as simply the name of a network; the sentence is not calling attention to the form of the name, the letters of which it is composed.

Correct: Some of it [the program], like the reflections on the early days of CNN—the call letters of which used to stand, we're told, for Chicken Noodle Soup in some quarters— is plain wonderful.

12K AVOIDING ADJECTIVES AS ANTECEDENTS

Do not write a sentence in which an adjective or an adjectival phrase is forced into serving as the antecedent of a pronoun. The antecedent of a pronoun must be a noun or the equivalent of a noun (such as a noun phrase or a nominative dependent clause).

Faulty: On Lou Reed's album *The Blue Mask*, he pays tribute to his mentor, the poet Delmore Schwartz.
The pronoun *he* has no explicit antecedent. *He* is obviously intended to refer to Lou Reed, but the name Lou Reed does not appear as a noun in the sentence; the name has been converted to the possessive form, *Lou Reed's*, which functions as an adjective.

Correct: On the album *The Blue Mask*, Lou Reed pays tribute to his mentor, the poet Delmore Schwartz.
A possessive pronoun may of course have a noun as its antecedent, as in *Lou Reed pays tribute to his mentor*; and a possessive pronoun may have a possessive noun as its antecedent, as in *Lou Reed's tribute to his mentor Delmore Schwartz is one of the high points of the album.*

Faulty: The Beanie Babies business is flourishing because many a child is crazy about them.
In this sentence, *Beanie Babies* is functioning adjectivally and thus cannot serve as the antecedent of *them*.

Correct: Selling Beanie Babies is a flourishing business because many a child is crazy about them.
Beanie Babies is now functioning as a noun—it's the object of the gerund *selling*—and therefore is unmistakably the antecedent of *them*.

Faulty: This is a very churchy place. There are 22 of them here, one for about every 300 residents, serving this southern New Mexico town about halfway between Albuquerque and the Mexican border.

(Gwen Florio, "Battle over the Bible Splits a N.M. Community," *Philadelphia Inquirer*, 28 Feb. 1998, p. A1)

Correct: This is a very churchy place. There are 22 churches here, one for about every 300 residents. ...
Correct: This is a very churchy place. There are 22 houses of worship here, one for about every 300 residents. ...
Correct: This is a very religious place. There are 22 churches here, one for about every 300 residents. ...

Faulty: But now, the administration's enforcement efforts are in disarray and it is expected to abandon 70 cases against adult homes after two judges determined that health inspectors had violated state law and regulations governing how they document their visits to the homes.

(Clifford J. Levy, "New York Suffers a Setback in Its Crackdown on Adult Homes for the Mentally Ill," *New York Times*, 14 Jan. 2004, p. A20)

Correct: But now, with its enforcement efforts in disarray, the administration is expected to abandon 70 cases against adult homes after two judges determined that health inspectors had violated state law and regulations governing how they document their visits to the homes.

12L ANTECEDENTS AND THE RELATIVE PRONOUN *WHICH*

Be careful with an adjectival dependent clause in which the subject is the relative pronoun *which*. Readers will expect the antecedent of *which* to be the noun or noun equivalent immediately preceding *which*. Remember that an adjectival dependent clause functions like an adjective: it modifies (describes or limits the meaning of) a noun. Therefore, the adjectival clause should directly follow the noun it is intended to modify. In the sentence *She wants to buy the new Belle and Sebastian album, which will go on sale tomorrow,* the noun *album* is clearly the antecedent of *which* (and *which* is the subject of the adjectival dependent clause *which will go on sale tomorrow*).

Pronoun-reference errors arise (a) when the noun immediately preceding *which* is not the antecedent of *which* or (b) when *which* lacks an explicit antecedent. Both of these conditions may exist in a single sentence.

> **Faulty:** She was twenty minutes late in arriving for the meeting, which annoyed the boss.
>
> *Meeting* appears to be the antecedent of *which*, because *meeting* is the noun immediately preceding the adjectival dependent clause. But it was the employee's late arrival, and not the meeting, that annoyed the boss.
>
> **Correct:** The boss was annoyed when she arrived twenty minutes late for the meeting.
> **Correct:** The boss was annoyed because she arrived twenty minutes late for the meeting.
> **Correct:** She annoyed the boss by arriving twenty minutes late for the meeting.
> **Correct:** Arriving twenty minutes late for the meeting, she annoyed the boss.
> **Correct:** Her arrival twenty minutes late annoyed the boss.

Sometimes a sentence includes no noun to which the relative pronoun *which* could refer even mistakenly. In the sentence *She once again arrived twenty minutes late, which annoyed the boss,* no noun in the independent clause could possibly be regarded as the antecedent of *which*. *Which*, in other words, lacks an explicit antecedent in the form of a noun or a noun equivalent (such as a noun phrase or a noun clause). But won't the reader obviously infer that the entire independent clause of the sentence (*she once again arrived twenty minutes late*) is in fact functioning as the implicit antecedent? Some editors would say yes—and would insist that the sentence does not need to be revised. (Their argument would be that there is no possibility of misreading the sentence, especially since the independent clause is very brief.)

Other editors, however, would consider the sentence unacceptable and would insist upon a revision such as *She annoyed the boss by once again arriving twenty minutes late* (a revision that edits the pronoun *which*—and the adjectival dependent clause—out of the sentence) or *She once again arrived twenty minutes late, annoying the boss* (a revision that substitutes the participial phrase *annoying the boss* for the adjectival dependent clause *which annoyed the boss*).

In short, some editors insist that *which* can never be used without an explicit antecedent. Other editors will accept a sentence in which the relative pronoun *which* lacks an explicit antecedent—provided that (a) the independent clause of the sentence is brief, (b) the reader will recognize the independent clause in its entirety as the implicit antecedent of *which,* and (c) the independent clause does not include any noun or noun equivalent that an unalert reader might mistakenly regard as the antecedent of *which.*

Faulty: Fashion loves a paradox, which may explain why some designers are turning to glass in all its fragile glory to give shoes a boost this season.

This sentence meets only the first two of the three criteria: a reader might initially think that *paradox,* and not the independent clause, is the antecedent of *which.*

(Richard Dorment, "Glass Slippers," *Interview*, Mar. 2004, p. 124)

Correct: Fashion loves a paradox. How else to explain why some designers are turning to glass in all its fragile glory to give shoes a boost this season?

Faulty: Few of them [movies about older women in relationships with younger men] make for reassuring viewing, which may be more a reflection of long-standing taboos than reality: Demi Moore and Ashton Kutcher, take heart.

(Graham Fuller, "Shots in the Dark," *Interview*, July 2004, p. 44)

The writer wants the entirety of the independent clause of the sentence to serve as the antecedent of *which,* but some readers will initially think that *viewing*—the gerund preceding the pronoun—is the antecedent. A quick fix is to reduce the independent clause to a noun clause, then eliminate the comma and the pronoun.

Correct: That few of them make for reassuring viewing may be more a reflection of long-standing taboos than of reality.

Faulty: He'd moved to the States from Ireland two years ago because of his father's finance job and had no real roots here, which often came in handy, especially during times like these.

(David Amsden, "The Siege of Fulton Avenue," *New York*, 14 June 2004, p. 100)

Correct: He had moved here from Ireland two years ago because of his father's finance job, and the fact that he had no real roots in the States often came in handy, especially during times like these.

Correct: He had moved here from Ireland two years ago because of his father's finance job, and his not having real roots in the States often came in handy, especially during times like these.

Correct: He had moved to the States from Ireland two years ago because of his father's finance job, and his rootlessness often came in handy, especially during times like these.

CHAPTER 13

FAULTY COMPARISONS

A comparison is logical when the two things being compared belong to the same class or category. One might compare one movie with another, one concert with another, one city with another. But writers often lose sight of what they are comparing with what, and they end up composing illogical, nonsensical sentences that attempt to compare unlike, noncomparable things. Such comparisons are called faulty comparisons.

13A APPLES-AND-ORANGES COMPARISONS

Faulty: Too many discrete songs, one after the other, is like reading a joke book or eating candies. They don't make an album, or a novel, or a meal.

(John Rockwell, "Beyond Singles and Concept Albums, Pop Yearns for a Long Form," *New York Times*, 2 Jan. 2004, p. B3)

The sentence is illogically comparing songs (things) with reading and eating (processes).

Correct: Listening to too many discrete songs, one after the other, is like reading a joke book or eating candies.

Faulty: According to readership surveys, the average annual income of *[Wall Street] Journal* readers is about two hundred thousand dollars—about twice that of the *[New York] Times*.

(Ken Auletta, "Family Business," *New Yorker*, 3 Nov. 2003, p. 55)

The writer is comparing the average annual income of readers with the average annual income of a newspaper.

Correct: According to readership surveys, the average annual income of *Journal* readers is about two hundred thousand dollars—about twice that of *Times* readers.

Faulty: Compared with old-style Japanese stores, which have a mishmash of merchandise crowding the shelves, the towering aisles here are filled with rows and rows of similar products—soda, sneakers, frying pans.

("Japanese Wowed by Their First Superstore," for Associated Press, in *New York Daily News*, 25 Apr. 2004, p. 38)

The sentence is comparing stores with aisles.

Correct: Compared with old-style Japanese stores, which have a mishmash of merchandise crowding the shelves, Seiyu has towering aisles filled with rows and rows of similar products—soda, sneakers, frying pans.

Faulty: Selling at an airport is different from a traditional mall.

<small>(Teresa F. Lindeman, "Storm Clouds Lifting," *Pittsburgh Post-Gazette*, 14 Apr. 2002, p. C2)</small>

The sentence is illogically comparing selling (an activity) with a mall (a place).

Correct: Selling at an airport is different from selling at a traditional mall.

Faulty: It is not a total surprise to learn that if California were a nation, it would boast the seventh-largest economy in the world, larger than China and just a bit behind Italy.

<small>(David S. Broder, "Where the Engines Are," *Washington Post*, 29 Mar. 1998, p. C7)</small>

The sentence incorrectly compares an economy with two countries.

Correct: It is not a total surprise to learn that if California were a nation, it would boast the seventh-largest economy in the world, larger than China's and just a bit behind Italy's.

Faulty: Compared with the end of 1999, which was still a good time for programmers, December 2003 data show a 14 percent increase in business and financial occupations, a 6 percent increase in computer and mathematical jobs, and a 2 percent drop in architecture and engineering jobs.

<small>(Virginia Postrel, "A Researcher Sees an Upside in the Outsourcing of Programming Jobs," *New York Times*, 29 Jan. 2004, p. C2)</small>

The writer is comparing a period of time with data.

Correct: Compared with data for the end of 1999, which was still a good time for programmers, December 2003 data show a 14 percent increase in business and financial occupations, a 6 percent increase in computer and mathematical jobs, and a 2 percent drop in architecture and engineering jobs.

Some apples-and-oranges comparisons violate the patterns *A's X is better than B's X* and *A's X is better than that of B.*

Faulty: Taco Bell's current advertising campaign is more innovative than Burger King.

The sentence is illogically comparing an advertising campaign with a fast-food chain.

Correct: Taco Bell's current advertising campaign is more innovative than Burger King's advertising campaign.

Better (More Concise): Taco Bell's current advertising campaign is more innovative than that of Burger King.

The antecedent of the pronoun *that* is *campaign.*

Better (More Concise): Taco Bell's current advertising campaign is more innovative than Burger King's.

The words *current advertising campaign* are implied after the possessive noun *Burger King's;* the construction is elliptical.

Faulty: The company developed a reputation for customer loyalty that rivaled higher-priced brands.

<small>(Scott Reeves, "Changes at Saturn Mark End of 'Different Kind of Company,'" for Associated Press, in *Pittsburgh Post-Gazette*, 30 Jan. 2004, p. B22)</small>

The writer is comparing a reputation with brands.

Correct: The company developed a reputation for customer loyalty that rivaled that of higher-priced brands.

Faulty: Three years ago, the unemployment rate in Santa Clara County dipped to 1.3 percent, far lower than the rest of the country.

<small>(Andrew Maykuth, "Google the Engine in an Industry That Could," *Philadelphia Inquirer*, 4 Jan. 2004, p. A14)</small>

Correct: Three years ago, the unemployment rate in Santa Clara County dipped to 1.3 percent, far lower than that in the rest of the country.

CAUTION

Do not succumb to the redundant comparative pattern of *A's X is better than that of B's.*

Faulty: Harold Bloom's demons are no more demonic than those of any other complex human being's.

<small>(Naomi Wolf, "The Silent Treatment," *New York*, 1 Mar. 2004, p. 29)</small>

Correct: Harold Bloom's demons are no more demonic than those of any other complex human being.

Correct: Harold Bloom's demons are no more demonic than any other complex human being's.

13B OMISSION OF THE SECOND *AS* FROM *AS* + MODIFIER + *AS* ELEMENTS

Beware of incomplete comparisons resulting from the faulty use of the *as* + **modifier** + *as* … [*or*/*if not*] **comparative modifier** + *than* pattern. Do not omit the second *as* from the *as* + **modifier** + *as* element.

> **Faulty:** Her new movie is as good or better than her previous one.
> **Correct:** Her new movie is as good as or better than her previous one.

Writers sometimes use commas to set off the phrase *or better than* (and similar phrases): *Her new movie is as good as, or better than, her previous one.*

Corrective additions to the following sentences have been boldfaced and bracketed.

- His [Stephen Glass's] stories had to be beyond belief so that his name would become known and admired, so he would be as big [**as**] or bigger than the nobodies he wrote about.
  (Marc Fisher, "The Strange Life of Stephen Glass," *Pittsburgh Post-Gazette*, 12 Nov. 2003, p. A21)

- It's true other regions have suffered as much [**as,**] if not more than[**,**] Pittsburgh during the recession and what some are calling the "job-loss" recovery.
  (Don Hammonds, "What Becomes an Image Most?," *Pittsburgh Post-Gazette*, 28 Dec. 2003, p. C3)

- He's playing with undiminished verve as the leader of a medium-sized big band, and he's singing Porter and Razaf as well [**as**] or better than anyone [**else**].
  ("Bobby Short," *Village Voice*, 17–23 Dec. 2003, p. 117)

  For the reason why the adjective *else* needs to be added to the sentence, see the final section of this chapter.

Sometimes the most concise revision involves rephrasing the sentence to eliminate the *as* + **adjective** + *as* … [*or*/*if not*] **comparative** + *than* pattern.

> **Faulty:** Because some [Pokémon] character cards are scarcer than others, they have been ascribed monetary value in trading and collectible stores, where they're in as much, if not more, demand than sports trading cards.
> (Cindi Lash, "In the Grip of Poké-Mania," *Pittsburgh Post-Gazette* online, 3 Oct. 1999, paragraph 18)
>
> The adjectival dependent clause at the end of the sentence botches the *as much as … if not more than* pattern.
> **Correct:** Because some character cards are scarcer than others, they have been ascribed monetary value in trading and collectible stores, where they're in as much demand as, if not in more demand than, sports trading cards.
>
> **Better (More Concise):** Because some character cards are scarcer than others, they have been ascribed monetary value in trading and collectible stores, where the Pokémon cards are selling as well as sports trading cards—and sometimes even outselling them.
>
> **Better (More Concise):** Because some character cards are scarcer than others, they have been ascribed monetary value in trading and collectible stores, where the Pokémon cards are selling as well as sports trading cards—and sometimes even better.

13C FAULTY COMPARISONS BEGINNING WITH *LIKE* OR *UNLIKE*

Be careful with any sentence that includes a prepositional phrase beginning with *like* or *unlike:* Make sure that the prepositional phrase is followed by a nounal or pronominal subject that belongs to the same category or class of things as the noun or pronoun serving as the object of the preposition in the prepositional phrase. In the following two-sentence paragraph, the writer correctly manages the comparison in the first sentence but botches the comparison in the second.

Faulty: Like computers, cellular phones have become an almost indispensable part of our lives. And like anything else we rely on—food, air, water, microwave ovens—the warnings about possible hazards have begun to crop up.

(Monica L. Haynes, "Cell Phones Stand Accused of Equipment Interference and Even Gas-Pump Blasts," *Pittsburgh Post-Gazette* online, 3 Nov. 1999, paragraph 6)

> In the first sentence, *computers* are compared, logically, with *cellular phones*—but in the second sentence, *anything else we rely on* is compared, illogically, with *warnings about possible hazards.*

Correct: And like anything else we rely on—food, air, water, microwave ovens—cell phones may pose hazards as well.

Correct: And as with anything else we rely on—food, air, water, microwave ovens—the warnings about possible hazards have begun to crop up.

Faulty: And the morbid truth is that, like James Dean, Jim Morrison and Jimi Hendrix, death has enhanced his [Kurt Cobain's] legend.

(Ernest A. Jasmin, "The Cobain We'll Never See," for *Tacoma [WA] News Tribune*, in *Fresno Bee* online, 4 Apr. 2004, paragraph 5)

> A writer can compare three famous men with another famous man—but not with death.

Correct: And the morbid truth is that, like James Dean, Jim Morrison, and Jimi Hendrix, Kurt Cobain is more legendary in death than he was in life.

Faulty: Like the Velvet Underground, Big Star's influence far outstripped their sales.

("The 500 Greatest Albums of All Time," *Rolling Stone*, 11 Dec. 2003, p. 164)

> A writer can compare one rock group with another, or the influence of one with the influence of another—but not a rock group with an influence.

Correct: Like the Velvet Underground, Big Star was far more influential than its record sales would suggest.

Faulty: Unlike other milestones of indecency—rock star Bono using the f-word at the 2003 Golden Globes, or Madonna and Britney Spears tongue-kissing on MTV—[Janet] Jackson chose to reveal herself before the largest TV audience of the year.

(David Bauder, "TV Hastens to Cover After Jackson Uproar," for Associated Press, in *Pittsburgh Post-Gazette*, 7 Feb. 2004, p. B8)

Correct: Unlike other milestones of indecency—rock star Bono's using the f-word at the 2003 Golden Globes, or Madonna and Britney Spears' tongue-kissing on MTV—Janet Jackson's "wardrobe malfunction" was witnessed by the largest TV audience of the year.

Faulty: Unlike the Bravo show, in which five gay men help a hapless straight man find his inner metrosexual, these advisers help gay men rediscover their outer alpha male.

(Alessandra Stanley, "Acting Straight for a Day, or How I Learned to Belch," *New York Times*, 23 Feb. 2004, p. B3)

Correct: Unlike the Bravo show's five gay men, who help a hapless straight man find his inner metrosexual, these advisers help gay men rediscover their outer alpha male.

Sometimes the quickest, easiest fix is to replace *like* with a phrasal preposition such as *as with, as in,* or *as at.*

- Like [**As with**] "Queer Eye [for the Straight Guy]," it is possible to watch more than one episode of "Straight Plan [for the Gay Man]" and still be amused.

  (Alessandra Stanley, "Acting Straight for a Day, or How I Learned to Belch," *New York Times*, 23 Feb. 2004, p. B3)

- Russ Kick is the editor of three previous Disinfo anthologies with titles like *You Are Being Lied To* and *Everything You Know Is Wrong.* Like [**As with**] those books, you needn't read 50 *Things [You're Not Supposed to Know]* in any particular order.

  (Mickey Z., "Flipping Out," *New York Press*, 17–23 Dec. 2003, p. 35)

- Like [**As at**] most extended-stay residences, an application is required.

  (Dakota Smith, "Boardinghouse Rules," *New York Post*, 20 Dec. 2003, p. 11R)

13D COMPARISONS LACKING *OTHER* OR *ELSE*

Avoid writing sentences of this sort: *Godiva is better than any gourmet chocolate.* By declaring that Godiva is better than any gourmet chocolate, the sentence is erroneously, illogically, removing Godiva from the category to which it belongs: The category of gourmet chocolate. That is, the sentence is implying that Godiva is not a gourmet chocolate. What the writer intends—but fails—to say is that *Godiva is better than any other gourmet chocolate;* that is, Godiva chocolate is superior to the other chocolates in the category of gourmet chocolate, such as Lindt, Droste, and Ghiradelli.

Here is another way to understand why the original version of the sentence is ungrammatical and illogical: The writer's purpose is to compare one member (Godiva) of a category (gourmet chocolate) with the other members of that category; but without including the word *other* in the sentence, the writer has inadvertently banished Godiva from the category of which it is a member. A sentence such as *Hershey is better than any gourmet chocolate,* however, is grammatically and logically sound (Hershey does not belong to the category of gourmet chocolate, so the word *other* would be out of place in this comparison), though lovers of chocolate would dispute the truthfulness of the statement.

Corrective additions to the following sentences have been boldfaced and bracketed.

- NBC-owned Bravo's "Queer Eye for the Straight Guy" has generated more buzz than any [**other**] show this summer.

  (Ed Bark, "Ratings Are Culling Summer Reality Glut," for *Dallas Morning News,* in *Pittsburgh Post-Gazette,* 2 Sept. 2003, p. C4)

- It's fair enough to give us a character who refuses to view himself or his life accurately, one who lives to embellish himself. Robert Anderson's "I Never Sang for My Father" does that better than any [**other**] work of stage or screen.

  Note: The Anderson work was both a play and a film.

  (Ed Blank, "'Big Fish' Fails to Evoke Sympathy," *Greensburg [PA] Tribune-Review,* 9 Jan. 2004, p. C5)

- I've had more complaints about Loews Waterfront and more personal bad experiences there than at any [**other**] site, past or present.

  (Ed Blank, "Moviegoer Won't Again Darken Door of Poorly Illuminated Loews," *Greensburg [PA] Tribune-Review* online, 15 Feb. 2004, paragraph 8)

- Watch Fox [News Channel] for a few hours and you encounter a conservative presence unlike anything [**else**] on TV.

  (Brian C. Anderson, "Liberal Media, on the Run," in *Pittsburgh Post-Gazette,* 7 Dec. 2003, p. E1)

- More than anyone [**else**], he has fused dancing and skating into a seamless whole, as seen again in the lyrical flow and beautiful contrapuntal patterns of "Sunrise," this show's opening group piece.

  (Anna Kisselgoff, "With Star Turns and Triple Turns, a Sail Through Time," *New York Times,* 6 Mar. 2004, p. A21)

CHAPTER 14

FAULTY PREDICATION

14A MISMATCHED SUBJECTS AND PREDICATES

A sentence is a group of related words consisting of both a subject and a predicate. The predicate, the part of the sentence beginning with a conjugated verb, declares something about the subject. Writers occasionally compose sentences in which the predicate is logically incompatible with the subject. Such a mismatch is called faulty predication. Consider the following example.

> **Faulty:** The governor's remarks at a photo opportunity honoring the heroic firefighters were the first time he has publicly apologized for the disarray in his administration.
>> The subject and the predicate are logically incompatible: *remarks* are not a *time*.
> **Correct:** The governor's remarks at a photo opportunity honoring the heroic firefighters included his first public apology for the disarray in his administration.
>> In this instance, the problem has been resolved by recasting the predicate.

Sometimes it is easier to resolve faulty predication by retaining the predicate as is and recasting the subject.

> **Faulty:** Waiting lists for a subsidized apartment can take months.
> **Correct:** Waiting for a subsidized apartment to become available can take months.

> **Faulty:** Gasoline sniffing is "the most accessible and efficient substance with which to achieve a mild altered state," Brady says.
> (Rohan Sullivan, "Aborigines Struggle to Keep Children, Culture Alive from Gas Sniffing," for Associated Press, in *Philadelphia Inquirer*, 5 Feb. 1998, p. A8)
>> The subject-predicate mismatch is *sniffing is ... the ... substance.*

Correct: Gasoline is "the most accessible and efficient substance with which to achieve a mild altered state," Brady says.

Faulty: At least 104 of the 379 troops killed by hostile fire in Iraq resulted from what the military calls improvised explosive devices, or I.E.D.'s, most of them since President Bush called major combat over on May 1.
(Eric Schmitt, "Despite New G.I. Tactics, Bombs Are Still Biggest Peril," *New York Times*, 5 Mar. 2004, p. A8)

> The subject-predicate mismatch is *at least 104 of the 379 troops ... resulted from what the military calls improvised explosive devices.*

Correct: The deaths of at least 104 of the 379 troops killed by hostile fire in Iraq resulted from what the military calls improvised explosive devices, or I.E.D.'s, and most of those deaths have occurred after President Bush called major combat over on May 1.

Faulty: Idle doodles on the stationery of the Rice Hotel in Houston are possibly the last time JFK put pen to paper.
(Patrice O'Shaughnessy, "Camelot for Sale, Again," *New York Daily News*, 1 Mar. 1998, p. 13)

> The subject-predicate mismatch is *doodles ... are possibly the last time.*

Correct: Idle doodles on the stationery of the Rice Hotel in Houston are possibly the last record of JFK's having put pen to paper.

Correct: Possibly the last time JFK put pen to paper, he doodled idly on the stationery of the Rice Hotel in Houston.

Faulty: Unfortunately, the news that we had all been dreading has come true.
(Leroy Sievers and the *Nightline* staff, "*Nightline* Daily E-Mail," 18 June 2004, paragraph 1)

> The subject-predicate mismatch is *news ... has come true.*

Correct: Unfortunately, the news that we have all been dreading has arrived.

Faulty: Pilgrim's 75 minutes of easy-listening soul searching goes on too long.
(Dan DeLuca, review of Eric Clapton's *Pilgrim*, *Philadelphia Inquirer*, 8 Mar. 1998, p. F12)

> The subject-predicate mismatch is *75 minutes ... goes on too long.*

Correct: Pilgrim's easy-listening soul-searching goes on too long. The album clocks in at seventy-five minutes.

Faulty: Setting the engine idle, once adjusted with the turn of a screw, is now controlled electronically.
(Mike Bucsko, "Mechanics Becoming Obsolete with New Technology," *Pittsburgh Post-Gazette* online, 16 Feb. 1998, paragraph 12)

> The subject-predicate mismatch is *setting ... is now controlled electronically.*

Correct: The engine idle, once adjusted with the turn of a screw, is now controlled electronically.

Faulty: His Arkansas classmates said he had bragged about being in gangs, but even 12-year-olds knew that a white boy in Arkansas bragging about being a member of the Crips or Bloods, big-city street gangs mostly made up of black youths, was far-fetched.
(Rick Bragg, "Jonesboro Dazed by Its Darkest Day," *New York Times*, 18 Apr. 1998, p. A7)

> The subject-predicate mismatch in the nominative dependent clause is *boy ... was far-fetched.*

Correct: ... a white boy in Arkansas bragging about being a member of the Crips or Bloods, big-city street gangs mostly made up of black youths, was not to be believed.

Correct: ... an Arkansas white boy's bragging about being a member of the Crips or Bloods, big-city street gangs mostly made up of black youths, was far-fetched.

Faulty: Dragging their bored, ignored kids along as they go from store to store in search of exquisite clothing or educational toys is hardly the optimal milieu for parent-child interaction.
(Barry Schwartz, "Choice Overload: The New Parenting Problem," for Slate.com, in *Pittsburgh Post-Gazette*, 2 May 2004, p. E2)

> The subject-predicate mismatch is *dragging ... is ... milieu.*

Correct: Dragging their bored, ignored kids along as they go from store to store in search of exquisite clothing or educational toys is hardly the optimal way for parents to spend time with their children.

Faulty predication is often the consequence of the writer's having forgotten what has been set down as the subject of a sentence.

Faulty: But four decades later, the debate about virtually every aspect of those "six seconds in Dallas" remains open to debate and theory, as evidenced by the wide-ranging presentations during the second day of the national symposium on the assassination being held at Duquesne University.

(Michael Fuoco, "40 Years Later, JFK Theories Still Abound," *Pittsburgh Post-Gazette*, 22 Nov. 2003, p. A1)

The sentence is also weakened by the misplaced modifier *being held at Duquesne University;* see chapter 8.

Correct: But four decades later, virtually every aspect of those "six seconds in Dallas" remains open to debate. . . .

CAUTION

The subject of a sentence must be logically compatible not only with the predicate but also with any appositive that follows the subject.

Faulty: Tyler, a city of about 83,000 people some 90 miles east of Dallas, is one of seven police departments using a digital video system from IBM's Global Services division and Coban Research and Technologies Inc., a small private company near Houston.

(Matt Slagle, "Digital Video Cameras in Cruisers Catching On with Police," for Associated Press, in *Pittsburgh Post-Gazette*, 8 July 2004, p. C11)

The trouble with the sentence is that its subject (*Tyler*) is understood in a different sense in relation to the appositive than it is understood in relation to the predicate. The appositive emphasizes Tyler as a city; the predicate emphasizes Tyler as a police department. The two senses are incompatible.

Correct: Tyler, a city of about 83,000 people some 90 miles east of Dallas, has one of seven police departments nationwide using a digital video system.

14B *THE COST … IS EXPENSIVE …*

The noun *cost* is frequently followed by incompatible predicates.

Faulty: The cost of prohibiting freshmen from having cars on campus could become very expensive due to a loss of tuition if prospective students decide to enroll at a different college.

(from a student's research paper)

Although a cost might be high or low, reasonable or unreasonable, a cost cannot be *expensive.*

Correct: Prohibiting freshmen from having cars on campus could become very expensive.

14C *THE REASON … IS BECAUSE …*

Avoid sentences that include the expression *the reason is because,* such as the sentence *The reason I'm late is because I overslept.* Such sentences are both redundant and ungrammatical. First, it is stylistically undesirable to use the subordinating conjunction *because* (which introduces a dependent clause providing the reason for something) in a sentence whose subject, *reason,* has already explicitly declared that a reason will be provided. (The writer ends up saying the same thing twice.) Second, the subject of the sentence is the noun *reason,* and the verb, *is,* is a linking verb. A linking verb equates the subject with a complement, which may take the form of a noun, a pronoun, an adjective, or a phrase or clause functioning as a noun or an adjective. In the sentence cited above, however, the clause *because I overslept* is an adverbial dependent clause—and thus it cannot function as a complement. Grammatically correct revisions include *The reason I'm late is that I overslept* (*that I overslept* is a nominative dependent clause and therefore can function as a complement) and *I'm late because I overslept.*

Faulty: Bryan E. Smith, 42-year-old driver of the minivan that struck Stephen King on June 19, said the reason he was indicted last week on aggravated assault charges is because the novelist is a celebrity.

("So They Say," *Pittsburgh Post-Gazette*, 6 Oct. 1999, p. E7)

Correct: ... the reason he was indicted last week on aggravated-assault charges is that the novelist is a celebrity.

14D *X IS WHEN ... AND X IS WHERE ...*

Two other sentence patterns to avoid are those starting with *X is when* and *X is where*. The clauses beginning with *when* and *where* are adverbial dependent clauses and thus cannot function as complements of a linking verb.

Faulty: Severe depression is when you feel completely helpless and hopeless.
Correct: Severe depression is a feeling of complete helplessness and hopelessness.

Faulty: An inferiority complex is where you feel that everybody else is superior to you.
Correct: An inferiority complex is the conviction that everybody else is superior to you.

CHAPTER 15

MISHANDLED ELLIPTICAL CONSTRUCTION

An elliptical sentence is a sentence from which the writer, aiming for conciseness and forceful-ness of expression, has intentionally omitted one or more words with the expectation that the reader will be able to restore the missing word or words. An elliptical sentence is grammati-cally sound when the reader can mentally fill the blank—that is, round out the elliptical con-struction—by inserting a word or words that have been presented elsewhere in the sentence. In Alexander Pope's famous 1711 declaration *To err is human, to forgive divine,* for instance, Pope deliberately omitted the linking verb between the infinitive *to forgive* (serving as the subject of a clause) and the adjective *divine* (serving as the complement of the clause), because he was confident that readers could fill the blank by carrying forward the verb *is,* which appears in the first clause of the sentence. But a writer cannot expect a reader to fill blanks with words that have not put in an appearance somewhere else in a sentence. A sentence in which the exact word or words to be inserted by the reader are not physically present elsewhere in the sentence is weakened by a faulty elliptical construction.

15A SUBJECTS NOT AGREEING IN NUMBER

A common form of faulty ellipsis occurs when the subject of a clause presented in full and the subject of an elliptical clause do not agree in number.

> **Faulty:** Cabinets were open, furniture missing.
>
> (Greg Sargent, "Husband Hunting," *New York,* 7 June 2004, p. 46)
>
> The plural verb *were* in the first clause cannot be carried forward to fill the slot between the subject and

the participle in the elliptical clause.

Correct: Cabinets were open, furniture was missing.

This is an asyndetonic compound sentence; see chapter 25.

Correct: Cabinets were open, pieces of furniture missing.

Faulty: If your nose is stuffed already, your itchy eyes on allergy red alert and your pockets full of wadded tissues—blame El Niño.

(Susan Ferraro, "Nothing to Sneeze At," *New York Daily News*, 12 Apr. 1998, p. 4)

The singular verb *is* in the first dependent clause cannot be carried forward to fill the slots between *eyes* and *on allergy red alert* in the first elliptical clause and between *pockets* and *full* in the second elliptical clause. Only plural verbs can fill those slots. An easy fix is to substitute a plural noun, such as *sinuses* or *nostrils*, for the singular subject *nose* in the first clause and then to pluralize the verb.

Correct: If your sinuses are stuffed already, your itchy eyes on allergy red alert, and your pockets full of wadded tissues—blame El Niño.

Faulty: His eyes shift everywhere, his movements are jerky, his speech rapid, his questions staccato and continuous, with no time out for answers.

(S. N. Behrman, *The Suspended Drawing Room* [New York: Stein and Day, 1965], p. 128)

The first two clauses of the sentence are phrased in full, and the third and fourth clauses are phrased elliptically—with the verbs omitted. The slot between *speech* and *rapid,* however, cannot be filled by carrying forward the plural verb *are.*

Correct: His eyes shift everywhere, his movements are jerky, his speech is rapid, his questions are staccato and continuous, with no time out for answers.

The sentence no longer includes any elliptical clauses.

Correct: His eyes shift everywhere, his movements are jerky, his remarks rapid, his questions staccato and continuous, with no time out for answers.

A plural noun replaces the singular noun *speech,* ensuring the correctness of the elliptical phrasing in the third and fourth clauses.

15B MAIN VERBS NOT IN ACCORD WITH AUXILIARY VERBS

Another form of faulty ellipsis arises when an auxiliary verb in an elliptical clause cannot accept the main verb used in a clause that has been phrased in full.

Faulty: To refer to Rickles, as people often have, as "the father of insult comedy" is perhaps a little far-fetched.

(Zoë Heller, "Don't Call Me Sir," *New Yorker*, 2 Aug. 2004, p. 35)

The slot following the auxiliary verb *have* in the elliptical adverbial dependent clause cannot be filled by carrying forward *refer.* An easy fix is to replace *have* with an auxiliary verb that can accept *refer* as the main verb.

Correct: To refer to Rickles, as people often do, as "the father of insult comedy" is perhaps a little far-fetched.

Faulty: Eurocopter says it also listened to customers when its rivals weren't.

(Daniel Michaels, "Helicopters Soar Overseas," *Wall Street Journal*, 2 Jan. 2004, p. A7)

The slot following the contraction *weren't* needs to be filled by *listening.*

Correct: Eurocopter says it also was listening to customers when its rivals weren't.

Faulty: The blame, as it mostly should and does, lies with the inhabitants of those corner offices.

(Jeff MacGregor, "What's Wrong with TV? Just Do the Math," *New York Times*, 9 Aug. 1998, section 2, p. 27)

The slot following the auxiliary verbs *should* and *does* cannot be filled by *lies.*

Correct: Most of the blame should lie with the inhabitants of those corner offices—and it does.

Correct: Most of the blame should—and does—lie with the inhabitants of those corner offices.

Faulty: Moreover, he says, he never has and never will agree to stay off certain subjects with an interviewee.

(Ginia Bellafante, "After the Break … ," *Time*, 6 Oct. 1997, p. 92)

The slot between the auxiliary verb *has* and the coordinating conjunction cannot be filled by *agree*.

Correct: Moreover, he says, he never has agreed and never will agree to stay off certain subjects with an interviewee.

15C VIOLATIONS OF THE PATTERN *ONE OF THE …* *IF NOT THE …*

A third common form of faulty ellipsis occurs in sentences that include the *one of the … if not the …* pattern.

Faulty: Now, at the end of the troubled, trembling 1993, he had plummeted from being one of the—if not *the*—most venerated, for all the right reasons, figures in his field to coming across like a small-minded wart.

(Victor Bockris, *Transformer: The Lou Reed Story* [New York: Simon & Schuster, 1994], p. 413)

The slot following the italicized article *the* cannot be filled with *most venerated … figures in his field*. It needs to be filled by a construction in singular form.

Correct: Now, at the end of the troubled, trembling 1993, he had plummeted from being one of the most rightfully venerated figures in his field, if not the most revered of them all, to coming across like a small-minded wart.

Faulty: You poets have made the Post-Gazette one of the few, if not the only, daily American newspaper that encourages and rewards your work.

(Bob Hoover, "Mystery Lovers Can Meet P. D. James," *Pittsburgh Post-Gazette* online, 11 Jan. 1998, paragraph 30)

Correct: You poets have made the *Post-Gazette* one of the few daily American newspapers, if not the only paper, to encourage and reward the work of poets.

15D UNSHAREABLE PREPOSITIONS AND ADVERBIAL PARTICLES

Faulty ellipsis occasionally arises in a series when two nouns or verbs that together form a compound element cannot share the same preposition or adverbial particle.

Faulty: Violation of this policy will result in disciplinary action, including, but not limited to, a warning, written reprimand, suspension, dismissal, expulsion, and/or mandatory participation and successful completion of a drug abuse assistance or rehabilitation program approved by an appropriate health or law enforcement agency.

(from a university memo)

The slot following *participation* needs to be filled by a preposition, but *of* cannot be carried backward to fill it. Only the preposition *in* can fill the slot.

Correct: Violation of this policy will result in disciplinary action, including, but not limited to, a warning, a written reprimand, suspension, dismissal, expulsion, and/or mandatory participation in and successful completion of a drug-abuse-assistance or rehabilitation program approved by an appropriate health or law-enforcement agency.

15E AMBIGUOUS ELLIPTICAL CONSTRUCTIONS

A mishandled elliptical construction occasionally results in ambiguity.

Ambiguous: *Taboo* makes out that the gay renegade [Leigh Bowery], a fantastic art installation personified, craved stardom as much as Boy George.

(John Heilpern, "Rosie and Boy's Big Identity Crisis," *New York Observer* online, 24 Nov. 2003, paragraph 12)

The troublesome elliptical construction is *as much as Boy George*, which can be filled out in two ways.

Clear: … craved stardom as much as Boy George craved it.
Clear: … craved stardom as much as he craved Boy George.

15F FAULTY ELLIPSIS IN TWO-SENTENCE SEQUENCES

Finally, an elliptical construction in one sentence sometimes requires that the reader fill a slot by carrying forward a word or a phrase from the previous sentence. But unless the previous sentence includes a word or a phrase that will fit exactly in the slot, the elliptical construction will be faulty.

> **Faulty:** When the syndicated "Blind Date" began four years ago, the producers were banned from showing gay men on dates. Now, they do.
>
> (Emily Nelson, "Whose 'Reality' Is This?," *Wall Street Journal*, 1 Mar. 2004, p. B4)
>
> > The slot following the auxiliary verb *do* at the end of the second sentence cannot be filled with any of the main verbs in the first sentence.
>
> **Correct:** When the syndicated *Blind Date* began four years ago, the producers were banned from showing gay men on dates. But they no longer are.

> **Faulty:** It'll be a tough act to follow, and Vernon's is the idiosyncratic type of voice that many one-hit wonders have had difficulty shaking. But even if he never does, DBC Pierre has made his mark.
>
> (Jem Aswad, review of DBC Pierre's debut novel, *Vernon God Little*, *Time Out New York*, 30 Oct.–6 Nov. 2003, p. 57)
>
> > The slot following the auxiliary verb *does* in the second sentence cannot be filled by any verb structure from the first sentence. An easy fix is to recast the first sentence by setting up a verb phrase that can be carried forward.
>
> **Correct:** It'll be a tough act to follow, because the trouble with a voice as idiosyncratic as Vernon's is that few one-hit wonders can shake it off. But even if he never does, DBC Pierre has made his mark.

CHAPTER 16

TWO SPECIAL PROBLEMS WITH *THAT*

16A OMISSION OF *THAT* FROM THE START OF A NOMINATIVE DEPENDENT CLAUSE

Do not omit the indefinite relative pronoun *that* from the beginning of a nominative dependent clause if the subject of the clause is likely to be misread as the direct object of a transitive verb in the clause immediately preceding. Despite the widespread notion that *that* is a superfluous and discardable word, the inclusion of *that* often improves the readability of a sentence.

Consider this sentence: *When a researcher discovers a new strain of the flu could threaten a large segment of the population, the ethics panel determines whether the public should be notified immediately.* Readers can initially misconstrue *strain* as the direct object of *discovers*. Only when they reach the helping verb *could* will they realize that they have misread the sentence. The inclusion of *that* between *discovers* and *a* will ensure that readers can traverse the sentence without stumbling. (The entire nominative dependent clause *that a new strain of the flu could threaten a large segment of the population* is the direct object of *discovers*.)

Corrective additions to the following sentences have been boldfaced and bracketed.

- Mr. Green noticed **[that]** the kids he continued to bring to practice with him improved greatly.

  (Lola Ogunnaike, "Class, Get in Touch with Your Inner Zappa," *New York Times*, 3 Nov. 2003, p. E-1)

- But on board his flight to Los Angeles, he found **[that]** the promised seat-back TVs were missing, and the bottled water ran out halfway there.

  (Paula Szuchman and Susan Carey, "Trouble in Low-Fare Land," *Wall Street Journal*, 13 Feb. 2004, p. W1)

- I think it [the movie] should be required viewing for every American, but as usual, I fear [**that**] the people who could learn the most from the issues it raises will avoid it like a fund-raiser for free abortions.

  (Rex Reed, "Moore's Magic: 9/11 Electrifies," *New York Observer* online, 28 June 2004, paragraph 9)

The indefinite relative pronoun *that* can usually be omitted following verbs such as *say, think,* and *hope,* because there is no possibility of misreading: *She said the food was overcooked. I thought the girl looked pale. He hopes the incumbent wins the election.*

If two or more nominative dependent clauses follow a transitive verb, be sure to phrase the clauses in parallel form (this principle is discussed in chapter 7).

> **Faulty:** I realized I was going to be late for the meeting and that there was nothing I could do.
> **Correct:** I realized that I was going to be late for the meeting and that there was nothing I could do.
> **Correct:** I realized that I was going to be late for the meeting and there was nothing I could do.
> In this revision, the first *that* is implicitly carried forward to the start of the second dependent clause, and the absence of a comma before *and* signals to the reader that what follows is another dependent clause and not a second independent clause.

Ambiguity can easily afflict sentences in which the writer is careless about the handling of *that.* Consider this sentence: *The personnel director explained that only twelve candidates had applied for the job and the president was in a hurry to fill the vacant position.* Is this intended to be a sentence with two nominative dependent clauses functioning as the direct object of *explained*? That is, did the personnel director explain (a) that only twelve candidates had applied for the job and (b) that the president was in a hurry to fill the vacant position? Or is *that only twelve candidates had applied for the job* to be construed as a nominative dependent clause, while *and the president was in a hurry to fill the vacant position* is to be construed as an independent clause? In other words, is the sentence intended to convey (a) that the personnel director explained that only twelve candidates had applied for the job and (b) that the writer of the sentence—not the personnel director—is declaring that the president was in a hurry to fill the vacant position? If the first interpretation is the desired one, the insertion of *that* after the coordinating conjunction *and* will eliminate the ambiguity. If the second interpretation is the desired one, the insertion of a comma before the coordinating conjunction *and* will clarify that what follows the conjunction is an independent clause (and not a nominative dependent clause functioning as a second direct object of *explained*).

16B ERRONEOUS DOUBLED *THAT*

Writers sometimes mistakenly insert *that* at both ends of a dependent clause: *He knows that if he oversleeps again that he might lose his job.* The second *that* is superfluous and ungrammatical. A comma should be inserted in its place.

In each of the two following sentences, the second, bracketed *that* should be replaced by a comma.

- The PA Department of Revenue knows that no matter how careful a taxpayer is about reporting their income on the Personal Income Tax return [that] mistakes and oversights can happen.

  (Pennsylvania Department of Revenue, *Commonly Asked Questions: Amending PA-40 Returns,* REV-630 PO [12-98], p. 1)

- Many think that when they enter a highway from an on ramp [that] the approaching right lane traffic is required to move to the left lane in order to allow them to enter the traffic flow without interruption.

  (Jay Ofsanik, "Signs, Signs, Everywhere a Sign," *AAA Motorist,* Westmoreland [PA] Region, Jan. 2004, p.16)

In the second sentence of the following excerpt, the third, bracketed *that* must be deleted, and it would be advisable to insert *then* in its place.

- Valentine's Day is this weekend; if you are alone, it is your fault. So embrace your responsibility, feel that pain, and consider that if you are without a companion at 35—when you still have a fairly decent body— [that] when you die at 80, there will certainly be no one at your bedside.

  (Joyce Wadler, "The Next Time He Called, Jean-Luc Had a Headache," *New York Times*, 13 Feb. 2004, p. A-27)

PART III:
PUNCTUATION: RULES, CONVENTIONS, AND ERRORS TO AVOID

CHAPTER 17

TERMINAL PUNCTUATION MARKS

The three punctuation marks that signal the end of a sentence are the period, the question mark, and the exclamation point.

17A THE PERIOD

The period marks the end of a declarative sentence and an imperative sentence, as well as the end of an intentional sentence fragment. The period also has two other important functions.

A period follows any initial in a person's name: *J. D. Salinger, S. J. Perelman, George W. S. Trow.* One blank space must follow each period. If a name is presented entirely in the form of initials, however, the periods can be dispensed with, and the initials can be presented without spaces between them: *JFK.*

A period follows many abbreviations, such as *Jan., Feb., St.,* and *Ave.* Other abbreviations, such as *e.g.* and *p.m.,* include one or more interior periods as well as a terminal period. No blank space follows an interior period. A third category of abbreviations, which are pronounced as if they were words and are known as acronyms, do not include periods: examples are *NASA, NASCAR,* and *NAFTA.* Nor do abbreviations like *FBI* and *CIA* include periods. The abbreviation of *United States of America* is more often presented without periods (*USA*) than with periods (*U.S.A.*); be consistent throughout a document. If you are uncertain about whether an abbreviation includes one or more periods, consult a good dictionary.

Any punctuation mark necessary after an abbreviation ending with a period will be positioned immediately after the period; no blank space will precede the punctuation mark. In a declarative or an imperative sentence that ends with an abbreviation terminating in a period, the period at the end of the abbreviation will also serve as the closing punctuation mark for the sentence.

- The applicants were told to arrive no later than 9:30 A.M.

If a sentence ends with a parenthesized abbreviation that requires a period, the closing parenthesis will be both preceded by and followed by a period.

- The class was studying the brief reign of Tutankhamen (1361–1352 B.C.).

On typed pages, two blank spaces traditionally follow a sentence-ending period—except in two special cases. (The first exception is a freestanding parenthesized or bracketed sentence, like this one, in which the closing parenthesis or bracket will be positioned right after the period; the next sentence will begin two spaces after the closing parenthesis or bracket.) The second exception is a sentence ending with quoted matter, "like this one." The closing quotation mark will immediately follow the period, and the next sentence will begin two spaces after the closing quotation mark. Many editors, however, now prefer only a single blank space after any sentence-ending period.

17B THE QUESTION MARK

A question mark should appear at the end of a direct question.

- Who is responsible?
- What now? she wondered.
  Note that the question mark alone precedes the clause of attribution in sentences with this pattern.

An indirect question should be punctuated with a period.

- She asked whether I could fill in for her on Saturday.

Sometimes the indirect question is expressed by one word alone.

- I know I still have the file, but the question is where.

Polite formal requests in question form are often punctuated with a period, not with a question mark.

- Would you please fill out and return the enclosed application form.

Sometimes a declarative sentence has an interrogative thrust and should thus be followed by a question mark.

- She said what?
- He left yesterday?

Sometimes a short direct question is embedded within a sentence, where it can function as the subject, a complement, or an adjective. A question mark should be inserted at the end of the short question wherever it appears in the sentence.

- What next? was the question all of us were pondering.
- The burning question is, Where do we go from here?
- She was weary of his Where-should-we-eat? and What-DVD-should-we-rent? questions.
  A sentence of this sort, however, could be rephrased: *She was growing weary of his always asking "Where should we eat?" and "What DVD should we rent?"*

Avoid asymmetrical punctuation in sentences in which questions function as nonrestrictive appositives. There are several alternative, preferable patterns.

> **Awkward:** The final question, Whom should we hire? went unanswered.
> **Better:** The final question (Whom should we hire?) went unanswered.
> **Better:** The final question—Whom should we hire?—went unanswered.
> **Better:** The final question, "Whom should we hire?," went unanswered.
> **Better:** The final question, about whom we should hire, went unanswered.

Each of the elements in a list of short questions not in sentence form should be followed by a question mark. Uppercase the initial letters of the first words of the questions if the questions have stand-alone, sentence-like status; lowercase the initial letters if the questions are clearly elements of the hosting sentence.

- She glumly considered her options: Get a divorce? Go back to school? Look for another job?
- Should she order a salad? or a sandwich? or something sweet?

If a trademark term includes a question mark at its end, another punctuation mark will often have to follow the question mark when the trademark term is included in a sentence.

- GUESS?, Inc., is run by Maurice and Paul Marciano.

A question mark is used to denote uncertainty.

- The aphorisms of Diogenes the Cynic (412?–323? B.C.) remain especially relevant today.

When a quotation expressing a question is inserted into a hosting sentence that is also a question, the sentence will have only one question mark, and it will be inserted before the closing quotation mark.

- Who asked, "Why are we doing this?"

A sentence like the one above, in which a question mark is forced into double duty, can usually be rephrased so that the question-within-a-question is expressed indirectly.

- Who asked why we're doing this?

In typescripts, a sentence-ending question mark is traditionally followed by two blank spaces, but many editors now prefer only a single blank space. The positioning of question marks in relation to closing quotation marks is discussed in more detail in Chapter 22.

17C THE EXCLAMATION POINT

Reserve the exclamation point for a sentence whose contents are genuinely astonishing or unexpected or emotionally potent. Avoid getting carried away with the exclamation point. Amateur writers all too often resort to it in an attempt to work up some excitement in a sentence whose ideas or details are anything but provocative or startling.

Unusually strong emotional reactions and urgent commands or warnings, of course, can call for exclamation points: *What a jerk! How dare you! Get me out of here! Get lost! Leave me alone! Move it! Duck! Look out!*

Similarly, interjections can be followed by exclamation points: *Ouch! Oof! Ow! Oh!*

As the examples demonstrate, justifiable exclamation points tend to appear at the close of very short, blunt sentences—sentences that express an unpremeditated, even involuntary outburst. A witheringly phrased sarcastic remark or sparklingly ironic utterance, however, is hardly in need of an exclamation point to boost its verbal wattage.

If a statement is both interrogative and exclamatory, use only the exclamation point.

- Will you stop that!

A trademark term that includes an exclamation point at its end will sometimes need to be followed by another punctuation mark.

- Yahoo!, Google, and Vivisimo are her favorite search engines.

But:

- Her favorite search engine is Yahoo!

The same is true of the titles of works (such as the musicals *Hello, Dolly!* and *Mamma Mia!*), as well as the names of organizations or groups, that end in an exclamation point. Writing about the alternative-rock band whose name is !!! may require sentences like the following.

- !!!, whose name is pronounced "chk chk chk," has been around since 1996.

Avoid using a bracketed exclamation point to express disgust or condescending amusement with the contents of a direct quotation. Such punctuational behavior is amateurish, even boorish.

- She calls herself "the doyenne [!] of the city's arts community."

In typescripts, a sentence-ending exclamation point is traditionally followed by two blank spaces, but, again, many editors now prefer a single blank space. When an exclamation point appears after the last word of an interruptive element set off by a pair of dashes or parentheses, the exclamation point precedes the closing dash or closing parenthesis. The positioning of exclamation points in relation to closing quotation marks is discussed in Chapter 22.

CHAPTER 18

THE COMMA

The comma signals the very briefest of necessary pauses, but no other punctuation mark is more vital to the meaning of the sentences you compose. The omission of commas to mark off boundaries between certain elements of a sentence often obscures the architecture of the sentence. Commas are thus necessary to prevent misreading and to enable a reader to achieve an instant grasp of the syntactic contours of a statement.

The thirty-eight principles discussed in this chapter will help you achieve precise, nuanced, reader-friendly, even elegant punctuation. Throughout, punctuational corrections of the illustrative sentences have been boldfaced and bracketed.

18A COMMAS: THE BASICS

1. Commas After Introductory Elements
Most introductory elements—which may take the form of single words, phrases, or adverbial dependent clauses—should be set off with commas. The commas improve the readability of the sentences.

A. Single-Word Adverbial Introductory Elements
A single-word adverbial element at the start of a sentence is almost always followed by a comma.

- Surprisingly[,] three films nominated for best picture garnered no acting nominations.
  (Sharon Waxman, "'King' Leads in Nods for Oscars," *New York Times*, 28 Jan. 2004, p. B5)

The adverb *then,* however, is rarely set off.

- First, all the lights went out in the apartment complex. Then a loud scream was heard.

Similarly, a comma is optional after *thus* or *hence* at the start of a sentence.

CAUTION

Do not insert a comma after an adverb at the start of an inverted sentence—a sentence in which the verb precedes, rather than follows, the subject.

- Nearby are several new big-box retailers.

Do not insert a comma after the coordinating conjunctions *and, but, yet, or, nor,* and *for* when such a conjunction is used as a transitional word at the beginning of a sentence. (But, as in this sentence, such a conjunction is occasionally followed by an interruptive element that needs to be set off with commas at both ends. See rule 15.)

The following sentence should lose the comma after *but.*

Faulty: But, getting radium, uranium and other radioactive elements was a bit tougher than buying potassium nitrate at the drug store.

(Bob Hoover, "Love Might Have Made the Difference Between Loser and Genius," *Pittsburgh Post-Gazette*, 22 Feb. 2004, p. E5)

A comma sometimes follows the coordinating conjunction *so* to signal a dramatic pause.

- So, what next?

B. Introductory Transitional Phrases

A transitional phrase such as *in fact, for example, as a result,* and *on the other hand* should be followed by a comma.

- On the contrary, her performance was heartrending and unforgettable.

C. Introductory Prepositional Phrases

It is advisable to insert a comma after an introductory prepositional phrase that is five words long or longer. American newspapers, however, are vividly inconsistent in their punctuation of single prepositional phrases—and of pairs and sequences of prepositional phrases—that appear at the beginning of sentences.

Consider the following four sentences, all of which appeared in the *New York Times* (the introductory prepositional phrases have been underlined).

- <u>But on New Year's Eve at the Bowery Ballroom</u> she also found time for more unusual wishes and pleas and dreams.

(Kelefa Sanneh, "Enjoying the Moment, Patti Smith Celebrates Time's Passage," *New York Times*, 3 Jan. 2004, p. A20)

- <u>Across the ski area's trail map</u> yellow bands stretch like caution tape, warning of cliff bans—but not making them off limits.

(Christopher Solomon, "For Skiers, Is Bigger Always Better?," *New York Times*, 2 Jan. 2004, p. D4)

- <u>In November</u>, you might have read in this space about a company called Travel Sentry that developed a lock technology in conjunction with the Transportation Security Administration and the luggage industry.

(Joe Sharkey, "On the Road: Luggage Lock Program Not Without a Few Hitches," *New York Times*, 30 Dec. 2003, p. C6)

- On the real-time television series "24" split screens put us in two places at once, watching the counterterrorist heroes and the villains they're chasing.

  (Caryn James, "Critic's Notebook: Splitting. Screens. For Minds. Divided," *New York Times*, 9 Jan. 2004, p. B7)

Only in the third example has the introductory prepositional phrase been set off with a comma—and that phrase is only two words long. In the other three sentences, many readers would surely welcome a boundary-marking comma between the lengthier introductory elements and the independent clauses.

Not setting off an introductory prepositional phrase can sometimes lead a reader to mistake a sentence for a sentence fragment.

- At the time the Great Salt Lake was unusually shallow because of a drought.

  (Melissa Sanford, "The Salt of the Earth Sculpture," *New York Times*, 13 Jan. 2004, p. B5)

  The prepositional phrase *at the time* can easily be misconstrued as the equivalent of the subordinating conjunction *while* or *when*—and a reader will then regard the entire word group as an adverbial dependent clause rather than as a complete sentence. If a comma is inserted after *at the time*, however, no reader will stumble.

A reader is also likely to stumble through the following sentence.

- Instead of leather seats in the base model you get leatherette.

  ("X Marks the Sweet Spot," *AAA Motorist*, Westmoreland [PA] Region, Jan. 2004, p.16)

  Is the second prepositional phrase (*in the base model*) modifying *seats*, or does it belong in the independent clause? The punctuational divider of a comma between *seats* and *in* will spare the reader the trouble of having to puzzle things out.

It is therefore recommended to use a comma to set off an introductory prepositional phrase, especially a longish one, as well as an introductory pair or sequence of prepositional phrases.

CAUTION

Do not insert a comma after one or more prepositional phrases at the start of an inverted sentence—a sentence in which the subject follows, rather than precedes, the verb.

- In 2000, came the power crisis.

  ("The Shame of Kaiser," editorial, *Seattle Times*, 20 Jan. 2004, p. B6)

D. Introductory Participial Phrases

A comma must follow a participial phrase at the start of a sentence.

- Coming from another performer[,] this message might have sounded tendentious or even self-serving. . . .

  (Kelefa Sanneh, "Enjoying the Moment, Patti Smith Celebrates Time's Passage," *New York Times*, 3 Jan. 2004, p. A20)

- Watching Conor Oberst[,] it's almost impossible to keep the words "new" and "Dylan" out of your head.

  (Scott Mervis, "Conor Oberst/Jim James/M. Ward," *Pittsburgh Post-Gazette*, 24 Feb. 2004, p. D5)

- Decked with gold and diamond jewelry[,] Chingy genially reveled in the success he has had rapping about his success.

  (Jon Pareles, "Bling-Bling, Party Party: Some Rappers Just Want to Have Fun," *New York Times*, 6 Mar. 2004, p. A22)

- Not being a seafood person (I'm allergic)[,] I had to pass.

  (R. Pierce Reid, as told to Melinda Ligos, "Frequent Flier: Lingering Odor of Smelt and a Damp Wool Suit," *New York Times*, 30 Dec. 2003, p. C6)

A. Do not insert a comma after a participial phrase that appears at the beginning of an inverted sentence—a sentence in which the subject follows, rather than precedes, the verb.

- Arranged on the walls of her bedroom are dreamy watercolors depicting an ecofeminist utopia.

B. Be sure to distinguish between a gerund phrase serving as the subject of a sentence and an introductory participial phrase. A gerund-phrase subject must not be followed by a comma.

- Deciding what to buy for a teenager's birthday can be exasperating.

E. Introductory Infinitive Phrases

A comma must follow an introductory infinitive phrase.

- To discourage shoplifters, the manager of the store installed four security cameras.

F. Introductory Appositives

Sometimes an appositive precedes the noun to which it is in apposition. Remember that an appositive is a noun or a noun phrase that provides information about another noun. If the appositive is nonrestrictive—that is, if it provides only supplementary, disposable information (see rule 33A)—a comma follows it.

- An avid bibliophile, she reads at least five books a week.

G. Introductory Absolute Constructions

A comma always follows an introductory absolute construction. An absolute construction consists of a noun (or a pronoun) and a participial phrase.

- Her palm pressed against her cheek, the girl watched her mother assemble the playhouse.

H. Introductory Adverbial Dependent Clauses

A comma should follow an adverbial dependent clause at the start of a complex or compound-complex sentence. The omission of the comma will puzzle or distract some readers, especially in a sentence such as the following.

> **Faulty:** When you gas up the attendant asks, "Can I re-duct-tape that windshield for you?"
>
> ("Top Ten Reasons to ... Replace Your Car," *Pennysaver*, Greensburg [PA] East 77 edition, 28 Apr. 2004, p. 19)
>
> > If the writer does not insert a comma to mark the boundary between the introductory adverbial clause and the independent clause, a reader can initially mistake *attendant* for the direct object of *gas up* instead of recognizing it as the subject of the independent clause.

The inclusion of the comma between an introductory dependent clause and the independent clause will never require a defense, but its omission most likely will. Remember that adverbial dependent clauses begin with subordinating conjunctions, the most common of which are *because, although, though, even though, if, unless, after, as, before, while, when, whenever, since,* and *until.*

The following sentences were published without commas after the introductory adverbial dependent clauses. Inserting a comma to mark off the borderline between the dependent clause and the independent clause improves the readability of each sentence and clarifies its structure.

- If we know only one thing about Sir Walter Raleigh[,] it is his gallant effort to preserve the equanimity of the queen's dainty foot on a stormy day.
  (Stuart Ferguson, "Bookshelf: Exploits and Execution," *Wall Street Journal*, 6 Jan. 2004, p. D10)

- Before you send your work out[,] have it read by a professional.
  (Gotham Writers' Workshop catalogue of courses, winter 2004, p. 24)

- Because gay relationships aren't based on defined roles or social conventions[,] everything is negotiated—from who pays for the groceries to who runs the house.
  (Michael Alvear, "How Heterosexuals Will Benefit from Gay Marriage," *Pittsburgh Post-Gazette*, 23 Nov. 2003, p. E2)

- When everyone gathers for Blake and Ross' surprise wedding[,] there will be nine Santas: Buzz, Frank, Danny, Gus, Alan, Rick, Josh, Edmund—and the real Santa Claus, who restores everyone's belief in the holidays.
  (Carolyn Hinsey, "He Has 'One Life' to Relive," *New York Daily News*, 19 Dec. 2003, p. 156)

- When I want up-to-the-minute fast-talking Englishmen running amok across their own class barriers[,] I think I'll go see a Guy Ritchie movie.
  (Max Watman, "Tickling Your Catastrophe," *New Criterion* online, Nov. 2003, paragraph 26)

A comma is especially helpful when two consecutive adverbial dependent clauses precede the independent clause.

- But since many consumers these days either buy or rent a movie as soon as it comes out on video[,] there is little interest in watching the movie by the time it's available on-demand on television a month later.
  (Martin Peers, "Merger Could Alter Hollywood Balance of Power," *Wall Street Journal*, 13 Feb. 2004, p. B1)

2. Commas Setting Off Sentence-Ending Participial Phrases

A sentence-ending participial phrase should be preceded by a comma—unless the participial phrase has a restrictive function (see rule 33C).

- Neither the editors nor the writers hew to fashionable choices[,] preferring instead to emphasize individual achievement.
  (Paula Deitz, undated subscription-solicitation letter for *Hudson Review*, p. 3)

- Among the findings: 25% of Italian children are now overweight or obese[,] making them the heaviest in Europe.
  (Ellen Hale, "Junk Food Super-Sizing Europeans," *USA Today*, 18 Nov. 2003, p. 13A)

- Cold temperatures can thicken your oil[,] making it difficult for engine parts to move.
  ("Slippery Roads and Cold Weather Mean Winter Driving Is No Joy Ride," *AAA Motorist*, Westmoreland [PA] Region, Jan. 2004, p. 18)

- But then the 2002 Olympics in Salt Lake City came along, and all of a sudden people across the United States were standing around the office water cooler[,] comparing notes on the game they had stayed up until 3 a.m. to watch.
  (Mark Yost, "Blame Canada: Curling Sweeps U.S.," *New York Times*, 2 Jan. 2004, p. D5)

  The coordinating conjunction *and* could be substituted for the comma after *cooler*.

3. Commas Separating Elements in a Series (*a, b, and c*)

When three or more elements are listed in a series, a comma should follow every element except the final one. All American daily newspapers and some magazines, however, omit the comma between the second-last element and the coordinating conjunction *and*.

- Tens of thousands of survivors remain homeless, hungry and vulnerable to disease.

  ("In Dark Hour, Humans Shine," editorial, *USA Today*, 29 Dec. 2003, p. 11A)

The comma inserted before *and* in a series is known as the serial comma. Some editors attempt to justify the omission of the serial comma by claiming that, since the word *and* is separating the two final elements in the series, the comma before *and* is redundant. But their reasoning is faulty. *And* is not separating the two final elements; *and,* a conjunction, is uniting them. In the following sentence, for instance, Sony and Dell appear to have merged.

- Tech players Microsoft, Hewlett-Packard, Sony and Dell, among others, will open online music stores in 2004.

  (Byron Acohido, "2004 May See 'Bit of a Gold Rush' for Digital Tunes," *USA Today*, 29 Dec. 2003, p. 4B)

In the following sentence, San Diego seems to be in Kentucky.

- Although widely syndicated across the country's major markets, [Howard] Stern was carried on only six of Clear Channel's 1,200 stations: Pittsburgh, Fort Lauderdale, Fla., Orlando, Fla., Rochester, N.Y., San Diego and Louisville, Ky.

  (Adrian McCoy, "Broadcast Giant Takes Whack at Shock Radio," *Pittsburgh Post-Gazette*, 27 Feb. 2004, p. A1)

In the next sentence, a cafeteria seems to be serving macaroni, cheese, and spinach as one dish.

- On this day, the popular meal was fried chicken, whipped potatoes and gravy, corn, homestyle macaroni and cheese and spinach.

  (Paula Reed Ward, "Post House Closing Doors," *Pittsburgh Post-Gazette*, 27 June 2004, p. C4)

The *a, b, and c* pattern is favored by most magazines and by most publishers of books—because it prevents misreading and ambiguity. A frequent problem with the *a, b and c* pattern is that the *b and c* elements can be mistaken for appositives.

- The company hired five copyright specialists, three lawyers and two paralegals.

Did the company hire five persons or ten? A comma before *and* will make it clear that ten were hired. A colon or dash after *specialists* will make it clear that five were hired. But if the punctuation is left as is, alert readers will not know whether *three lawyers* and *two paralegals* are to be construed as the second and third elements in a series or whether *three lawyers and two paralegals* is to be construed as an appositive providing additional information about the five copyright specialists who were hired.

   A similar problem afflicts the following sentence.

- In the late 1980's, Asian manufacturers began turning out basic memory chips, undercutting American chip makers' prices and inciting a fierce policy debate.

  (Virginia Postrel, "Economic Scene: A Researcher Sees an Upside in the Outsourcing of Programming Jobs," *New York Times*, 29 Jan. 2004, p. C2)

    Are the phrases beginning with *undercutting* and *inciting* intended to serve as the second and third elements in a series? If so, a comma before *and* will clarify the writer's purpose. But if the two final phrases are intended to function with appositional force, a dash, rather than a comma, after *chips* will clarify the writer's intention.

A second problem arising from the widespread use of the *a, b and c* pattern is that a trio of words or phrases not intended as a series can easily be mistaken for a series.

- Thanks in part to poverty-level wages, hunger and homelessness are up sharply, according to the new U.S. Conference of Mayors survey.

  (Holly Sklar, "Two Different Americas Set to Ring in New Year," *Pittsburgh Post-Gazette*, 28 Dec. 2003, p. C2)

At first, readers are likely to regard *hunger* and *homelessness* as the second and third objects of the preposition *to* rather than recognize *hunger and homelessness* as the compound subject of the independent clause. Not until readers reach the predicate of the sentence will they realize that they have misread the opening.

Finally, the *a, b and c* pattern can obscure the structure of a lengthy sentence.

- And he details its [the fire's] wide-ranging aftermath, which prompted a comprehensive reform of labor and worker-safety laws, recast Tammany Hall from a political machine that had once broken strikes into one that allied itself with the workers and set a young legislator named Alfred E. Smith on the road that would lead to the governor's mansion and the 1928 Democratic presidential nomination.
(Eric Fettmann, "$75 per Victim," *New York Post*, 11 Jan. 2004, p. 30)

Without a comma between *workers* and *and*, readers can easily misregard the verb phrase beginning with *set a young legislator on the road* as the second half of the predicate of the adjectival dependent clause beginning with *that allied itself with the workers*. A comma after *workers* will make it immediately clear that the adjectival dependent clause beginning with *which* has a three-part predicate: *prompted ... , recast ... , and set. ...*

4. Commas Between Two or More Consecutive Adjectives Before a Noun

Commas always separate two or more coordinate adjectives positioned before a noun. Commas never separate two or more cumulative adjectives positioned before a noun.

Coordinate adjectives are consecutive adjectives that individually modify the noun they precede. Commas must be inserted between coordinate adjectives.

TIP: There are two easy ways to determine whether two or more consecutive adjectives are coordinate adjectives.

1. If the coordinating conjunction *and* is inserted between the adjectives and the resulting phrase sounds perfectly natural, the adjectives are coordinate.

- She is a loyal, loving friend. She is a loyal and loving friend.

2. If the positions of the adjectives are reversed and the resulting phrase sounds perfectly natural, the adjectives are coordinate.

- She is a loyal, loving friend. She is a loving, loyal friend.

The following phrases include coordinate adjectives.

- a long, frustrating day
- an underweight, fidgety teenager
- a slow-spoken, solemn juror

Coordinate adjectives need to be distinguished from cumulative (or noncoordinate) adjectives, which are never separated by commas. Cumulative adjectives do not individually modify the noun they precede. Instead, in a pair of cumulative adjectives, the adjective right before the noun modifies the noun, and the first adjective in the pair modifies the duo formed by the second adjective and the noun. Thus in the sentence *She lives in an old brick house*, *brick* modifies *house*, and *old* modifies *brick house* as a duo.

> **TIP:** There are two easy ways to determine whether two or more consecutive adjectives are cumulative.
>
> 1. If the coordinating conjunction *and* is inserted between the adjectives and the resulting phrase sounds unnatural or awkward, the adjectives are cumulative.
>
>> **Awkward:** She lives in an old and brick house.
>> **Better:** She lives in an old brick house.
>
> 2. If the positions of the adjectives are reversed and the resulting phrase sounds unnatural or awkward, the adjectives are cumulative.
>
>> **Awkward:** She lives in a brick old house.
>> **Better:** She lives in an old brick house.

The following phrases include cumulative (noncoordinate) adjectives.

- a deep personal interest in the matter
- a decaying manufacturing town
- laughable political commentary
- a little white lie

In the following sentence, the adjectives *damp* and *wool* are cumulative adjectives, so the comma separating them must be deleted.

- I walked around NASA for the next two days in a damp, wool suit.
  (R. Pierce Reid, as told to Melinda Ligos, "Frequent Flier: Lingering Odor of Smelt and a Damp Wool Suit," *New York Times*, 30 Dec. 2003, p. C6)

> **TIP:** Determining whether consecutive adjectives are coordinate or cumulative can be difficult—especially when three or more adjectives precede a noun. You may find it helpful to refer to the following pattern. Any set of adjectives conforming to this sequence will be presented without commas: **quantity + age + size [or weight or length] + color + material + subtype[s] of thing.**
>
>> - three new large green plastic garbage cans
>> - two brand-new navy-blue oxford-cloth shirtwaist dresses
>
> Commas usually separate consecutive adjectives denoting the distinctive features of a thing.
>
>> - a pair of unpleated, wrinkleproof, relaxed-fit casual slacks

The presence or absence of a comma between two consecutive adjectives can make all the difference in what a sentence means.

- Paul Simon is quoted as saying that the idea for "The Capeman," his first, extremely problematic Broadway musical, came to him in an instant.
  (Vincent Canby, "'Capeman' Doesn't Fly, Despite the Music," *New York Times* online, 8 Feb. 1998, paragraph 1)

  > With the comma between *first* and *extremely problematic*, the sentence is telling us that, at the time of writing, Simon had created only one Broadway musical and it happened to be extremely problematic. Without the comma, the sentence would be telling us that *The Capeman* was the first of at least two extremely problematic Broadway musicals created by Simon.

5. Commas With Direct Address

Commas set off the names of persons being written to or spoken to in direct address. Commas also set off words like *sir* and *ma'am*. Finally, commas set off plural nouns denoting groups of people being addressed directly.

- Mom and Dad, I have something to tell you.
- Sir, you'll need to follow me into the examination room.
- Come here, Diane, and tell me what's wrong.

6. Commas After Interjections

Only two punctuation marks are used after interjections (words like *ouch, whoops,* and *drat)*— the comma and the exclamation point.

- Wow, I love your jacket.
- Whew! That was a close call.

7. Commas in Elliptical Constructions

Use a comma to indicate that one or more words have been intentionally withheld from a sentence with the expectation that the reader can fill in the missing word or words. Such a sentence is called an elliptical sentence.

- In 2002, the chain opened thirty-nine restaurants; in 2003, fifteen; in 2004, twenty; and in 2005, eleven.

8. Commas Preceding Nominative Dependent Clauses From Which the Indefinite Relative Pronoun *that* Has Been Omitted

A comma often takes the place of the indefinite relative pronoun *that* when a form of the linking (equational) verb *to be* is followed by a nominative dependent clause.

- The trouble is, the company's turnover rate has increased exponentially.

If the sentence included the pronoun *that,* no comma would precede the pronoun.

- The trouble is that the company's employee-turnover rate has increased exponentially.

9. Commas With Correlative Conjunctions

Do not use a comma before the second half of a correlative-conjunction pair (such as *not only ... but also; not ... but; either ... or; and neither ... nor*) unless an independent clause follows each half of the correlative-conjunction pair. The commas before *but* in the following two sentences should thus be deleted.

> **Faulty:** The answers to these questions not only affect the personal satisfaction with the sale, but also how much the seller might get for a business.
>
> (Mark A. Stein, "Selling a Family Enterprise: Tough to Decide and to Do," *New York Times,* 19 Feb. 2004, p. C6)
>
> Note that the sentence is also weakened by faulty parallelism; see chapter 7.

> **Faulty:** But his film has been embraced by Christian leaders not just as a faith-affirming experience, but also as a backlash against a permissive, godless world of media and entertainment.
>
> (Alessandra Stanley, "'Passion' [Contd]: A Timid Debate," *New York Times,* 20 Feb. 2004, p. B26)

The comma in the following sentence is correct, because each half of the correlative-conjunction pair is followed by an independent clause (the first of which is in inverted form).

- Not only has she revitalized our advertising department, but she has become our most forward-thinking manager.

10. Commas That Prevent Misreading

As you recall from our discussion of introductory elements (rule 1), the omission of a boundary-marking comma often obscures, rather than clarifies, the structure of a sentence.

> **Faulty:** Not long into the dispute about 300 protesters left a rally in Mellon Square and marched toward the USX Tower offices of Donald O'Connor, the labor lawyer who represented management.
> (Jim McKay, "Executive in the Spotlight: Billy Joe Jordan," *Pittsburgh Post-Gazette*, 23 Feb. 1998, p. E5)
>> Because there is no comma between *dispute* and *about*, the reader can initially misconstrue *about 300 protesters* as an adjectival prepositional phrase modifying *dispute* instead of recognizing *protesters* as the subject of the sentence. The insertion of a comma after *dispute* will resolve the problem.

11. Commas With *that is, namely, i.e.,* and Similar Phrases and Abbreviations

A comma always follows *that is, i.e., e.g.,* and similar phrases and abbreviations. A comma often precedes such elements as well, but stronger punctuation (such as a semicolon or a dash) is usually more desirable, especially if the construction following the element is a long phrase or an independent clause.

- His hobby is numismatics, i.e., coin collecting.
- He's a numismatist; that is, he collects coins.
- She especially enjoys reading innovative, experimental writers—for example, Gordon Lish, Ben Marcus, Sam Lipsyte, Diane Williams, and Brian Evenson.

12. Commas in Constructions Such as *the simpler the better*

If such a construction is short and consists of two phrases, omit the comma between the two halves. If the two halves of the construction are longer phrases or are clauses, the comma is necessary.

- The bigger the better.
- The bigger they come, the harder they fall.

13. Commas Between Identical Words

Readability improves when a comma separates two consecutive uses of the same word.

- What happened, happened.
- What it is, is nothing short of miraculous.

But it is often better to rephrase such a sentence.

- It is nothing short of miraculous.

14. Commas With Contrasted Phrasing

Commas set off phrases or clauses being contrasted.

- Basketball, not soccer, was her favorite sport in college.
- But not all tasks lend themselves to self-serve, and you wonder whether some increases in worker productivity come from the customer's sweat[,] not the worker's.
  (Ann Belser, "Untold Story of Worker Productivity: Let the Consumer Do It," *Pittsburgh Post-Gazette*, 7 Sept. 2004, p. A1)

15. Pairs of Commas Enclosing Interruptive and Parenthetical Elements

An interruptive or a parenthetical element—which may take the form of a single word (such as *however* or *therefore*), a short transitional expression (such as *for example* or *as a result*), a phrase, or a nonrestrictive dependent clause (see rules 33D and 33E)—must be set off by punctuation at both ends. An element is said to be interruptive or parenthetical if it is not essential to the meaning of the sentence. It is added to the sentence as a kind of bonus—and thus it often enhances the reader's understanding of the main point of the sentence.

- Cell phones, though, may have changed our lives for the worse.
- There was a time, not too long ago, when she had been considered a promising athlete.
- It's possible, and even likely, that subscribers won't immediately notice the rate increase.
- It was a propitious, if unmemorable, start for his campaign.

Explanatory interrupters are a special subcategory of interruptive elements. An explanatory interrupter consists of the coordinating conjunction *or* and a noun or noun phrase that functions like an appositive, renaming or clarifying the noun that precedes the interrupter. Explanatory interrupters must be set off punctuationally at both ends.

- Mad-cow disease, or bovine spongiform encephalopathy, has killed almost a hundred and fifty people worldwide.

All too often, interruptive elements appear with asymmetrical punctuation—that is, the interruptive elements are set off punctuationally at only one of their two ends. Such mispunctuation is very likely to occur when an interruptive element includes, at its end, another interruptive element—especially one that is enclosed within parentheses. The boldfaced, bracketed commas correct the asymmetrical punctuation of interruptive elements in the following sentences.

- Roscoe does have land[,] though, and people are still buying and building.
  (Sandra Hurtes, "Weekender: Roscoe, N.Y.," *New York Times*, 2 Jan. 2004, p. D8)

- Gold and silver also shine their way into more dainty, or ladylike[,] watches.
  (Kristi L. Gustafson, "Watches Make a Timely Fashion Statement," for *Albany Times Union*, in *Seattle Post-Intelligencer*, 20 Jan. 2004, p. C1)

- That said, the notion of pairing roasted turnips with squid, or stuffing a ravioli with mashed rutabaga and tossing in some Serrano ham[,] is brilliant.
  (Pascale Le Draoulec, "Surprises Under Chestnut Shell," *New York Daily News*, 19 Dec. 2003, p. 86)

- "Masked and Anonymous," directed by the "Seinfeld" vet Larry Charles and probably written largely by Dylan himself (the credited scriptwriters seem to be pseudonyms)[,] takes place in a near-future America torn apart by revolution; Jack Fate (Dylan) is a washed-up rock star who gets roped into a benefit concert by the unscrupulous promoter Uncle Sweetheart (John Goodman).
  (Ben Greenman, capsule film review, *New Yorker*, 4 Aug. 2003, p. 17)

- Mr. Cox, once a designer for Tommy Hilfiger, and Mr. Silver, a former daytime talk-show producer (who insists that he hoped to write a book about that experience called "But Do They Have Teeth?")[,] have made bright color contrasts their trademark while keeping cuts and shapes uncomplicated.
  (Ginia Bellafante, "The Newest Stars to Watch in 2004," *New York Times*, 30 Dec. 2003, p. C20)

  The parenthesized element is also weakened by a misplaced participial phrase (*called "But Do They Have Teeth?"*); see Chapter 8.

Another common form of the mispunctuation of interruptive elements occurs when the writer mispositions the second of the two commas setting off the interruptive element. In each of the following examples, the mispositioned comma is enclosed between braces, and that comma should be deleted from the sentence. The correctly positioned second comma is bracketed and boldfaced.

- One of the sickest, and funniest[,] black comedies in years{,} stars Billy Bob Thornton as a misanthropic department store Santa. . . .

  (Jack Mathews, capsule film review of *Bad Santa, New York Daily News*, 19 Dec. 2003, p. 70)

- But for commuters who drive to, and then park{,} in[,] Pittsburgh, it is the winter of their discontent.

  ("Parking Decked," editorial, *Pittsburgh Post-Gazette*, 14 Jan. 2004, p. A18)

Finally, writers sometimes completely forget to punctuate an interruptive element, and their failure to insert the two commas can distort the meaning of a sentence.

Faulty: Shock radio is getting its mouth washed out with a heavy-duty bar of soap—not as expected by the guardians at the Federal Communications Commission but by the nation's top radio conglomerate.

(Adrian McCoy, "Broadcast Giant Takes Whack at Shock Radio," *Pittsburgh Post-Gazette*, 27 Feb. 2004, p. A1)

Because the writer has neglected to set off the phrase *as expected* with a comma at each end, the sentence is telling us, erroneously, that it was the radio conglomerate, and not the guardians, who were doing the expecting. But the writer's intention is not to emphasize either the conglomerate or the guardians as expectants. With commas around *as expected*, the sentence will make it clear that there was an expectation on the part of the general public that shock jocks would be censured and censored.

TIP: Some single-word interrupters (such as *therefore*, *thus*, *perhaps*, and *indeed*) and some short-phrase interrupters (such as *of course* and *in fact*) often appear without commas, especially when the interrupter follows the verb of the sentence or when the interrupter is positioned between an auxiliary verb and a main verb.

- You are therefore likely to find the update useful.
- You should in fact receive the package this afternoon.
- Your suggestions are indeed welcome.
- You will of course be compensated for your services.

---

16. Commas With Clauses of Attribution

Use a comma between a clause of attribution (such as *she said*) and a full-sentence direct quotation. The clause of attribution can appear at the beginning of the sentence or at the end.

- She said, "I'm not sure we've made the wisest decision."
- "I'm not sure we've made the wisest decision," she said.

TIP: In American punctuational practice, periods and commas are always inserted inside, not outside, the closing quotation marks.

Use a pair of commas to set off a clause of attribution that is inserted between the two halves of a full-sentence direct quotation. Each half of the quotation must be enclosed by a pair of quotation marks.

- "There were a few warning signs I should've heeded," she said, "but I don't regret marrying him."

> **TIP:** Use a colon, not a comma, between a clause of attribution and a multisentence direct quotation (see chapter 19).
>
> • She added: "He could be so openhearted and beguiling. Then his dark side would take over."

Do not use a comma after a clause of attribution that is followed by the indefinite relative pronoun *that* and a direct quotation. The indefinite relative pronoun and the quotation together form a nominative dependent clause functioning as the direct object of the verb of attribution in the independent clause. The initial letter of the first word in the direct quotation will not be capitalized unless the first word is a proper noun or proper adjective (either of which always requires capitalization) or the pronoun *I*.

> **Faulty:** [The record's jacket] claims of Johnson that, "He even creates his own thunder and lightning storm."
> (Michael Devine, "Bin There, Heard That," *Pittsburgh City Paper*, 26 May–2 June 2004, p. 61)
>
> The comma after *that* should be deleted, and the *H* in *He* should be lowercased.

The same principles of punctuation and capitalization apply when the attribution is provided within an adjectival dependent clause. The following sentence should lose the comma after *that*.

> **Faulty:** At the time, I talked with Robert Frederick, assistant director of the Center for Business Ethics at Bentley College in Waltham, Mass., who worried that, "CEOs have moved themselves into a new class of American aristocracy."
> (Steve Massey, "What They Make, and Why We Tell You," *Pittsburgh Post-Gazette*, 23 May 2004, p. E3)

Rule 33A discusses punctuational patterns for direct quotations functioning as appositives. Rule 37 discusses punctuational patterns for sentences in which direct quotations function as structural components of sentences, such as subjects, objects, and complements.

Do not insert a comma after a clause of attribution that is followed by an indirect quotation. (An indirect quotation provides a paraphrase, rather than the exact words, of a statement. An indirect quotation is never enclosed by quotation marks. The initial letter of the first word of an indirect quotation is not capitalized unless the indirect quotation appears at the beginning of the sentence or unless the first word is a proper noun, a proper adjective, or the pronoun *I*.)

> • She said we'll need to hire two more paralegals.

If a clause of attribution follows an indirect quotation, a comma must separate the two elements.

> • We'll need to hire two more paralegals, she said.

> **TIP:** When you are converting a first-person direct quotation to an indirect quotation, remember to shift the first-person pronouns to third-person pronouns, and make sure that the tense of the verb in the indirect quotation is consistent with that of the verb in the clause of attribution.

If a clause of attribution is inserted between the two halves of an indirect quotation, the clause of attribution must be enclosed by a pair of commas.

- The best she could do, she said, was to recommend that he read the fine print more carefully the next time.

TIP: A comma should be inserted between a form of the linking verb *to be* and a question that is in either direct-quotation or indirect-quotation form and that is functioning as a complement. (In a very formal context, a colon may be substituted for the comma.) The initial letter of the first word of the question does not need to be uppercased unless the first word is a proper noun or a proper adjective. It is not considered an error, however, to capitalize the first word of the question. When the question is fairly long or the context is very formal, capitalizing the first word is often desirable.

- The question is, whom should we hold responsible?

17. Commas Separating Clauses in Compound, Complex, and Compound-Complex Sentences

See chapter 25.

18. Commas With Dates

When the sequence of month, day, and year appears anywhere in a sentence except at the end (where a period, a question mark, or an exclamation point will follow), a comma must follow the year.

- That package of antiterrorism measures [the USA Patriot Act], rushed into law following the Sept. 11, 2001[,] attacks, is set to expire next year.
  (Bob Hoover, "Take Action to Amend 215's Abuses," *Pittsburgh Post-Gazette*, 22 Feb. 2004, p. E4)

When the name of the day of the week is followed by the month and the day of the month, use a pair of commas to enclose the unit formed by the month and the day of the month.

- Still, the news that Elliott Smith died on Tuesday[,] October 21[,] from a self-inflicted knife wound was no less heartbreaking, even if it was somehow half-expected.
  (Leah Greenblatt, "Elliott Smith 1969–2003," *Time Out New York*, 30 Oct.–6 Nov. 2003, p. 109)

When the month is followed by the year, it is now standard to omit any punctuation.

- May 2003 was our most profitable month.

A comma following the month, however, must be paired with a comma following the year.

- Our May, 2003, sales figures were our most impressive yet.

18A

When the day of the month precedes the name of the month and the year, the date is presented without commas.

- The 24 September 2005 performance was unforgettable.

19. Commas With Place Names

Everybody knows that a comma separates the name of a town or city from the name of a county, a state, a province, or a country. Fewer seem to know, however, that another comma must follow the name of the county, state, province, or country—except when the place name appears at the end of a sentence.

- The Duluth, Minnesota[,] band Low bucks the trend with the fierce grace only a pioneering sadcore group could muster, filling a box set with songs that, for the most part, can stand chin-up with the group's stellar catalog.
  (Josh Modell, review of Low's *A Lifetime of Temporary Relief: 10 Years of B-Sides & Rarities*, Onion online, 4 Aug. 2004, paragraph 1)

- Elizabeth Smart was born in Ottawa, Canada[,] in 1913.
  (biographical note in Grafton Books [London, U.K.] 1988 paperback reprint of Elizabeth Smart's *By Grand Central Station I Sat Down and Wept*)

A pair of commas must also be used in sentences in which the name of a neighborhood, community, or district is followed by the name of the borough or larger municipal entity of which it is a part.

- Mayor Bloomberg throws out the first pitch of a Little League game in Bayside, Queens[,] yesterday—one of two rare Saturday public appearances by Hizzoner, who's often out of town on weekends.
  (Stefan C. Friedman, "Mike Makes a Play at Home," *New York Post*, 25 Apr. 2004, p. 7)

EXCEPTION

When a participle or participial phrase is attached to the name of the county, state, or country, the second comma is omitted.

- Until fall 2003, international success had eluded the Glasgow, Scotland-based company.

Such asymmetrical punctuation, however, is inelegant, so it is better to rephrase the sentence.

- Until fall 2003, international success had eluded the company, which is based in Glasgow, Scotland.

---

20. Commas in Addresses

All of the components of a mailing address are separated by commas—except the state abbreviation and the ZIP Code.

- Please mail the catalogue to Jane Hersch, 1428 North Krome Avenue, Apartment 5-C, Grand Forks, ND 58201.

21. Commas With Names

When a person's name is presented with the last name preceding the first name, a comma separates the two, but no comma separates the first name from the middle name or the middle initial.

- Marr, Suzanne H.

22. Commas With *Jr.* and *Sr.*

Honor the punctuational preference of the man whose name includes the abbreviation. If he inserts a comma between his last name and the abbreviation, follow his lead. If he presents his full name without the comma, do not insert one.

- Sammy Davis, Jr.
- John G. Craig Jr.

TIP: Commas do not set off Roman numerals, such as *II* and *III*, that follow last names.

- Samuel William Hurston III was born in Chicago.

If a man includes the comma before the abbreviation, a comma will also follow the abbreviation when his name is included in a sentence.

- Sammy Davis, Jr., died in 1990.

If a man does not include the comma before the abbreviation, a comma will not follow the abbreviation when his name is included in a sentence.

- For many years, John G. Craig Jr. wrote a weekly column in the *Pittsburgh Post-Gazette*.

TIP: When a sentence ends with an abbreviation whose final element is a period, that period will also serve as the period for the sentence.

- We hired Jonathan David, Jr.

A question mark or an exclamation point, of course, may follow a sentence-ending abbreviation whose final element is a period.

- What possessed us to hire Jonathan David, Jr.?

---

23. Commas With Academic Degrees, Honorary Degrees, and Military Titles

A pair of commas encloses such elements, except at the end of a sentence, where a comma precedes the element and a period follows.

- Ellen Fenton, Ph.D., was the first panelist to speak.
- The guest speaker was Laurel Mason, M.F.A.

When such an abbreviation appears in the title of a work, such as a television series, a comma does not follow the abbreviation unless the syntax of the sentence requires it.

- The TV series *Marcus Welby, M.D.* starred Robert Young.
- The TV series *Marcus Welby, M.D.*, which starred Robert Young, first aired in September 1969.

24. Commas With Job Titles and Official Titles

When a person's name is followed by a job title, the job title should be set off with commas at both ends—except when the sentence ends with the job title.

- Leanne Brach, vice-president of marketing, was honored at the convention.
- The featured speaker was Lauren Morrissey, chief executive officer.

When a title is presented without an article and precedes the title holder's last name, no comma separates the title from the name.

- General Lawrence held a press conference yesterday.

There are two principles to heed when a title precedes a person's name. First, when the article *a* or *an* precedes the title, the person's name must be set off with commas.

- An administrative assistant, Todd Pfizer, caught the error.

Second, when the article *the* precedes the title, the person's name is set off with commas unless one holder of the job title is being distinguished from another.

- The assistant manager, Todd Pfizer, caught the error.
  This sentence makes it clear that the organization has only one assistant manager.
- The assistant manager Todd Pfizer caught the error.
  This sentence makes it clear that the organization has more than one assistant manager.

25. Commas With *Inc.*

If the full, official name of a business includes either the word *Incorporated* or the abbreviation *Inc.*, follow the company's lead in inserting or omitting a comma.

- Gateway, Inc.
- Dell Inc.

If a business includes the comma in its name, a comma will also follow *Inc.* when the name of the business is included anywhere in a sentence except at the end.

- Alfred A. Knopf, Inc., is John Updike's publisher.

If a business does not include the comma in its name, a comma will not follow *Inc.* when the name of the business is included in a sentence.

- Dell Inc. is based in Round Rock, Texas.

The same principles apply to the names of businesses that include the word *Limited* or the abbreviation *Ltd.*

26. Commas Following *etc.* and *et cetera*

A comma always precedes *etc.* and *et cetera,* and a comma must also follow (unless the sentence ends with *etc.* or *et cetera*).

- Wristwatches, bracelets, necklaces, etc., are not to be worn in the manufacturing plant.

TIP: It is redundant to insert *etc.* or *et cetera* at the end of a series introduced by *such as, like, for example,* or *for instance,* because such introductory words make it clear that the list that follows is selective, not exhaustive.

> **Faulty:** The decline in Pittsburgh's economic fortunes over the past 20 years has left a residue of wonderful institutions such as the museums, libraries, sports franchises, etc. that are outsized for the current population.
> (Bruce Johnson and Denise Johnson, "Leadership Key to Making Pittsburgh Forward Looking," *Pittsburgh Post-Gazette,* 23 May 2004, p. C2)

> **Correct:** The decline in Pittsburgh's economic fortunes over the past 20 years has left a residue of wonderful institutions, such as the museums, libraries, and sports franchises, that are outsized for the current population.

27. Commas Following *yes* and *no* and Similar Words

A comma should follow *yes, no,* and any casual term such as *yeah, nope,* and *nah.*

- Yes, I understand your side of the argument.
- Yeah, I saw it all happen.

A comma should also precede any such word when it appears in the body of a sentence.

- And, yes, I'll try to show up on time.

> **TIP:** *No, thanks* is the polite declining of an offer. *No thanks* is a declaration of ingratitude.

28. Commas Following Greetings and Felicitations

A comma should follow a greeting or a felicitation. All too often, especially in e-mails, the comma is carelessly omitted.

- Hi, Ottessa.
- Hello, Ottessa.
- Congratulations, Ottessa!

29. Commas in the Salutations and Complimentary Closings of Letters and E-Mails

In an informal or a semiformal letter or e-mail, the salutation—as well as the complimentary closing—should be followed by a comma.

- Dear Claudia,
- Sincerely,

In a more formal letter or e-mail, a colon follows the salutation.

30. Commas in Numbers of Four or More Digits

The insertion of commas improves the readability of long numbers that specify quantities. Working backward from the final digit, insert a comma before each set of three digits.

- The population has increased to 250,394,792.

31. Commas in Phrasing That Specifies a Person's Height

A comma does not separate the two parts of a phrase that presents a person's height in feet and inches.

- He is six feet two inches tall.

32. Commas in Relation to Quotation Marks

Commas, like periods, are inserted inside, not outside, closing quotation marks.

- The T-shirt slogans that drew the most protests were "Boys Are Stupid," "Girls Rule, Boys Drool," and "Boys Are Smelly."

18B COMMAS: THE SUBTLETIES

33. Commas Setting Off Nonrestrictive Elements

A restrictive element in a sentence narrows down, limits, or restricts the meaning or scope of the word or group of words immediately preceding it. The information presented in a restrictive element is crucial to the meaning of the sentence, because the information is necessary to distinguish one person, place, or thing from another. A restrictive element must never be set off with any form of punctuation. (A restrictive element is also called an essential or a defining element.)

A nonrestrictive element, in contrast, provides supplementary but disposable information about the word or group of words immediately preceding it. The information presented in a nonrestrictive element is not crucial to the meaning of the sentence. Think of the information it presents as bonus information—a little something extra for the reader. A nonrestrictive element is always set off punctuationally. If the nonrestrictive element appears in the middle of a sentence, the element must be set off at both ends with a pair of commas, a pair of parentheses, or a pair of dashes. If the nonrestrictive element appears at the end of a sentence, it must be preceded by a comma or by a dash, or it must be enclosed within parentheses. (A nonrestrictive element is also called a nonessential or nondefining element.)

Restrictive and nonrestrictive elements can take several forms. They can be appositives, prepositional phrases, participial phrases, adjectival dependent clauses, and adverbial dependent clauses.

A. Nonrestrictive vs. Restrictive Appositives

An appositive is a noun or a noun phrase that renames or provides further information about another noun. An appositive almost always follows, rather than precedes, the noun or noun phrase to which it is in apposition.

Examine the punctuation of the following paragraph.

- Melissa's mother, Ellen, is an attorney. Her stepmother, Frieda, is a medical secretary. Her father, Carl, is a computer programmer. Her brother Jason plays in a rock band. Her other brother, David, is in college. Her sister, Greta, is a freshman in high school.

In the paragraph, the names *Ellen, Frieda, Carl, Jason, David,* and *Greta* are all functioning as appositives. *Ellen, Frieda,* and *Carl* are set off at both ends with commas because the names are not essential to the sentences in which they appear. Melissa has only one mother, only one stepmother, and only one father—so their names are merely supplementary information. Those three names are nonrestrictive appositives. Furthermore, it is obvious from the contents of the paragraph that Melissa has two brothers. In the fourth sentence, *Jason* is not set off with commas, because the reader needs to know which of her two brothers plays in a rock band. The name *Jason,* in other words, is needed to distinguish one brother from the other. *Jason* is thus a restrictive appositive. In the fifth sentence,

David is set off with commas because the name is not vital to the meaning of the sentence; the complete subject of the sentence, *her other brother,* sufficiently identifies him as Melissa's second male sibling. *David* is therefore nonrestrictive. Finally, the fact that *Greta* is set off with commas in the last sentence makes it clear that Melissa has only one sister. The name of the sister is not essential to the meaning of the sentence. *Greta* is a nonrestrictive appositive.

The following mispunctuated excerpt is from a review of a performance by the postpunk trio the Yeah Yeah Yeahs, which consists of a singer, a guitarist, and a drummer.

- It was a triumphant performance, led by the singer Karen O, who teased the audience by feigning oblivion: onstage she acts as if she's alone in her bedroom, wriggling and flailing and squawking. ... While the drummer Brian Chase bashed out rudimentary rhythms, the guitarist Nick Zinner found restrained ways to add noise and melody.

  (Kelefa Sanneh, "Oblivious to the Ballroom, As If She Were Home Alone," *New York Times*, 13 Jan. 2004, p. B3)

  The names of the singer, the drummer, and the guitarist are nonrestrictive (the sentences are not distinguishing one singer in the band from another, or one drummer in the band from another, or one guitarist in the band from another), and thus they should be set off with commas at both ends.

The following sentences were mispunctuated when they appeared in the publications listed.

- Prince Charles took his youngest son[,] Harry[,] to a rehabilitation clinic to show him the dangers of drug and alcohol abuse, after the young prince admitted having smoked marijuana and getting drunk when he was 16, a Sunday newspaper reported.

  ("World Briefs: Prince Harry and Drugs," *Pittsburgh Post-Gazette*, 13 Jan. 2002, p. A8)

  A father can have only one youngest son, so the son's name is nonrestrictive. The sentence is also weakened by an error in the use of comparative and superlative adjectives; see chapter 9.

- The Clash was always the most ambitious of punk bands, and its 1979 double album[,] London Calling[,] was easily the London quartet's most visionary statement.

  (Ethan Brown, "Revolution Rock," *New York*, 13 Sept. 2004, p. 86)

  The Clash released only one double album in 1979, so the title of the album is nonrestrictive.

- Seinfeld, who's planning a low-key celebration with his wife, Jessica, and children[,] Sascha and Julian Kal, tried to shrug off the ribbing, but couldn't resist having a little dig at his advancing years.

  (Heather Gilmore, "Yep, I'm 50!," *New York Post*, 25 Apr. 2004, p. 3)

  Commas correctly enclose Jessica, but the omission of a comma after children implies, misleadingly, that at the time of writing, Seinfeld had more than two children. The phrase Sascha and Julian Kal needs to be set off punctuationally at both ends.

- Lawrence Russell Brewer Sr., left, and his son John weep as the jury deliberates the fate of Brewer's other son[,] Lawrence Russell Brewer Jr.[,] yesterday in Bryan, Texas.

  (photo caption accompanying Michael Graczyk, "A Second Racist Sentenced to Death in Dragging Case," for Associated Press, in *Pittsburgh Post-Gazette*, 24 Sept. 1999, p. A10)

  John is restrictive. But Lawrence Russell Brewer Jr. is nonrestrictive—because the phrase that precedes the name (Brewer's other son) sufficiently identifies the person being referred to. Commas should therefore surround Lawrence Russell Brewer Jr.

- Over the decades, there have also been several non-definitive attempts to stage and film "1984," a tale which unspools mostly inside the mind of its alienated protagonist[,] Winston Smith, a Ministry of Truth employee in the mythic nation of Oceania.

  (Misha Berson, "'1984': The Way We Live Now?," *Seattle Times*, 20 Jan. 2004, p. E1)

  The novel has only one alienated protagonist. His name functions as a nonrestrictive appositive.

- Less than a month after his debut album[,] "It's Dark and Hell Is Hot[,]" topped the pop chart in its first week, DMX was arrested and charged with raping an exotic dancer at a friend's apartment.

  (Tony Norman, "Gangsta Rap Cools It Down," *Pittsburgh Post-Gazette*, 7 July 1998, p. B1)

    A recording artist can have only one debut album. Its title is a nonrestrictive appositive.

- Olympic swimmer Jenny Thompson treated her mother, Margrid, and coach John Collins to the Broadway show, *The Producers*.

  (Jill Lieber, "The Sport of Giving," *USA Today*, 26 Dec. 2003, p. 2C)

    Delete the comma before the title of the musical. With the comma, the sentence makes the preposterous declaration that there was only one show on Broadway at the time of writing. And if Thompson has only one coach, his name should be enclosed by commas.

TIP: When a sentence includes the title of a work (such as a book or a movie) that consists of a noun followed by a nonrestrictive appositive, a comma precedes but does not follow the appositive—unless the title is followed by another nonrestrictive element (as in the third example below).

- *I, Robot* was a popular science-fiction movie released during the summer of 2004.
- The science-fiction film *I, Robot* was released during the summer of 2004.
- *I, Robot*, a science-fiction film released during the summer of 2004, was based on stories by Isaac Asimov.

Quotations sometimes serve as appositives. Do not use any punctuation to set off a quotation that is restrictive in function. In each of the following examples, the comma before the quotation must be deleted, because the quotation is essential to the meaning and completeness of the sentence.

- Now every newscast has experts opining on the question, "Is it safe to feed beef to your family?"

  (Walter Shapiro, "Too Little Regulation and Too Much Hysteria Feed Food Fears," *USA Today*, 26 Dec. 2003, p. 8A)

- This is the kind of deal that should remind consumers of the adage, "If it seems too good to be true, it probably is."

  ("Profit Center," editorial, *Pittsburgh Post-Gazette*, 29 Sept. 2003, p. A16)

TIP: When a noun or noun phrase is preceded by *a* and is followed by an appositive, the appositive is always nonrestrictive and needs to be set off with punctuation.

- She is the author of a memoir, *My Years with Cal*.

When a noun or noun phrase is preceded by *the* and is followed by an appositive, the appositive is usually restrictive and should not be set off with punctuation.

- She is the author of the memoir *My Years with Cal*.

Occasionally, however, the appositive following a noun or noun phrase that is preceded by *the* is nonrestrictive and thus needs to be set off with punctuation.

- She plans to move to the state capital, Boise.

When an appositive follows a noun or noun phrase that is not preceded by the article *a*, *an*, or *the*, the appositive is restrictive and is not set off punctuationally. *Jerry Garcia* is a restrictive appositive in the following sentence.

- Guitarist Jerry Garcia was a brilliantly inventive improviser.

The comma before *Philip Wylie* should be deleted from the following sentence.

- The preoccupation with a monstrous mom who threatened to engulf and devour the family was a phenomenon contemporary psychologists called "momism," a name coined by febrile patriot and anti-Communist, Phillip [sic] Wylie, in his bestselling book Generation of Vipers.

(Mary F. Corey, *The World Through a Monocle: The New Yorker at Midcentury* [Cambridge, MA: Harvard University Press, 1999], p. 165)

B. Nonrestrictive vs. Restrictive Prepositional Phrases

The failure to use punctuation to set off nonrestrictive prepositional phrases results in illogical sentences and sentences that distort the writer's intended meaning. In the sentence *She lived in San Francisco until her death in 2002,* for example, the prepositional phrase *in 2002* is functioning restrictively. It is distinguishing the woman's death *in 2002* from her death in some other year. In other words, the sentence is implying that the woman died more than once. Surely, however, that is not the writer's intended meaning. The prepositional phrase *in 2002* is in fact providing only supplementary information, not essential information. Inserting a comma before the prepositional phrase will resolve the problem.

Similarly, the sentence *The suspect was arrested at his home in Detroit* is correct only if the writer wants the reader to understand that the suspect has more than one home. The prepositional phrase *in Detroit* is restrictive: it is distinguishing one of the suspect's homes from one or more other homes of his. If the writer wants the reader to understand that the suspect has only one home, a comma must be inserted before *in Detroit.* Consider the following two-sentence passage.

- When he married Marianne, in May 1999, he was enthralled by her brilliance. After they divorced, in 2003, the two remained close friends.

Without the comma after *Marianne,* the first sentence would be implying that he married Marianne more than once—that their May 1999 marriage is being distinguished from another marriage of theirs. Without the comma after *divorced,* the second sentence would imply that the couple were divorced more than once.

These sentences were mispunctuated when they appeared in newspapers and magazines.

- On his first job[,] as an elevator operator at the Gimbels department store during the 1960s, he rallied other young operators to fight for the right to wear beards.

(Jim McKay, "Executive in the Spotlight: Billy Joe Jordan," *Pittsburgh Post-Gazette,* 22 Feb. 1998, p. E5)

A person can have only one first job, so the three consecutive prepositional phrases (*as an elevator operator at the Gimbels department store during the 1960s*) together form a nonrestrictive element.

- He was 53 and earning a salary of $93,000 a year when he was fired[,] in 1993.

(Marylynne Pitz, "Age Bias Award Let Stand in Court," *Pittsburgh Post-Gazette,* 24 Feb. 1998, p. E9)

The article makes it clear that the man was fired only once. Without the comma before *in 1993,* however, the prepositional phrase *in 1993* is forced into a restrictive role, distinguishing one instance of his having been fired from another.

- When it first came out[,] in 1972, Don McLean's elliptical epistle "American Pie" got puzzled and pored over like ancient runes by fans and rock critics alike.

  (Parke Puterbaugh, review of the reissue of Don McLean's *American Pie*, *Rolling Stone*, 21 Aug. 2003, p. 78)

- [Warren] Zevon's first round of stardom[,] in the 1970s and early 1980s[,] ended with his dive into severe alcoholism.

  (David Fricke, review of four Warren Zevon reissues, *Rolling Stone*, 4 Dec. 2003, p. 147)

- Since its founding[,] in 1985, Arts for Transit has installed nearly 140 works (and counting) of public art in [subway] stations throughout its labyrinthine 722-mile system.

  (Roberta Smith, "The Rush-Hour Revelations of an Underground Museum," *New York Times*, 2 Jan. 2004, p. B37)

- After his final prison stint ended[,] in 1969, he decided to turn his life around, he says.

  (Vanessa O'Connell, "How Troubled Past Finally Caught Up With James Minder," *Wall Street Journal*, 8 Mar. 2004, p. A1)

- Between designing collections, Herrera also has launched fragrances: Carolina Herrera[,] in 1988; Carolina Herrera for Men[,] in 1991; Flore[,] in 1994; and Aqua Flore[,] in 1996.

  (Rod Stafford Hagwood, "Carolina in the City: Designer Herrera and Daughter Collaborate on a Scent Named for Manhattan Area Code," *Sun-Sentinel*, 11 Feb. 1998, p. 1E)

- As the most expensive dial-up Internet service on the market[,] at $23.90 a month, AOL is loathe [sic] to bother subscribers with pop-up and other take-over-the-screen ads.

  (Julia Angwin, "As Ads Plunge, Marketing Head to Leave AOL," *Wall Street Journal*, 9 Jan. 2004, p. A9)

Be especially careful with sentences in which prepositional phrases are providing supplementary, not essential, information about people or things being ranked.

In the following sentence, the punctuation makes it clear that at the time of writing, Terry Swigoff had directed only three feature films.

- *Bad Santa* was Terry Swigoff's third feature film, after *Crumb* (1994) and *Ghost World* (2001).

  If the writer had neglected to insert the comma after *film*, the sense of the sentence would be that *Bad Santa* was the third of three feature films Swigoff made after having made *Crumb* and *Ghost World*. In other words, the sentence would be telling us that at the time of writing, the director had made at least five feature films.

The following sentences were mispunctuated when they appeared in newspapers, and the result was that they misstated the facts and muddled the reader's sense of how many entities were being ranked.

- Burger King, the No. 2 burger chain[,] behind McDonald's, spent $358.6 million on ads in 2002 and $244.9 million during the first 10 months of 2003. ...

  (Suzanne Vranica and Brian Steinberg, "Burger King Takes Y&R Off Menu," *Wall Street Journal*, 23 Jan. 2004, p. A13)

  Without the comma after *chain*, the sentence is telling us that Burger King is one of two hamburger chains trailing McDonald's in sales.

- Target, the third largest discount department store chain in the United States[,] behind Wal-Mart and Kmart, is plotting its entry into the market with at least two openings scheduled for 1999 and plans for at least half a dozen stores overall.

  (Joyce Gannon, "On Target," *Pittsburgh Post-Gazette*, 22 Jan. 1998, p. C1)

  Without the comma after *United States*, the sentence is telling us that Target is one of three discount-department-store chains trailing behind Wal-Mart and Kmart.

- Lexington's smoke-free ordinance for restaurants, bars, bowling alleys, nightclubs, laundries and other enclosed public places is a first for Kentucky, the No. 2 tobacco-producing state[,] behind North Carolina.

  ("Clearing the Air," editorial, *Pittsburgh Post-Gazette*, 29 Apr. 2004, p. A-16)

- Type 1 diabetes affects about one million Americans, with about 13,000 new cases each year, making it the second-largest childhood disease in the U.S.[,] after asthma.

  (Michael Waldholz, "Researchers' Goal: Stopping Diabetes Before Kids Get It," *Wall Street Journal*, 1 Mar. 2004, p. A12)

C. Nonrestrictive vs. Restrictive Participial Phrases

A participial phrase is a phrase beginning with a participle—a verbal adjective. Remember that participles take two forms: present participles always end in -*ing*, and past participles usually end in -*d* or -*ed*. Be sure to use punctuation to set off nonrestrictive participial phrases.

- Hartman is halfway finished with another play[,] called "Mad Honey."

  (Marylynne Pitz, "$10,000 Grants Surprise Three Local Artists," *Pittsburgh Post-Gazette*, 24 Jan. 2004, p. C8)

    Without the comma, the sentence is telling us that the playwright will have written at least two plays with the same title.

- But all that fades away when Carol, the nicest, most efficient server on the planet, hands you Monterey Bay's famous menu[,] featuring 26 kinds of fish, prepared just about any way you want.

  (Mackenzie Carpenter, "Monterey Bay Cruise," *Pittsburgh Post-Gazette*, 30 Jan. 2004, p. W21)

    The restaurant has only one famous menu, so the participial phrase describing the contents of the menu must be treated as nonrestrictive.

- The initiative comes after a bad year for manned space exploration that included the breakup of the space shuttle Columbia[,] killing all seven astronauts on board[,] and a devastating report by the Columbia Accident Investigation Board that blamed NASA management for cutting corners on safety.

  (Ann McFeatters, "Bush Sets Sight on Moon and Mars," *Pittsburgh Post-Gazette*, 15 Jan. 2004, p. A3)

    Without the commas, the participial phrase *killing all seven astronauts on board* is distinguishing one Columbia tragedy from another Columbia tragedy—but there was, of course, only one.

D. Nonrestrictive vs. Restrictive Adjectival Dependent Clauses

An adjectival dependent clause is a dependent clause that functions like a single-word adjective and directly follows the noun or pronoun it is describing. Adjectival dependent clauses usually begin with the relative pronouns *that, which, who, whom,* and *whose*. Occasionally, though, an adjectival dependent clause begins with *where, when,* or *why*.

Examine the punctuation in the following paragraph.

- My friend who works at a bookstore gave me a book that was delivered to the store yesterday. The book, which is an anthology of poems and short stories about heartbreak, is five hundred pages long. The book's editor, who lives in Los Angeles, got the idea for the anthology after suffering a devastating breakup with his longtime girlfriend, who left him for another man. The book is dedicated to the woman whom the editor now intends to marry.

The first sentence of the paragraph includes two restrictive adjectival dependent clauses. The first (*who works at a bookstore*) specifies which friend gave the writer the book, and the second (*that was delivered to the store yesterday*) specifies which book was given to the writer. In other words, the first adjectival clause distinguishes one friend from the writer's other friends, and the second adjectival clause distinguishes one book from many other books. The information in the adjectival clauses is essential to the meaning of the sentence, so the restrictive clauses have not been set off punctuationally.

The adjectival dependent clause in the second sentence is not distinguishing one book from another. The subject of the second sentence (*the book*) clearly refers to the book introduced in the previous sentence. The information in the adjectival clause, in other words, is not crucial to the meaning of the sentence. The clause is nonrestrictive and has therefore been set off with commas.

The third sentence in the paragraph includes two nonrestrictive adjectival dependent clauses. The clause *who lives in Los Angeles* offers merely supplementary information about the subject of the sentence (*the book's editor*), and *who left him for another man* offers merely supplementary information about *his longtime girlfriend*. The adjectival clauses have thus been set off punctuationally.

In the final sentence, *whom the editor now intends to marry* is a restrictive adjectival clause: It specifies which woman the book is dedicated to. The adjectival clause is therefore not preceded by a comma.

The sentences that follow were mispunctuated when they appeared in newspapers and other sources. The first example is from an article about the singer Michael Jackson.

- The 45-year-old singer[,] who had international hits with the albums "Thriller" (1982), "Bad" (1987) and "Dangerous" (1991)[,] saw his career begin to collapse in 1993, amid allegations he molested a boy.

  (Jeff Wilson, "Jackson Ranch Searched amid Abuse Reports," for Associated Press, in *Pittsburgh Post-Gazette*, 19 Nov. 2003, p. A10)

  > Because the adjectival clause contains internal punctuation, it would be stylistically desirable to set off the clause with a pair of dashes or a pair of parentheses (see Chapter 20).

- The babies range in size from Alexis, the smallest, weighing 6 pounds, up to Kenneth, the largest[,] who weighs 9 pounds, 5 ounces.

  ("Life at Home with Seven Babies Is Busy, Not Chaotic," for Associated Press, in *Pittsburgh Post-Gazette*, 16 Mar. 1998, p. A20)

- Writing dialogue is as simple as talking, right? Wrong. Few understand this concept better than dramatists[,] who must tell their stories primarily through dialogue.

  (Gotham Writers' Workshop catalogue of courses, winter 2004, p. 23)

  > Dramatists, by definition, are writers who tell their stories primarily through dialogue, so the adjectival clause is nonrestrictive.

- He started a partnership with another poet[,] who goes by the pseudonym Tehut-Nine, who had been a fellow student, and they formed a self-publishing company, SunRASon Productions.

  (Dinitia Smith, "A Hip-Hop Author in Search of a Publisher Finds One on the A Train," *New York Times*, 6 Jan. 2004, p. B7)

  > Without the comma before *who*, the sentence is declaring, erroneously, that both men share the same pseudonym. (To smooth out the phrasing, delete the comma after *Tehut-Nine* and insert the coordinating conjunction *and*.)

Make sure that a nonrestrictive adjectival dependent clause is set off punctuationally at both ends.

- William Ivey Long, who is apparently the only person allowed to design costumes in New York this season (his work has appeared in "Little Shop of Horrors," "The Boy from Oz," and "Never Gonna Dance"—all within the last three months)[,] has done a very restrained, smart group for this play.

  (Howard Kissel, "Nothin's Comin' Up 'Rose's,'" *New York Daily News*, 19 Dec. 2003, p. 67)

- He escorted grieving parents[,] who were never to see their daughters again, out the door.

  (Dinitia Smith, "Cultural Theorists, Start Your Epitaphs," *New York Times*, 3 Jan. 2004, p. A15)

TIP: Many writers use the relative pronouns *that* and *which* interchangeably, but it is better to reserve *that* for restrictive clauses and *which* for nonrestrictive clauses. In the first two of the following examples, it would be advisable to substitute *which* for *that*; in the third example, it would be advisable to substitute *that* for *which*.

- [The movie] "Big Fish" has two aces. One is its moving conclusion, that [which] would be a thousand percent stronger had the film made its many characters more sympathetic.

  (Ed Blank, "'Big Fish' Fails to Evoke Sympathy," *Greensburg [PA] Tribune-Review*, 9 Jan. 2004, p. C5)

- In 2000 he played the title role in a Broadway production of "Macbeth," that [which] was panned by critics and lasted only 10 days.

  ("Kelsey Grammer May Join 'Producers,'" *New York Times*, 14 Jan. 2004, p. B3)

  > The relative pronoun **that** could be mistaken for the pronoun **that**—and some readers could thus initially misconstrue the sentence as a mispunctuated compound sentence.

- New York restricts the sale of toy guns to those models that are brightly-colored and which [that] have closed barrels.

  (Mike Bucsko, "Fake Handguns Sparking Fears That Are All Too Real," *Pittsburgh Post-Gazette*, 21 Feb. 2004, p. A1)

  This sentence, of course, could be rephrased: *The only toy guns that can be sold legally in New York are brightly colored models with closed barrels.*

E. Nonrestrictive vs. Restrictive Adverbial Dependent Clauses at the End of a Sentence

An adverbial dependent clause at the end of a sentence is not preceded by a comma if the clause sets any limitations on the meaning of the independent clause. Such a dependent clause is restrictive: It provides information essential to the sense of the sentence as a whole. That is, the meaning of the sentence would change if the clause were punctuationally detached from the independent clause.

An adverbial dependent clause at the end of a sentence is preceded by a comma, however, if the contents of the clause provide information that is only supplementary to the meaning of the independent clause. This sort of dependent clause is nonrestrictive: It must be punctuationally detached from the independent clause, because it is not presenting essential information. That is, the clause could be deleted from the sentence without changing the meaning of the sentence.

The following sentence is not stating categorically that David will be fired.

- David will be fired unless his performance improves.

Instead, the adverbial dependent clause *unless his performance improves* is restrictive: It specifies the circumstances under which David will be fired. The adverbial dependent clause has therefore not been preceded by a comma.

Similarly, in the following sentence, the adverbial dependent clause *if any merchandise is defective* is restrictive: It stipulates the special condition that will entitle customers to a refund.

- Our customers are always entitled to a refund if any merchandise is found to be defective.

The adverbial dependent clauses in the following sentences, however, are nonrestrictive: They provide merely supplementary information and should have been preceded by commas.

- One of the dumbest time-travel adventures of all time is adapted from Michael Crichton's best seller about a group of archeology students miraculously transported to the 14th century[,] where they have to rescue their professor in the midst of a war between the French and English.

  (Jack Mathews, capsule film review of *Timeline*, *New York Daily News*, 19 Dec. 2003, p. 70)

- In the winter I usually feel myself getting drowsy near 4:30 p.m.[,] when it starts to get dark.

  (Bernd Heinrich, "Hibernation, Insulation and Caffeination," *New York Times*, 31 Jan. 2004, p. A31)

- [Howard] Dean, a political science major, arrived at the New Haven campus in 1967[,] when Bush was a struggling third-year student with his eye on the presidency—of the Delta Kappa Epsilon fraternity.

  (Bill Hutchinson, "Yale Was Dean's Study and Bush's Fun House," *New York Daily News*, 19 Dec. 2003, p. 111)

Sentence-ending adverbial dependent clauses that begin with *even though, although,* and *though* are almost always nonrestrictive. Such clauses are known as concessive clauses. A comma should precede the concessive clause in the following sentence.

- A Nashville native who now lives in Southlake, Texas, Samuels says he's always had a natural curiosity about the Internet[,] although his computer science undergraduate degree from Abilene Christian University focused on business, not technical applications.

(Carol Memmott, "A Starter, a Surfer, and an Ex-Secretary Reform Travel," *USA Today*, 17 Mar. 1998, p. 7E)

Occasionally, however, the contents of a concessive clause are felt to be essential to a sentence. Such a clause is not preceded by a comma.

- They wore shorts even though the temperature was in the forties.
- The company continued to market the product even though serious concerns had been raised about its safety.

Sentence-ending adverbial dependent clauses that begin with *while* are almost always nonrestrictive when *while* is used as a synonym for *and*.

- Members of the first group voiced approval of the new version of the software, while members of the second group were less pleased.

Sentence-ending adverbial dependent clauses that begin with *if* and *even if* are not always restrictive.

- There's some chicken salad in the refrigerator, if you're hungry.
  Whether you are hungry or not, the chicken salad is still in the refrigerator— so the contents of the adverbial dependent clause are not essential to the meaning of the sentence.

Sentence-ending adverbial dependent clauses beginning with *because* (and also with *since* and *as* when those two subordinating conjunctions are used as synonyms for *because*) can be especially troublesome. The most precise discussion of such clauses appears in Wilson Follett's *Modern American Usage*, a magisterial guide edited and completed by Jacques Barzun. We are indebted to Follett for our explanations that follow.

If the independent clause is stated in positive terms, the adverbial dependent clause beginning with *because* can be either nonrestrictive or restrictive.

- We hired her, because she has a degree in marketing.
- We hired her because she has a degree in marketing.

In both sentences, the main point is that the woman was hired. But the sentences differ subtly in intent. The first sentence stresses the fact that she has been hired; the reason for her having been hired is considered to be nonessential, and thus the adverbial dependent clause is preceded by a comma. The second sentence stresses the reason why the woman was hired. Here the contents of the adverbial dependent clause are crucial to the writer's intentions, so the dependent clause is not set off with a comma; it is treated as a restrictive clause.

In the second of the following two sentences, the reason for the writer's avoidance is considered to be of less importance than the act of avoidance itself.

- I kept avoiding him because I knew he'd been talking behind my back.
- I kept avoiding him, because I knew he'd been talking behind my back.

It is up to the writer to decide whether the contents of a clause beginning with *because* are vital to the meaning of a sentence. Most often, such clauses are regarded as restrictive.

- He moved to El Paso because he liked the dry climate.
- According to the results of the survey, people avoid the neighborhood because they perceive it as a high-crime area.

In each of the three sentences below, the independent clause relates a circumstance or a state of being, and the adverbial dependent clause specifies the cause of the circumstance or state of being. The adverbial dependent clause in each sentence has been treated as a nonrestrictive element because the writer wants to place the emphasis on the circumstance or state of being itself, not on its cause.

- He was more demoralized than his colleagues, because he had invested much more time in the project.
- She was by nature a fierce individualist, because she had grown up as one of three children in a single-parent household.
- It's difficult to appreciate just how revolutionary the rock band Pavement was in its heyday, because so much of today's music has appropriated the band's innovations and ushered its sound into the mainstream.

Each of the three preceding sentences could, of course, be presented without the comma; but, as noted, the emphasis of the sentence would undergo a subtle change. Only the writer can determine whether a comma is necessary to express the intended shade of meaning. The careful writer is always attentive to nuance.

When the independent clause that precedes the *because* clause is stated in negative terms, two possibilities arise. If the adverbial dependent clause is stating the reason why something has not happened or why something is not true, the clause is nonrestrictive and is preceded by a comma. But if the adverbial dependent clause is ruling out a reason why something has happened or why something is true, the clause is restrictive, and a comma must not precede the dependent clause.

Compare the following sentences.

- We did not hire her, because she had a degree in marketing.
- We did not hire her because she had a degree in marketing.

The independent clause of the first sentence is stating that the woman was not hired. That is the important point of the sentence. The dependent clause is merely providing the reason why she was not hired. The reason is not essential to the meaning of the sentence, and thus the adverbial dependent clause is punctuated as a nonrestrictive element.

The important point of the second sentence is that the woman was hired—but for a reason other than that she had a degree in marketing. The adverbial dependent clause is vital to the sense of the sentence; without the dependent clause, the sentence would be declaring that the woman had in fact not been hired. The dependent clause is therefore not set off punctuationally.

Examine the following two-sentence excerpt.

- I wouldn't recommend eating at the Grotto because the menu is entirely heart-healthy and vegetarian. Go there because the desserts are out of this world.

    The first sentence makes it clear that eating at the Grotto is being recommended for a reason other than the fact that the menu consists entirely of heart-healthy and vegetarian items. The adverbial dependent clause is therefore restrictive. (If the writer had inserted a comma before *because*, the dependent clause would be nonrestrictive, and the sentence would have a profoundly different meaning: The sentence would be advising the reader not to eat at the Grotto.) The second sentence explains why the writer is recommending the restaurant. In the second sentence, the adverbial dependent clause is also restrictive.

Each of the following two sentences needs a comma before the nonrestrictive adverbial dependent clause beginning with *because*.

- The corporation does not release financial information, because it is privately owned.
- We can't start the performance on time, because the musicians haven't yet arrived.

The sentences below were mispunctuated when they appeared in newspapers and in magazines (the sentence-ending adverbial dependent clauses are nonrestrictive).

- Kerry, who played the eligible-Washington-bachelor game for many years, says he wasn't eager to remarry[,] because he felt protective of his daughters and the failure of his first marriage made him unwilling to commit again.

  (Meryl Gordon, "Hurry, Kerry," *New York*, 24 Nov. 2003, p. 49)

- It's not necessary to have a car in Cold Spring[,] because there is so much within walking distance.

  (Mary C. Bounds, "Weekender: Cold Spring, N.Y.," *New York Times*, 13 Feb. 2004, p. D7)

- In 1984, the runner and author James Fixx, who helped popularize the health benefits of jogging, dropped dead of a heart attack while running, leading to widespread smugness by those, including some doctors, who thought the new craze was folly. But, of course, running did not stop[,] because Americans had found out for themselves that it promotes fitness and health.

  ("Fat Wars," editorial, *Pittsburgh Post-Gazette*, 16 Feb. 2004, p. A10)

  > Without the comma, the sentence would be declaring that running did in fact stop—but for a reason other than that provided in the dependent clause. With the comma, the sentence declares that Americans did not give up jogging, and the dependent clause explains why they did not.

- The Amish aren't overweight[,] because they work their asses off.

  (Dawn Patton, "I've Had My Fill of the Atkins Diet," *Pittsburgh City Paper*, 4–11 Feb. 2004, p. 5)

  > Without the comma, the sentence is declaring, illogically, that the reason the Amish are not overweight is something other than the fact that they are such industrious workers. Even with the comma, however, the sentence is clumsy. It could be revised as *The reason the Amish aren't overweight is that they work their asses off.*

TIP: If a nonrestrictive adverbial dependent clause appears in the middle of a sentence, treat it as you would treat any interruptive element: Set it off punctuationally at both ends. The writers of the following sentence did not punctuate the adverbial dependent clause that separates the subject of the independent clause from its predicate.

- The golden era of Fitzgerald, Hemingway and Faulkner[,] when fiction was a staple of many mainstream magazines[,] is long gone.

  (Margo Hammond and Ellen Heltzel, "The Fall of Fiction," *Pittsburgh Post-Gazette*, 22 Feb. 2004, p. E2)

It is not uncommon to find a sentence in which more than one nonrestrictive element has been left unpunctuated.

Faulty: A former chiropractor from Coraopolis who caused a furor in Georgia a decade ago when he paid $200,000 to clear his criminal record has been arrested again in Ohio.

(Torsten Ove, "Chiropractor Who Cleared Record with Cash Arrested Again," *Pittsburgh Post-Gazette*, 20 Aug. 2003, p. B3)

> The sentence includes an unpunctuated nonrestrictive adverbial dependent clause (*when he paid $200,000 to clear his criminal record*) and an unpunctuated nonrestrictive prepositional phrase (*in Ohio*).

Correct: A former chiropractor from Coraopolis who caused a furor in Georgia a decade ago, when he paid $200,000 to clear his criminal record, has been arrested again, in Ohio.

F. False Restrictives

Writers—journalists, especially—who attempt to compress much information into the smallest possible space often unintentionally force a nonessential or nonrestrictive detail into playing a restrictive role. That is, a supplementary, disposable detail is forced to function as if it were distinguishing one person or thing from another. The sentence *Aaron's biologist father and neuroscientist mother have instilled in the boy a deep curiosity about the world* implies that Aaron has at least two fathers (one of whom is a biologist) and at least two mothers (one of whom is a neuroscientist). Logic can be imparted to the sentence by revising it as *Aaron's father, a biologist, and his mother, a neuroscientist, have instilled in the boy a deep curiosity about the world*.

The following sentence unwittingly implies that a television-news network was launched more than once.

Faulty: Fox's ratings, already climbing since the station's 1996 launch, really began to rocket upward after September 11, 2001, and blasted into orbit with the second Iraq war.

(Brian C. Anderson, "Liberal Media, on the Run," *Pittsburgh Post-Gazette*, 7 Dec. 2003, p. E1)

The writer appears to be distinguishing the network's 1996 launch from its launch in some other year. *1996* is a false restrictive. The sentence could be revised as *Fox's ratings, already climbing since the station's launch, in 1996, really began to rocket upward.* . . .

The meaning of each of the following sentences is distorted by a false restrictive.

Faulty: George Harrison wrote a lot of great songs and had a lot of talented friends, and they converged for a tribute to the late Beatle at London's Royal Albert Hall exactly one year after his 2001 death.

(Austin Scaggs, review of *The Concert for George*, *Rolling Stone*, 11 Dec. 2003, p. 219)

Harrison died only once. The ending of the sentence might be revised as *after his death, in 2001.*

Faulty: Still, *Life and Death* is a haunting profile of Wuornos during the months before her October 2002 execution.

(Nicole Keeter, review of *Aileen: Life and Death of a Serial Killer*, *Time Out New York*, 8-15 Jan. 2004, p. 89)

Wuornos was put to death only once. The ending of the sentence might be revised as *during the months before her execution, in October 2002.*

Faulty: The title of the Clash's 1980 double-LP critique of British social ills came from the intro to a World War II–era BBC World Service program: "Hello, America. This is London calling."

(Shirley Halperin and Bud Scoppa, "The Tales Behind the Titles," *Rolling Stone*, 11 Dec. 2003, p. 92)

The Clash released only one double-LP critique of British social ills. A possible revision is *The title of the Clash's double-LP critique of British social ills, which was released in 1980, came from.* ...

A false restrictive occasionally arises when coordinate adjectives are presented as if they were cumulative adjectives (see rule 4).

Faulty: His beautiful younger wife is at work at her design job, his life and art have stopped.

(John Homans, "Blue's Clues," *New York*, 15 Dec. 2003, p. 58)

The sentence is erroneously distinguishing the man's beautiful younger wife from at least one other younger wife of his. Insert a comma after *beautiful*.

Faulty: On his dark third album, Browne explored, in the words of one *Rolling Stone* reviewer, the "romantic possibility in the shadow of apocalypse."

("The 500 Greatest Albums of All Time," *Rolling Stone*, 11 Dec. 2003, p. 162)

Jackson Browne released only one third album, but the sentence is illogically distinguishing his dark third album from another third album of his. Insert a comma after *dark*.

Faulty: Will Smith is gettin' jiggy in his new deluxe $1.8 million trailer.

(Marianne Garvey, "Big-Rig Willy," *New York Post*, 20 June 2004, p. 3)

Smith's new deluxe $1.8 million trailer is not being contrasted with an older deluxe $1.8 million trailer of his, so a comma should be inserted between *new* and *deluxe*. And since a *deluxe* $1.8 million trailer is not being contrasted with some other sort of $1.8 million trailer, a comma is also needed between *deluxe* and *$1.8 million*. The sentence is thus providing three facts about the trailer: it's new, it's deluxe, and it cost $1.8 million.

34. Alternatives to the *a, b,* and *c* Pattern for a Series

Writers need not confine themselves to the *a, b, and c* pattern for presenting a series, which is discussed in rule 3. There are three alternative patterns.

A. *a, b, c*

This pattern can be used to secure two effects.

1. Use this pattern when the subsequent items in the series are restatements of, revisions of, or variations on the first element.

   - The editor thought that the chapter had many gaps, omissions, lacunae.
   - Lauren hated anything fake, sham, inauthentic.
   - Melissa had a fondness for oddballs, misfits, eccentrics.

2. Use this pattern to imply that the series could be extended further—that the list is not necessarily complete (the abbreviation *etc.* is implied).

   - Morrissey's songs are full of loneliness, isolation, unrequited love, heartbreak, despair, self-doubt, self-incrimination.
   - She collected old postcards, handbills, placards, restaurant menus, business stationery.
   - His diary entries are rich in gossip, self-analysis, crankery, confessions, evasions.

B. *a and b and c*

This pattern throws extra emphasis on each item in the series.

   - She has brains and beauty and brilliance.
   - I was young and obtuse and bewildered.
   - He spent his final years in a haze of drug abuse and disease and bitterness.

C. *a, and b, and c*

This pattern throws even greater emphasis on each member of the series—and slows down the sentence.

   - He was empty-headed, and hesitant, and unexcitable.
   - She misses the skyline, and the crowds, and the clamor.

35. Defensible Splits of Compound Predicates

Do not insert a comma before a coordinating conjunction separating the two halves of a compound predicate—unless you have a very good justification for doing so.

The following two sentences should lose the commas splitting the compound predicates.

> **Faulty:** You know those people on your street who maintained a beautiful old house, but were always bickering?
> (Nicole Brodeur, "The Market Still Thrives on Conflict," *Seattle Times*, 20 Jan. 2004, p. B1)

> **Faulty:** Those who are fortunate enough to be employed often have to work long hours, or string together two and three jobs to make ends meet.
> (Bob Herbert, "The Other America," *New York Times*, 23 Jan. 2004, p. A25)

There are, however, five defensible reasons for using a comma to split a compound predicate.

1. To prevent confusion or misreading.

> **Faulty:** The drunken lout taking a swing at her missed and hit a bystander instead.

Insert a comma after *missed*, so that readers will not initially regard *missed* as one of two transitive verbs with *bystander* as their direct object. The verb *missed* is functioning intransitively in the sentence.

Faulty: I received an e-mail from the manager, who said the other waitress called in sick and asked me to fill in for her.

Insert a comma after *and*, so that the reader does not mistake *waitress* as the subject of *asked*.

TIP: Sentences like the two above can always be rewritten to avoid a split compound predicate: *The drunken lout who took a swing at her missed his target and hit a bystander instead. I received an e-mail from the manager saying the other waitress had called in sick and asking me to fill in for her.*

Faulty: Recent discussions of this important social trend fail to face up to a key source of the problem and prescribe the wrong solution.

(James J. Heckman and Amy L. Wax, "Home Alone," *Wall Street Journal*, 23 Jan. 2004, p. A14)

Without a comma before *and*, the sentence can be construed as saying that the discussions also fail to prescribe the wrong solution.

2. To achieve an emphatic contrast or drama or gravity.

- He was gravely ill, or at least claimed to be.
- Every man is a consumer, and ought to be a producer.
  (Ralph Waldo Emerson, in "Wealth")

3. To clarify the structure of a sentence in which the first verb phrase already includes a coordinating conjunction in a pair or series.

- Lonnie is short, squabby, and coarse, and wears Hawaiian shirts under wide-lapelled corduroy suit jackets.

4. To emphasize the passing of time (in other words, the action in the second half of the predicate takes place considerably later than the action in the first half).

- She evicted him from his apartment, and fell head over heels for him.

5. To emphasize that the two parts of the predicate are not of equal importance.

- She was hard of hearing, and had amassed a fortune worth several million dollars.

18C ERRONEOUS COMMAS

36. Single Commas Separating Subjects From Predicates

Never insert a lone comma between a subject and a predicate. (Remember, however, that a nonrestrictive, interruptive element—a single word, a phrase, or a dependent clause—often appears between the subject and the predicate of a sentence. Such elements are set off punctuationally at both ends.)

Each of these sentences must lose the comma separating the subject from the predicate.

Faulty: Today, the permanent collection of Albuquerque's airport, features 112 artworks from more than 80 New Mexico artists.

(Sharon McDonnell, "Art Exhibits Help Make Time Fly Between Flights," *New York Times*, 20 Dec. 2003, p. C6)

Delete the comma after *airport*.

Faulty: The trend of watches doubling as jewelry, is especially noticeable in the movement from the plain silver and gold watches to those with embellishments and jewels, like those favored by rap artists.

(Kristi L. Gustafson, "Watches Make a Timely Fashion Statement," for *Albany Times Union*, in *Seattle Post-Intelligencer*, 20 Jan. 2004, p. C6)

Delete the comma after *jewelry*.

Faulty: The all-new xDrive intelligent all-wheel-drive system, sets new standards in agility for all-wheel-drive vehicles.

("X Marks the Sweet Spot," *AAA Motorist*, Westmoreland [PA] Region, Jan. 2004, p. 16)

Delete the comma after *system*.

Faulty: What Mr. Dean has never had to answer to in the Democratic primary, perhaps because the other candidates are too embarrassed to ask, is how a presidential contender whose campaign is dedicated to relieving the economic squeeze on working class families, believes that socking these folks with a $1,400 to $1,800-a-year tax hike will make their financial situation less stressful.

(Stephen Moore, "Take a Hike," *Wall Street Journal*, 2 Jan. 2004, p. A8)

Delete the comma after *families*.

EXCEPTION

A comma separating a subject from a predicate is occasionally needed to ensure the clarity of a sentence or to prevent misreading.

- The culture that fell, fell.

(James McCourt, cited in Liz Brown, "Road Warrior," *Time Out New York*, 8–15 Jan. 2004, p. 111)

A comma-free version of this sentence would most likely confuse readers. (See rule 13.)

---

37. Commas With Quotations Serving as Structural Components of Sentences

Do not use a comma to set off a nondialogic quotation that is functioning as a structural component of the sentence into which it has been integrated. That is, do not use a comma to set off a quotation functioning as the subject of a clause; as the predicate of a clause; as the complement of a linking verb (unless the quotation takes the form of an interrogative sentence); as a restrictive appositive; as the direct object of a transitive verb that is not functioning as a verb of attribution; as the objective complement of a transitive verb; as the retained objective complement of a transitive verb; as the object of a gerund or the object of a participle (unless the quotation is fairly long); or as the object of a preposition.

In each of the following two sentences, the quotation is functioning as the subject. Each sentence should lose the comma before the linking verb.

Faulty: "Before we get started, you should know that I had a vasectomy," are Harvey's first words to her.

(Peter M. Nichols, "New DVDs: Making a Relaxed, Low-Key Film in Madcap Tokyo," *New York Times*, 3 Feb. 2004, p. B8)

Faulty: "Char belongs to the people now," is how another of Char's friends put it.

(Steve Fishman, "The Dead Wives Club, or Char in Love," *New York*, 31 May 2004, p. 20)

The following sentences are punctuated correctly.

Correct: Her objection to the new policy is that it "diminishes the accountability of each teacher in the school district."

The quotation serves as the predicate of a nominative dependent clause.

Correct: The slogan on his T-shirt was "I bring nothing to the table."

Do not use a comma to set off a declarative-sentence quotation functioning as the complement of a linking verb.

Correct: The unspoken question is, "Who's really in charge?"

A complement taking the form of a question, however, should be preceded by a comma.

Correct: A job candidate should be prepared to answer the question "Where do you see yourself five years from now?"

Do not use a comma to set off a quotation functioning as a restrictive appositive (see rule 33A).

Do not use a comma to set off a quotation serving as the direct object of a transitive verb that is not functioning as a verb of attribution. In the next example, the quotation functions as the direct object of *offer* and thus should not be preceded by a comma. (When the comma is removed, the initial letter of the first word of the quotation will need to be lowercased.)

Faulty: Still untitled, the publisher promises the book will offer, "An ultimate close-up look at the evolution of Miramax Films into one of the great Hollywood success stories."
(Michael Cader, "Weinstein's Memoirs," *New York Sun*, 14-16 May 2004, p. 13)

The sentence is also weakened by a misplaced modifier (the phrase *still untitled* should be modifying *book*, not *publisher*), and the sentence would benefit from the insertion of the indefinite relative pronoun *that* between *promises* and *the*.

A quotation serving as an objective complement should not be set off with a comma. The two sentences below, both from the same article in a newspaper, are mispunctuated.

Faulty: Various candidates for the Democratic nomination for president called President Bush, "A miserable failure," "a liar," or compared him to the Taliban.

Delete the comma after *Bush*, and lowercase the first word of the first quotation. (The sentence also suffers from faulty parallelism; see the first principle discussed in chapter 7.)

Faulty: This past March, John Kerry was caught on camera calling the GOP, "The most crooked, lying group I've ever seen."
(Douglas MacKinnon, "No Time for Nastiness," *Pittsburgh Post-Gazette*, 4 July 2004, p. E2)

Delete the comma after *GOP*, and lowercase the initial letter of the first word of the quotation.

A quotation functioning as a retained objective complement should not be set off with a comma. The difference between an objective complement and a retained objective complement can be understood by examining the positioning of the noun *failure* in the sentences *He considered the movie a failure* and *The movie was considered a failure*. In the second sentence, which is a passive-voice reworking of the first sentence, the objective complement now follows the verb instead of following the object. The noun or noun equivalent that follows the passive-voice verb construction in such a sentence is called a retained objective complement.

Faulty: When Disney recently rolled out an internal system for handling payroll, accounting and other tasks it was named, "Project Tomorrowland."
(Bruce Orwall and Emily Nelson, "Hidden Wall Shields Disney's Kingdom: 80 Years of Culture," *Wall Street Journal*, 13 Feb. 2004, p. A8)

Delete the comma after *named*. *Project Tomorrowland* is the retained objective complement.

Do not use a comma to set off a short quotation functioning as the object of a gerund (as in the first example below) or as the object of a participle (as in the second example).

- As an executive, she is capable of withstanding "every conceivable form of stress and pressure."
- She was one of nearly two hundred protesters chanting "Resign now!"

If the quotation serving as the object of a gerund or the object of a participle is considerably longer than the ones in the examples above, a comma may precede the quotation.

Finally, do not use a comma to set off a quotation functioning as the object of a preposition.

Faulty: Concerned citizens wrote to newspapers with comments like, "If this is the start, where will it end?"

(Neil MacFarquhar, "A Kiss Is Not Just a Kiss to an Angry Arab TV Audience," *New York Times*, 5 Mar. 2004, p. A3)

Delete the comma following *like*.

38. Commas Following Participles Such as *entitled*

Do not use a comma to separate a participle such as *entitled* or *called* from the title of a work, which may be italicized or presented between quotation marks.

Faulty: Mr. Bush must have missed that classic "Twilight Zone" episode where the aliens arrive with a book entitled, "To Serve Man."

(Maureen Dowd, "Are They Losing It?," *New York Times* online, 27 June 2004, paragraph 17)

Delete the comma following *entitled*.

CHAPTER 19

THE SEMICOLON AND THE COLON

19A THE SEMICOLON

The semicolon is a punctuational divider, a separator. It partitions off a segment of a sentence more forcibly than a comma can—but without the finality, the closure, of a period. With one exception (discussed on page 237), the semicolon is used correctly only when it marks off the boundary between grammatically parallel elements—that is, elements of identical grammatical status. The use of the semicolon is confined primarily to separating independent clauses in compound and compound-complex sentences and to separating items in a series when one or more of the items include interior punctuation.

Semicolons Separating Independent Clauses Within a Sentence

Use a semicolon to separate two independent clauses closely related in meaning.

- His heart told him to move to New York City; his head told him to stay put.
- I saw Megan only three times after her divorce; once was at a dance recital in Berkeley.

Use a semicolon to separate two independent clauses joined by a conjunctive adverb (such as *however* or *consequently*) or by a transitional phrase (such as *for example* or *on the other hand*) that clarifies the logical interrelationship between the clauses. The use of a comma, rather than a semicolon, between two such independent clauses results in a comma splice. A comma must follow the conjunctive adverb (see chapter 25).

- He pleaded with her for hours; nevertheless, she left on the 5:10 p.m. flight to Boston.

- A month or so later, they were back together; in fact, they plan to marry in October.

A semicolon, rather than a comma, is sometimes used to separate independent clauses joined by a coordinating conjunction if one or both of the independent clauses include interior commas.

- After seven hours on an Amtrak train, Leatrice, barely awake, still despondent, struggled out into the throngs of Midtown; but even in the cold drizzle, she began feeling hopeful again.

CAUTION

The use of a comma, rather than a semicolon, between independent clauses not joined by a coordinating conjunction results in the catastrophic sentence-structure error known as a comma splice (see Chapter 25).

Remember that there are only seven coordinating conjunctions: *and, but, yet, or, nor, for,* and *so.*

Semicolons Separating Elements in a Series

Use a semicolon between items in a series if one or more of the items include interior punctuation.

- Her favorite movies are *Requiem for a Dream* (2000), directed by Darren Aronofsky; *Ghost World* (2001), directed by *Terry Swigoff; The Royal Tenenbaums (2001),* directed by Wes Anderson; and *Lost in Translation* (2003), directed by Sofia Coppola.

CAUTION

Do not use a semicolon to introduce a series.

Faulty: Next came the three editorial assistants; one with a desk (Jannika Hurwitt), one with a rolling chair (Lucas Matthiessen), and one perched uncertainly between the tiny bathroom, the front door, and the sliver of a storage room (me).

(David Michaelis, "The Last Gentleman," *New York Observer* online, 6 Oct. 2003, paragraph 2)

A colon should replace the semicolon.

The next sentence is especially confounding.

Faulty: "Intense" is the word that probably best describes guitarist Vernon Reid; his thick, speedy shards of sound, his devout personality, his educational dedication to his Black Rock Coalition.

(A. D. Amorosi, "Vernon Reid & Masque," *New York Press Summer Guide,* 26 May–1 June 2004, p. 138)

Either a series of three elements (*shards, personality, dedication*) has been misintroduced with a semicolon instead of with a colon, or a series of four elements (*guitarist, shards, personality, dedication*) has been punctuated inconsistently (only the second of the elements in the four-element series has been preceded by a semicolon; commas precede the third and fourth elements).

The absence of semicolons can obscure the structure of a lengthy, complicated series and thereby confuse the reader.

Faulty: More than 130 families are bringing gently used items, including name brand clothing items from Abercrombie, The Gap, Gymboree, Limited Too, Peg Perego baby equipment, and toys, books, videos, games and DVDs.

(Marjorie Wertz, "Sale to Feature Used Children's Items," *Greensburg [PA] Tribune-Review*, 13 Apr. 2004, p. A8)

The *and* before the phrase *toys, books, videos, games and DVDs* signals that the writer regards that five-noun list as constituting one of the units—the final unit—in a larger series; but the reader doesn't instantly discern that the first unit (a list of four brands of clothing) ends with *Limited Too*, because that brand name is not preceded by a closure-imparting *and*. The second unit in the series, the reader soon realizes, consists of only a single element: *Peg Perego baby equipment.*

Correct: More than 130 families are bringing gently used items, including name-brand clothing items from Abercrombie, The Gap, Gymboree, and Limited Too; Peg Perego baby equipment; and toys, books, videos, games, and DVDs.

Faulty: Although widely syndicated across the country's major markets, [Howard] Stern was carried on only six of Clear Channel's 1,200 stations: Pittsburgh, Fort Lauderdale, Fla., Orlando, Fla., Rochester, N.Y., San Diego and Louisville, Ky.

(Adrian McCoy, "Broadcast Giant Takes Whack at Shock Radio," *Pittsburgh Post-Gazette*, 27 Feb. 2004, p. A1)

The writer is inconsistent and untidy in presenting place names. The omission of *Pa.* is understandable, because the sentence appeared in a Pittsburgh newspaper, but the absence of any punctuation and an abbreviation after *San Diego* will throw some readers off, if only for a fraction of a second.

Correct: Although widely syndicated across the country's major markets, Stern was carried on only six of Clear Channel's 1,200 stations: Pittsburgh; Fort Lauderdale, Fla.; Orlando, Fla.; Rochester, N.Y.; San Diego, Calif.; and Louisville, Ky.

Semicolons Before *that is*, *for example*, and Similar Expressions

A semicolon is sometimes used before *that is, for example,* and similar expressions, as well as before the abbreviations *i.e.* and *e.g.,* even if what follows is not an independent clause. (A comma follows *that is,* similar expressions, and the abbreviations.) This is the only use of the semicolon that does not involve separating grammatically parallel elements. Either a comma or a dash, however, could be used instead of a semicolon in the following sentence (a third alternative is to omit *that is* and the comma, and then insert a colon after *shrinkage*).

- The upper-level managers of the retail chain are increasingly concerned with shrinkage; that is, shoplifting by employees.

TIP: No blank space precedes a semicolon. One blank space follows a semicolon.

Erroneous Semicolons

The most common misuse of the semicolon involves forcing it to separate groups of words that are not grammatically equivalent.

Faulty: With your gift to the United Way Community Fund you help increase self-sufficiency for people facing a disaster; like Debbie, who arrived home one day to find her apartment heavily damaged by fire.

(*Living Proof: Your Gift Makes a Difference*, United Way of Southwestern Pennsylvania brochure, C-2, 1999)

An independent clause precedes the semicolon; a prepositional phrase and an adjectival dependent clause follow the semicolon. The semicolon should be replaced by a comma or (if the writer wants to set off the second part of the sentence emphatically) by a dash. (Notice, too, that a comma should follow the pair of prepositional phrases at the beginning of the sentence.)

Faulty: The city has a $90 million liability on its books for self-insured compensation claims; a problem that could be addressed by privatizing this department.

(Mark Mustio, "Tough Love for the City," *Pittsburgh Post-Gazette*, 1 Jan. 2004, p. A17)

An independent clause precedes the semicolon; an appositive (to which an adjectival dependent clause has been attached) follows the semicolon. The writer can expand the appositive into an independent clause by inserting *this is* before *a problem*, or the writer can replace the semicolon with either a comma or a dash.

Faulty: To have been a pioneer prairie farmer in the 1800s, cracking hard soil with a hand plow; to have been a seamstress working 14-hour days for starvation wages in a sweatshop in the 1800s; these and many other past life circumstances were surely stressful.

(Gregg Easterbrook, "Modern Life: How to Cope," for Los Angeles Times, in Pittsburgh Post-Gazette, 29 Feb. 2003, p. E1)

> The first semicolon is correct (it separates two grammatically parallel infinitive phrases, the second of which has internal punctuation), but the second semicolon (preceding a summational independent clause) needs to be replaced by a dash (see chapter 20) or a colon.

TIP: Avoid semicolonic overkill. Many editors consider the semicolon an old-fashioned punctuational device so use it cautiously and sparingly.

> **Faulty:** The clock is ticking; my boss calls; the cab comes.
>
> (Susan Spano, "Make a List, Check It Twice Before You Leave on Vacation," for Los Angeles Times, in Pittsburgh Post-Gazette, 28 Dec. 2003, p. G3)
>
> The semicolons (inserted between three very brief independent clauses) slow down the sentence when the writer seems to want to emphasize the swift passing of time. Replacing the semicolons with commas will speed up the sentence. The sentence can even do without a conjunction before the final clause, because all three clauses are short and grammatically parallel, and can thus be presented asyndetonically (see Chapter 25).
>
> **Correct:** The clock is ticking, my boss calls, the cab comes.

19B THE COLON

The colon is an introducer. Think of it as an arrow pointing forward to a list, a clarification, an explanation, an elaboration, an example, or a one-sentence or multi-sentence quotation. The business of the colon, in short, is to serve notice that something important awaits the reader. The phrasing that precedes a colon sets up an expectation that is fulfilled by the phrasing that follows the colon.

Colons Introducing Items in a Series

A colon is used correctly to introduce a series only if the group of words preceding the colon is an independent clause (the equivalent of a grammatically complete sentence).

- Ben Marcus is the author of three books: *The Age of Wire and String, Notable American Women,* and *The Father Costume.*

A colon is also used to introduce a series preceded by phrasing such as *the following* or *as follows* at the end of an independent clause.

- The recommendations are as follows: dress appropriately, arrive fifteen minutes before your appointment, and be prepared to answer difficult questions about your background.

CAUTION

Do not use a colon (or any other punctuation) to introduce a series that functions as the direct object of a transitive verb, as the complement of a linking verb, or as the object of a preposition.

> **Faulty:** Companies with whom we have worked include: PricewaterhouseCoopers, Nickelodeon, and Pembroke Consulting.
>
> (Gotham Writers' Workshop catalogue of courses, Winter 2004, p. 14)

When the items in a series are arrayed vertically, however, a colon correctly introduces the list, even if the phrasing that precedes the list is not an independent clause.

Correct: Companies with whom we have worked include:
PricewaterhouseCoopers
Nickelodeon
Pembroke Consulting

Note that no commas follow the items in the series, the coordinating conjunction *and* is not positioned before the final item, and no period appears at the end of the sentence.

A colon can also be used after a series that precedes an independent clause. (The dash, however, is more common in such sentences.)

- *Time, Newsweek, BusinessWeek, U.S. News & World Report:* These magazines are just a part of her weekly reading regimen.

Colons Introducing Restatements, Clarifications, and Examples

A colon is used to introduce an independent clause, a phrase, or a single word that restates, clarifies, enlarges on, or provides an example of the statement (usually a generalization) declared in the independent clause at the start of the sentence.

- Every new employee is taught one important principle: Customers must be treated courteously.
- Every new employee is taught one important principle: the need to treat customers courteously.
- Every new employee is taught one important principle: courtesy.

TIP: There are only two cases in which you need to capitalize the initial letter of the first word following a colon.

1. Use capitalization if the word following the colon is a proper noun or a proper adjective (a noun or an adjective always requiring capitalization).

- Last night I finally realized something I should have figured out long ago: Jacob can't be trusted.

2. Capitalize the word following the colon if the independent clause preceding the colon is setting up or introducing a sequence of two or more closely related sentences.

- You'll need to keep three things in mind as you begin to write your essay: Give yourself plenty of time. Don't fall prey to self-doubt. And stay focused on your purpose.

In all other sentences in which the equivalent of a complete sentence follows the colon, the capitalization of the first word after the colon is optional. Be consistent in the capitalization throughout any piece of writing.

Colons Introducing Quotations

A colon follows an independent clause that introduces a single-sentence direct quotation.

- Henry David Thoreau had a very dark view of ordinary humanity: "The mass of men lead lives of quiet desperation."

> A comma instead of a colon after *humanity* would be dead wrong: The result would be a comma-splice error. A semicolon, though grammatically correct, would be stylistically awkward and inappropriate.

CAUTION

Do not use a colon before a quotation that functions as a restrictive appositive. No punctuation should precede such a quotation (see rule 33A in chapter 18).

Faulty: The book's ultimate contribution may be asking the simple question: "What was it like before urban renewal?"

(Christopher Briem, "Root Shock," *Pittsburgh Post-Gazette*, 27 June 2004, p. E4)

If the article *the* in *the simple question* were replaced by *a*, the colon before the quotation (which would now be functioning nonrestrictively) would be correct, as would a comma.

The colon is the correct punctuation mark to introduce a direct quotation consisting of more than one sentence.

- Henry David Thoreau wrote: "The mass of men lead lives of quiet desperation. What is called resignation is confirmed desperation."

A convention in academic writing is to set off longer, multisentence quotations by indenting on both sides and using a smaller type. Quotation marks do not enclose such passages, which are known as block quotations. (A quotation within such a passage would, of course, be punctuated with quotation marks.) A colon follows the sentence that introduces such a passage.

TIP: Do not use a colon following transitional words or phrases such as *namely, for example,* and *that is* or following the abbreviations *e.g.* and *i.e.* The colon itself implies that an example, an explanation, or a clarification will follow—so a transitional word or an abbreviation would be redundant.

Faulty: Her favorite writers are metafictionists: e.g., Gordon Lish, Donald Barthelme, David Markson.

Correct: Her favorite writers are metafictionists: Gordon Lish, Donald Barthelme, David Markson.

Miscellaneous Colon Usage

The colon has several miscellaneous functions.

1. A colon, not a comma, follows the salutation in a formal letter.

- Dear Ms. Wallace:
- To Whom It May Concern:
- Colleagues:

2. A colon follows each of the four headings in standard memo format.

TO:
FROM:
DATE:
SUBJECT:

3. A colon separates the hour from the minutes when the time is presented in numeral form.

- 3:13 a.m.

4. A colon separates the title of a book from its subtitle.

- *Gynecology: The Metaethics of Radical Feminism*, by Mary Daly

5. The colon is used in complete Internet addresses—that is, URLs.

- http://www.google.com

6. A colon separates the name of a speaker from his or her statement in certain formattings of dialogue and in transcripts of interviews. Quotation marks are not used—except when a speaker is quoting someone else.

    Clark: Can you talk a little about the genesis of your book?
    Smithson: The idea came to me while I was jogging a few days after 9/11.

7. A colon separates the numbers specifying the chapter and the verse in a book of the Bible.

- Luke 23:4

Conservative standard typescript format requires that two blank spaces follow a colon that separates elements of a sentence, but one blank space has become more common. No blank space follows a colon that appears in an Internet address, in a numeral expressing the time of day, and in a notation specifying the chapter and verse of a book of the Bible.

CHAPTER 20

PARENTHESES AND DASHES

20A THE PARENTHESES

Parentheses are the curvilinear punctuational device by means of which you can insert into an already complete statement a pinch of information that is less important than the surrounding information but that rounds out the sentence in a satisfying way. That is, a pair of parentheses encloses secondary, incidental, digressive, or supplemental material, such as examples or clarifications, as well as afterthoughts or reconsiderations Any parenthesized matter is thus non-restrictive or nonessential: It is not vital to the meaning of the sentence to which it is added. Instead, it is a bonus bestowed upon the reader.

- Robert Quine (1942–2004) was the most extraordinarily eloquent lead guitarist in punk-rock history.

- She loved obscure, unusual words like *fard* (which means "to apply makeup") and *eldritch* (which means "weird").

- His poetry (if that term is elastic enough to encompass his ham-handed, subliterate efforts) mostly concerns his romantic frustrations.

- We are awaiting word from the Department of Motor Vehicles (DMV).

- She was the most qualified candidate (or so she claimed).

Parentheses are also used to surround numbers or letters that precede the elements in a series.

- You'll need to bring the following documents: (1) your Social Security card, (2) your birth certificate, and (3) your driver's license.

  Note that in this pattern, a comma and a blank space precede the opening parenthesis in the second element. This is the only circumstance in which another punctuation mark precedes an opening parenthesis within a sentence.

Be careful with the positioning of other punctuation marks in relation to the closing parenthesis in a pair of parentheses. (If an entire sentence is parenthesized between two sentences in a paragraph, the terminal punctuation mark—the period, question mark, or exclamation point—is inserted before the closing parenthesis, as in this sentence.) If a parenthesized element is inserted between two parts of a sentence (as in this sentence, in which the parenthesized element follows an introductory adverbial dependent clause in a complex sentence), any necessary punctuation mark following the parenthesized element will be inserted after the closing parenthesis. If a parenthesized element is inserted at the end of a sentence, the terminal punctuation mark—a period, a question mark, or an exclamation point—will be inserted after the closing parenthesis (as in this sentence).

Any writer who decides to insert the equivalent of an entire sentence between two parts of a sentence (this pattern appears frequently in the work of professional writers) will not insert a period before the closing parenthesis, as this sentence illustrates, unless the parenthesized sentence ends with an abbreviation requiring a period. But if the parenthesized sentence-within-a-sentence is a question or an exclamatory statement, a question mark (are you reading very attentively?) or an exclamation point (we know you are!) needs to be inserted before the closing parenthesis. The initial letter of the first word of the parenthesized sentence-within-a-sentence will not be capitalized unless it is a proper noun or a proper adjective or unless the parenthesized sentence begins with the pronoun *I*. No punctuation mark is ever inserted before an opening parenthesis—with the exception of the pattern illustrated at the bottom of page 242.

A common error is the omission of appropriate punctuation after the closing parenthesis. Insert after the closing parenthesis whatever punctuation would be necessary following the last word before the parenthetical element if the parenthetical element were removed from the sentence.

> **Faulty:** While Blue Smoke is clearly a hit with diners (it's still necessary to reserve weeks in advance) critics have derided everything from the restaurant's hokey urban cowboy décor to the authenticity of its menu. ...
> (Brad Goldfarb, "All the Dish: Where the Food Is Smokin' and Lip-Smackin'," *Interview*, Aug. 2002, p. 85)
>
> **Correct:** While Blue Smoke is clearly a hit with diners (it's still necessary to reserve weeks in advance), critics have derided everything from the restaurant's hokey urban cowboy décor to the authenticity of its menu. ...

Punctuational trouble often arises when a writer resorts to parentheses to cram the equivalent of two or more sentences between two parts of the hosting sentence or when a writer tries to squeeze the equivalent of two or more sentences between parentheses right before the end of the hosting sentence. The result is almost always awkward and unsightly—and, more often than not, the writer misplaces the final period, as in each of the following examples.

> **Faulty:** My sister and I were forced to wait outside the casino while my parents gambled (which I didn't understand, either—we played penny-ante card games at home all the time. I didn't see what the big deal was.)
> (Jim Knipfel, "Boobs and Ruin," *New York Press*, 2–8 June 2004, p. 22)
>
> Even if the period following *was* is repositioned on the other side of the closing parenthesis, the sentence will still be ungainly, because the parenthetical element includes an undesirable internal period, after *time*. That period can be replaced by a comma and the coordinating conjunction *so*.

Better: My sister and I were forced to wait outside the casino while my parents gambled (which I didn't understand, either—we played penny-ante card games at home all the time, so I didn't see what the big deal was).

The sentence, however, still has a lopsided appearance (the parenthesized portion is longer than the unparenthesized portion), and the sentence is still weakened by the lack of an explicit antecedent for the pronoun *which*.

Faulty: This is the Sir Paul who wants to be known as the principle [sic] author of the very worst Beatles song ("Yesterday"—you know he's petitioned to have its authorship read "McCartney and Lennon" rather than the traditional "Lennon and McCartney." That tells you everything. Let him have it, Yoko.")

(Ron Rosenbaum, "Long, Winding Road for Phil Spector—Guilty of Genius," *New York Observer* online, 8 Dec. 2003, paragraph 24)

It might be advisable to import the title of the song into the hosting sentence, then bring that sentence to a halt. The three remaining sentences can then be presented as stand-alone units sheltered between one set of parentheses.

Better: This is the Sir Paul who wants to be known as the principal author of the very worst Beatles song— "Yesterday." (You know he's petitioned to have its authorship read "McCartney and Lennon" rather than the traditional "Lennon and McCartney." That tells you everything. Let him have it, Yoko.)

If you decide, however, that you do have sufficient justification for parenthesizing two or more sentences between two parts of a hosting sentence, heed these four guidelines: (a) be sure to lowercase the first word of the first parenthesized sentence (unless the first word is a proper noun, a proper adjective, or the pronoun *I*); (b) be sure to insert a period after each of the parenthesized sentences except the final one (unless, that is, any of the sentences call for a question mark or an exclamation point); (c) be sure to capitalize the first word of the subsequent parenthesized sentences; and (d) do not insert a period at the end of the final parenthesized sentence (a question mark or an exclamation point, however, may be necessary).

Leave one blank space before and after a parenthetical statement within a sentence unless punctuation is needed immediately following the closing parenthesis. Traditional typescript requires two spaces after the closing parenthesis of a stand-alone parenthetical statement (in which the terminal punctuation mark always falls inside the closing parenthesis), but it is becoming more common to use one space.

20B THE DASH

The dash is the most dramatic punctuation mark you can deploy within the interior of a sentence. Use it sparingly.

The dash is usually formed on the computer keyboard by pressing the hyphen key twice. (Do not confuse the hyphen with the dash. Hyphens are discussed at length in chapter 24.) No blank space should precede—or follow—any dash, as this sentence illustrates.

Dashes are used either singly or in pairs. A single dash is a marker of discontinuity or abruption: It indicates a dramatic shift (such as in tone or in the direction of a thought) within a sentence. A pair of dashes sets off an interruptive element at both ends and thus functions somewhat like a pair of commas or a pair of parentheses.

The Single Dash

A single dash is used to signal an abrupt change or shift (usually a downshift) in the progression of a thought, in tone, or in the level of diction or style.

- He's the perfect companion—at least for now.
- I met her when I was—oh, let's just say I was younger.
- He's an explicator of oneiric symbologies—he can tell you what your dreams mean.

A single dash is also used within a quotation to indicate that the speaker did not complete a statement.

- Heather said, "The door opened, and then he—"

Such a sentence lacks any terminal punctuation following the dash.

A dash is sometimes used instead of a comma or a semicolon before phrasing that begins with *that is* or *for example* or with the abbreviation *i.e.* or *e.g.*

- Her uncle is a philatelist—i.e., a stamp collector.

The single dash has also taken on three of the functions of the colon, although the dash lacks the formality of the colon. First, a dash can be used to introduce a series that follows an independent clause.

- We hired fifteen new employees—seven computer programmers, five paralegals, and three administrative assistants.

Second, a dash can be used between a series at the beginning of a sentence and a summational independent clause that ties the elements of the series together.

- Patience, common sense, punctuality—these are the qualities she most prizes in an assistant.

Third, a dash can be used between an independent clause expressing a generalization and an independent clause, a phrase, or a single word that restates, explains, or provides an example of the generalization.

- There is only one drawback to the new software—it is prohibitively expensive.
- There is only one drawback to the new software—its price tag.
- There is only one drawback to the new software—price.

The Pair of Dashes

Like a pair of commas or a pair of parentheses, a pair of dashes can be used to set off an interruptive (that is, a nonessential or nonrestrictive) word, phrase, or dependent clause within a sentence. The three punctuational patterns differ, however, in the degree of emphasis they place on the interruptive phrasing.

Parenthesizing the interruptive element places the least amount of emphasis on it.

- Her brother (an intern at MTV) wants to move to California.

Using a pair of dashes to set off the interruptive element places the greatest amount of emphasis on it.

- Her brother—an intern at MTV—wants to move to California.

Enclosing the interruptive element between commas makes no change in emphasis; that is, the information in the interruptive element is no more important, and no less important, than the other information in the sentence.

- Her brother, an intern at MTV, wants to move to California.

Another distinction that is drawn between parentheses and dashes setting off interruptive elements is that the dashes signify that the enclosed matter is more important and relevant to the sentence than any matter set off with parentheses. Choose the punctuational pattern appropriate to the amount of emphasis you want to place on the interruptive element.

Use either a pair of dashes or a pair of parentheses to set off an interruptive element that includes interior commas. Using commas to set it off would obscure the structure of the sentence.

Confusing: Belle and Sebastian's first three albums, *Tigermilk, If You're Feeling Sinister,* and *The Boy with the Arab Strap,* are usually considered to be the group's best.

The punctuation does not clarify the design of the sentence. The sentence consists of three main segments: a subject, an appositive phrase, and a predicate. The commas, however, slice the sentence five ways. A reader could even mistakenly infer that the sentence concerns a total of six albums, only three of which have been mentioned by name.

Better: Belle and Sebastian's first three albums—*Tigermilk, If You're Feeling Sinister,* and *The Boy with the Arab Strap*—are usually considered to be the group's best.

Better: Belle and Sebastian's first three albums (*Tigermilk, If You're Feeling Sinister,* and *The Boy with the Arab Strap*) are usually considered to be the group's best.

Use a pair of dashes to set off an interruptive element that includes both commas and parentheses.

- Belle and Sebastian's first three albums—*Tigermilk* (1996), *If You're Feeling Sinister* (1996), and *The Boy with the Arab Strap* (1998)—are usually considered to be the group's best.

Never set off an interruptive element with a dash at one end and a comma at the other. The resulting sentence will lack punctuational symmetry.

Faulty: The tiles come in every imaginable shape—squares, circles, hexagons, rectangles, and they can be cut to virtually any size.

(Bill Morris, "The Quarry Men," *New York Daily News,* 11 Jan. 2004, Lifeline p. 6)

> **Correct:** The tiles come in every imaginable shape—squares, circles, hexagons, rectangles—and they can be cut to virtually any size.

Asymmetrical punctuation is defensible, however, when a conjunctive adverb (a word such as *however* or *therefore*) follows the interruptive element. The design of such a sentence requires that a semicolon precede the conjunctive adverb.

- Incunabula released three critically acclaimed albums—*Lunettes, My Lies, and Sordor;* nevertheless, the band never caught on with the listening public.

Any such sentence could be recast with parentheses instead of dashes.

- Incunabula released three critically acclaimed albums (*Lunettes, My Lies, and Sordor*); nevertheless, the band never caught on with the listening public.

CAUTION

Never include more than one pair of dashes in a sentence. The inclusion of three or more dashes will obscure the contours of the sentence. A pair of parentheses vividly cups a word, phrase, or clause—because the opening and closing halves of the pair are mirror images of each other. An opening dash and a closing dash, however, are typographically indistinguishable. Therefore, a reader confronting a sentence with multiple dashes cannot immediately discern which phrasing functions as inserted, interruptive matter and which constitutes the primary, surrounding text.

> **Confusing:** The movie's subject matter—the unglorified miseries of the alienated and the often painful consequences of being "different"—and its soundtrack—obscure ragtime, acoustic blues, Indian rock-and-roll—limited its appeal to mainstream American teenagers.
> **Clear:** The movie's subject matter (the unglorified miseries of the alienated and the often painful consequences of being "different") and its soundtrack (obscure ragtime, acoustic blues, Indian rock-and-roll) limited its appeal to mainstream American teenagers.

In the publishing world, the kind of dash discussed in this chapter is known as an em dash, because its length is the same as that of the letter *m*. The em dash is distinguished from an en dash, which is slightly longer than a hyphen but shorter than an em dash. The en dash (so named because it is as long as the letter *n*) is discussed at the end of Chapter 24.

CHAPTER 21

THE APOSTROPHE

The apostrophe is used in contractions (*shouldn't*), in possessives (*Jennifer's brilliance*), in expressions that have the force of a possessive (*a summer's day*), and in certain plurals (*Ph.D.'s*).

The apostrophe is often inserted where it does not belong—most often in the plural form of a noun not used possessively.

- GOOD ALE'S
  (advertisement for McSorley's Old Ale House, *New York Daily News*, 19 Dec. 2003, p. 94)

- First thing's first: Gus Van Sant's Palme D'Or winner, though a rapturous and terrifying memorial to the Columbine massacre, brings nothing to the discussion on high-school violence.
  (Scott Tobias, capsule film review of *Elephant*, *Onion*, 18 Dec. 2003–1 Jan. 2004, p. 24)
  No apostrophe is needed in *thing's*.

Yet the apostrophe is often carelessly omitted where it is needed to signal possession.

- Established Program seeks women to carry couples [**couples'**] biological babies 21–45
  (*Pennysaver*, a classified-advertisement weekly, Greensburg [PA] East 77 edition, 28 Apr. 2004, p. 3)

- LADIES [**LADIES'**] DENIM TOPS
  (*Pennysaver*, a classified-advertisement weekly, Greensburg [PA] East 77 edition, 28 Apr. 2004, p. 3)

- ELECTRICIAN: 21 YEARS [**YEARS'**] EXPERIENCE
  (*Pennysaver*, a classified-advertisement weekly, Greensburg [PA] East 77 edition, 28 Apr. 2004, p. 3)
  This item could also be rephrased as ... *21 YEARS of EXPERIENCE*.

21A CONTRACTIONS

The apostrophe is used to indicate the omission of one or more letters in a contraction.

- isn't, weren't, won't, can't, wouldn't, haven't, I'd, we'll, they'll

Rule 1: Avoid using two apostrophes in one contraction. Instead of writing *I'd've gone,* write *I would've gone* or *I'd have gone.* Instead of writing *I wouldn't've done it otherwise,* write *I wouldn't have done it otherwise.*

Rule 2: Do not confuse *it's* (the contraction of *it is*) with *its* (a possessive pronoun). There is no such word as *its'.* (This sentence is correct: *It's fun to watch the cat play with its toy.*)

Rule 3: Do not confuse *you're* (the contraction of *you are*) with *your* (a possessive pronoun), or *they're* (the contraction of *they are*) with *their* (a possessive pronoun) or with *there* (an adverb and an expletive). (These sentences are correct: *You're supposed to bring your own beverage. They're not supposed to be parking their cars over there!*)

Rule 4: Do not misspell *could've, might've, should've,* and *would've* (the contractions of *could have, might have, should have,* and *would have*) as *could of, might of, should of,* and *would of.* Similarly, do not misspell *may have* and *must have* as *may of* and *must of.* The preposition *of* makes no sense—grammatically or logically—after a helping verb.

Rule 5: Avoid the contractions *we'd, he'd, she'd,* and *they'd,* except in very casual contexts; and avoid *it'd* in any context.

Not all contractions involve verbs. Check a good dictionary when you are unsure of how to form other contractions.

- o'clock
- rock 'n' roll
- ma'am

Use an apostrophe to indicate the omission of the first two digits from a numeral specifying a year.

- She will graduate in the class of '17.

21B POSSESSIVES: THE BASICS

Use an apostrophe to convert a noun to the possessive form. (A possessive noun preceding another noun functions as an adjective.)

> **TIP:** It is no longer considered awkward or undesirable to use an apostrophe and *-s* to indicate that something inanimate is the possessor of something else. Thus *the program's purpose* is now as acceptable as *the purpose of the program.*

1. To form the possessive of a singular noun not ending in *-s,* add an apostrophe and *-s:*

- the reader's questions, the girl's handwriting, Rachel's pottery
- Xanax's side effects, the dominatrix's day off, Groucho Marx's wit
- Paul Theroux's style, Molyneaux's suggestion
- Bruno Schulz's drawings, Joseph Mankiewicz's movies

- Gabriel García Márquez's magic realism
- the building's fire escape, a month's salary, a moment's notice
- bachelor's degree, master's degree

CAUTION

Do not use a plural noun where a singular-possessive noun is called for.

> **Faulty:** The cities downtown business district is in decline.
> **Correct:** The city's downtown business district is in decline.

---

2. To form the possessive of a singular noun ending in -s, add an apostrophe and -s.

- the boss's office
- the waitress's schedule
- the witness's testimony

The apostrophe is added to a singular proper noun ending in -s regardless of whether or not the conversion to the possessive form adds an extra syllable to the word. (This is the editorial policy of distinguished publishing houses and magazines, such as Alfred A. Knopf, Inc., and *New Yorker*.)

- Otis's sense of humor, Ross's magazine, James's elegance, Thomas's career
- William Gass's novels, Yeats's poetry, Gayl Jones's novels
- George Lucas's movies, Sinclair Lewis's satires, David Davis's opinions
- Alice Adams's books, Joyce Carol Oates's prolificacy, Ben Marcus's fiction
- William Dean Howells's novels, Diane Williams's novellas
- Carson McCullers's imagination, Julian Barnes's essays
- W. C. Fields's movies, Rosa Parks's heroism, Andre Dubus's short stories

For example:

Awkward: Los Angeles's weather
Better: the weather in Los Angeles

Awkward: Kansas's largest city
Better: the largest city in Kansas

Awkward: Memphis's tourist attractions
Better: the tourist attractions in Memphis

Awkward: St. Louis's mayor
Better: the mayor of St. Louis

Awkward: New Orleans's population
Better: the population of New Orleans

Exception: the United States' reputation

3. To form the possessive of a plural noun ending in -s, add only the apostrophe.

- the employees' lounge, the girls' father, the paralegals' supervisor, the bosses' meeting
- five dollars' worth, four days' pay, three weeks' paid vacation
- two months' salary, only five hours' sleep, for old times' sake
- the Petersons' house, the Joneses' boat, the Whites' children
- the Beatles' final album, the Rolling Stones' lead singer, the Smiths' final tour

> **TIP:** A few nouns ending in *-s*—such as *series* and *species*—are identical in their singular and plural forms.
>
> - one new TV series; several new TV series
>
> Their singular-and plural-possessive forms are also identical.
>
> - one new TV series' cast; the three new TV series' casts

Faulty: An equally bright 13-year-old at a Mott Haven school was showing off a movie prop pistol to some buddies in the boy's room on Dec. 10.

("Crime Blotter: Missing the Boat," *New York Press*, 17–23 Dec. 2003, p. 4)

Correct: ... in the boys' room [i.e., restroom] on Dec. 10.

Faulty: Fueled by our student's enthusiastic word of mouth and a "Best of the Web" rating by Forbes, our online classes now reach thousands of students in dozens of countries.

(Gotham Writers' Workshop catalog of courses, Winter 2004, p. 2)

Correct: Fueled by our students' enthusiastic word of mouth. . . .

Faulty: The Walton's combined $102.5 billion—up from $94 billion in 2002—nearly matches the wealth of the three richest men: Microsoft cofounders Bill Gates ($46 billion) and Paul Allen ($22 billion) and mega-investor Warren Buffet ($36 billion).

(Holly Sklar, "Two Very Different Americas Set to Ring in New Year," *New York Times*, 28 Dec. 2003, p. C-2)

Note: The Waltons are Wal-Mart founder Sam Walton's widow and four children.

Correct: The Waltons' combined $102.5 billion. . . .

> **TIP:** When the last word in the multiword name of an organization, the multiword name of a corporation, or a multiword place name is a plural noun ending in *-s*, form the possessive by adding only an apostrophe. (The phrasing is often smoother if you recast a construction to avoid the use of the apostrophe.)
>
> **Awkward:** the Academy of American Poets' membership list
> **Better:** the membership list of the Academy of American Poets
>
> **Awkward:** Carnival Cruise Lines' headquarters
> **Better:** the headquarters of Carnival Cruise Lines
>
> **Awkward:** Pleasant Hills' shopping plazas
> **Better:** shopping plazas in Pleasant Hills
>
> **Awkward:** Brooklyn Heights' cachet
> **Better:** the cachet of Brooklyn Heights
>
> **Awkward:** Carroll Gardens' crime problem
> **Better:** the crime problem in Carroll Gardens

4. To form the possessive of a plural noun not ending in *-s,* add an apostrophe and *-s*.

- children's playthings, women's rights, men's foibles

Consider the following example.

Faulty: Long before I became an editor of *The Hudson Review*, I read the magazine regularly for its concern with quality literature in contrast to the daily fare served up by newspapers and political magazines that, unfortunately, occupy most peoples' thoughts and conversations.

(Paula Deitz, undated subscription-solicitation letter for *Hudson Review*, p. 2)

Correct: ... occupy most people's thoughts and conversations.

5. To form the possessive of a singular compound noun, add an apostrophe and -s following the final element.

- my sister-in-law's poetry
- the jack-in-the-box's spring
- the governor-elect's agenda

6. To form the possessive of a plural compound noun, add only an apostrophe if the compound ends in -s. But if the compound does not end in -s, add an apostrophe and -s.

- big-box stores' returned-merchandise policies
- my in-laws' holiday party

It is sometimes better to rephrase an awkward possessive of a plural compound noun.

Awkward: my sons-in-law's annual get-together
Better: the annual get-together of my sons-in-law

7. When you are forming the possessive of a longish noun phrase, it is often stylistically desirable to use a prepositional phrase beginning with *of* instead of attaching an apostrophe and -s to the end of the noun phrase. (The object of the preposition *of* will name the thing or person that is possessing something or someone.)

Awkward: The governor of Pennsylvania's re-election campaign began today.
Better: The re-election campaign of the governor of Pennsylvania began today.

Awkward: The car I borrowed from my neighbor's windshield wipers aren't working.
Better: The windshield wipers of the car I borrowed from my neighbor aren't working.

Awkward: The flower vendor on the corner's mother won the lottery.
Better: The mother of the flower vendor on the corner won the lottery.

To express joint ownership (that is, two or more persons together own one thing), convert the final noun in the pair or series to the possessive form. To express individual ownership by two or more persons (that is, two or more persons each individually own one thing), convert each noun in the pair or series to the possessive form and pluralize the noun that specifies what is owned.

- Elisa and Stacey's deluxe condominium (Elisa and Stacey live together)
- Elisa's and Stacey's deluxe condominiums (Elisa and Stacey each has her own deluxe condominium)
- my mother and father's time-share property (they own the property together)
- my brother's and sister's CD collections (each of the siblings has a CD collection)

Avoid confusing or awkward constructions.

Faulty (Misleading): Detroit and Philadelphia's crime rate
Correct: Detroit's and Philadelphia's crime rates
Better: the crime rates of Detroit and Philadelphia

TIP: In a joint-possessive phrase in which both a proper noun and a pronoun identify the owners of something, both the proper noun and the pronoun must be in possessive form.

- Jason's and my RV; my and Jason's RV
  Jason and I together own an RV.

Possessives, Indefinite Pronouns, and Reciprocal Pronouns

Do not insert apostrophes in the possessive personal pronouns. Use apostrophes to convert indefinite pronouns and reciprocal pronouns to possessive form.

1. The possessive personal pronouns ending in *-s* do not have apostrophes: *ours, yours, his, hers, theirs.* (Nor does the possessive pronoun *its* have an apostrophe.)

2. An indefinite pronoun requires an apostrophe when the pronoun is used possessively.

   - the time of one's life
   - no one's idea of fun
   - to everybody's surprise
   - the other's feelings (singular possessive)
   - the others' feelings (plural possessive)

3. The possessive form of an indefinite pronoun followed by the adjective *else* is indicated by an apostrophe and *-s* after *else.*

   - everybody else's successes
   - anybody else's achievement

4. The possessive forms of the reciprocal pronouns—*each other* and *one another*—are *each other's* and *one another's.*

   - The roommates respected each other's privacy.
   - We need to tolerate one another's differences.

Note the errors in the following excerpt from the request filed for the annulment of the very brief marriage of Britney Spears and Jason Allan Alexander.

   - The newlyweds "did not know each others [**other's**] likes and dislikes, each others [**other's**] desires to have or not have children and each others [**other's**] desires as to State of residency."
     (cited in Lola Ogunnaike, "Britney Spears, After a Dip into Marriage, Is Free for Whatever Future May Hold," *New York Times*, 6 Jan. 2004, p. B3)

21C POSSESSIVES: THE SUBTLETIES

1. Because one writes *an acquaintance of mine* and not *an acquaintance of me,* one should also write *an associate of Brian's* instead of *an associate of Brian.* The doubled possessive form of *a coworker of Lauren's, colleagues of ours,* and *an ex-spouse of hers* is called the double genitive. Failure to use the double-genitive form can result in imprecision.

   - *a painting of Jennifer* is a painting that depicts Jennifer
   - *a painting of Jennifer's* is either a painting by Jennifer or a painting that Jennifer owns

2. Attributive nouns are presented without apostrophes. Attributive nouns are said to function adjectivally rather than possessively. Plural attributive nouns sometimes appear in the names of organizations, holidays, and publications.

   - Veterans Administration, Department of Veterans Affairs
   - Veterans Day
   - Boys & Girls Clubs of America
   - Girls and Boys Town, Boys Town National Research Hospital
   - Administrative Professionals Day
   - American Booksellers Association
   - *CliffsNotes*

The use of attributive nouns (vs. possessives) is sometimes irregular.

- Miami Childrens Hospital, Children's Hospital of Pittsburgh
- Disabled Employees Assistance Program, workers' compensation
- National Grandparents Day, Mother's Day, Father's Day
- *Publishers Weekly, Boys' Life* and *Girls' Life* magazines

The names of rock bands and sports teams can be used attributively.

- a Rolling Stones concert
- the new Strokes CD
- a Pittsburgh Steelers victory

The sports departments of some newspapers report the scores for *girls soccer, girls basketball, girls softball, boys basketball, boys baseball,* etc. But other newspapers continue to use the possessive forms: *girls' soccer, girls' basketball, girls' softball,* etc.

Some readers will consider attributive nouns to be mispunctuated, so caution and consistency are urged in the use of such forms.

3. A noun in possessive form cannot be followed by an appositive that is not in possessive form.

> **Faulty:** Her friend's (the girl visiting from Chicago) car broke down.
> **Correct:** The car of her girl friend who is visiting from Chicago broke down.

> **Faulty:** Alisdair MacLean's (the guitarist and singer in the Clientele) songwriting is exquisite.
> **Correct:** The songwriting of Alisdair MacLean, the guitarist and singer in the Clientele, is exquisite.

> **Faulty:** The laptop computer I'm borrowing is my uncle's, Michael Montclair.
> **Correct:** The laptop computer I'm borrowing belongs to my uncle, Michael Montclair.

> **Faulty:** The long strand of hair on his sweater looked a lot like Monica's, my ex-girlfriend.
> **Correct:** The long strand of hair on his sweater looked a lot like Monica's, my ex-girlfriend's.
> **Correct:** The long strand of hair on his sweater looked a lot like that of Monica, my ex-girlfriend.

It is perfectly acceptable for an appositive in possessive form to follow a noun or nouns in nonpossessive form.

- My friend Jacob's favorite bar is McSorley's.
- The singer-songwriter Morrissey's 2004 album was entitled *You Are the Quarry.*

4. The noun or pronoun preceding a gerund is usually presented in possessive form (this rule is discussed more thoroughly in chapter 10).

- She was annoyed by Jason's talking throughout the movie.
- Ursula was puzzled by his falling asleep so early.

5. The possessive of a name ending in a Roman numeral is formed by adding an apostrophe and -*s* to the numeral.

- William J. Gleason II's public-service record

The possessive of a name ending in *Jr.* or *Sr.* is formed by adding an apostrophe and -*s* to the abbreviation if no comma separates the name from the abbreviation.

- James Thorton Jr.'s career

If a comma separates the name from the abbreviation, however, or if commas precede and follow the abbreviation, adding an apostrophe and -*s* will result in an awkward-looking construction. If possible, rephrase the construction so that an apostrophe is not needed.

- The outstanding performance of Jon Smithson, Jr., surprised us all.

6. Certain standard expressions depart from the conventions governing the apostrophe.

  - for goodness' sake
  - for appearance' sake

7. To form the possessive of a proper noun ending in -s that names a figure from the Bible or from classical antiquity, insert only an apostrophe after the -s if the noun consists of more than one syllable.

  - Jesus' teachings
  - Moses' importance
  - Socrates' influence
  - Achilles' tendon
  - Sophocles' dramas
  - Catullus' poetry

But if the name consists of only a single syllable, form the possessive by adding an apostrophe and -s.

  - Zeus's powers

21D POSSESSIVES: SPECIALIZED USES

1. The possessive form of a title presented between quotation marks is indicated with an apostrophe and an -s following the closing quotation marks.

  Awkward: "Sweet Jane"'s opening chords
  Better: the opening chords of "Sweet Jane"

2. The possessive form of the title of a work or the name of a newspaper or magazine presented in italics is indicated with an apostrophe and an -s in roman type.

  - the *New Yorker*'s coverage of the war
  - *Citizen Kane*'s box-office performance

21E APOSTROPHES IN CERTAIN PLURALS

1. With decades and with italicized letters and numbers used plurally, conservative practice favors the use of the apostrophe before the -s. But such elements are now commonly and acceptably presented without the apostrophe. Be consistent throughout a document.

  - The Smiths were the best alternative-rock band of the 1980's [or: 1980s].
  - His calligraphic *g*'s and *q*'s [or: *g*s and *q*s] are eccentrically elaborate.
  - She draws a horizontal line through her *7*'s [or: *7*s].

The plural of an uppercase letter is not usually formed with an apostrophe; nor is the letter italicized.

  - Are students still being taught the three Rs?
  - She was quick to learn her ABCs.

2. The apostrophe is standard in the plural form of an italicized word or of an abbreviation that includes more than one period.

- There were eight *because*'s in one short paragraph.
  The -s ending is presented in roman type, not in italics.
- We hired three C.P.A.'s and two M.B.A.'s.

3. The plurals of abbreviations, in capital letters, that do not include periods are presented without apostrophes.

- TVs, PCs, ATMs, SUVs, YWCAs, IOUs, URLs, MCs, DJs [*but:* pj's]

4. The plurals of letters that designate academic grades are presented without apostrophes.

- Her transcript includes mostly As and Bs.

21F APOSTROPHES IN ABBREVIATIONS THAT FUNCTION AS VERBS

The third-person-singular form of the present tense of a verb that is fashioned from an abbreviation is indicated with an apostrophe followed by -*s*.

- She O.K.'s most of my requests for days off.

The past tense of a verb that is formed from an abbreviation is indicated with an apostrophe followed by -*d*.

- She O.K.'d my suggestion.
- He was K.O.'d early in the match.
- He OD'd on heroin.

CHAPTER 22

QUOTATION MARKS AND ITALICS

22A QUOTATION MARKS: THE BASICS

Quotation marks are the means by which we distinguish somebody else's words from our own in a piece of writing. Quotation marks, that is, enclose a direct quotation—the exact words of a writer or speaker. Quotations can vary in length from single words to multisentence passages.

Quotation marks always appear in pairs. Each pair consists of the inward-curving, opening quote (") and the outward-curving, closing quote (").

As discussed in rule 16 of chapter 18, a clause of attribution (such as *Henry David Thoreau wrote*) explains who wrote or uttered a statement being quoted. A clause of attribution can precede a single-sentence quotation, it can follow such a quotation, or it can be inserted between two halves of the quotation. When the clause of attribution precedes the quotation, the clause is followed by a comma.

- Henry David Thoreau wrote, "The mass of men lead lives of quiet desperation."

When the clause of attribution follows the quotation, the clause is preceded by a comma.

- "The mass of men lead lives of quiet desperation," wrote Henry David Thoreau.

When the clause of attribution is inserted between two halves of the quotation, one comma will precede the clause and another comma will follow it.

- "The mass of men," wrote Henry David Thoreau, "lead lives of quiet desperation."

Rule 37 in chapter 18 discusses how you determine whether a comma should precede a quotation that does not consist of a complete sentence. Chapter 19 explains how to use a colon to introduce a multisentence direct quotation.

Quotation marks do not enclose an indirect quotation. An indirect quotation is a paraphrase of a writer's or speaker's statement.

> **Direct Quotation:** She said, "I can't drive you to the station."
> **Indirect Quotation:** She said she couldn't drive me to the station.

Putting quotation marks around an indirect quotation usually misrepresents the speaker's or writer's original statement.

> **Faulty:** She said, "She couldn't drive me to the station."
> The sentence is misleading: The speaker, a woman, is declaring that some *other* woman could not drive the speaker to the station.

Integrating a Fragmental Quotation Into a Sentence

When you are tucking only a portion of a direct quotation into a sentence, make sure that the pronominal point of view of the excerpt does not clash with the point of view of the hosting sentence.

> **Faulty:** She said she was relieved to have "at long last made my position absolutely clear."
> The hosting sentence is presented from the third-person point of view; the fragmental quotation, however, is presented from the first-person point of view. You cannot simply substitute *her* for *my* without misrepresenting the speaker's statement: she was talking about herself, not about some other woman.
> **Correct:** I am relieved to have at long last made my position absolutely clear.
> In this example, the speaker's utterance is included in its entirety.
> **Correct:** She said she was relieved to have "at long last" made her position "absolutely clear."
> Here, only the words that seem especially important are isolated for quotation.
> **Best:** She said she was relieved to have made her position clear.
> In this final example, the speaker's statement is paraphrased and the quotation marks are eliminated. This is the best alternative when, as in this example, there is nothing remarkable about the speaker's choice of words.
> **Faulty:** She insists that she didn't want to "repeat myself," having never done a sequel.
> (Jada Yuan, "Girl Overboard," *New York*, 13 Sept. 2004, p. 54)
> **Correct:** She insists that she didn't want to repeat herself, having never done a sequel.

THOUGHTS VS. SPOKEN OR WRITTEN STATEMENTS

If a statement is merely thought, rather than spoken or written, quotation marks are not needed.

- I must have done something wrong, she thought to herself as she walked to her car.
- Did I do something wrong? she wondered as she walked to her car.
- I can't believe I messed up again! she thought as she walked to her car.

Using quotation marks to enclose the woman's thoughts cannot be considered an error—but it is likely to strike readers as punctuational overkill. (Some writers italicize such thoughts, but the italics, too, are unnecessary.) However you decide to punctuate—or not punctuate—such thoughts, be sure to be consistent throughout a piece of writing.

22B PUNCTUATION MARKS AND CLOSING QUOTATION MARKS

Typographical convention in the United States requires that periods and commas always be inserted before the closing quotation marks—regardless of whether a direct quotation consists of an entire sentence, a phrase, or a single word.

This convention, however, is widely violated.

Faulty: And just like the ending of the song you'll be "alive and doing fine".

(Jay Ofsanik, "Signs, Signs, Everywhere a Sign," *AAA Motorist*, Westmoreland [PA] Region, Jan. 2004, p. 16)

Faulty: Also new this year is a contest for children to win "The Hippest Room on Earth", compliments of Radio Disney.

("What's Happening," *AAA Motorist*, Westmoreland [PA] Region, Jan. 2004, p.18)

Semicolons and colons are always inserted after the closing quotation marks.

- The first poem she memorized was Ezra Pound's "In a Station of the Metro"; the second was Philip Larkin's "This Be The Verse."

- She was fond of quoting the second line of Wordsworth's sonnet "The World Is Too Much with Us": "Getting and spending, we lay waste our powers."

A dash is inserted before the closing quotation mark if the dash signals to the reader that the speaker has not finished his or her statement.

- "He pulled out a knife and—" she said, gasping.

A dash follows the closing quotation mark when the dash belongs not to the quotation but to the sentence hosting the quotation.

- She said, "He pulled out a knife"—and then she started to sob.

A question mark or an exclamation point is inserted before the closing quotation mark if the quotation itself is a question or an exclamatory statement.

- She said, "How can I be sure that you're telling the truth?"

- She shouted, "I believed you!"

A question mark or an exclamation point is inserted after the closing quotation mark, however, if the entire sentence (of which the direct quotation is only a part) is a question or an exclamatory statement.

- Did she really say, "You can take this job and shove it"?
- How dare he call me a "cybergeek"!

Doubled Punctuation and Closing Quotation Marks

A quotation ending with a question mark or an exclamation point sometimes also requires a comma before the closing quotation mark. Such doubled punctuation improves the readability of the sentence.

If a quotation ending with a question mark or an exclamation point is immediately followed by a clause of attribution, no comma is inserted.

- "Where are you calling from?" she asked.
- "Listen to me!" she shouted.

If a quotation ending with a question mark or an exclamation point is immediately followed by a participial phrase, a dependent clause, or a long independent clause beginning with a coordinating conjunction, insert a comma before the closing quotation mark.

- She asked, "You did what?," trying to make him feel guilty.
- She shouted, "Come back!," as if he were finally ready to listen to reason.

When quotation marks enclose the title of a work (such as the title of a song) that ends with a question mark or an exclamation point, insert a comma before the closing quotation mark if the title is followed by a nonrestrictive element (that is, an element that needs to be set off with commas at both ends).

- The Smiths' "How Soon Is Now?," first released in 1984, remains the band's most familiar song.

Similarly, when quoted matter ending with a question mark or an exclamation point functions as a nonrestrictive appositive or appears at the end of a nonrestrictive phrase or dependent clause, insert a comma before the closing quotation mark.

- The Smiths' most familiar song, "How Soon Is Now?," was first released in 1984.

Consider the following examples.

Faulty: January is crammed with fresh contortions on the reality genre, from Fox's "My Big Fat Obnoxious Fiancé" (a woman has to pass off a horrible boor as the love of her life to family and friends) to "Can You Be a Pornstar?" a self-explanatory reality show on adult pay-per-view cable channels.

(Alessandra Stanley, "Contestants, Meet the King of the Jungle," New York Times, 8 Jan. 2004, p. B1)

Correct: … "Can You Be a Pornstar?," a self-explanatory reality show on adult pay-per-view cable channels.

Faulty: Though he's Google-adept, as he proves when he's playing "Gotcha!", one does wonder what Mr. Peck knows.

(Adam Begley, "The King of Splatter Crit Lays Down His Weapon," New York Observer online, 28 June 2004, paragraph 8)

Correct: Though he's Google-adept, as he proves when he's playing "Gotcha!," one does wonder what Mr. Peck knows.

22C OTHER USES OF QUOTATION MARKS

Quotation marks have several specialized functions. When you are calling attention to a word as a word—that is, when you are emphasizing the word as an object or emphasizing the combination of letters that constitute the word—you can insert the word between quotation marks. Italics, however, are more commonly used.

- The noun "enormity" is often misused.
- The noun *enormity* is often misused.

Do not, however, put quotation marks around a slang word or a figure of speech that is not being pointed to or emphasized as a word or figure of speech. That is, if you are not calling attention to the term as an object and instead are merely using the term to express its commonly understood meaning, do not use quotation marks. Using them would be the equivalent of saying to the reader, "Look at how hip I am—I'm using slang," or "I'm sorry—I know this phrase is stale, but I'm using it because I just can't think of anything better." A careful writer will spare the reader such annoyances.

Unacceptable: She was wearing lots of "bling-bling."

Unacceptable: I have "issues" when it comes to men.

Unacceptable: You can definitely say we're "birds of a feather."

An unusually casual word or phrase inserted into a rather formal sentence or an unusually formal word or phrase inserted into a casual or semiformal sentence may be presented between quotation marks. Quotation marks may also enclose a word that has been liberated from its customary context and whisked into a context in which it is both apt and unexpected.

- The teacher entering the boys' lavatory discovered two students "huffing"—inhaling aerosol sprays to achieve a form of intoxication.
- The journalists turned their attention to the "perp walk" of the disgraced executive.

Quotation marks do not enclose the words *yes* and *no* unless such a word is part of a written or spoken statement.

- It seems that she can never say no to her son.
- After he proposed, she shouted, "Yes!"

Quotation marks enclose interjections that approximate nonverbal sounds.

- "Brrr," she said, shivering.
- We heard an audience member's "Ssshhh" as the movie started.

When you are calling attention to a single letter of the alphabet, it is better to italicize the letter than to put quotation marks around it.

Correct: The "j" looked like a "y."
Better: The *j* looked like a *y*.

Quotation marks enclose a nickname inserted between a first name and a last name or between a middle name (or middle initial) and a last name.

- Clifford S. "Jokeman" Bartells

22D QUOTATION MARKS IN PASSAGES OF DIALOGUE

When you are writing dialogue (as in a short story), the convention is that each character's speech should be presented in a separate paragraph. That is, start a fresh paragraph whenever someone else begins to speak.

"Didn't you see that?" Emily said.

"What?" I said.

"You missed it?" Emily said.

"What are you two talking about?" Gretchen said.

Departures from this convention—the inclusion of several speakers' dialogue in a single paragraph—are likely to confuse the reader, even if the attribution has been handled carefully.

When one person is speaking at length and the speech consumes more than one paragraph, begin each paragraph with an opening quotation mark, but withhold the closing quotation mark until the end of the last sentence of the last paragraph of the person's speech.

22E SINGLE QUOTATION MARKS

Single quotation marks—formed by pressing the apostrophe key on a computer keyboard—enclose a quotation within a quotation. A comma or a period is always inserted before the closing single quotation mark.

- The grieving widower said, "My wife's last words were 'Remember me.'"

A question mark or an exclamation point follows the closing single quotation mark but precedes the closing double quotation mark if the quotation-within-a-quotation is a declarative statement but the entire quotation itself is a question or an exclamatory statement.

- Jacob asked, "Did Sarah say, 'I can't do it'?"

A question mark or an exclamation point precedes both the closing single quotation mark and the closing double quotation mark if the quotation-within-a-quotation (a) is a question or an exclamatory statement and (b) is positioned at the end of the hosting quotation.

- Erik said, "I heard Jennifer scream, 'Why can't I ever count on anybody?'"

22F CAPITALIZING THE FIRST WORD OF A QUOTATION

Be sure to observe the conventions that determine whether the first word of a quotation should be capitalized. A full-sentence quotation begins with a capital letter when the quotation is preceded by, followed by, or interrupted by a clause of attribution.

- Henry David Thoreau wrote, "Beware of all enterprises that require new clothes."

The first word of a full-sentence quotation serving as an appositive must also be capitalized.

- Henry David Thoreau's admonition "Beware of all enterprises that require new clothes" is especially relevant in our consumeristic society.

There are two types of sentences, however, in which the first word of a full-sentence quotation is not capitalized—unless the first word is a proper noun, a proper adjective, or the pronoun *I*. First, when a full-sentence quotation has been integrated into the structure of a hosting sentence so that the quotation is not functioning as an appositive, the first word is lowercased.

- Henry David Thoreau urged his readers to "beware of all enterprises that require new clothes."

Second, when the clause of attribution is followed by the indefinite relative pronoun *that*, the first word of the quotation will not be capitalized. Furthermore, no punctuation will separate the pronoun *that* from the quotation.

The quotation in the following sentence is punctuated correctly, but the initial letter of the first word of the quotation should be lowercased.

Faulty: Mr. Cox makes a good point when he says that "If by making idle threats that are always taken seriously by people who are just scared, we can impose enormous costs on the country, and the terrorists can impose enormous costs on the country. . . ."

("The Color of Terrorism," editorial, *Pittsburgh Post-Gazette*, 6 Jan. 2004, p. A12)

Faulty: Dr. Johnson observed that "Every man thinks meanly of himself for not having been a soldier, or not having been to sea."

(Fred Smoler, "The Soldier Inside All Men," *New York Post*, 11 Jan. 2004, p. 30)

22G ITALICS: THE BASICS

Italic type, the forward-slanting alternative to roman type, is the means by which an individual letter or numeral, a word, or a span of phrasing can be typographically distinguished from the surrounding phrasing.

Italics are used to call attention to a word as a word.

- Homer Simpson's interjection *d'oh* seems to be a contraction of *duh* and *oh*.

Italics are used to call attention to a single letter or numeral.

- His *i*'s look like *j*'s; his *7*'s are unmistakable.

Italics are also used for foreign words or phrases that have yet to become a part of the English language. (The dictionary entries for such words will usually tell you whether italics are needed.) Many foreign words have settled into our vocabulary for good; terms like *per diem, per se, non sequitur,* and *status quo* are no longer italicized. Nor are italics used any longer for Latin abbreviations such as *e.g.* and *i.e.*

The names of legal cases are italicized.

- *Roe v. Wade*

Italics can also be used to emphasize a word or a phrase within a sentence—but this use is often dismissed as a gimmick and an affectation. It is better to reshape a sentence so that any desired emphasis is built into its very contours than to rely on italics to direct the reader's attention to whatever the writer considers most important. (The end of a sentence is the most emphatic position; the beginning is the second most emphatic; the middle is the least emphatic.)

If italics are called for in phrasing that has already been set in italics, use roman type for the italics-within-italics.

- *Patterns of Symbolism in Hemingway's* The Sun Also Rises *and Early Short Fiction*

PUNCTUATIONAL CONVENTIONS

Italics are not the only typographical means of distinguishing a word or phrasing from surrounding text. **Boldfacing** is another. Boldface is a bulkier-looking, darker type than surrounding type and is used for emphasis and for headwords in glossaries. Like italicizing, boldfacing is best used sparingly.

Several typographical conventions govern the punctuation of italicized (or boldfaced) phrasing. Any comma, semicolon, colon, or period following italicized (or boldfaced) phrasing should be italicized (or boldfaced) as well. Use standard, roman parentheses or brackets to enclose phrasing that has been entirely or partially italicized or boldfaced unless the result looks off-kilter. Use roman type for quotation marks unless an entire quotation has been italicized (or boldfaced), in which case the quotation marks should be italicized (or boldfaced) as well. Italicize (or boldface) a question mark or an exclamation point ending a sentence only if the entire sentence has been italicized (or boldfaced) or if the question mark or exclamation point clearly belongs with italicized (or boldfaced) phrasing appearing at the end of the sentence, as in the following example.

• Her favorite movie is *Who Is Killing the Great Chefs of Europe?*

22H TITLES AND NAMES OF WORKS AND PUBLICATIONS

In academic writing that conforms to the conventions of the Modern Language Association (MLA), the titles of certain categories of works are always presented between quotation marks, and the titles of other categories of works are always italicized.

According to the MLA, the categories of titles that should be enclosed by quotation marks include titles of essays, newspaper articles, magazine articles, essays, chapters in books, sections or other divisions of books, encyclopedia articles, lectures, speeches, short poems, short stories, unpublished works (such as manuscripts and theses), e-mails, episodes of TV series, episodes of radio series, and songs.

The categories of titles that should be italicized include titles of books (except the Bible and the books within the Bible, as well as the designations Old Testament and New Testament), pamphlets, full-length plays, films, videotapes, paintings, sculptures, comic strips, most long musical compositions, operas, ballets and works of choreography, and record albums (full-length CDs)—as well as the names of print-edition and online newspapers (the article *the* at the beginning of the name of a newspaper, however, does not need to be italicized), the names of print-edition and online magazines and journals, TV series, radio programs, and legal cases. The names of aircraft, ships, submarines, trains, spacecraft, and satellites are also italicized.

The distinction between the use of quotation marks and the use of italics in the presentation of titles boils down to this: Quotation marks are used for the titles of short works and of works that are part of longer works; italics are used for the titles of long works composed of shorter works and for the titles of long indivisible works.

The titles of documents of unusual historical significance—such as the Declaration of Independence, the United States Constitution, the Bill of Rights, and the Gettysburg Address— are neither italicized nor enclosed between quotation marks, but their principal words are capitalized. The same is true of the names of college courses.

Finally, neither quotation marks nor italics are used for the title of a classical-music work whose name specifies its musical form and often specifies a number or a key (or sometimes both). The significant words in the title are capitalized.

• Bach's Toccata and Fugue in D Minor

Bear in mind that the guidelines for the presentation of titles discussed in the paragraphs above are the prescriptions of the Modern Language Association. The distinction between quotation marks and italics for the presentation of titles is not universally observed. In fact, some newspapers and magazines use quotation marks for all titles (other than the names of magazines and newspapers, which are presented without any typographical distinction). Be consistent in the presentation of titles throughout a piece of writing.

CHAPTER 23

SPECIALIZED PUNCTUATION MARKS

23A ELLIPSES

Ellipses, also known as ellipsis points and suspension points, are a punctuational device composed of a trio of spaced periods. (Always make sure that all three periods fit on a single line of text.) Ellipses have two important functions. First, they are used in dialogue to indicate that a speaker has not brought an utterance to completion or to indicate that there are awkward pauses in the utterance.

- The witness said, "She followed me into the stockroom and then pulled . . ."

In such sentences, one blank space precedes the ellipses, but no blank space separates the final period of the ellipses from the closing quotation mark. Furthermore, no additional period is added as terminal punctuation.

- "I didn't ... I mean, did I? ... I don't know if ... ," she began. "I can't, you know, just ... I mean, I really shouldn't even think of ..."

In the example above, note that the question mark precedes the second set of ellipses and that after the third set of ellipses, one blank space precedes the comma. (One blank space would also precede a question mark or an exclamation point following ellipses that indicated that a question or an exclamatory statement remained unfinished.)

The second use of the ellipses is to indicate that one or more words have been omitted from a direct quotation because the quoter considers them irrelevant to his or her purpose. (It would be unscrupulous and indefensible, of course, to delete any phrasing if the result would in any way misrepresent, or even reverse, the meaning of the source being cited.)

- Ursall goes on to state that "neither of the suggestions ... addresses the underlying cause of the problem."

Here the reader infers that one or more words have been deleted between *suggestions* and *addresses*. Note that one blank space precedes and follows the ellipses.

If you delete one or more words from the beginning of a quotation, you do not need to use ellipses—unless the document you are writing is unusually formal, in which case no blank space will separate the opening quotation mark from the first ellipsis period but one blank space will follow the final ellipsis period. If you delete one or more words from the end of a quotation positioned at the end of the hosting sentence, however, you need to use both a period and ellipses if the quoted matter has the status of a grammatically complete sentence. No blank space will precede the period.

- Two weeks later, she wrote in her journal, "I'm enduring another crisis of increativity. . . ."

If you are deleting one or more words from the end of a quotation that has the status of a grammatically complete sentence and that ends with a question mark or an exclamation point, position the terminal punctuation mark after the ellipses.

- In another entry, she wrote, "Will I ever find a way out ... ?"

Note that in this sentence one blank space precedes and follows the ellipses.

If the quoted matter at the end of a hosting sentence is a sentence that was left grammatically incomplete in the source (in other words, the phrasing in the source is a sentence fragment), the hosting sentence will end with three ellipses but not also with a period (again, note that a blank space separates the final word from the ellipses).

- Two pages later appears an unfinished entry in which she merely wrote, "Not if I have to go through with ..."

If you are deleting phrasing before a comma in a direct quotation, leave one blank space before the first ellipsis period and one blank space between the final ellipsis period and the comma.

- "After resuming work ... , she recruited a pair of collaborators."

If you are deleting phrasing after a comma in a direct quotation, leave one blank space between the comma and the first ellipsis period and one blank space after the final ellipsis period.

- "Between April 2003 and March 2005, ... she composed forty-seven songs."

TIP: Do not use ellipses when you are integrating single-word or phrasal quotations into a hosting sentence. It will be obvious to readers that you are citing only portions of one or more sentences from a source.

- She said the imagery of the poem was "incandescent" and "stunningly original."

Sometimes ellipses are used to indicate that one or more sentences have been omitted between two grammatically complete sentences included in a quotation.

- What surprised us were two statements in her single-paragraph journal entry for April 24: "I wrote the song in less than an hour. ... The lyrics came to me fully formed."

Here the reader infers that the two cited sentences did not appear consecutively in the source. Note that a period precedes the ellipses. No blank space precedes the sentence-ending period, but one blank space precedes and follows the ellipses.

A final use of ellipses is to indicate the omission of one or more lines from a multiline quotation from a poem when the quotation has not been run in with the text of a paragraph but instead has been presented as an extract. The omitted line or lines are marked by a line of spaced periods equivalent in length to the line immediately above it.

> In Diane Stevenson's poem "Resurrection," the act of knitting becomes a means of recovering, reclaiming, the body of a departed loved one:
>
> > Here are the many soft fists of yarn.
> >
> > . . . .
> >
> > [A]nd from this morning's knot, a back is formed,
> >
> > and grows, row by row, each stitch and loop of wool.

CAUTION

Both uses of the ellipses that we have discussed involve their insertion within direct quotations. Avoid using ellipses as a substitute for a dash in other kinds of sentences.

> **Awkward:** The job seemed to interest him . . . for the moment.
> **Better:** The job seemed to interest him—for the moment.

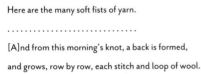 BRACKETS

Brackets—the squared-off cousins of parentheses—are a highly specialized punctuational device. In those rare sentences that call for one set of parentheses to be inserted within another, brackets are used for the inner parentheses.

- (She appeared in *The Best Years of Our Lives* [1946] and *Something to Live For* [1952].)

Brackets are also used to insert clarifying, explanatory, or interpretative phrasing into a direct quotation. The brackets signal to the reader that the writer citing someone else's words has added something to a quotation to enrich the reader's understanding. When a sentence with a pronominal subject is isolated from its context in a published source, for instance, the antecedent of the pronoun may need to be inserted between brackets.

- The article says that "he [the governor] had been unaware of the new allegations."

A noun in a quotation occasionally needs clarification.

- According to Fallmann's recollection, "The alternative version [of "Run Through Your Windows"] included no percussion whatsoever."

It is sometimes also permissible for a writer citing a source to use brackets to substitute a more precise word for an imprecise word in the original statement. Such substitutions are especially useful when the source is an interview in which a person was speaking off the top of his or her head and thus did not have the luxury of pausing to find exactly the right word. In the following quotation, the writer has replaced the vague noun *thing* with *side effect*.

- "Another [side effect] we have to worry about is dizziness," she said.

When only a portion of a direct quotation is inserted into a hosting sentence, the quoter occasionally needs to make an adjustment to one or more words in the quotation so that the quoted phrasing will grammatically fit within the structure of the hosting sentence. Brackets alert the reader to any such changes in the form of a word within a quotation.

Original Sentence: Let me propose a more subtle alternative interpretation of the ending of the film.

Adjusted Quotation: Morton "propose[s] a[n] ... alternative interpretation of the ending of the film."
It was necessary to reconjugate the verb so that it would agree with the subject of the hosting sentence, and because the adjectival phrase *more subtle* was omitted, the article *a* needed to be converted to *an*. The brackets enclose only the letters that have been added to words. Note that there is no blank space before either of the opening brackets, because in each case the bracketed material belongs to a word. One blank space follows each closing bracket.

A final use of the brackets is to insert the Latin word *sic,* meaning "thus," to alert the reader to an error in a quotation that the writer has transcribed accurately from a written source. The bracketed [*sic*] should be positioned directly after the erroneous word or punctuation mark.

- The memo stated that "one out of every four employees in the company are [*sic*] going to be laid off because of the steep, unexpected, and, frankly, even catastrophic drop-off in orders."

Use *sic* sparingly—and only with good reason. Overusing it will seem to suggest that you delight in finding fault with your sources and displaying your superiority to them. In the example above, the writer could have quoted only the remark-worthy or memorable phrasing of the sentence from the memo, tactfully ignoring the subject-verb agreement error.

- The memo stated that the "steep, unexpected, and, frankly, even catastrophic drop-off in orders" will result in the layoffs of twenty-five percent of the company's workforce.

The principles that determine the positioning of other punctuation marks in relation to closing brackets are similar to those for closing parentheses, which are discussed in chapter 20. When you are inserting brackets before a closing parenthesis, follow these punctuational patterns.

- (She appeared in *Girl With a Pearl Earring* [2003].)
- (She wrote, "It had no appreciable affect [*sic*].")

23C THE SLASH

This forward-slanting punctuational device—also called the virgule, the solidus, and the diagonal—is of limited use, yet it is widely misused and widely misunderstood.

Its most important function is to separate alternatives. In this capacity, it has the force of the conjunction *or.*

- and/or
- he/she
- him/her
- his/her
- student/educator discount

Yet many writers carelessly use the slash as if it meant *and.* Journalists are especially fond of using it to indicate that a person or thing is functioning in two or more capacities (*owner/operator; singer/songwriter; producer/director; actor/producer/director; action/adventure film*) when in fact the hyphen is the only appropriate punctuation mark in such constructions: *owner-operator; singer-songwriter; producer-director; actor-producer-director; action-adventure film.* Any such two-word construction can be recast by replacing the hyphen with *and* (*owner and operator*), and that is the preferred pattern.

There are four other important uses of the slash.

1. Slashes are used when dates are presented informally, with a numeral specifying the month.

- 9/11
- 10/24/99

2. A slash is used to separate the two parts of a fraction.

- 5/6
- 3/16

3. Slashes are used in Internet addresses.

- http://www.webdelsol.com/5_trope

TIP: When an entire Internet address will not fit at the end of a line of text, make the line break after any single slash.

---

4. Slashes are used to mark off the line breaks in poetry when quoted lines are inserted into a hosting sentence.

- Diane Stevenson's poem "Discover Paradise" makes subtle use of slant rhymes in lines 1 and 2 ("His ashes are the ashes of sleep, / and he is the dream") and again in lines 9 and 10 ("and from the small place / left whole in his brain").

More casually, slashes are used in the expression *24/7* and sometimes in the date of a double issue of a magazine (*June/July 2005*), although the use of an en dash between the two parts of the date is preferred. In casual contexts, the slash can also be used between the names of two entities in phrasing that emphasizes rivalry, competition, conflict, or opposition: *the Harvard/ Yale rivalry.*

There is no blank space before or after any slash—except when you are indicating line breaks in a poem, in which case there should be a blank space before and after each slash.

CHAPTER 24

THE HYPHEN

24A HYPHENS: THE BASICS

The hyphen has two uses—one of them simple, the other complicated. The simple use of the hyphen is to divide a multisyllabic word that does not fit in its entirety at the end of a line of text. The dictionary entry for any such word will tell you how to break the word. The complicated use of the hyphen is to unite words, or word elements, together into compounds, such as *ex-husband, pro-war, anti-Semitic, court-martial, hand-me-downs, stir-crazy, slow-spoken, long-distance* (in the phrase *long-distance service*), and *under-the-table* (in the phrase *under-the-table payments*). Notice that there is no space before or after a hyphen when it is used to form a compound. Knowing when to insert hyphens into compound elements is an important part of writing clear, readable sentences.

24B HYPHENS AND COMPOUND NOUNS

Whenever you are using a compound noun—a noun assembled from two or more words—you need to determine whether the compound should be presented as two words, in what is called an open compound (such as *soul mate, half sister,* and *bag lady*), or as a hyphenated compound (such as *drive-by, great-grandmother,* and *two-timer*), or as a single word known as a closed or solid compound (such as *makeover, stepmother,* and *busboy*). A good dictionary will usually answer such questions for you. You merely need to form the habit of consulting one. The prevailing trend is toward closed compounds (*lifestyle* instead of *life-style* or *life style*), but some compounds are still in the early phases of their development (*mind-set,* for instance, is gradually morphing into *mindset*). It is important, though, that you be consistent in spelling such words throughout a document. Compound proper nouns specifying the double nature of a person's heritage are often hyphenated (*African-American; Italian-American*) and sometimes not (*French Canadian*); let a good dictionary be your guide. A closed-compound noun preceded by an adjective (or by a noun functioning adjectivally) sometimes needs to be broken in two, its first half becoming the second half of a hyphenated adjectival compound: a homeowner with a second home is a *second-home owner;* a shopwindow in a pet shop is a *pet-shop window;* a bookshelf for reference books is a *reference-book shelf.*

24C HYPHENS AND COMPOUND VERBS

For compound verbs, two general principles should be heeded. First, when a verb attracts an adverbial particle—as in *clean up, turn down, work out, phase in,* and *sign off*—the verb phrase should not be hyphenated. (The nounal forms of such phrases, however, usually are closed compounds: *cleanup, turndown, workout, signoff.*) Second, when a noun, an adjective, or an adverb is added before a verb to form a phrasal verb, the resulting compound usually needs to be hyphenated: *trash-talk, cherry-pick, hand-wash, slow-cook, stir-fry, quick-freeze, deep-fry.*

TIP: Many such compound verbs have worked their way into dictionaries; so, as stated above, it is good to get in the habit of referring to one. Some compound verbs are still too new to have settled into a universally agreed-upon form: The closed-compound verb *homeschool* appears in *Merriam-Webster's Collegiate Dictionary;* the hyphenated-compound verb home-school appears in *Webster's New World College Dictionary.* (Again, be consistent in the spelling of such words throughout a document.)

24D HYPHENS AND ADJECTIVAL COMPOUNDS

The most complicated business conducted by hyphens is uniting words into adjectival compounds that precede nouns. Many writers neglect to hyphenate such compounds, and the result is ramshackle sentences that often frustrate the reader. In each of the following examples, the adjectival compound has been italicized.

- credit-card debt
- low-carbohydrate diet
- over-the-counter medications
- do-it-yourself projects
- once-in-a-lifetime opportunities

The words constituting these compound modifiers are often pairs of nouns or combinations of nouns and adjectives (including participles, which function as adjectives).

  Adjectival compounds sometimes include prepositional phrases and adverbs as well. The reader needs to recognize that any such compound functions just like a single-word adjective, so it needs to be fastened together with one or more hyphens. The hyphens signal that the reader should take in the compound in one sweep—and thus regard it as one unit with interlocking parts rather than as two or more separate units. (Many hyphenated adjectival compounds have become permanent additions to dictionaries—among them are *quick-witted, stone-faced, slow-footed, full-fledged, deep-seated, empty-handed, ill-fated, weak-minded, well-meaning, long-range,* and *short-term*—so, again, a trip to a dictionary is always well advised.) Correct hyphenation ensures that readers will get the right idea about the function of words within a sentence, as well as about their interrelationships with the other components of the sentence.

There is a world of difference, after all, between an *infectious disease expert* and an *infectious-disease expert* (the former is a disease expert who is infectious; the latter is an expert in infectious diseases), between an *adult film star* and an *adult-film star* (the former is a movie star who is an adult, not a child or an adolescent; the latter is a star of adult films), between a *homeless outreach worker* and a *homeless-outreach worker* (the former is an outreach worker who is homeless; the latter is an outreach worker who helps the homeless), between a *suspicious activity report* and a *suspicious-activity report* (the former is an activity report whose contents arouse suspicion; the latter is a report about suspicious activity), and between *dumb blonde jokes* and *dumb-blonde jokes* (the former are bad jokes about blondes; the latter are jokes about dumb blondes).

- Build Your Own Salad Bar

  (from a restaurant window sign)

    This sign from a New York City restaurant unintentionally invites diners to construct a salad bar rather than to assemble their own salads. A more precise sign would read *Build-Your-Own-Salad Bar.*

- The lost lottery ticket story sounded too fantastic to be true.

  (L. A. Johnson and Lillian Thomas, "Truth Is, in Truth, Often Not the Norm," *Pittsburgh Post-Gazette,* 11 Jan. 2004, p. A1)

    Notice how the insertion of two hyphens (between *lost* and *lottery* and between *lottery* and *ticket*) would improve the readability of the following sentence.

Readability diminishes when unhyphenated nouns are piled atop one another.

Faulty: The mayor was skeptical about the landmarks preservation commission agenda.
The first three of the four consecutive nouns together constitute a single adjectival compound modifying *agenda.*
Correct: The mayor was skeptical about the landmarks-preservation-commission agenda.
The hyphens increase readability by making it clear that the adjectival compound is modifying *agenda.*
Correct: The major was skeptical about the agenda of the landmarks-preservation commission.
Only one hyphen is needed in this revision; *landmarks-preservation* is an adjectival compound modifying the noun *commission.*

The insertion of two hyphens, which have been bracketed and boldfaced, improves the reader-friendliness of the following sentence.

- Last year, shoppers dropped $28.9 billion into the specialty[-]car[-]equipment industry, up 7.7% from 2002.

  (Rebecca Louie, "He'll Pimp Your Ride," *New York Daily News,* 16 May 2004, p. 8)

24E HYPHENATION OF ADJECTIVAL COMPOUNDS THAT PRECEDE NOUNS

Adjectival Compounds That Begin With Nouns

Noun + Noun Noun

home-improvement loans; customer-support services; blood-sugar levels; junk-food diet; age-discrimination verdict; crisis-management expert; weight-loss methods; crime-prevention program; computer-repair technician; life-size statue; art-history professor; health-food store; video-game arcade; cream-cheese frosting; community-college student; human-rights issues; feature-length film; Saturday-morning cartoons; a fairy-tale life; chocolate-chip cookies; ice-cream cone; button-fly jeans

Noun + Noun + Noun Noun
computer-virus-detection software; radio-talk-show host; lead-hazard-reduction grants; breast-cancer-prevention campaign; motor-vehicle-death rate

---

CAUTION
Remember that we are illustrating patterns in which hyphens are inserted into adjectival compounds that precede nouns. Such compounds lose their hyphens, however, when they are no longer positioned before nouns.

- He bought a chocolate-cake mix.
- He baked a chocolate cake.
- Emily writes situation-comedy scripts.
- Emily writes scripts for a situation comedy.
- The widow attended a group-therapy session.
- The widow found group therapy helpful.

Noun + Conjunction + Noun Noun
a father-and-son business; country-and-western music; a law-and-order issue; a cat-and-mouse game

Noun + Noun + Conjunction + Noun Noun
a guitar-bass-and-drums combo

TIP: Be sure to hyphenate adjectival compounds that begin with the indefinite pronoun all.

- an all-encompassing proposal
- an all-inclusive policy

Noun + Adjective Noun
commercial-free broadcast; fashion-forward buyers; lightning-quick response; computer-savvy kindergartner; reader-friendly prose; street-smart teenager

Noun + Participle Noun
Spanish-speaking residents; attention-getting behavior; a money-grubbing hack; an ego-deflating remark; eye-opening results; job-seeking graduates; life-threatening injuries; stomach-turning violence; male-bashing jokes; thought-provoking questions; snow-cleared streets; air-conditioned bedroom; Philadelphia-based corporations; a Los Angeles-based actor; fleece-lined jacket; time-tested methods

Noun + Preposition [or Adverbial Particle] Noun
hands-on experience; the heads-up sign

Adjectival Compounds That Begin with Adjectives

Adjective + Noun Noun
early-morning appointment; one-hit wonders; five-year wait; first-time offender; sexual-harassment case; no-parking zone; minimum-wage hike; maximum-security prison;

medical-equipment company; full-page advertisement; middle-class voters; public-school superintendent; red-carpet treatment; real-estate agent; high-contrast colors; free-speech advocates; social-studies teacher; civil-liberties lawyer; hot-air balloons; punk-rock groups; bare-bones approach; special-effects footage

Adjective + Noun + Noun **Noun**
three-month-subscription offer; a high-school-graduation party; high-blood-pressure medications

Adjective + Noun + Gerund **Noun**
crude-oil-processing plant

Adjective + Adjective + Noun **Noun**
public-high-school student; junior-high-school library

Adjective + Participle **Noun**
full-figured fashions; low-flying airplane; youthful-looking singer

Adjectival Compounds That Begin With Participles

Participle + Noun **Noun**
cutting-edge fashion; closed-door session; returned-merchandise policy; baked-goods sale; used-CD store; used-car salesman

Participle + Participle **Noun**
closed-minded people

Participle + Preposition [or Adverbial Particle] **Noun**
locked-in freshness; built-in quality; tired-out athletes; washed-up singer; stripped-down version; a beat-up sofa

Adjectival Compounds That Begin with Verbs

Verb + Conjunction + Verb **Noun**
slash-and-burn measures; a do-or-die attitude

Helping Verb + Main Verb **Noun**
a get-acquainted reception; a get-lost gesture

Verb + Noun [or Pronoun] **Noun**
a tell-all memoir

Verb + Adverb [or Adverbial Particle] **Noun**
drop-dead gorgeousness; a come-hither look; a drive-thru window

Verb + Adjective **Noun**
a stay-put attitude

Phrasal Verb + Conjunction + Phrasal Verb **Noun**
a pay-up-or-shut-up attitude

> **TIP:** Be sure to hyphenate an adjectival compound that consists of, or includes, an infinitive when such a compound precedes a noun.
>
> - my to-do list
> - her soon-to-be-published memoirs

Adjectival Compounds That Begin With Adverbs

The rules for hyphenating adjectival compounds that begin with adverbs are more complicated than the rules presented thus far.

Never insert a hyphen between an adverb ending in *-ly* and an adjective or a participle when they together form an adjectival compound that precedes a noun. The first hyphen in the following sentence should thus be deleted.

> **Faulty:** Leaders of Pittsburgh suburbs whose fortunes are closely tied to the financially-troubled city are faced with a double-edged sword of accepting remedies that may negatively impact their residents but prove beneficial to the region over the long haul.
>
> (Bill Toland, "Leaders Discuss City/Suburb Tug-of-War," *Pittsburgh Post-Gazette*, 17 Apr. 2004, p. A9)

Similarly, phrases such as the following should appear without hyphens: *particularly attractive alternatives; admittedly foolish decisions; highly touted cure; a relatively recent development; a brilliantly original comedy; an internationally famous actress; a usually fatal disease; a slightly different dress; a newly formed organization.*

Be careful, however, to distinguish between adverbs ending in *-ly* and adjectives ending in *-ly*. The phrase *friendly-looking salesclerk* requires a hyphen because *friendly* is an adjective, not an adverb. (Among the other adjectives that end in *-ly* are *womanly, manly, scholarly, homely, timely, ugly, likely, costly, deadly, lonely, ghastly, ghostly, sisterly,* and *brotherly*.)

Occasionally, an *-ly* adverb is part of an adjectival compound that takes the form **-ly adverb + participle + noun** and that is positioned before a noun. Hyphens are needed throughout such a compound.

- a sexually-transmitted-disease epidemic

But it is often better to rephrase such a compound.

- an epidemic of sexually transmitted diseases

When a flat adverb and a participle combine to form an adjectival compound that precedes a noun, the compound must be hyphenated. (Remember that flat adverbs are a subclass of adverbs that do not end in *-ly* and that are indistinguishable from adjectives in their form.) The pattern is **flat adverb + participle noun**.

- a quick-thinking employee
- slow-moving traffic

But:

- slowly moving traffic

The following two principles apply to adjectival compounds that begin with adverbs not ending in *-ly*.

1. When an adverb preceding an adjective or a participle could be mistaken for an adjective, insert a hyphen between the adverb and the adjective or participle. Consider the phrase *less expensive* in the following two sentences.

- She bought less expensive clothing.
- She bought less-expensive clothing.

The first sentence means that she cut back on her shopping for expensive clothing; *less* is an adjective (it is the first in a pair of cumulative adjectives modifying the noun *clothing*). But the second sentence means that she bought clothes costing *less* than some other kind; *less* is an adverb. Only the writer of such sentences is in the position to know whether *less* is to be read as an adjective or as an adverb, so it is up to the writer to know when the hyphen is needed.

The adjectival compounds in the following sentences need hyphens to clarify the meaning.

Faulty: She is the best educated applicant.
The sentence is not intended to mean that of all the educated applicants, she is the best; the sentence is intended to mean that she is the applicant with the best education.
Correct: She is the best-educated applicant.
A hyphen between *best* and *educated* ensures that the sentence conveys the intended meaning:

Faulty: She owns the most used appliances.
The sentence is not intended to mean that she owns the greatest number of secondhand appliances; the sentence is meant to convey that she owns the kinds of appliances that are most frequently used.
Correct: She owns the most-used appliances.
A hyphen between *most* and *used* will clarifies the writer's intention.

Faulty: The teacher asked for more specific examples.
The sentence is not intended to mean that the teacher asked for a larger quantity of specific examples; the sentence is intended to mean that the teacher asked for examples that were more specific than the ones already provided.
Correct: The teacher asked for more-specific examples.
A hyphen between *more* and *specific* resolves the problem.

The words that are especially likely to cause ambiguity or misreading are *best, better, more,* and *most.*

2. When an adjectival compound consists of an **adverb + modifier + participle** combination, make sure that the reader can instantly tell whether the modifier in the central position is functioning as an adjective or as an adverb.

The following phrases each need a hyphen so that the reader knows that the words coming after *very, rather,* and *fairly* are adverbs, not adjectives.

Faulty: a very good looking waiter
Correct: a very good-looking waiter

Faulty: a rather ill fated boy
Correct: a rather ill-fated boy

Faulty: a fairly well trained volunteer
Correct: a fairly well-trained volunteer

In each case, the first adverb is not modifying a single word (*good, ill,* or *well*) but instead is modifying an adjectival compound composed of a second adverb and a participle. A hyphen is needed to unite the two parts of the compound into a single unit.

A great many adverbs not ending in *-ly* can appear at the beginning of adjectival compounds modifying nouns. Some of the adverbs require hyphenation, but most do not. Below is a checklist of the most common patterns. The checklist is based on hyphenation practice in the *New Yorker,* a magazine whose punctuation is especially precise, even exquisite.

All too + adjective noun *not hyphenated* (an all too wonderful offer; an all too likely risk; an all too easy question)

Almost + adjective [or participle] noun *not hyphenated* (an almost unbelievable account; an almost finished manuscript; some almost satisfying moments)

Already + adjective noun *not hyphenated* (an already available position)

Already + participle noun *not hyphenated* (the already recorded tracks)

Altogether + adjective [or participle] noun *not hyphenated* (the one altogether disappointing album)

Always + adjective noun *not hyphenated* (the always empty house)

As yet + adjective [or participle] noun *not hyphenated* (the as yet untitled song)

At once + adjective [or participle] + *and* + adjective [or participle] noun *not hyphenated* (the at once peculiar and entrancing stranger)

Best + participle noun *hyphenated* (the singer's best-known song; the best-looking couple; the best-guarded secret)

Better + participle noun *hyphenated* (a better-known song)

Better than + adjective noun *not hyphenated* (better than average salaries) *or hyphenated* (better-than-average Smiths songs) Both patterns can be found in the *New Yorker;* a writer merely needs to be consistent within a particular document. (Note: *Better* in these examples is an adjective, but because it can sometimes be difficult to classify the function of *better* within a phrase, we decided to include this pattern with adjectival phrases beginning with adverbs.)

By now + adjective noun *not hyphenated* (a by now familiar figure)

Equally + adjective noun *not hyphenated* (an equally impressive record)

Equally + adverb + participle + adjective noun *hyphenated only between adverb and participle* (an equally long-simmering departmental conflict)

Even + adjective noun *not hyphenated* (an even worse example)

Even + adverb + adjective noun *not hyphenated* (even halfway great performances)

Even more + adjective [or participle] noun *not hyphenated* (the even more lazy employee; an even more shocking spectacle)

Ever + adjective noun *hyphenated* (the ever-game actress) *or not hyphenated* (ever dependable means of transportation) Both patterns can be found in the *New Yorker;* a writer merely needs to be consistent within a particular document.

Ever + comparative adjective noun *hyphenated* (ever-larger paintings)

Ever more + adjective noun *not hyphenated* (our ever more regrettable inclinations)

Ever + **participle noun** *hyphenated* (ever-increasing debt; ever-rising prices)

Ever so + **adjective noun** *hyphenated* (an ever-so-pale complexion) *or not hyphenated* (the ever so polished diction) Both patterns can be found in the *New Yorker*; a writer merely needs to be consistent within a particular document.

Extra + **adjective noun** *hyphenated* (extra-large portions)

Far + **comparative adjective noun** *not hyphenated* (a far longer essay)

Far from + **adjective noun** *not hyphenated* (her far from miraculous performance)

Far more + **participle noun** *not hyphenated* (a far more relaxing evening)

Good enough **noun** *not hyphenated* (a good enough specimen of her work)

Halfway + **adjective noun** *not hyphenated* (a halfway decent proposal)

Just + **participle noun** *not hyphenated* (the just opened restaurant)

Least + **adjective [or participle] noun** *not hyphenated* (the least conspicuous member; the least understood reason)

Less + **adjective noun** *not hyphenated* (a less significant reason; less imaginative students) In the latter example, *less* should not be misread as an adjective pertaining to quantity, because the appropriate adjective would be *fewer*.

Less + **participle noun** *not hyphenated* (less fevered followers) See the note in the entry above.

Lesser + **participle noun** *hyphenated* (a lesser-known actor)

Less than + **adjective noun** *not hyphenated* (a less than spectacular movie)

Little + **participle noun** *hyphenated* (a little-known caricaturist) A *little known caricaturist* would be a known caricaturist who is small in stature.

Long + **participle noun** *hyphenated* (the long-delayed sequel; his long-suffering wife)

Long + **participle + adverbial particle noun** *hyphenated* (the long-drawn-out response)

More + **adjective [or participle] noun** *not hyphenated* (the more famous sister; a more conspicuous success; a more interesting alternative; more conventional films; more aggressive women) But notice the ambiguity in the last two examples. Whenever there is any possibility of the reader's mistaking the adverb *more* for the adjective *more*, it is better to insert a hyphen after the adverb: Thus *We need more economical alternatives* is a sentence meaning that we need a greater number of alternatives that are economical; and *We need more-economical alternatives* is a sentence meaning that we need alternatives that are more economical than the ones we have right now.

More + **adjective + participle noun** *hyphenated* (a more open-minded supervisor) If the noun were the plural *supervisors,* ambiguity could arise: *more open-minded supervisors* could mean either a greater number of supervisors who are open-minded or supervisors who are more open-minded than some others; it would be to the reader's advantage for you to recast the phrase so that it conveys the intended meaning.

More or less + **adjective noun** *not hyphenated* (a more or less pointless exercise)

More + **participle noun** *not hyphenated* (one of her more thrilling performances; a more concentrated effort; progressively more complicated examples; the more promising students) Be attentive to any possible ambiguity; see the first two entries about compounds beginning with *more.*

More than + **adjective noun** *not hyphenated* (her more than generous offer)

More than enough + **noun** *not hyphenated* (more than enough chocolate)

Most + **adjective noun** *not hyphenated* (the most significant result; a most instructive example; the most recent entry; one of her most dangerous stunts) Note that the sentence *Her research yielded the most significant results* is ambiguous. If *most* is to be read as an adverb, it would be to the reader's advantage if you inserted a hyphen after *most,* because *most* could otherwise be read as an adjective pertaining to quantity.

Most + **adverb** + **adjective noun** *not hyphenated* (the most nearly complete collection)

Most + **participle noun** *not hyphenated* (her most interesting suggestion; the most accomplished pianist) Note that *She offered the most interesting suggestions* is ambiguous; see the note in the first *most* entry above.

Most + **participle** + **adverbial particle noun** *hyphenated only between participle and adverbial particle* (the most sought-after designer)

Much + **comparative adjective noun** *not hyphenated* (in much deeper water)

Much more + **participle noun** *not hyphenated* (a much more refined performance)

Much + **participle noun** *hyphenated* (one of the much-quoted remarks) *or not hyphenated* (a much travelled part of the state) Both patterns can be found in the *New Yorker;* a writer merely needs to be consistent within a particular document.

Near + **adjective noun** *hyphenated* (near-permanent damage; near-perfect pitch; near-legendary performance)

Never + **adjective noun** *not hyphenated* (her never unremarkable stories)

Next to + **adjective noun** *hyphenated* (the next-to-impossible task)

No longer + **adjective noun** *not hyphenated* (the no longer fashionable address)

None too + **adjective noun** *not hyphenated* (none too welcome glimpses of her private life)

Not + **adjective noun** *not hyphenated* (a not uncommon result)

Not + **adverb** + **adjective noun** *not hyphenated* (a not particularly vivid account)

Not altogether + **adjective noun** *not hyphenated* (the not altogether tidy fellow; a not altogether satisfactory plot)

Not quite + **adjective noun** *hyphenated* (the not-quite-dead lobster)

Not so + **adjective noun** *not hyphenated* (not so young men) *or hyphenated* (not-so-good Jackson Pollocks) Both patterns can be found in the *New Yorker;* a writer merely needs to be consistent within a particular document.

Not too + **adjective noun** *not hyphenated* (a not too bright idea; a not too brief report)

Not very + **adjective noun** *not hyphenated* (a not very solid job; a not very successful attempt)

Not yet + **adverb** + **participle noun** *not hyphenated* (the not yet successfully marketed replacement)

Not yet + **participle noun** *not hyphenated* (the not yet published article)

Now + **adjective [or participle] noun** *not hyphenated* (the now unhappy child; the now vanished style; the now forgotten painter)

Often + **adjective noun** *not hyphenated* (her often undiscussable problems)

Often + **participle noun** *not hyphenated* (the often maligned suburb)

Once + **adjective noun** *hyphenated* (a once-famous journalist)

Once + **adjective** + **adjective noun** *hyphenated only between once and first adjective* (the once-monthly afternoon meetings)

Once + **participle noun** *not hyphenated* (a once promising director; a once flourishing career; a once reviled sculpture)

Perhaps + **adjective noun** *not hyphenated* (a perhaps unavoidable collision)

Pretty + **adjective noun** *not hyphenated* (a pretty weak argument; a pretty accessible venue)

Quite + **adjective noun** *not hyphenated* (a quite innocent mistake)

Rather + **adjective noun** *not hyphenated* (a rather peculiar suggestion; the rather dim voice)

Rather more + **adjective noun** *not hyphenated* (a rather more substantial book)

Really + **adjective noun** *not hyphenated* (really good desserts)

Single best + **participle noun** *hyphenated only between* best *and participle* (her single best-known painting)

Single most + **adjective noun** *not hyphenated* (the single most helpful piece of advice)

Somewhat + **adjective noun** *not hyphenated* (my own somewhat facetious remark; a somewhat different perspective)

Still + **adjective noun** *not hyphenated* (the still fashionable neighborhood)

Then + **adjective noun** *not hyphenated* (the then new technology)

Too + **adjective noun** *not hyphenated* (too thin women; a too blunt manner)

Too + **adverb** + **participle noun** *not hyphenated* (her too little known poems)

Very + **adjective [or participle] noun** *not hyphenated* (very short sleeves; the very elegant house; the very real threat; a very depressed patient)

Well + **participle noun** *hyphenated* (well-behaved children; well-read students; well-known performers; well-regarded pundits)

Yet another + **noun** *not hyphenated* (yet another embarrassment; yet another oddball)

Adjectival Compounds That Present the Names of Colors

An adjectival compound that presents the name of a color should be hyphenated when it precedes a noun: *a robin's-egg-blue blouse; chrome-yellow stationery; a battleship-gray desk; olive-green trousers; orchid-pink buttons; greenish-blue curtains; light-blue shirts; a pale-yellow sweater; a dark-brown jacket; stone-white trousers.*

Here are two other common patterns: stripes (*a red-and-white striped shirt; a green-and-yellow striped awning*) and combinations of two or more colors (*a bright-green-and-purple shirt; black-and-white photographs; a red-white-and-blue design*).

Adjectival Compounds That Consist of, or Contain, Prepositional Phrases

An adjectival compound consisting of, or including, a prepositional phrase should be hyphenated when it precedes a noun: *on-site snack bar; on-premises bakery; in-house repairs; under-the-table payments; across-the-board pay raises; off-the-cuff remarks; a beyond-the-pale performance; an up-to-the-minute style; a by-the-skin-of-her-teeth escape; an off-the-beaten-track restaurant; an on-again, off-again romance; face-to-face confrontation; top-of-the-line models; state-to-state calls; a rags-to-riches story; run-of-the-mill musicians; turn-of-the-century music; an ill-at-ease waiter; a go-for-broke attitude; back-to-back classes; Paris-to-London flights; Chicago-to-San Francisco train service; a 3:30-to-3:45 appointment; a 10 a.m.-to-noon broadcast.*

Longer Adjectival Compounds

There are often two ways to present longer adjectival compounds (some of which are the equivalent of complete sentences). The first way is to hyphenate them throughout.

- a little-bit-of-everything assortment
- an all-you-can-eat buffet
- a so-bad-that-it's-good movie
- a three-strikes-and-you're-out policy
- an I-couldn't-care-less attitude
- an earn-while-you-learn opportunity

The second way is to enclose the compound within quotation marks. In this case, no hyphens should be inserted.

- a "little bit of everything" assortment
- an "all you can eat" buffet
- a "so bad that it's good" movie
- a "three strikes and you're out" policy
- an "I couldn't care less" attitude
- an "earn while you learn" opportunity

Many long adjectival compounds, of course, can be presented only in the first way, with hyphens.

- a thirty-five-thousand-dollar-a-year job
- a pair of one-hundred-percent-cotton trousers

TIP: Sometimes a noun will be preceded by two or more consecutive hyphenated adjectival compounds.

- a hard-core mope-rock fan
- a Sunday-morning talk-show host
- a six-week high-school driver-training class

24F UNHYPHENATED ADJECTIVAL COMPOUNDS

There are three categories of adjectival compounds that are not hyphenated.

1. Multi-word proper nouns that are functioning as adjectival compounds and that precede nouns are not hyphenated (remember that a proper noun is a noun always requiring capitalization): *Operation Desert Storm veterans; a New York City resident; a Cleveland Heights delicatessen; Peter Pan collars; a Best Buy executive; the No Child Left Behind Act; an Equal Employment Opportunity Commission report.*

But there are some exceptions: *the 1948 Arab-Israeli War.* When in doubt, consult a dictionary, an almanac, or an encyclopedia.

2. Names of chemical compounds that are functioning as adjectives and that precede nouns are not hyphenated: *a sodium bicarbonate toothpaste; a hydrogen peroxide rinse.*

3. Foreign phrases that are functioning as adjectival compounds and that precede nouns are not usually hyphenated, regardless of whether the phrases appear in italics or not: *an ad hoc panel; average per capita income; an au courant shopper; a de facto government; a bon voyage gift; ad hominem attacks.*

TIP: Hyphens should be inserted in adjectival compounds that appear in titles of works and in headlines of newspaper articles, even if the headlines are formatted for standard capitalization.

Faulty: Single Mom Overwhelmed by Recording Industry Suit

(headline, *Pioneer Press* online, 26 May 2004)

Recording can initially be misread as a gerund whose object is *Suit* rather than as the first half of an adjectival compound modifying *Suit.* A hyphen between *Recording* and *Industry* dispels any confusion: *Single Mom Overwhelmed by Recording-Industry Suit.*

Faulty: Umbilical-Cord Blood Stem Cell Transplants Lag

(headline, Reed Abelson, for *New York Times,* in *Pittsburgh Post-Gazette,* 29 May 2004, p. A3)

A reader can initially be confused about which words are functioning as nouns, which functioning as adjectives, and which are functioning as verbs. The article makes it clear that the topic is the use of umbilical-cord blood in stem-cell transplants, so the hyphenation should be as follows: *Umbilical-Cord-Blood Stem-Cell Transplants Lag.*

Faulty: Cleaner Gasoline Rule Is Criticized

(headline, *Pittsburgh Post-Gazette,* 20 Feb. 1998, p. B8)

It is not the gasoline rule that is cleaner (*cleaner* and *gasoline* are not intended to be regarded as cumulative adjectives, as the unpunctuated phrasing suggests); it is the gasoline that is cleaner—and the rule being criticized is one that requires cleaner gasoline. Thus the words *Cleaner* and *Gasoline* need to be yoked together with a hyphen to form an adjectival compound modifying *rule: Cleaner-Gasoline Rule Is Criticized.*

> **Faulty:** Off-Duty Officer, Wife Bottle Up Roadway Attack Suspect
>
> (headline, *Greensburg [PA] Tribune-Review,* 13 Jan. 1998, p. A1)
>
> > This title, intended to be playful, is perplexing at first glance. The reader can initially mistake *roadway* for the direct object of the verb phrase *bottle up*, but then the syntactical relation of *attack* suspect to the rest of the sentence is obscured. Is *attack* a second verb with *off-duty officer* and *wife* as the subjects? If so, the headline is mispunctuated. The reader soon realizes, however, that *attack* is serving adjectivally; it is the second half of the adjectival compound *roadway-attack,* modifying *suspect,* which is the intended direct object of *bottle up.* A hyphen between *roadway* and *attack* eliminates the confusion: *Off-Duty Officer, Wife Bottle Up Roadway-Attack Suspect.*

24G HYPHENATION OF ADJECTIVAL COMPOUNDS THAT FUNCTION AS COMPLEMENTS

Adjectival compounds can also function as the complements (predicate adjectives) of linking verbs. Adjectival-compound complements come after, rather than precede, the nouns they describe—and the rules governing the hyphenation of adjectival-compound complements are not as cut and dry as the rules governing the hyphenation of adjectival compounds that are positioned before nouns. Newspapers, magazines, and publishers of books differ in how they treat such compounds. There are a few commonsensical principles, however, to guide you.

1. Hyphenated adjectival compounds that have found their way into dictionaries can retain the hyphens when the compounds are used as complements. The hyphenation of such compounds can never be considered wrong. But editors sometimes consider such hyphens fussy and distracting—a form of punctuational overkill. Thus *He just turned forty and feels over the hill* and *He just turned forty and feels over-the-hill* are both acceptable, but the hyphens in the three-word adjectival-compound complement are disposable. When an adjectival compound not only is included in a dictionary but also forcibly impresses itself upon the mind as a single unit, however, it should be hyphenated as a complement.

    - The software is user-friendly.
    - Her friends are far-flung.
    - The design is eye-catching.
    - She is no longer camera-shy.
    - His manner was matter-of-fact.
    - The performance was fine-tuned.

2. Adjectival-compound complements in which the first word might initially be misconstrued as a stand-alone word should be hyphenated to eliminate misreading. It is in the best interest of your readers for you to hyphenate the complements in sentences such as these:

    - He was wide-eyed.
    - The model is full-scale.
    - The problem is deep-rooted.
    - She was ill-humored.
    - She is extremely good-looking.
    - She is quick-witted.
    - The boy is high-spirited.
    - The supervisor is low-key.

- She remains open-minded.
- She's the best-known of the writers in her generation.
- The TV is off-limits.
- He is dead-serious.

Without the hyphens, these sentences can easily lead the reader to think—if only for a fraction of a second—that *he was wide, the model is full, the problem is deep, she was ill, she is extremely good, she is quick, the boy is high, the supervisor is low, she remains open, she's the best, the TV is off,* and *he is dead.* The reader needs a signal that the adjective following the linking verb is not operating solo but instead is hooked up with a noun, an adjective, or a participle. The hyphen clues the reader in.

Similarly, when an adjectival-compound complement consists of a phrase, hyphens can help the reader instantly grasp the meaning of the entire sentence.

- Her performance was over-the-top.
- She is well-thought-of.
- The girl is up-to-date.

Without the hyphens, the sentences can cause the reader to stumble for a nanosecond, thinking that *her performance was over, she is well,* and *the girl is up.* It is therefore advisable to hyphenate adjectival-compound complements wherever the hyphens can help ensure instant readability. (Hyphens would obviously not be used, however, in sentences such as *The performance was over at ten o'clock* and *The girl is up to trouble.*)

3. Most adjectival-compound complements formed with *well* or *ill* do not need hyphens—unless such a complement is describing a human being and *well* or *ill* might initially be misread as referring to physical or emotional health. The following sentences are thus fine without the hyphens.

- The thriller is well paced.
- The chairs are well made.
- The songs were well sung.
- The point is well taken.
- The suggestion was well intended.
- The restaurant is well lighted.
- The gift was well concealed.
- The presentation was remarkably well balanced.
- The lecture was well organized.
- The move was ill advised.
- The project was ill conceived.

Some adjectival compounds formed from *well* and a participle have long been included in dictionaries, however, and have become permanent compounds that always require hyphenation. Among them are *well-meaning* and *well-read.*

TIP: If, in a sentence including two or more adjectival compounds formed from *well* and a participle, one of the compounds (such as *well-meaning*) requires a hyphen and one or more of the other compounds (such as *well organized*) do not require hyphenation, it is better to hyphenate them all than to risk distracting a reader with inconsistent hyphenation.

- She was well-meaning and well-organized.

---

4. Adjectival-compound complements that specify the age of someone or something are not hyphenated, unless the number itself requires a hyphen.

- The girl is four years old.
- Uncle Harry is ninety-two years old.

5. Adjectival-compound complements that present the names of colors are not hyphenated.

- The trousers were olive green.
- The shirt was fulvous yellow.

But:

- The film was black-and-white.

6. When an adjectival-compound complement consists of a noun or a gerund followed by a participle, the compound is not hyphenated unless it could be misread (*I am hearing-impaired* needs the hyphen so that a reader doesn't initially regard *am* as a helping verb and *hearing* as the main verb).

7. When an adjectival-compound complement consists of a participle followed by an adverbial particle such as *out* or *up*, the phrase is not hyphenated.

- They were worn out from the trip.

24H HYPHENATION OF PHRASES THAT INCLUDE NUMBERS AND FRACTIONS

Cardinal Numbers

Hyphens are required in the spelled-out forms of cardinal numbers between (and including) twenty-one and ninety-nine—regardless of whether the numbers are functioning as nouns or as adjectives.

Other numbers are not hyphenated—even when they are used adjectivally before nouns.

- thirty-four; thirty-four applicants
- seventy-eight; seventy-eight employees
- twelve hundred; twelve hundred patents
- two hundred and forty-seven; two hundred and forty-seven pairs of shoes
- three thousand five hundred and twenty-six; three thousand five hundred and twenty-six residents
- a hundred and thirty-three million; a hundred and thirty-three million gallons
- three and a half; three and a half hours
- half a million; half a million dollars
- five and a half million; five and a half million copies

TIP: When the abbreviation *No.* is followed by a numeral in an adjectival compound preceding a noun, no hyphen is used.

- the No. 1 box-office attraction

Hyphenate an adjectival compound formed by the combination of a cardinal number and a noun when the compound precedes another noun.

- an eighteen-screen cineplex

- thirty-seven-cent stamps
- a nine-hundred-dollar laptop
- five-hundred-word essays
- a hundred-and-seventy-five-pound patient
- a one-and-a-half-hour lunch
- a three-hour-and-thirty-six-minute film
- a twenty-four-hour supermarket
- a two-hundred-and-twenty-five-thousand-gallon tank
- a hundred-and-eighty-five-thousand-square-foot store

TIP: Observe the following conventions for the hyphenation of phrasing that presents a person's age.

- She is thirty-two years old.
- We hired a twenty-four-year-old woman.
- She was baby-sitting a four-year-old.
- She has two children: a three-and-a-half-year-old and a six-year-old.

Here are four other common patterns involving cardinal numbers.

odd, **preceded by a number** *hyphenated* (thirty-odd applicants; two hundred-odd members; 200-odd residents) A hyphen must be inserted before *odd,* which means *"slightly more than the round number specified."*

percent, **in an adjectival phrase preceding a noun** *not hyphenated* (a thirty percent share of the audience; a 30 percent share) *or hyphenated* (a thirty-percent decrease; a 30-percent decrease) Either pattern is correct, but the first is more common; be consistent throughout a document.

percent, **in a noun phrase** *not hyphenated* (thirty-four percent of the population voted in the primaries; fifty-eight and a third percent voted in the general election)

plus, **preceded by a number** *hyphenated* (forty thousand-plus fans; 100-plus applicants)

Hyphens in Expressions Providing Times of Day and in Names of Decades

When a number and *o'clock* together function as a noun phrase, no hyphen is used.

- My appointment is at two o'clock.

When a number and *o'clock* together form an adjectival compound preceding a noun, a hyphen should be inserted before *o'clock.*

- I have a two-o'clock appointment.

Observe the following conventions for the hyphenation of phrasing in which the time of day is spelled out.

- It was eight-thirty.
- It was half past eight.
- My appointment was rescheduled for a quarter past seven.

Spelled-out numbers expressing the names of decades should be hyphenated.

- the eighteen-sixties
- the nineteen-nineties

Insert a hyphen after the prefix *mid* when it is attached to the spelled-out name of a decade or to the name of a decade presented in numeral form.

- from the mid-sixties to the mid-nineties
- from the mid-1960s to the mid-1990s

Adjectival Compounds Providing Measurements

Observe the following conventions for the hyphenation of phrasing that provides measurements.

- a two-inch-wide insect
- The insect was two inches wide.
- a fifty-eight-foot-long mural
- The mural was fifty-eight feet long.
- a ten-inch-by-thirteen-inch canvas
- The canvas was ten inches by thirteen inches.
- a fifteen-by-nineteen-inch mat
- The mat was fifteen inches by nineteen inches.
- a quarter-inch-thick mat
- The mat was a quarter of an inch thick.
- twelve-ounce cans
- 12-ounce cans
- 12 oz. cans
- a fifty-pound bag
- a 50-pound bag
- a 50 lb. bag

Ordinal Numbers

When an ordinal number (such as *first, second,* or *third*) combines with an adjective to form an adjectival compound preceding a noun, the compound must be hyphenated.

- the second-best employee
- the second-ugliest thing in the room
- the third-floor cafeteria
- fourth-rate musicians
- the fifth-richest woman in the country

When an ordinal number combines with an adverb and an adjective to form an adjectival compound preceding a noun, no hyphen is used.

- the second most disagreeable person I've met in this town

When a compound consisting of an ordinal number and an adjective functions as the complement of a linking verb, the compound is not hyphenated.

- The city is the third largest.

> **TIP:** The spelled-out forms of ordinal numbers greater than one hundred are hyphenated.
> - the hundred-and-seventy-fourth anniversary
> - the five-hundredth anniversary

When an ordinal number and *century* together function as a noun phrase, no hyphen precedes *century*.

- He flourished in the twelfth century.
- Welcome to the twenty-first century.

When an ordinal number and *century* together form an adjectival compound preceding a noun, a hyphen should be inserted before *century*.

- Twenty-first-century technology is dauntingly complex.
- The thirty-fifth-anniversary celebration was well attended.

When *early*, *late*, or *mid* is positioned at the start of an adjectival compound that is composed of an ordinal number and *century* and that precedes a noun, insert hyphens throughout the adjectival compound.

- mid-nineteenth-century paintings
- early-twentieth-century music
- late fifth-century carvings
- late-Ice Age tools
- early-Iron Age artifacts

> **TIP:** Observe the following conventions for the hyphenation of phrasing about students in grades one through twelve.
> - She is in the eleventh grade.
> - She is an eleventh-grade student.
> - She is an eleventh-grader.

Fractions

Hyphenate a fraction that is functioning as a noun.

- My portion was only one-third.
- She received three-quarters of the vote.
- Seven-tenths is the expected concentration.

> **EXCEPTION**
>
> When either the top half or the bottom half of a fraction itself requires a hyphen, do not hyphenate the fraction.
> - The length was only five thirty-seconds of an inch.

When a fraction combines with a noun to form an adjectival compound that precedes a noun, hyphens are needed throughout the compound.

- She bought a three-quarter-length coat.

When a whole number combines with a fraction either to form a noun phrase or to form an adjectival compound functioning as a complement, the coordinating conjunction *and* should not be hyphenated at either end.

- Thirty-two and four-fifths was not an impressive result.
- She hiked twenty-one and a half miles in one afternoon.
- She spent five and three-quarters hours on the job.
- Its length was three and three-fourths inches.

When a whole number combines with a fraction and a noun to form an adjectival compound that precedes a noun, hyphens are needed throughout the compound.

- She took a twenty-one-and-a-half-mile hike yesterday.

When a fraction functions adverbially before a participle such as *finished, done,* or *completed* in an adjectival-compound complement, a hyphen should not precede the participle.

- The project was three-fifths completed.

Phrases That Include *half*

1. When *half* functions as an adjective preceding a noun or a gerund, it is not followed by a hyphen.

- She gave me a half smile.
- A half hour should be sufficient.
- She won without half trying.

2. When *half* functions as an adverb modifying a verb, it is not followed by a hyphen.

- She half walks, half runs.
- He half sings, half speaks the lyrics.

TIP: Avoid ambiguity. Does the sentence *The students were half bored* mean that half of the students were bored or that all of the students were partially bored? If the latter interpretation is the intended one, the insertion of a hyphen between *half* and *bored* will dispel any confusion. But if the former interpretation is intended, it is better to rephrase the sentence: *Half of the students were bored.*

---

3. When *half* functions as an adverb modifying an adjective in an adjectival compound that precedes a noun, a hyphen must follow *half.*

- It was a half-friendly, half-hostile gesture.
- The half-German, half-Italian manager speaks three languages.
- We watched a half-hour sitcom.

(Sometimes the adjectival compound to which *half* belongs is more elaborate in structure: *a half-century-old building.*)

4. When *half* functions as an adverb modifying either an adjective or a participle in an adjectival-compound complement, *half* is not followed by a hyphen.

- The concert was half over.
- Is the glass half empty or half full?
- She seemed only half awake.
- I felt half ignored.

TIP: Observe the following conventions for the hyphenation of phrasing that includes the words *half* and *dozen.*

- a half-dozen novels
- half a dozen novels
- a half dozen of the novels

Phrases That Include *quarter*

1. When *quarter* functions as a noun, it is not followed by a hyphen.

- She flourished for a quarter of a century.

2. When *quarter* functions as an adjective preceding a noun, it is not followed by a hyphen.

- She flourished for a quarter century.

3. When *quarter* combines with a noun to form an adjectival compound modifying a noun, *quarter* must be followed by a hyphen.

- She signed up for a quarter-hour session.

4. When *quarter* functions adjectivally within an adverbial phrase (such as *a quarter hour ago*), it is not followed by a hyphen.

- She finished a quarter hour earlier than expected.

241 MISCELLANEOUS PATTERNS

There are six miscellaneous patterns that involve hyphenation.

cum, **between nouns** *hyphenated* (a chef-cum-musician) *Cum* means "plus."

first-come, first-served; first-come-first-served *hyphenated* (first-come, first-served basis; first-come-first-served basis) Both forms are correct.

full-time and part-time; full time and part time *not hyphenated* (she works part time) *or* *hyphenated* (I have a full-time job) A hyphen is not used when the phrase funcations adverbially; a hyphen is used when a phrase functions adjectively before a noun.

person functioning in a double capacity *hyphenated* (a singer-songwriter) Do not use a slash mark, which means *or,* not *and.*

person functioning in a triple capacity *hyphenated* (a director-actor-screenwriter) Do not use slash marks.

turned, **between nouns** *not hyphenated* (an author turned actor) *or hyphenated* (an author-turned-actor) Either form is correct, but be consistent throughout a document.

24J SUSPENSIVE HYPHENS

Suspensive hyphens can be used when two or more adjectival compounds preceding a noun have a second term in common. The use of the suspensive hyphen eliminates the unnecessary repetition of the second term. (A blank space follows each suspensive hyphen.)

- full- and part-time employees
- second- and third-rate musicians
- two- and four-year colleges
- elementary- and middle-school children
- first- and second-generation college graduates
- fifteen- and thirty-minute breaks
- middle- and lower-class families
- middle- and upper-middle-class students
- first- and business-class seats
- nineteenth- and twentieth-century architects
- smoke- and water-damaged merchandise
- 500- and 1,000-meter races
- four-inch- or five-inch-diameter pipes
- three-sixteenth- and one-quarter-inch-thick blades
- one-, two-, or three-bedroom apartments
- a study of 16-, 17-, and 18-year-olds

The suspensive hyphen is also used when two or more single-word adjectives differ only in their prefixes. Hyphens are not included in the adjectives spelled out in full (unless the adjectives are always hyphenated).

- pre- and postmodern paintings
- over- and underappreciated employees

CAUTION

Never insert a hyphen immediately before or after the conjunction *and* or *or* in a suspensive-hyphen compound. A blank space must precede and follow the conjunction. The phrase *14- and 18-foot-high ceilings* means *14-foot-high ceilings and 18-foot-high ceilings*. Do not mispunctuate the phrase as *14-and-18-foot-high ceilings*, which means *ceilings between 14 and 18 feet high.*

The suspensive hyphen is also used when only one of two consecutive compounds requires a hyphen before the shared second term.

- in the mid- to late 1990s
- from the early to mid-sixties

CAUTION

Suspensive hyphens cannot be used when two or more adjectival compounds preceding a noun have the first term in common.

> **Faulty:** "American Idol," when you get down to it, is just a much better-conceived and -produced version of talent contests like "Star Search" and "Ted Mack's Original Amateur Hour."
>
> (Rick Kushman, "TV Can Do Worse Than Reality Shows," for *Sacramento Bee*, in *Pittsburgh Post-Gazette*, 30 June 2004, p. C5)
>
> **Correct:** ... is just a much better-conceived and better-produced version. . . .

Suspensive hyphens can also be used when two or more adverbial compounds have a second term in common.

- increased nine- or tenfold

24K HYPHENATION OF ADVERBIAL-COMPOUND PHRASES

Hyphenate adverbial-compound phrases only if they are hyphenated as adverbs in a dictionary.

- The girl was selling raffle tickets door-to-door.
- The meetings were scheduled back-to-back.
- The two of us didn't see things eye to eye.
- We saw them walking arm in arm.
- They made money hand over fist.
- He was head over heels in love.
- The houseguest expected to be waited on hand and foot.
- He finally saw her up close.

24L A FINAL NOTE: THE EN DASH

The publishing world draws a distinction between the hyphen and a very specialized punctuational device known as the en dash, which is a little longer than the hyphen but not as long as the regular dash (which in the publishing world is called the em dash). The dashes get their names from their lengths: The en dash is as wide as the letter *n*; the em dash is as wide as the letter *m*. Many writers use a hyphen where those in the publishing world would use an en dash. Following is a quick survey of the uses of the en dash in the publishing world.

The en dash stands in for the preposition *to* in inclusive phrases (such as *pages 212–215; the years 1998–2004; May 2004–March 2005;* and *1:00–4:30*), as well as in phrasing such as the *Pittsburgh–Chicago train* and *London–New York flights.* The en dash is also used in reporting sports scores: *We beat Central 34–12.* (The hyphen, however, is used between numbers that are sequential—such as the digits in telephone numbers—rather than inclusive.)

The en dash improves the readability of an adjectival compound if one or more of its components are unhyphenated compounds (*post–Vietnam War policies; San Francisco–area residents; Los Angeles–New York flights; the Vladimir Nabokov–Edmund Wilson correspondence*) or if at least one of its components is a hyphenated compound (*public-school–private-school rivalries; Wal-Mart–expansion strategies*).

CAUTION

The use of an en dash or a hyphen in phrasing such as *from May 2004-August 2005* and *from 9:00 a.m.-5:30 p.m.* is always incorrect. The en dash or hyphen needs to be replaced by the preposition to: *from May 2004 to August 2005; from 9:00 a.m. to 5:30 p.m.*

CHAPTER 25

PUNCTUATING COMPOUND, COMPLEX, AND COMPOUND-COMPLEX SENTENCES

We have thus far been examining each of the punctuation marks individually. Now we want to examine the more elaborate orchestration of punctuation marks in sentences that include more than one clause—compound sentences, complex sentences, and compound-complex sentences. (For a full discussion of the types of clauses and an introduction to the four types of sentence structure, see chapter 4.)

25A COMPOUND SENTENCES

A compound sentence is a sentence consisting of at least two independent clauses and no dependent clauses. In a compound sentence, all of the independent clauses receive equal emphasis and are of equal importance.

Pattern 1: independent clause + comma + coordinating conjunction + independent clause + period. The most common way to punctuate a compound sentence is to insert a comma and a logically appropriate coordinating conjunction between the two clauses.

  • The end of a relationship is usually stressful for anyone, but Eloise was having an especially difficult time.

Remember that there are only seven coordinating conjunctions in the English language: *and*, expressing an additive relationship; *but* and *yet*, presenting a contrastive relationship; *or* and *nor*, separating alternatives; *for*, presenting a cause or a reason; and *so*, presenting a result, an effect, or a consequence.

Only is not a coordinating conjunction, but it is punctuated like one when it joins two independent clauses.

- It's a very beautiful dress, only it doesn't fit me anymore.

When both of the independent clauses are brief, the comma before the coordinating conjunction can be omitted—if the omission will not diminish the readability of the sentence.

- She revealed very little emotion and the ceremony seemed to bore her.

The omission of the comma before the coordinating conjunction in a compound sentence sometimes leads to misreading.

- Volunteers will help man the sale and a special pre-sale for expectant and first-time mothers is set for 6–9 p.m. Friday.
  (Marjorie Wertz, "Sale to Feature Used Children's Items," *Greensburg [PA] Tribune-Review*, 13 Apr. 2004, p. A8)

    The absence of a comma before *and* will initially lead some readers to regard *pre-sale* as a second direct object of man rather than as the subject of the second independent clause.

- It [the economy] is impenetrable to the unversed and those trained in it are the conversational equivalent of honking geese.
  (Dennis Roddy, "The 2004 Post-Election Analysis," *Pittsburgh Post-Gazette*, 30 Nov. 2003, p. E1)

    The reader can at first misconstrue *those trained in it* as a second object of the preposition *to*, rather than recognize it as the subject of the second independent clause.

The following compound sentences are also misreadable.

- There are 21 communities directly served by the [water] authority and three others buy water wholesale from it.
  (Jim McKay, "Water Authority Talks Stall," *Pittsburgh Post-Gazette*, 1 Mar. 1998, p. F4)

- They [e-tickets] eliminate the cost of replacing lost tickets and overnight delivery services aren't needed to send tickets to employees in remote locations.
  (Donna Rosato, "Fliers Flock to Airlines' E-tickets," *USA Today*, 17 Mar. 1998, p. 1A)

In each of the four examples above, the insertion of a comma before the coordinating conjunction will resolve the problem.

A comma rarely precedes the coordinating conjunction in a compound sentence whose first independent clause is imperative (expressing a command) and whose second independent clause is declarative.

- Give it a try for a few days and you'll see what I mean.

Pattern 2: independent clause + semicolon + independent clause + period. A second way to punctuate a compound sentence is to insert a semicolon between the two independent clauses. The semicolon tells the reader that the two independent clauses are closely related—but it doesn't explicitly articulate the nature of the interrelationship between the two clauses.

- Her brother works for an animal shelter; her sister works for a mortgage company.

Pattern 3: independent clause + semicolon + conjunctive adverb + comma + independent clause + period. A third way to punctuate a compound sentence is to insert a logically appropriate conjunctive adverb (or transitional phrase) between the two independent clauses. A semicolon will precede the conjunctive adverb, and a comma will follow it.

- Jennifer works for a mortgage company; however, she's looking for a less stressful job.

Here are the most commonly used conjunctive adverbs and transitional phrases, grouped according to the logical interrelationships they clarify between independent clauses.

To express an additive relationship: *also, in addition, additionally, furthermore, first, second, finally*

To express a contrastive relationship: *however, nevertheless, on the other hand, in contrast*

To express a cause-and-effect relationship: *therefore, thus, consequently, as a result*

To introduce an example: *for example, for instance*

To intensify: *in fact, indeed, after all*

To make a comparison: *similarly, likewise, in like manner*

To express a time relationship: *meanwhile, soon, then, afterward, later, now*

To introduce a clarification: *in other words, that is, that is to say*

To introduce a conclusion or summary: *in conclusion, in short, to sum up, in sum, in brief*

Pattern 4: independent clause + semicolon + coordinating conjunction + independent clause + period. A fourth way to punctuate a compound sentence is to insert a semicolon before a coordinating conjunction joining two or more independent clauses if one or more of the independent clauses have interior punctuation (the semicolon is a much stronger and more prominent punctuational divider between the independent clauses).

- She has recently opened restaurants in Denver, Des Moines, St. Paul, and Akron; and she has been scouting sites in Toledo and Cleveland.

Comma-Splice Errors

The omission of a coordinating conjunction after the comma between two independent clauses results in a serious sentence-structure error known as a comma-splice error.

- I have lived in Seattle for 16 years, my mother and brother moved here a year after.

  (Judy Nicastro, "How Nice [or Mean] Is Seattle Nowadays?," *Seattle Post-Intelligencer*, 17 Jan. 2004, p. B5)

  The insertion of *and* after the comma will resolve the problem.

- The suit said the exits are sometimes padlocked, employees spray pepper spray into crowds and have allowed fireworks to be set off inside.

  (Karen Farkas, "Cuyahoga Falls Says Boot Scoot'n Saloon Raises Ruckus, Asks Court to Shut It Down," *Cleveland Plain Dealer*, 12 Feb. 2004, p. B3)

  One suggestion for correcting the sentence is replacing the comma with a semicolon.

Another type of comma-splice error occurs when the writer is careless about punctuating the clause of attribution inserted between two sentences of a multisentence quotation.

- "Every child needs a good home," Ray said, "every child is a blessing."

  (*Living Proof: Your Gift Makes a Difference*, United Way of Southwestern Pennsylvania brochure, C-2, 1999)

  Because both halves of the quotation are independent clauses, the comma following *said* needs to replaced either by a semicolon or by a period (if the period is chosen, the initial letter of *every* in the second half of the quotation will of course need to be capitalized). Bear in mind that commas would enclose a clause of attribution such as *Ray said* if it were inserted between two parts of a quotation consisting of a single independent clause: *"Every child," Ray said, "needs a good home."*

A different sort of comma-splice error occurs when a conjunctive adverb or transitional phrase, rather than a coordinating conjunction, follows the comma between two independent clauses.

- "Does your dog think? Does your dog have emotions? Is your dog conscious? Your initial reaction to the questions may be a resounding yes, however, consider these questions carefully."

    (from a course description in the Franklin & Marshall College catalogue, cited in "Tony & Tacky," *Wall Street Journal*, 9 Jan. 2004, p. W11)

    Even though *however* is synonymous with *but*, the two words belong to different classes of conjunctions, each with its own special punctuation pattern. A semicolon should replace the comma between *yes* and *however*.

- The judge is hesitant to grant her petition, after all it was unprecedented for a teenager to be granted guardianship.

    (Laura Urbani, "Trio of Performances Excels in 'Gracie's Choice,'" *Greensburg [PA] Tribune-Review*, 12 Jan. 2004, p. B10)

    This sentence needs a semicolon, not a comma, after *petition*; and a comma must follow *after all*.

- Mussels are to Munch as Kryptonite is to Superman, thus Munch fears most anything mollusk.

    ("Munch Goes to Roland's Seafood Grill," *Pittsburgh Post-Gazette*, 7 May 2004, p. W35)

    This sentence needs a semicolon, not a comma, between *Superman* and *thus*.

TIP: *Thus* and *then* are two conjunctive adverbs that do not need to be followed by a comma.

Fused-Sentence Errors

A less common error that results from the mispunctuation of a compound sentence is the fused-sentence error. In a sentence afflicted with a fused-sentence error, there is no punctuation whatsoever to mark the boundary between two independent clauses. The clauses are thus said to be fused together. A fused-sentence error can be corrected by using any of the patterns for punctuating a compound sentence.

- Her brother works for an animal shelter her sister works for a mortgage company.

Other Patterns for Punctuating Compound Sentences

A colon, a dash, or a pair of parentheses can also be used to set off the second independent clause in a compound sentence. (These punctuation marks are discussed in more detail in chapter 19 and chapter 20.)

Compound Sentences and Colons

Insert a colon between two independent clauses when the second clause restates, clarifies, or amplifies the statement made in the first clause, or when the second clause provides an example to support the generalization stated in the first clause: **independent clause + colon + independent clause + period**.

- Yesterday there was yet another problem with the computer: It somehow got infected with the Blaster worm.
- Attending "singles only" get-togethers was like going shopping: Both experiences left her feeling demoralized.
- Her life was melodramatic: Her father was an alcoholic, her mother was a compulsive shopper, and her brother was a job hopper.

Compound Sentences and Dashes

A dash can function much like a colon between independent clauses—but the dash is always less formal than a colon: **independent clause + dash + independent clause + period**.

- Jacob's life had no stability—he was too impulsive to hold on to any good things coming his way.
- Emily is an excellent manager except in one respect—her perfectionism drives everyone else crazy.

A dash can also be used between contrastive clauses (the dash will give more emphasis to the contrast than a semicolon would).

- She isn't maternal to her children—she's more like a freewheeling sister.

A further use of the dash is to signal an abrupt change, often a descent, in tone or level of diction.

- She's intelligent, ambitious, complex, unpredictable—she's cool.

Compound Sentences and Parentheses

Use a pair of parentheses to enclose the second independent clause if you want to reduce it to the status of a hushed afterthought: **independent clause + opening parenthesis + independent clause + closing parenthesis + period**.

- She was our most consistently impressive employee (she was hired away by a rival firm late last year).

Asyndetonic Compound Sentences

Finally, there is a special kind of compound sentence in which nothing more than a comma is needed between the independent clauses: **independent clause + comma + independent clause + period**.

Such a sentence is called an asyndetonic compound sentence. Asyndeton is the intentional omission of a conjunction between independent clauses. (Julius Caesar's victorious declaration *I came, I saw, I conquered* is the most famous asyndetonic sentence in history.) If you are aiming for more sophistication in your style, consider adding asyndetonic compound sentences to your repertoire of sentence types—but be sure to distinguish between legitimate asyndetonic compound sentences and compound sentences weakened by comma-splice errors.

An asyndetonic sentence is one in which the independent clauses are relatively short and are either parallel or antithetical. (Compound sentences afflicted with comma-splice errors lack parallel or antithetical structure in their independent clauses.)

Here are examples of asyndetonic sentences with parallel clauses.

- Some rejoiced, others wept.
- She couldn't eat, she couldn't sleep.

Asyndetonic compound sentences often consist of parallel clauses embedded within a *not only X but Y* structure, with the coordinating conjunction *but* only implied.

- Not only is he selling out, he's burning out.
- Not only was the movie the sleeper hit of the summer, it was a turning point in the director's career.

Here are examples of asyndetonic sentences with antithetical clauses.

- That was then, this is now.
- United we stand, divided we fall.
- He doesn't need a girlfriend, he needs a mother.
- It wasn't his appearance that bothered her, it was his attitude.

25B COMPLEX SENTENCES

A complex sentence consists of only one independent clause and one or more dependent clauses. The dependent clauses can function as adjectives, as adverbs, or as nouns.

Adjectival Clauses and Complex Sentences

Complex sentences that include adjectival clauses are discussed in rule 33D of chapter 18. Let's take a closer look at four patterns.

Pattern 1: first half of independent clause + comma + nonrestrictive adjectival dependent clause + comma + second half of independent clause + period. A pair of commas is used to set off a nonrestrictive adjectival dependent clause that is wedged between two parts of an independent clause.

- Her best friend, who works for a major airline, is being transferred to Los Angeles.

Pattern 2: independent clause + comma + nonrestrictive adjectival dependent clause + period. A single comma separates an independent clause from a nonrestrictive adjectival dependent clause that is positioned at the end of a sentence.

- She's going to miss her best friend, who is moving to Los Angeles.

Pattern 3: first half of independent clause + restrictive adjectival dependent clause + second half of independent clause + period. No commas set off a restrictive adjectival dependent clause when it separates two parts of an independent clause.

- Her friend who works for a major airline is being transferred to Los Angeles.

Pattern 4: independent clause + restrictive adjectival dependent clause + period. Here, no comma separates an independent clause from a restrictive adjectival dependent clause that is positioned at the end of a sentence.

- She is going to miss her friend who is moving to Los Angeles.

Adverbial Clauses and Complex Sentences

Let's look at four patterns for including adverbial clauses in complex sentences. (Complex sentences that include adverbial dependent clauses are also discussed in chapter 18.)

Pattern 1: adverbial dependent clause + comma + independent clause + period. When an adverbial dependent clause introduces the independent clause, a comma should separate the two clauses (see rule 1 in chapter 18).

- After we hired him, he enrolled in some evening courses at the community college.

Pattern 2: independent clause + comma + nonrestrictive adverbial dependent clause + period. When the adverbial dependent clause follows the independent clause, you insert a comma between the clauses only if the adverbial clause is nonrestrictive (see rule 33E in chapter 18).

- We didn't hire him, because he lacked the appropriate educational credentials.

Pattern 3: independent clause + restrictive adverbial dependent clause + period.

- We won't hire him unless he agrees to further his education.

Pattern 4: first half of independent clause + comma + nonrestrictive adverbial dependent clause + comma + second half of independent clause + period. In this final pattern, a nonrestrictive adverbial dependent clause is inserted between two halves of an independent clause.

- He performed well during the interview and, if his luck holds out, will be offered the job.

Nominative Dependent Clauses and Complex Sentences

Complex sentences in which a nominative dependent clause functions as the direct object of a transitive verb of attribution are discussed in chapter 18. A comma never separates the verb of attribution from the indefinite relative pronoun *that* at the start of a nominative clause (see rule 16 in chapter 18).

- She said that the mayor had not yet seen the revised report.

The only pattern we have not yet discussed is the pattern involving nominative dependent clauses whose internal structure is complex.

When the combination of an adverbial dependent clause and an independent clause is embedded within a nominative dependent clause functioning as the direct object or as the complement of the verb in an independent clause, no punctuation is needed within the nominative dependent clause.

- She insisted that if students pay attention they should do well in her course.
- Her thinking seems to be that as long as we meet or exceed the daily production quotas everything will be fine.

The advantage of such a pattern is that it keeps the contents of the nominative clause intact as a unit. But there is nothing wrong with inserting a comma between the two halves of the nominative clause—that is, between its adverbial-dependent-clause element and its independent-clause element. A comma could thus be inserted after *attention* in the first example above and after *quotas* in the second. Furthermore, the adverbial dependent clauses *if students pay attention* and *as long as we meet or exceed the daily production quotas* could each be set off with commas at both ends.

25C COMPOUND-COMPLEX SENTENCES

A compound-complex sentence consists of at least two independent clauses and at least one dependent clause. Punctuation patterns for compound-complex sentences vary from those with minimal or light punctuation (sometimes called "open" punctuation) to those with heavy punctuation (sometimes called "close" punctuation).

Introductory Adverbial Dependent Clauses in Compound-Complex Sentences

There are five patterns in which an adverbial dependent clause appears at the start of a sentence.

Pattern 1: adverbial dependent clause + independent clause + coordinating conjunction + independent clause + period. There is no punctuation whatsoever between clauses.

- When Samantha was nine her parents split up and her father moved to New Jersey.

Misreadable sentences, however, occasionally result from this pattern.

- After we finished eating our supervisor asked us to start a new project and that kept us busy for the rest of the day.

    At first glance, *supervisor* appears to be the object of the gerund *eating*. Inserting a comma between *eating* and *our* will resolve the problem. Thus, the second pattern is often preferable.

Pattern 2: adverbial dependent clause + comma + independent clause + coordinating conjunction + independent clause + period. Misreading can result from this pattern as well.

- When you awaken, don't move from your sleeping position and keep your eyes closed.

  (Virginia Linn, "A Dream Journal 'How-To,'" *Pittsburgh Post-Gazette*, 7 Dec. 2003, p. A17)

  Readers can initially misconstrue *keep* as a second main verb to be attached to the combination of the helping verb *do* and the contracted adverb *not*. That is, readers can mistakenly think that they are being told not to keep their eyes closed. The insertion of a comma between *position* and *and* will improve the readability of the sentence.

Pattern 3: Adverbial dependent clause + comma + independent clause + comma + coordinating conjunction + independent clause + period. The third—and most common—pattern is often the most reader-friendly.

- After she divorced her husband, she moved to San Francisco, but she never found happiness.

Pattern 4: adverbial dependent clause + comma + independent clause + semicolon + coordinating conjunction + independent clause + period. The fourth pattern—the most formal of them all—is usually resorted to only if one or both halves of the sentence have heavy interior punctuation.

- After she divorced her husband, she moved to San Francisco, enrolled in college, and became an animal-rights activist; but she never found happiness.

Pattern 5: adverbial dependent clause + comma + independent clause + semicolon + conjunctive adverb + comma + independent clause + period. This final pattern involves the use of a conjunctive adverb, rather than a coordinating conjunction, to join the two independent clauses.

- After she divorced her husband, she moved to San Francisco; however, she never found happiness.

Internal Adverbial Dependent Clauses in Compound-Complex Sentences

There are five patterns in which an adverbial dependent clause is positioned between two independent clauses.

Pattern 1: independent clause + comma + coordinating conjunction + adverbial dependent clause + independent clause + period. This is a common pattern in the *New Yorker* magazine. The advantage of this pattern is that it is clean and uncluttered. The sole comma serves as the divider between the two principal parts of the sentence.

- She spent the afternoon in her studio, and after she was finished painting she spoke to her mother on the phone.

The pattern is not advisable, however, when the subject of the second independent clause can initially appear to be the object of a verb (or of a verbal or preposition) at the end of the adverbial dependent clause, as in the following examples.

Ambiguous: She spent the afternoon in her studio, and after she was finished painting her mother called. Unless *painting* is followed by a comma, *mother* can be misread as the object of *painting* rather than as the subject of the second independent clause.

Clear: She spent the afternoon in her studio, and after she was finished painting, her mother called.

Ambiguous: Second, he [President Bush] needs to explain that we are losing in Iraq, and if we continue to lose the U.S. public will eventually demand that we quit Iraq, and it will then become Afghanistan-on-steroids, which will threaten everyone.

(Thomas L. Friedman, "Restoring Our Honor," *New York Times* online, 6 May 2004, paragraph 8)

Unless a comma follows the infinitive *to lose*, which is functioning intransitively, the reader can mistakenly regard *U.S. public* as the object of the infinitive instead of recognizing it as the subject of the second independent clause in the sentence.

Clear: Second, he needs to explain that we are losing in Iraq, and if we continue to lose, the U.S. public will eventually demand that we quit Iraq, and it will then become Afghanistan-on-steroids, which will threaten everyone.

Pattern 2: independent clause + comma + coordinating conjunction + adverbial dependent clause + comma + independent clause + period. The second pattern is the most common for punctuating complex sentences in which the adverbial dependent clause is positioned between two independent clauses.

- She is probably the most daringly experimental novelist of the past two decades, and even though you might not always instantly grasp her meaning, you can't help being bowled over by her virtuosity.

Pattern 3: independent clause + comma + coordinating conjunction + comma + adverbial dependent clause + comma + independent clause + period. This more formal—and somewhat old-fashioned—pattern uses heavier punctuation. In this pattern, the adverbial dependent clause is set off at both ends, and thus it has a punctuational symmetry lacking in the previous patterns.

- She is probably the most daringly experimental novelist of the past two decades, and, even though you might not always instantly grasp her meaning, you can't help being bowled over by her virtuosity.

Pattern 4: independent clause + semicolon + coordinating conjunction + comma + adverbial dependent clause + comma + independent clause + period. Even more formal is pattern four, which substitutes a semicolon for the comma following the first independent clause.

- She is probably the most daringly experimental novelist of the past two decades; and, even though you might not always instantly grasp her meaning, you can't help being bowled over by her virtuosity.

One variation on this pattern eliminates the comma following the coordinating conjunction.

Pattern 5: independent clause + semicolon + conjunctive adverb + comma + adverbial dependent clause + comma + independent clause + period. In another variation on the pattern above, a conjunctive adverb can be substituted for the coordinating conjunction.

- She is probably the most daringly experimental and different novelist of the past two decades; however, even if you might not always instantly grasp her meaning, you can't help being bowled over by her virtuosity.

PART IV:
MECHANICS AND USAGE

CHAPTER 26

CAPITALIZATION

Determining whether words should be capitalized can sometimes seem dauntingly complicated. Do you write *Irish Setter* or *Irish setter*, *Cold War* or *cold war*, *Lou Gehrig's Disease* or *Lou Gehrig's disease*, *Rhodes Scholar* or *Rhodes scholar*, *Roman numerals* or *roman numerals*, *Cubism* or *cubism*, *Art Deco* or *art deco*, *Oxford cloth* or *oxford cloth*, *The Bronx* or *the Bronx*, *Third World* or *third world*, *X-ray* or *x-ray*, *Indian Summer* or *Indian summer*, *Election Day* or *election day*, *Right wing* or *right wing*, *Fourth and Main Streets* or *Fourth and Main streets*? Fortunately, your dictionary can usually guide you, because many of the words and compounds that are most likely to stump a writer will be found there, with authoritative advice on whether to uppercase or lowercase. (Your dictionary will also be of help when you need to know, for instance, whether the painter of the *Mona Lisa* was *Leonardo Da Vinci* or *Leonardo da Vinci*.)

When the dictionary comes up short, your own good sense can often tell you whether to capitalize or not. Occasionally, though, neither a dictionary nor common sense will be enough, and that is when a set of guiding principles and patterns comes in handy. Some matters are commonsensical (the need to capitalize the names of organizations, companies, institutions, governmental bodies, and such), and at the end of this chapter you will find a checklist to consult when you find yourself puzzled and a trip to the dictionary might not help. Bear in mind that some conventions of capitalization are entirely arbitrary and vary from publisher to publisher—for instance, *Republican Party* in one magazine versus

Republican party in another; *Midwesterner* in one, *midwesterner* in another. Be consistent throughout a piece of writing.

26A PROPER NOUNS AND PROPER ADJECTIVES

The most important guiding principle of capitalization is that all proper nouns and most proper adjectives are uppercased; all other words, including common nouns, are lowercased. A proper noun is a noun that specifies a particular member of a group of people or things (see chapter 1).

A proper noun may consist of more than one word. A proper noun and a common noun often combine to form the complete name of something—*Allegheny River, Bellevue Hospital*—and in such formations, both the proper noun and the common noun are capitalized. After the full name of something has been stated in a piece of writing, however, subsequent references can be shortened to the common noun, which will no longer be capitalized: *the river, the hospital.*

> **TIP:** For a long time, it was the practice of companies and institutions to be referred to by capitalized common nouns in phrasing such as *the Bank* and *the University* in documents produced by the companies or institutions. This practice, however, has been dying out. It is preferred that a foundation, for instance, refer to itself as *the foundation,* not as *the Foundation.*

A proper adjective is an adjective formed from a proper noun. *California,* for example, gives us *Californian* (which can also function as a noun). Most proper adjectives are capitalized. (Some phrases formed with proper adjectives, however, have begun evolving from proper to common status: *French fries, french fries; Dutch treat, dutch treat.*)

26B TERMS FOR MEMBERS OF NUCLEAR AND EXTENDED FAMILIES

The nouns *mother, father, grandmother,* and *grandfather,* along with their synonyms and variants, are lowercased when they are preceded by a possessive noun or a possessive pronoun; they are uppercased when they function like names.

- Has your mother met Louise's father, who is Darcie's grandfather?
- I'll ask Mom or Grandma about your dad's shoe size.
- I saw your grandmother Rose yesterday.

The nouns *aunt* and *uncle,* as well as *cousin,* are uppercased only when they are not preceded by a possessive noun or a possessive pronoun and when they are followed by a first name.

- She invited Cousin Jessie, Uncle Jacob, and a few other uncles and aunts.
- I saw my aunt Lauren at the reception.

Do not capitalize *brother, sister, son,* or *daughter* unless the word is part of a company name or trademark term.

- the Olsen sisters; Smith Brothers cough drops

26C NOUNS FUNCTIONING AS PERSONAL NAMES

Terms of affection like *baby* and *sweetheart* are lowercased. Nicknames are uppercased.

- Hey, sweetie, have you talked to Big Gravy lately?

Nouns like *coach, doctor, captain, lieutenant,* and *professor* are capitalized when they function like names and when they are used in direct address.

- I'll see you tomorrow, Coach.
- He said, "Listen, Doctor, I've been having some serious back pain."

There is no need to capitalize *sir, madam,* and *ma'am*—unless the words appear in positions where uppercasing is needed for another reason (such as in the salutation of a letter: *Dear Sir or Madam*).

26D NAMES OF RACES, ETHNIC GROUPS, NATIONALITIES, PEOPLES, AND SOCIAL CLASSES

Lowercase *black* and *white,* but uppercase *Negro* and *Caucasian.* Uppercase the names of ethnic groups, nationalities, and peoples: *Hispanics, Latinos, Germans, Asians, Filipinos, Native Americans.* It is not necessary to insert a hyphen in compounds like *African American* and *Italian American,* but consistency is desirable. Do not capitalize the names of social classes, such as the *middle class.*

26E TITLES AND POSITIONS

Two important principles govern the capitalization of titles that denote positions in the workforce, in government, in the military, in religious organizations, and in academia.

First, when a formal, official title is positioned before a person's last name, the title is uppercased.

- Governor Pataki; Mayor Bloomberg; General Schwarzkopf; Reverend Jackson; Judge Singerman; Professor Thomas; Officer Ryan

This pattern, in which the title and the last name form a single identifying unit, should be reserved for persons who hold positions of authority. When a title or, more often, an occupational designation is followed by a full name that functions as an appositive, the title is lowercased.

- former mayor Lucille Gaines
- divorce attorney Harold White
- senior editor Liane James
- animal-control officer Jane Perkins
- our customer-service representatives, Joyce Garner and Mike Ellman
- the regional director of sales, Randall Lane

Second, when a title is positioned after a person's name, the title is usually lowercased.

- Carl Thorn, chairman of the board
- Edward Rendell, the governor of Pennsylvania
- Allen Singerman, judge
- Melinda Thomas, professor of art history

In exceptionally formal contexts, a title following the name may be uppercased.

- Lisa Lehman, the Vice President of Marketing, addressed the stockholders.

But in all other contexts, it is no longer necessary to capitalize even the noun president in sentences about the president of the United States when the noun appears after the name.

- George W. Bush, former president of the United States

26F PLACE NAMES

Do not uppercase *east, west, north,* or *south* when the word merely specifies a direction. Uppercase such a word when it points to a particular region of the country: *three miles east of the college; the southbound lane; driving north on the turnpike; heading out West again; moved back to the Northeast; birds of the East.*

Uppercase such words when they are part of the formal name of a place: *the Southwest; the West Coast; the South; the South Side; the Upper East Side.*

Lowercase adjectives of direction in phrases such as *northern Florida* and *western Pennsylvania.*

Nounal variants of place names like *the Midwest* are usually uppercased: Follow your dictionary and be consistent with nouns like *Midwesterner* and *Easterner.*

Adjectival forms of place names like *the Midwest* and *the South* are usually uppercased: *Midwestern values; Southern hospitality.*

The adjective *greater* is uppercased when it precedes the name of a city to signify an entire metropolitan area: *Greater Philadelphia.*

Uppercase informal place names: *the Bible Belt; the Rust Belt; the Big Apple; Silicon Valley; the Golden Triangle.*

When two or more place names presented consecutively share the same common-noun final term, lowercase the final term: *Canandaigua and Seneca lakes; the Hudson and Lehigh valleys.*

But there is always an exception: *Lakes Erie and Superior.*

26G NAMES OF BUILDINGS, OTHER STRUCTURES, STREETS, AND SPACES

Capitalize *building* or a similar word if it is part of the official name of a structure or place: *the Fulton Building; the Sears Tower; Fifth Avenue Place; Two Girard Plaza; Rittenhouse Square; the Continental Room; the Washington Monument; the Brooklyn Bridge; the Holland Tunnel; Time Warner Center; Pennsylvania Turnpike.*

Each would be subsequently referred to as *the building, the monument, the bridge, the square,* etc.

When you are naming an intersection, two or more thoroughfares, or two or more structures (including buildings and monuments), lowercase the final, shared common-noun term: *Fifth and Market streets; Seventh and Eighth avenues; the Jefferson and Lincoln memorials; the Eastgate and Southpointe malls; the Woolworth and Singer buildings; the Plaza and Helmsley Palace hotels.*

When the name of a street includes a hyphenated number, uppercase only the first half of the compound: *East Thirty-fourth Street.*

26H GOVERNMENT TERMS

Do not uppercase *federal, government,* or *administration* unless the word appears as part of the name of an organization: *federal government; federal case; Federal Reserve Bank; the Clinton administration; Occupational Safety and Health Administration.*

26I *THE* AS PART OF A NAME

Sometimes *the* is part of the name of a city or town and thus is capitalized: *The Hague; The Plains, Ohio.*

But *the* is not uppercased in the names of countries: *the United States; the United Kingdom; the Philippines.*

Nor is *the* capitalized in *the Vatican.* Both *the Bronx* and *The Bronx* are correct, but be consistent throughout a document.

Lowercase *the* in the names of institutions and companies: *the University of Pennsylvania; the Foundation for Contemporary Performance Arts.*

The definite article is not capitalized in the names of rock groups (*the Who*). An exception is the alternative-rock group *The The.*

26J TRADEMARK TERMS AND NAMES OF BUSINESSES

Trademark terms, such as *Xerox* and *Kleenex,* are always capitalized. Do not uppercase a common noun following a trademark term unless the common noun is part of the full, formal name of the product: *Coca-Cola; Pepsi-Cola; Doritos snack chips; Crest toothpaste; Papermate pen; Dell laptop.*

Do not uppercase a common noun such as *restaurant* or *tavern* unless the common noun is part of the full, formal name of a business: *Red Lobster restaurant; Joe's Crab Shack.*

26K TITLES OF WORKS

Uppercase the first word and the final word of the title and also of the subtitle of a work—as well as all other words except the articles (*a, an, the*), prepositions consisting of up to four letters, coordinating conjunctions, and the *to* of an infinitive.

- The Urge to Splurge: A Study of Consumer Behaviors and Misbehaviors
- Against the Grain: An Anthology of Essays About Deviating from the Norm

Do not forget to capitalize linking verbs (such as *is*), pronouns (such as *it*), and subordinating conjunctions (such as *when* and *if*).

Do not forget to capitalize any article that is the first word of a title: *A Separate Peace; The Catcher in the Rye.*

But there are some exceptions: *the Bible; the New Testament; the Talmud.*

It is not necessary to capitalize *the* in the name of a newspaper or magazine, even if the definite article is part of the full, official name. The lowercased *the* will not be italicized: *the Philadelphia Inquirer; the Washington Post; the Atlantic Monthly.*

Uppercase a word that may look like a short preposition but is functioning as an adverbial particle—that is, it follows a verb and is not followed by an object of a preposition.

- Stand Up and Be Counted
- Looking Out for Number One

Sometimes the adverbial particle will follow a verb in a hyphenated compound.

- New Hope for Shut-Ins

When a hyphenated compound is included in a title, uppercase the first word in the compound. Uppercase subsequent words in the compound except articles, coordinating conjunctions, and prepositions. Do not uppercase the second part of a spelled-out whole number or fraction.

- *Twenty-five Tried-and-True Recommendations for Over-the-Hill and Out-of-It Parents*

If a hyphenated compound in a title begins with a prefix such as *pro-*, *anti-*, *non-*, or *re-*, uppercase the word following the prefix only if it is a proper noun or proper adjective.

- *Pro-life Protesters and the Law*

Whether to italicize the title of a work or present the title between quotation marks is discussed at the end of chapter 22.

26L SALUTATIONS AND COMPLIMENTARY CLOSINGS IN FORMAL LETTERS

Capitalize all important words in the salutation—that is, all words except prepositions, articles, and coordinating conjunctions.

- Dear Department of Customer Service:

Capitalize only the first word in a complimentary closing.

- Sincerely yours,
- Yours very truly,

26M COMPOUNDS WHOSE FIRST ELEMENT IS A SINGLE LETTER

Capitalize the single-letter element in compounds such as *A-frame* and *T-shirt*.

26N MISCELLANEOUS PATTERNS

The following checklist, arranged alphabetically, will help you determine which categories of words and phrases should be uppercased.

Abbreviations of names of companies, government organizations, etc. Follow the lead of the individual entity: *KFC; IBM; Nasdaq; NASA.*

Academic degrees. Capitalize the name of the degree only when it follows a person's name: *Leona Hammond, Bachelor of Arts; she earned a bachelor's of arts; a bachelor's degree.*

Age. *the Bronze Age; the late Bronze Age; the Middle Ages; the Age of Reason; the Ice Age; an ice age; the atomic age; the digital age.*

Astronomical terms. *the moons of Jupiter; the solar system; Halley's comet; Comet Hale-Bopp; the universe.* Capitalize *sun, moon,* and *earth* when they appear in phrasing with the capitalized names of other heavenly bodies: *a movie about colonizing the Moon and Mars.*

Awards. *honor roll; dean's list; Medal of Honor; Nobel Prize; Pulitzer Prize; MacArthur Fellowship; Academy Award; Oscar; Grammy; Emmy; Tony.*

Centuries. *the twentieth-first century; the eighteen-hundreds.*

Chemical elements and compounds. *hydrogen; sodium nitrite.*

Computer-network terms. *the Internet; the Net; the World Wide Web; the Web; website (some styles use Web site); web page; Weblog; blog; cyberspace; e-mail.*

Computer software. Treat as trademark terms: *WordPerfect; PowerPoint.*

Congress. *the United States Congress; Congress; congressional; the two houses of Congress.*

Courses (academic). *Introduction to Psychology; Psychology 200; a psychology course; an English course; English 101.*

Courts. *the Court* (only for the U.S. Supreme Court); *the state supreme court.*

Decades and historical periods. *the twenties; the nineteen-nineties; the Roaring Twenties; the Jazz Age; the Me Decade; the Go-Go Nineties.*

Departments (school or university). *Department of Philosophy; Philosophy Department; department chairwoman; departmental policies.*

Diseases. *measles; German measles; irritable bowel syndrome (IBS); Down's syndrome; Parkinson's disease; AIDS.*

Earth. *Planet Earth; Earth; the earth; down to earth.*

Epochs (geologic time). *the Holocene epoch.*

Eras. *Paleozoic era; the Victorian era.*

Generations. *baby boomers; Generation X.*

Governmental programs. *Social Security; welfare; food stamps; Medicare.*

He [God]; His [God's]. In standard usage, pronouns with *God* as the antecedent are lowercased. Capitalization is sometimes necessary, however, to prevent ambiguity: *The minister discussed His purpose.*

Historical documents. *the Constitution; the Bill of Rights; the Second Amendment.*

Historical events. *the Industrial Revolution; the Great Depression; a depression; a recession.*

Holidays. *New Year's Day; Thanksgiving; Thanksgiving Day; the Fourth of July.*

House of Representatives (federal). *the House.*

Languages: *English; French; Italian; Russian.*

Laws, acts, treaties, pacts, accords. *Megan's Law; Americans with Disabilities Act; Comprehensive Test Ban Treaty; Warsaw Pact; Camp David Accords.*

Medications. Lowercase the generic names of drugs; uppercase brand names: *ibuprofen; moexipril; Advil; Univasc.*

Military branches. *the U.S. Army; the Army* (in references to the U.S. Army); *U.S. Navy; the Navy* (in references to the U.S. Navy); *armies in conflict; nineteenth-century naval battles.*

Parts of a book mentioned within the book. *Table of Contents; Preface; Introduction; Chapter 4; Appendix; Glossary; Index.*

Periods (geologic time). *the Jurassic period.*

Radio stations. Call letters are capitalized: *WABC; KYW; WOR.*

Religious terms. *God; a god; the Lord; the church; Christianity; Christians; Mormons; Muslims; the Bible; biblical; the New Testament; the book of Job; the Talmud; the Koran; heaven; hell; the Crucifixion; Holy Father; Holy Communion; communion; holy water; Holy Week; the Last Supper; the Second Coming.*

Scientific laws, theorems, etc. *the Pythagorean theorem; Occam's razor; Hooke's law.*

Scientific phenomena. *Brownian motion; Doppler effect; Saint Elmo's fire; Van Allen belt.*

Seasons. *winter; fall; fall term 2005; fall 2005 schedule.*

Senate (federal). *the Senate; senatorial.*

Speeches. Capitalize titles of speeches of major significance: *the Gettysburg Address; the State of the Union address; George W. Bush's second inaugural address.*

Sporting events. *the World Series; Boston Marathon; the Super Bowl; the Olympics; the Special Olympics.*

Subjects (academic). *mathematics; math; arithmetic; science; physics; English; Spanish; French.*

Time zones. *Eastern standard time (EST); central standard time.*

TV networks. *the History Channel; Cable News Network (CNN); Home and Garden Television.*

TV stations. Call letters are capitalized: *WABC; KDKA.*

Wars. *World War II; the Second World War; the Cold War; the Vietnam War; the Gulf War; the war on terror.*

Yes and *no. I told her yes. We were advised to say no.*

260 CAPITALIZATION OF ELEMENTS IN A SENTENCE

The first word of a sentence is always uppercased, even if it is one of the rare proper nouns (such as the trademark name *iPod*) whose initial letter is normally lowercased.

- IPods are revolutionizing the world of recorded music.

Uppercase the first word of a sentence parenthesized between two complete, freestanding sentences. Lowercase the first word of a complete sentence parenthesized, or set off with dashes, between two parts of a hosting sentence or parenthesized before the period of the hosting sentence—unless the first word of the parenthesized sentence is a proper noun or a proper adjective, which requires capitalization (see chapter 20).

Uppercase the first word of a complete-sentence direct quotation that is not preceded by the indefinite relative pronoun *that*. Do not uppercase the first word of a complete-sentence direct quotation preceded by the pronoun *that* unless the first quoted word is a proper noun or a proper adjective. Do not uppercase the first word of a direct quotation that is not a complete sentence unless the first quoted word is a proper noun or a proper adjective—or unless the quotation has the force of a complete sentence: *She said, "Not today, Eric."* Uppercase the first word of a complete-sentence direct quotation that is divided by a clause of attribution (such as *she said*); uppercase the first word of the second half of the quotation only if it is a proper noun or a proper adjective. If you are citing lines of a poem, retain all of the uppercasing in the poem. The conventions for handling direct quotations are discussed in chapter 22.

> **TIP:** Capitalization is occasionally used to give a word or phrase a heightened importance in a particular context.
>
> - She had dated her share of men, but she decided that Jacob was The One.

Capitalization of the first word following a colon is required only if the first word is a proper noun or a proper adjective. If the colon is followed by the equivalent of a complete sentence, the first word of it may be capitalized, but such capitalization is optional. (Be consistent throughout a document.) See chapter 19.

CHAPTER 27

THE PRESENTATION OF NUMBERS

You can easily resolve the matter of whether to spell out a number or use a numeral if you commit yourself to one of two easy-to-use methods for the presentation of numbers, then follow its guidelines consistently throughout a document.

27A WHEN NUMBERS ARE USED INFREQUENTLY

The first method is better suited for documents in which numbers should appear only occasionally. If a number can be spelled out in two words or fewer, spell it out. All whole numbers between zero and one hundred will therefore be presented as words. So should numbers like *twenty-five thousand* and *ninety-nine million,* because such numbers can be presented in two words. Numerals should be used for all other numbers.

- Enrollment in the course is limited to thirty-six students.
- The company has 1,080 employees.
- We mailed thirty-five hundred brochures.
- The three research assistants together worked 596 hours on the project.

If a sentence includes a pair or series of related items, and the number in one would normally be spelled out and the number in another would normally be presented in numerals, use numerals for all of the items.

> **Awkward:** She read ninety-two novels and 127 biographies last year.
> **Better:** She read 92 novels and 127 biographies last year.

27B WHEN NUMBERS ARE USED FREQUENTLY

The second method is better for documents in which it will be necessary to include many numbers. (This method is especially useful for business, technical, and scientific documents.)

Numerals are more reader-friendly than spelled-out numbers, so the only numbers that are presented as words should be the whole numbers zero through nine; numerals should be used for all other whole numbers.

  · We opened seven new branches last year.
  · We hired 36 new technicians.

Use numerals even for round numbers.

  · 85,000 residents

A round number in the millions or higher is more reader-friendly if the zeros are replaced by the word *million, billion,* etc.

  · a population of 11.8 million
  · the next 200 billion years

If a sentence includes a pair or series of related items, and the number in one is below ten and the number in another is above ten, use numerals for all of the items.

  Awkward: We hired seven secretaries, 11 technicians, and 15 telemarketers.
  Better: We hired 7 secretaries, 11 technicians, and 15 telemarketers.

Present an ordinal number in the form of a numeral followed by the appropriate suffix.

  · the 18th attempt

Two Important Guidelines Common to Both Methods

First, never start a sentence with a numeral. Either spell out the number at the start of the sentence, or rewrite the sentence so that the numeral is no longer in the opening position.

  Faulty: 134 books were added to the library's fiction collection in May.
  Awkward: One hundred and thirty-four books were added to the library's fiction collection in May.
  Better: The library added 134 books to its fiction collection in May.

Second, when one number directly precedes another, the smaller of the two should be spelled out to improve the readability of the sentence.

  · We bought thirty-seven 120-pound bags.
  · The guidebook lists 132 five-star restaurants.

> **TIP:** It is now acceptable for a sentence to begin with a numeral specifying a year, but the year can always be repositioned later in the sentence.
> **Correct:** 2005 was the turning point for me.
> **Better:** The turning point for me was 2005.

27C COMMAS IN LARGE NUMBERS

The insertion of commas often improves the readability of large numbers.

- a salary of $34,500; 56,000 residents; 145,000 volumes; 246,500,000 stars

Commas are not inserted into numbers specifying years, account numbers, policy numbers, serial numbers, and other identification numbers—numbers that do not designate quantities.

- 2006; account number 309783; policy number 7892398

27D HYPHENS IN NUMBERS AND IN FRACTIONS

The guidelines for hyphenating numbers and fractions are presented in chapter 24. A hyphen should not be used to divide a numeral at the end of a line of text, but if such a break cannot be avoided, split the numeral after a comma. A spelled-out number may be divided.

27E NUMBERS IN DIALOGUE

Spell out numbers (other than any number specifying a year) in dialogue, including transcripts.

27F OTHER GUIDELINES

Below is detailed advice on how to present common categories of information that include numbers.

Addresses. Use numerals for building and apartment numbers: *134 North Pine Street, Apartment 6.* Spell out the number if a building's address is also its official name: *One Fifth Avenue.* Use numerals for room numbers.

Ages (of persons). Except in journalistic, business, and technical contexts, spell out ages: *forty-eight years old; a twenty-three-year-old; aged ninety-seven.*

Dates. The year should always be presented in numeral form, except in unusually formal documents (such as wedding invitations). Present complete dates as *October 24, 2000* or *24 October 2000.* Avoid *October 24th, 2000;* and although *on October 24th* and *the 24th of October* are acceptable (note that the year is not included in either construction), *October 24* is preferred. When neither the month nor the year is specified, spell out the number in ordinal form: *on the twenty-fourth.* Avoid the *10/24/00* or *10-24-00* patterns except in informal contexts. (The exception is *9/11,* which is appropriate even in formal contexts.) An apostrophe may be used instead of the first two digits of a year, but only in casual contexts: *the class of '02.* Decades may be spelled out (*the nineteen-nineties*) or presented in numeral form (*the 1990s*). Spell out a number specifying a century: *the seventeenth century; seventeenth-century poetry.* The abbreviation B.C. follows a year or a time span: *78 B.C.; 275–255 B.C.* The abbreviation A.D. precedes a year: A.D. *45.*

Decimals. The decimal point should be preceded by a zero if the quantity is less than one (*3.4; 0.46; from 0.74 to 1.97*), except in common terms such as *.45-caliber pistol.*

Fractions. Spell out fractions that are not attached to a whole number: *three-fifths of the manuscript; two-thirds of the workforce.* When a fraction specifies a physical portion, do not hyphenate it: *She threw away three quarters of the pizza.* When a fraction is attached to a whole number, spell it out only if it requires few words: *two and a half hours.* Otherwise, use numerals: *9½ × 11½ inches.* The hyphenation of fractions is discussed in chapter 24.

Highways. Use numerals: *Interstate 80* or *I-80; U.S. Route 22.*

Measurements. Except in business, technical, and scientific contexts (where numerals are preferred), spell out numbers between zero and one hundred: *ninety-four pounds; 165 pounds; thirty-two miles; ninety-eight degrees in the shade; six feet one inch tall; six inches by nine inches.* A numeral must precede an abbreviation or sign: *19 mpg; 64 oz.; 192 lb.; 5′ 9″; 6½″ × 9″.* (Periods and commas—as well as colons, semicolons, dashes, and parentheses—follow, not precede, the signs for inch and foot.)

Money (U.S.). A spelled-out amount must include the word *dollars* or *cents: fifty-nine dollars; twenty-seven cents.* An amount presented as a numeral must include the dollar sign or the cents sign: *$5; $23.89; from $.08 to $.81; from $20 to $50; from $19.01 to $20.00.* For very large, approximate amounts, combine numerals and the spelled-out words *million, billion,* etc.: *$3.3 billion; from $36 billion to $67 billion.*

Parts of books. Use numerals: *Chapter 7; Unit 9; page 53; pages 45-68; Volume 8.*

Percentages. In business, technical, and scientific contexts, use a numeral followed by the % symbol or the word *percent: 34%; 56 percent.* In other contexts, the number and the word *percent* should be spelled out: *thirty-five percent.*

Proper nouns. Spell out a number that is formally part of a proper noun: *First Federal Savings and Loan.*

Ratios. *4-1; 4:1; a ratio of four to one; a fifty-fifty proposition.*

Sports scores. Use an en dash (see chapter 24) between scores: *13–7.* Or substitute the preposition *to* for the en dash: *13 to 7.*

Street and avenue numbers. Spell out street and avenue numbers between first and ninety-ninth: *Eighth Avenue; Seventy-fourth Street; 115th Street.*

Temperatures. In a technical context, the temperature is expressed by a numeral followed by the degree symbol: *67° F.*

Times of day. When you are not spelling out the times (*seven-thirty; a quarter before eleven this morning; half past nine; nine o'clock; shortly after five*), use numerals followed by A.M. and P.M. (*12:09 A.M.; 3 P.M.; from 11:00 A.M. to 6:45 P.M.*); never write *three o'clock* A.M. or *three* A.M. Use the words *noon* and *midnight* instead of numerals.

Voting results. Treat such tallies exactly as you would treat sports scores.

CHAPTER 28

ABBREVIATIONS

Keep abbreviations to a minimum in your writing, because they are almost always undesirable shortcuts that give your sentences an impatient, dashed-off air and an unfinished look. Some abbreviations are not only handy but entirely untroubling: the traditional courtesy titles that precede a person's name (*Ms., Mrs., Mr., Dr., Prof., the Rev.*) and abbreviations that can follow the name (such as *Jr., Sr., M.D., D.D.S., B.S., M.F.A.,* and *Ph.D.*). But be sparing with all other abbreviations, and use them only when you are confident that your reader will know what they stand for. Many readers confuse *e.g.* with *i.e.* (the former means "for example"; the latter means "that is"), so it is better to avoid either, except in academic writing. The abbreviated names of organizations can also spell trouble. The abbreviation *NEA*, after all, is used by both the National Endowment for the Arts and the National Education Association; and *ABA* is shared by the American Bar Association, the American Booksellers Association, and the Amateur Boxing Association. Do not drop any such abbreviation into a sentence unless you are certain that the context will instantly make clear which organization you are referring to.

Abbreviated forms of the names of organizations and of technical terms can serve a useful purpose when they eliminate cumbersome repetition throughout a piece of writing, but it is best to spell out the name or term in full for the first mention and slip the abbreviation between parentheses immediately following the name so that readers can make the acquaintance of the abridged form.

- Most of the employees found the cost-of-living adjustment (COLA) inadequate.

A passage including several different abbreviations put in an appearance is much less readable than a passage in which only one or two abbreviations reappear several times.

Abbreviations that are uppercased from beginning to end fall into two classes. The first type, the acronym, has the status of a word, because it is pronounced as one: *NASCAR, NIMBY, PIN, AIDS, OPEC, ASCAP, UNICEF.* The other type of fully capitalized abbreviation, known as an initialism, requires that the speaker pronounce each letter in the sequence individually: *USDA, VWF, WWF, WMD, HDTV, HIV, DUI, STD.* Only a few fully uppercased abbreviations include periods; among them are *U.S., U.K.,* A.D., and B.C. The plurals of unpunctuated fully capitalized abbreviations are formed by attaching a lowercase *-s: PCs, PINs.* Be sure to choose the appropriate indefinite article to precede an entirely fully capitalized abbreviation. The choice of *a* or *an* is determined not by the first letter of the abbreviation but instead by the first sound: *a URL, a UPS truck; an MP3 file, an NFL team.*

Older abbreviations tend to be lowercased, and they often include periods (*lb., in., ft., vol.*), though some are unpunctuated (*mpg, mph*). The plural forms of lowercased punctuated abbreviations of measurement (such as *in., ft., lb., mi., min.*) are identical to the singular forms (*6 in.; 20 lb.*). The plurals of other entirely lowercased abbreviations that end with a period are formed by adding *-s* before the period (*bldgs., blvds.*).

Some abbreviations of phrases include a mix of uppercased and lowercased letters; if they include interior periods, such abbreviations are pluralized by attaching an apostrophe and *-s: Ph.D.'s; R.Ph.'s.* The same is true of the plurals of entirely uppercased abbreviations with interior punctuation: *M.D.'s; M.A.'s.* (There is no space before or after an abbreviation's interior period.)

The plural of *Mr.* is *Messrs.* The plural of *Mrs.* is *Mesdames* (with no period). The plural of *Ms.* is *Mss.* or *Mses.* (though the plurals are rarely used). The plural of *Dr.* is *Drs.*

The publication-related abbreviations *col.* (column), *ed.* (edition), *ex.* (example), *fig.* (figure), *no.* (number), and *vol.* (volume) form their plurals by the insertion of *-s* before the period: *cols., eds., exs., figs., nos., vols.* The plural of *p.* (page) is *pp.* The plural of *MS* (manuscript) is *MSS* (neither the singular form nor the plural form ends in a period).

The abbreviation of *versus* is *vs.*—except in the names of legal cases, where *v.* is used: *Roe v. Wade.*

The state abbreviations favored by the United States Postal Service each consist of two uppercased, unpunctuated letters: *CA, NY, OH, PA, WY.* (You can find the complete list in the front matter of almost any telephone directory.)

Use A.M. (or *a.m.*) and P.M. (or *p.m.*) only after times of day presented in numeral form (*8* A.M.; *3:35* P.M.). Never write *early in the* A.M. or *late in the* P.M.

When a declarative sentence ends with an abbreviation that includes a period at its end, a single period suffices.

- The next train is scheduled to arrive at 10:19 A.M.

When an interrogative or exclamatory sentence ends with an abbreviation that includes a period at its end, a question mark or an exclamation point follows the period of the abbreviation.

- Is the train still scheduled to arrive at 10:19 A.M.?

CHAPTER 29

GLOSSARY OF COMMONLY MISUSED WORDS

The entries in this glossary will guide you in your use of words that are most frequently mishandled in newspapers, magazines, newsletters, brochures, letters, and e-mails, as well as on websites and in blogs. Corrections to sentences cited from published sources have been bracketed and boldfaced.

a vs. *an* before *historian, historic, historical,* and *history*
A, not *an*, is the appropriate indefinite article to precede these four words beginning with *h*. (*An* precedes a word beginning with *h* only if the *h* goes unpronounced, as in *an hour*.)

affect vs. *effect*
Both words have highly specialized uses, but it is in their simpler, everyday employment that the words are commonly misspelled. *Affect* is a verb that means "to influence" or "to bring about a change in"; *effect* is a noun that means "consequence" or "result." Thus, A affects B; A has an effect on B.

aggravate (and *aggravation*)
Aggravate means "to make worse." (A synonym is *exacerbate*.) Do not use *aggravate* as a synonym for *annoy, irritate,* or *bother*.

- The air pollution aggravates her asthma.
- In some countries, so many people are using cell phones that the aggravation [**annoyance**] level has reached critical mass.
  (Torsten Ove, "Will Etiquette Keep Pace with Advancing Technology?," *Pittsburgh Post-Gazette* online, 26 July 1998, paragraph 82)

almost

See *most*.

alternate vs. *alternative*

These two words—the first of which functions as an adjective, a noun, and a verb, and the second of which functions as an adjective and a noun—are not synonymous. An *alternate* is the one and only substitute for something else at a given time. (Someone or something alternates, or goes back and forth, between two things: A and B.) An *alternative* is one of two or more substitutes for something else. (B and C are alternatives to A.)

among vs. *between*

Although the usual distinction drawn between these two prepositions is that *among* should be used in statements involving three or more persons or things (as in *honor among thieves*) and *between* should be limited to statements involving only two persons or things (as in *Let's keep this a secret between you and me*), the matter is in fact a little more complicated.

Among is used in statements involving three or more persons or things when not every single person or thing is interacting with every other person or thing in the group: *The principal tried to encourage discussion among the students in her school.*

Between is of course used in statements involving only two persons or things, but it is also used in statements involving three or more persons or things when every single person or thing is interacting with every other person or thing in the group: *She divides her time between New York, Paris, and Prague.* In other words, if all members of a group interrelate either literally or figuratively on a one-on-one basis, *between* is the appropriate preposition.

- But this view is fading, indicating that relations among [between] minorities may be just as prickly as white-black relations have been. . . .

  (Maria T. Padilla, "Are Ethnic Groups Just As Likely to Discriminate?," *Orlando Sentinel* online, 1 July 1998, paragraph 7)

- Yasmina Reza's one-act play "Art," which opens here this winter, is about a white-on-white abstract painting that nearly ruins a friendship among [between] three men.

  (Louis Menand, "What Is 'Art'?," *New Yorker*, 9 Feb. 1998, p. 39)

amount vs. *number*

Use *number*, not *amount*, when countable units are involved. Use *amount* when an indivisible mass is involved.

- His store remained open, selling flashlights and an inordinate amount [**number**] of scented candles.

  (Dan Barry, "At 99 Cents, Mystery Sells Cheap," *New York Times*, 14 Jan. 2004, p. A19)

- Due to the large amount [number] of books sent to the newspaper yearly, the policy on self-published books also works to narrow the candidates for review.

  (Bob Hoover, "Reviewers Mostly Draw the Line at Self-Published Submissions," *Pittsburgh Post-Gazette*, 16 Nov. 2003, p. E4)

anticipate vs. *expect*

Expecting something involves only looking ahead to it. Anticipating something involves taking action in preparation for it. (The action may be literal or figurative; it may be taking place entirely in the mind of the anticipator.)

- Anticipating ruthless competition, the store manager slashed the prices of all merchandise.

In the following sentence, the phrase *anticipating and planning for* is a redundancy; the writer should omit either half of the construction.

- Legislators in Harrisburg have a history of poorly anticipating and planning for the state's changing economic fortunes.

  ("Pray for No Rain," editorial, *Pittsburgh Post-Gazette*, 3 Mar. 1998, p. A10)

- It is anticipated [**expected**] that the organization will raise twenty-five thousand dollars during its two-month fund-raising campaign.

anxious vs. *eager*

If you remember that *anxious* means "afflicted with anxiety," you will never use *anxious* when the context calls for *eager*.

- The girl was eager to return to school.
- The girl was anxious about returning to school.

anyplace

Avoid the use of *anyplace*. Substitute the two-word phrase *any place* (*Do you know of any place that still sells typewriters?*) or *anywhere* (*I couldn't find my address book anywhere*) or *somewhere* (*Can you think of somewhere special?*).

as vs. *because*

The subordinating conjunction *as* is perfect for expressing the temporal relationship of simultaneity (*As I drove to work, I kept thinking about her suggestion*). It is less desirable as a conjunction expressing cause-and-effect relationships, because a reader might be seeing a temporal relationship where the writer wants the reader to be thinking of a causal relationship: *As I was preparing for a change of career, I took a computer-science course.* The ambiguity in such sentences can be resolved by replacing *as* with either *because* or *while*. (The subordinating conjunction *since* is also widely used to express cause-and-effect relationships as well as temporal relationships, and ambiguity can thus arise in sentences such as *Since she was appointed chairperson, our morale began to suffer.* Substitute either *because* or *after*.)

as far as vs. *as for*

As far as is a subordinating conjunction: It needs to be followed by a subject and a predicate that together constitute an adverbial dependent clause. *As for* is a two-word preposition that needs to be followed by a noun, a pronoun, or a noun phrase. Many writers and speakers mistakenly substitute *as far as* for *as for*.

Faulty: As far as her love life, things are improving.
Correct: As far as her love life is concerned, things are improving.
Correct: As for her love life, things are improving.

a while vs. *awhile*

You can wait *awhile* or wait *a while* (in each instance, the italicized construction is functioning adverbially), but you can wait only *for a while*. That is, when *while* is used as a noun functioning as the object of a preposition, *while* must stay detached from *a*.

- Every once in awhile [**a while**], when they aren't writing legislation concerning the resale of used underpants or kowtowing to beet-faced conventioneers, New York's City Council actually sets about trying to do something worthwhile.

  ("Way to Legislate, Guys!," *New York Press*, 2–8 June 2004, p. 7)

- Even for the most ardent enthusiast, the adrenaline rush of Wall Street gets old after awhile [**a while**].

  (Corilyn Shropshire, "Former Wall Streeter Has a Strategy to Give Back," *Pittsburgh Post-Gazette*, 24 June 2004, p. C11) *bad* vs. *badly*

See chapter 2.

because

See *as* and *just because*.

between

See *among*.

center around

The phrasal verb *center around* is illogical. Substitute *revolve around* or *center on*.

- "Curb [Your Enthusiasm]"—centered around [**revolved around** or **centered on**] ordinary-looking, mostly married 40- and 50-year-olds—is suddenly the frothy, outré HBO series; it has relegated "Sex and the City" to the status of "Bonanza."
  (Alessandra Stanley, "Sexy Women Out; Cantankerous Guy In," *New York Times*, 2 Jan. 2004, p. B34)

- His concern about money centered always around [**always centered on**] the baby he'd fathered in Paris and been stuck with by his fellow founders.
  (David Michaelis, "The Last Gentleman," *New York Observer* online, 6 Oct. 2003, paragraph 33)

complement vs. *compliment*

Do not confuse the verb *complement* (which means "to render complete or perfect") with the verb *compliment* (which means "to make a favorable remark about").

- There are only so many ways to say "pass the butter," Ronald Reagan's speech-writer observes. "The more ornate and highly stylized you get—'How I desire to have within my grasp the yellow fatted food that so compliments [**complements**] the taste of bread'—the more foolish you sound."
  (Don Feder, "State of the President: Hollow Rhetoric," *Jewish World Review* online, 27 Jan. 1998, paragraph 3)

comprise

As Wilson Follett succinctly explained in *Modern American Usage,* "the whole comprises the parts," not vice versa. Do not use *comprise* as a synonym for *constitute, compose,* or *make up.*

- On Pitt's main campus, there are 25,461 students, and among them, black students are the largest minority. They account for 2,056 of the 3,473 minority pupils, Pitt spokesman Ken Service said. Blacks thus comprise [**constitute** or **make up**] 8 percent of the total.
  (Bill Schackner, "Graduation Rates Lag for Black Students at Pitt," *Pittsburgh Post-Gazette*, 20 Feb. 1998, p. A13)

- PAT will hold public meetings next month to discuss specifics, although the four routes that will comprise [**constitute**] the eastern suburban service have already been proposed.
  (Joe Grata, "East Suburbs Get PAT Minibuses," *Pittsburgh Post-Gazette*, 25 Feb. 1998, p. B2)

continual vs. *continuous*

These two adjectives are not synonymous. *Continual* means "happening again and again"; *continuous* means "occurring without any interruption; nonstop."

- Her continual efforts to improve herself merit high praise.
- The continuous availability of the Internet is a distraction for many.

convince vs. *persuade*

You can *convince* someone *that* something is the case, and you can convince someone *of* the truthfulness or validity or importance of something. But you *persuade* somebody *to do* something or *to refrain from doing* something. *Persuade*, in other words, means "to urge." *Persuade*, not *convince*, is the appropriate verb to be followed by an infinitive.

- I also convinced [**persuaded**] my principal to include a list of my awards and honors along with my transcript.

  (Benjamin Kaplan, "How to Go to Harvard Free," *New York Times*, 5 Apr. 1998, section 4A, p. 17)

- Jean Georges chef Tony DiSalvo said he enjoys the fish, but has a hard time convincing [**persuading**] customers to try it.

  (Lizzy Ratner, "Redfish Redux," *New York Observer* online, 24 Nov. 2003, paragraph 11)

- If it [the film] convinces [**persuades**] one nonvoter to think, it will serve a purpose.

  (Rex Reed, "Moore's Magic: 9/11 Electrifies," *New York Observer* online, 28 June 2004, paragraph 9)

could care less vs. couldn't care less

The latter verb phrase—*couldn't care less*—means that one has achieved the least degree of caring about something.

- Sure enough, the chapter on the twins is a devastating portrait of two spoiled teenagers who could [**couldn't**] care less about their parents' dedication to public service, seeing it only as something that gets in the way of their having fun.

  (Mackenzie Carpenter, "Laura Bush Remains a Mystery," *Pittsburgh Post-Gazette*, 22 Feb. 2004, p. E5)

couple

Do not forget to follow *couple* with the preposition *of*—unless you are using the noun to denote a romantic or married pair.

- A couple [**of**] days after Hemmer had been there, he asked Hughes if he would make a good Marine.

  (Sarah Bernard, "Anchor Dreams," *New York*, 1 Dec. 2003, p. 52)

didn't used to

Didn't used to, not *didn't use to,* is the correct form. But it looks peculiar, and it is easily avoided.

Awkward: He didn't used to be so sneaky
Better: He wasn't always so sneaky.

different from vs. different than

Do not use *than* after *different* whenever *from* can easily be substituted.

- Besides, give Jagger credit for surviving this long, given that his chosen professional field has an actuarial table not much different than [**from**] that of a third-world country.

  (Russ Smith, "Wasted Space," *New York Press*, 17–23 Dec. 2003, p. 23)

When *different* is followed by an adverbial dependent clause and *from* cannot be substituted, *different than* is now considered perfectly acceptable.

- She looks little different than she did a decade ago.

Any such sentence, of course, can be recast with *different from*.

- She looks little different from how she looked a decade ago.

dilemma

Do not use *dilemma* as a synonym for *problem, quandary,* or *predicament*. Reserve it for the circumstance in which someone is forced to make a choice between two unpleasant alternatives.

- The toothache presented her with a dilemma: Should she visit the dentist or try to ride out the pain?
- I once again find myself in the dilemma [**predicament**] of having to buy a new computer.

disinterested vs. uninterested

The words are not synonymous. *Disinterested* means "impartial, unbiased, having no personal stake in an outcome." *Uninterested* means "not interested."

due to

Due to (a phrase formed of an adjective and a preposition) correctly follows a linking verb; but it should not be used after an intransitive verb or after the direct object of a transitive verb (where it is replaceable by *because of, owing to,* or a similar phrase).

- Her success is due to her persistence.
- The group disbanded due to [**because of**] friction between the singer and the guitarist.
- The singer, who's been hounded by rumors of ill-health after canceling her first tour date due to [**because of**] the flu and reports of backstage fainting spells, didn't get a wink of sleep Wednesday night.
  (Elisa Lipsky-Karasz, "Salivating Cyber-Snobs," *New York Post*, 20 June 2004, p. 119)

each other vs. *one another*

Use *each other* in statements involving only two persons.

- The couple comforted each other.

Use *one another* in statements involving three or more persons.

- The teammates consoled one another after losing the final game.

eager

See *anxious*.

effect

See *affect*.

enormity vs. *enormousness*

Enormity has nothing to do with size; *enormity* means "extreme wickedness" (as in *the enormity of her crimes*). *Enormousness* means "the quality of being huge." (*Immensity* is a synonym for *enormousness*.)

- The rapper LL Cool J, in his memoir "I Make My Own Rules," describes being at a birthday gala for Quincy Jones, attended by Sidney Poitier, Oprah Winfrey, and others, at which Rickles made a fulsome toast, congratulating Jones on the beauty of his wife and on the enormity [**immensity**] of his professional success, but concluding that, in spite of everything, he was "still a black man."
  (Zoë Heller, "Don't Call Me Sir," *New Yorker*, 2 Aug. 2004, p. 34)

equally vs. *equally as*

The *as* in *equally as* is always redundant and always wrong.

- Garth Brooks got to be the king of country music by giving his fans what they want. So it comes as little surprise that he is equally as good [**is equally good**] at telling people what they want to hear.
  (Jerry Sharpe, "Garth Loves How the Irish Hang onto Lyrics," *Pittsburgh Post-Gazette*, 2 Mar. 1998, p. D1)

everyday vs. *every day*

The single-word form is an adjective.

- Take advantage of everyday low prices.
- She's less at ease with the practical, the everyday.

The two-word phrase is an adverb.

- You'll find low prices every day.
- She walks to work every day.

expect

See *anticipate*.

experience (as a verb)

Experience is often forced to serve as an imprecise and pretentious substitute for a verb like *feel* or *suffer* or even *have*. *She experienced a setback* is hardly an improvement over *She suffered a setback*. *Experience* is especially clumsy when the experiencer is inanimate.

> **Awkward:** The [space]craft experienced malfunctions in key areas. . . .
> ("Space Race," editorial, *Pittsburgh Post-Gazette*, 28 June 2004, p. A8)
> **Better:** The spacecraft malfunctioned. . . .

famous vs. *notorious*

Famous means "well-known"; *notorious* means "well-known but not highly regarded or respected." (*Notorious* has a very negative connotation.)

> • Howard Stern is both famous and notorious.

farther vs. *further*

Reserve *farther* for physical, geographic, objectively measurable distances; reserve *further* for nonphysical distances.

> • A further problem is that the new warehouse is twenty miles farther from the plant than the old warehouse.

fewer vs. *less*

The distinction between *fewer* and *less* is similar to the distinction between *number* and *amount*. Use *fewer* when countable units are involved; use *less* when an indivisible mass is involved. The signs hanging above express-checkout lanes at supermarkets should read *Ten Items or Fewer*, not *Ten Items or Less*.

> • Fewer than fifty people showed up for the ceremony.
> • Less than half of the cake has been eaten.

There is an exception: When a quantity that is ordinarily thought of as a sum of units is instead thought of in bulk, as a single mass, *less* is the appropriate choice.

> • I had less than ten dollars left.
> • I had worked for less than three years.

for free

The preposition *for* is of course redundant; something that is *for free* is simply *free*. But the two-word phrase has its legitimate uses. Try removing the second *for* from the following sentence, and you will see that the omission throws off the rhythm.

> • Yesterday, the PAT board unanimously endorsed a feasibility study for the creation of a bicycle station—a building where commuters can safely store their bicycles for free and enjoy a range of amenities.
> (Jonathan D. Silver, "Port Authority to Construct Free Station for Bicyclists," *Pittsburgh Post-Gazette* online, 22 July 1998, paragraph 2)

got vs. *gotten* as past participles of *get*

The distinction usually drawn is that *have got* emphasizes the state of possession (*You've got a friend in Pennsylvania*) and *have gotten* emphasizes the act of taking possession (*We've gotten our hands on a perfect specimen*). But the redundancy of *have got* is best avoided (the sentence *She has got to be kidding* nicely preserves the rhythms and stresses of conversational English, but it is better to write *I have a friend* than *I have got a friend*); and *have gotten* is often clunky and inexact (it is better to write *She has found a new job* than *She has gotten a new job*).

- Staffers have gotten [**have received** *or* **have accepted** *or* **have recruited**] help from alumni, particularly in such states as California, Florida, Hawaii, Massachusetts, Texas and Florida, Porter said.

  (Bill Schackner, "Alumni Recruiters Pay Off for Pitt," *Pittsburgh Post-Gazette*, 19 Feb. 1998, p. C3)

- Without Starr, Clinton might not have gotten [**have scored**] a $10 million advance. And his wife, now a senator from New York, might not have gotten [**have received**] $8 million for her autobiography.

  (Ann McFeatters, "The Tome of His Life," *Pittsburgh Post-Gazette*, 27 June 2004, p. E7)

graduate (as a verb)

A person *graduates from* high school or college. Do not write *She graduated high school in 2005.*

hark back, harken back, hearken back

Hark back has emerged as the preferred phrasal verb to mean "to return (figuratively) to the past" or "to call to mind something from the past."

- The store's new signature line of small appliances harks back to the streamlined designs of Art Deco.

hopefully

Use the adverb *hopefully* to mean "full of hope" or "in a hopeful manner." Do not use it to mean "I hope," "let's hope," "he or she hopes," or "it is to be hoped." In the first example below, *hopefully* is used correctly.

- It is sometimes better to travel hopefully than to arrive.

  (fortune-cookie message)

- The party gets partisan on the Beastie Boys' first record since 1998's *Hello Nasty*, this election year's first—and hopefully [(**let's hope**)] not last—politically minded gemstone.

  (Stephen Mooallem, capsule review of *To the 5 Boroughs*, *Interview*, July 2004, p. 42)

if vs. *whether*

These two words are often used interchangeably, but good writers use *if* to mean "in the event that" or "in case" and reserve it for adverbial dependent clauses that stipulate a condition, and they use *whether* in nominative dependent clauses that involve two alternative courses of action.

- Be sure to tell the manager if you disagree with the assessment.

  This sentence makes it clear that there is no need to get in touch with the manager unless—that is, except in the event that—you disagree.

- Be sure to tell the manager whether you disagree with the assessment.

  This sentence makes it clear that you need to get in touch with the manager in either case—that is, regardless of whether you disagree with the assessment or agree with it.

If can sometimes lead to ambiguity, as in this headline.

- Who Judges If a Convict Is Retarded?

  (headline, *Pittsburgh Post-Gazette*, 17 May 2004, p. A1).

Is the headline asking who should be the judge presiding over a case when a retarded convict is on trial, or is it asking who should make the determination that a convict is retarded? The writer most likely meant the latter. If so, *whether* is preferable to *if.*

individual (as a noun)

Individual remains a pretentious synonym for *person*. Reserve the noun for contexts in which one person is being contrasted with a larger group.

- We discussed the individual's responsibility to his or her peers.

- Excessive ozone can cause shortness of breath, coughing, headaches, nausea and respiratory discomfort, especially for the young or old or individuals [people] with pre-existing respiratory problems.
  (Don Hopey, "El Niño Has Experts Predicting Warm, Dry, Smoggy Summer," *Pittsburgh Post-Gazette*, 18 May 1998, p. B8)

in terms of

The phrase *in terms of* is almost always deadwood.

> **Awkward:** In terms of maturity, is the child ready to start kindergarten?
> **Better:** Is the child mature enough to start kindergarten?

into

In casual American speech, the preposition *into* has come to mean "involved with" or "enthusiastic about." But avoid writing sentences such as *She's into Brazilian folk music* when the context is not casual.

just because (at the beginning of a dependent clause serving as the subject of a sentence)

An adverbial dependent clause, as we saw in chapter 4, functions exactly as a single-word adverb functions, and thus it cannot function as the subject of a sentence. You are therefore better off avoiding sentences like the following, except in the most casual contexts.

> **Awkward:** Just because the fair doesn't officially open until Aug. 25, doesn't mean there's nothing to do.
> (Julia Cleary, "Rounding Up the County Fairs," *Pittsburgh Post-Gazette* online, 17 July 1998, paragraph 27)
>
> > The comma before the second *doesn't* should be deleted. You can easily revise such sentences by converting the adverbial dependent clause to a nominative dependent clause or by refashioning both the dependent and independent clauses.
>
> **Better:** The fact that the fair doesn't officially open until Aug. 25 doesn't mean there's nothing to do.
> **Better:** Even though the fair doesn't officially open until Aug. 25, there's still plenty to do.

latter

Latter, as a noun or as an adjective, refers to the second of two things mentioned previously. Do not use it to refer to the last of three or more things mentioned earlier; substitute *the last, the last-named*, or *the last-mentioned* instead.

- Williams, who holds an engineering degree from Carnegie Mellon University, has been at Alcosan since 1984, as shift engineer, solid process superintendent and director of operations and maintenance. The latter [last-named] position put her in charge of the treatment plant, 85 miles of sewer lines and 160 employees.
  (Jon Schmitz, "Alcosan Board Names Director," *Pittsburgh Post-Gazette* online, 24 July 1998, paragraph 11)

lay vs. *lie*

If you understand the distinction between transitive and intransitive verbs discussed in chapter 1, you will never mishandle these two frequently abused verbs.

Lay, a transitive verb, always takes a direct object: *I am going to lay my cards on the table. I am going to lay down the law. I am going to lay my head down.* The present-participial form is *laying;* the past-tense and past-participial forms are *laid*.

Lie, an intransitive verb, never takes a direct object: *I am going to lie down for a nap. I'm going to lie low for a while.* The present-participial form is *lying: The magazine was lying on the floor.* The past-tense form is *lay: He lay in bed until noon.* The past-participial forms are *lain: She had lain in a hospital bed for six weeks.*

- Why doesn't she just go away, lay [lie] on a couch somewhere with her little son, Monty, and leave track and field to the next generation?
  (Filip Bondy, "Jones Able to Jump for Joy," *New York Daily News*, 26 Aug. 2003, p. 36)

- One-hundred-thousand people are predicted to pay their last respects to Ronald Reagan as he lay [**lies**] in state in the Capitol Rotunda on Thursday and Friday.

  ("Mourning in America: Reagan's Legacy," editorial, *Greensburg [PA] Tribune-Review*, 8 June 2004, p. A6)

  The hyphens in *one-hundred-thousand* should be deleted; see chapter 24.

less

See *fewer*.

like

Do not force the preposition *like* to serve as a conjunction. Substitute *as* or *as if* or (sometimes) *that*.

- But for now, it sounds like [**as if**] status quo is the goal.

  (Rachel Donadio, "McGrath Decamping from Intransigent Times Book Review," *New York Observer* online, 24 Nov. 2003, paragraph 6)

- It seems like [**that**] everything you buy these days is hidden behind more layers than a Vidalia onion.

  (Matt Smith, "Tale of the Tape, and Tape and Tape," *Pittsburgh Post-Gazette*, 8 July 2004, p. A7)

majority

Avoid using this word to mean a portion of a single inanimate thing.

- The majority of [**Much of**] the lecture was concerned with recidivism.
- The majority of [**Much of**] the book documented the relationship of social behavior and genetics in animals, such as ants and chimpanzees.

  (Anita Srikameswaran, "Pulitzer Prize Winning Biologist to Speak at Lecture Series," *Pittsburgh Post-Gazette*, 30 Mar. 1998, p. A7)

most vs. almost

Except in the most casual of contexts, do not use the adverb *most* in place of *almost*.

- Most [**Almost**] every fan in attendance was wearing a Bright Eyes T-shirt.

nor

In the chapters on punctuation, we discussed the insertion of coordinating conjunctions like *nor* between consecutive independent clauses. This entry is concerned with the use of *nor* as a conjunction linking two or more words or phrases. If a writer has included a negative word (such as *no* or *not* or *never*) before the first element of a pair or series, there is a temptation to balance it with a *nor* before the second element in the pair or before the final element in the series. But the force of the first negative word works its way forward throughout the entire sentence, and thus *or* is the appropriate choice. (*Nor* would, in effect, introduce a double negative into the sentence.)

- The alleged incident did not occur inside the crowed store nor [**or**] involve one of its employees.
- But the courts are not a fun place to the people who go there seeking redress, nor [**or**] to the many players roped into their costly, frustrating, drawn-out dramas.

  (Sally Kalson, "Dauer Should Play Cop in Traffic Jam in the Tunnel of Justice," *Pittsburgh Post-Gazette* online, 23 Feb. 1998, paragraph 16)

Occasionally, a phrase such as *and not any, and not a,* or *and not an* must be substituted for *nor any, nor a,* or *nor an*.

- The story has a dark, dreamlike quality, and author Reiken tells it with no melodrama nor any [**and not a**] word out of place.

  (John Skow, "The Odd Sea," *Time*, 10 Aug. 1998, p. 88)

notorious

See *famous*.

number

See *amount.*

of

The preposition *of* is always wrong and always redundant in sentences such as *It's not that big of a deal* and *He's not that smart of a guy.* Such sentences are grammatically complete and correct without *of.*

off of

Off of is merely a wordy variant of *off.* The latter is preferred.

- Thomas Harris has a good reason to get off of [**get off**] drugs. He's afraid to die alone.
  (Ann Belser, "Fighting Addiction," *Pittsburgh Post-Gazette*, 20 Feb. 1998, p. B1)

one another

See *each other.*

oral

See *verbal.*

persuade

See *convince.*

presently

Most experts on usage would prefer that we reserve this adverb as a synonym for *soon* (as in *I'll be there presently*). The word is most commonly used, however, as a synonym for *now. Presently* is in fact a word easily avoided. In a sentence such as *She is presently employed by Microsoft,* the word is disposable, and in any sentence where the reader feels the need for a clarifying adverb, *currently* will do nicely.

- Are you presently [**currently**] charged with a crime punishable by a sentence of more than one year?
  (Juror-Qualification Questionnaire, Westmoreland County [PA] Jury Commissioners' Office)

principal vs. principle

The noun *principal* most often means "the person in charge of a school" or "an important player in a drama or conflict." The adjective *principal* means "most important" or "primary." The noun *principle* means "rule" or "basic truth." The most common error in the use of these words is the insertion of the noun *principle* where the adjective *principal* is called for.

- This is the Sir Paul who wants to be known as the principle [**principal**] author of the very worst Beatles song ...
  (Ron Rosenbaum, "Long, Winding Road for Phil Spector—Guilty of Genius," *New York Observer* online, 8 Dec. 2003, paragraph 24)

proved vs. proven

Use *proved* following a helping verb (*The medication has proved to be effective for most patients*); reserve *proven* for adjectival use (*a proven cure*).

- Free lunches provided to some county employees have proven [**proved**] to be costly.
  (Mark Belko, "IRS Bills County for Free Lunches," *Pittsburgh Post-Gazette*, 25 Feb. 1998, p. B1)

- But during the last five years, Lack clearly had proven [**proved**] that he was ready for the job.
  (Phyllis Furman, "Proud as a Peacock," *New York Daily News*, 1 Mar. 1998, p. 45)

the reason ... is because ...

The construction *the reason ... is because ...*, which is discussed at length in chapter 14, is always ungrammatical and always redundant. The quickest fix is the substitution of *that* for *because.*

- The comic explained to everyone that the only reason she took this gig was because [that] she once confused Sting with Phil Collins on her show.

  (George Rush and Joanna Molloy, "Faces Were Red, Rosie Was Blue at Big Benefit," *New York Daily News*, 29 Apr. 1998, p. 14)

- One of the reasons we're not interested in anything that happened before we were born is precisely because [that] we want to remain ever children.

  (Mark Steyn, "Present-Tense Culture," *New Criterion*, Apr. 1997, pp. 14–15)

represent

Avoid using *represent* as a synonym for a verb derived from the infinitive *to be* or for a verb like *constitute*. To *represent* means "to stand for, to be exemplary of"—that is, to be merely part of something greater in scope or significance than what is being offered to the reader's attention.

- By 1949, women represented [made up *or* constituted] 45% of the readership.

  (Mary F. Corey, *The World Through a Monocle: The New Yorker at Midcentury* [Cambridge, MA: Harvard University Press, 1999], p. 179)

respective and *respectively*

These two words are used correctly only when a sentence includes two pairs or series of items and the writer wants to ensure that readers can easily relate each member of the first pair or series to a corresponding member of the second pair or series.

- The three largest lakes in North America, Lakes Superior, Huron and Michigan, span 31,700, 23,000 and 22,300 square miles respectively.

  ("Less Than Great," editorial, *Pittsburgh Post-Gazette*, 13 Mar. 1998, p. A18)

Respective or *respectively* has no place in a sentence lacking two corresponding pairs or series. The following sentence should thus lose *respective*.

- New York's John F. Kennedy International Airport and San Francisco International Airport are about 15 miles from their respective downtowns.

  (Kara K. Choquette, "Tips for Getting Around in an Unfamiliar Town," *USA Today*, 17 Mar. 1998, p. 6E)

It can be argued that *respective* or *respectively*, even when used correctly, is not always necessary to ensure that readers will draw reliable conclusions about which items in the first pair or series correspond to which items in the second pair or series. Thus, many a sentence with two corresponding pairs or series can do without *respective* or *respectively*, which can seem heavy-handed.

- School Districts 30 and 24, which include Jackson Heights and Corona, have[, respectively,] the highest and second-highest number of school-age children from Mexican families in the city.

  (Kevin McCoy, "City's Neighborhoods Savor Mexican Flavor," *New York Daily News*, 21 June 1998, p. 35)

- On his desk is a picture of his wife and three daughters—Emily, Amanda and Catherine, ages 9, 7, and 4 [, respectively]—taken at their Westchester County estate.

  (Dave Salstonstall, "At Last, a Cole Day in July: Designer's Line Is Hot," *New York Daily News*, 26 July 1998, p. 32)

Readers should expect that the writer of a sentence including two such pairs or series will have taken special care in sequencing the elements of each. In a sentence such as the following, however, the inclusion of *respectively* helps readers understand that each person played only one instrument.

- The Smiths' Johnny Marr, Andy Rourke, and Mike Joyce were masters of their instruments—guitar, bass, and drums, respectively.

since

See *as*.

sneaked vs. *snuck*

The past-tense and part-participial forms of *sneak* are *sneaked*. Avoid *snuck* except in dialogue or in sentences aiming for the most casual and colloquial of effects.

- Bone-weary of ritualistic public appearances and responsibilities beyond her years, she snuck [**sneaked**] off for a couple of days in Rome to live as a commoner ...

  (Ed Blank, "'Chasing Liberty' Screenplay Is Uninspired," *Greensburg [PA] Tribune-Review*, 9 Jan. 2004, p. C5)

someplace

Avoid this word. The word you want is *somewhere: Let's go somewhere special.*

'til vs. *till*

Till or *until* is the word you want. Either can function as a subordinating conjunction and as a preposition.

- In real estate, nothing is done 'til [**until**] the lease is signed. ...

  (Teresa F. Lindeman, "Developers See Lots of New Stores," *Pittsburgh Post-Gazette*, 24 June 2004, p. C11)

uninterested

See *disinterested*.

verbal vs. *oral*

Verbal is often used when *oral* is the logical choice. *Verbal* means "involving words, either written or spoken," but *oral* means "involving the spoken word only." An *oral agreement* is therefore one whose terms have not been set down on paper. The article from which the following sentence was extracted made it clear that nothing had yet been put in writing.

- The president of the Damascus-Bishop Tube Co., Brent A. Ward, said yesterday his company has reached a verbal [an oral] agreement with Georgia-Pacific Corp. to purchase 31 acres in Munhall that were formerly part of the old USX Corp. steel mill.

  (Ken Zapinski, "Munhall Site About to See Steel Again," *Pittsburgh Post-Gazette*, 19 Feb. 1998, p. F1)

wean

The verb *wean* is often used in the phrase *weaned on*, meaning "raised on," "reared on," or "brought up on." But many object to this usage and argue that the verb should be confined to its original meaning: "to bring to an end a baby's dependence on its mother's milk" or, figuratively, "to end someone's dependence on something." Therefore, the prepositions that logically follow *weaned* are *off* and *from*, not *on*.

- Infants Weaned [**Brought Up**] on TV 'Cannot Concentrate'

  (headline, Andrew Clennell, *Guardian Unlimited* online [U.K.], 6 Apr. 2004)

when

Avoid using this subordinating conjunction when you are expressing temporal relationships other than simultaneity. Writers often choose *when* in sentences where *after* would make more sense.

- When [**After**] an employee fell to his death, the news reports first portrayed him as the victim of an accident.

where

Everybody knows that the subordinating conjunction *where* expresses a relationship of place and that the subordinating conjunction *when* expresses a relationship of time, but, unfortunately, writers often use the words interchangeably. It is better to confine these two words to their logical, commonsensical meanings.

- Be prepared for instances where [**when**] you'll have to think on your feet.
- There have been incidents where [**when** or **in which**] two jets almost collided above busy airports.
- But on a sweltering August afternoon where [when] the thermometer inside Nas's Escalade indicates that the outside temperature is 100 degrees, they (almost) blend in with the camping and barbecuing masses.

  (Ethan Brown, "Hookmaster," *New York*, 13 Sept. 2004, p. 85)

while

The subordinating conjunction *while* primarily expresses the temporal relationship of simultaneity (*She wrote while her children slept*), but writers often use *while* as a substitute for *but* (to express a contrastive relationship) or as a substitute for *and* (to express an additive relationship). The sense of simultaneity is so dominant in *while,* however, that the temporal relation can arise in a reader's mind when the writer wants the reader to be thinking about an additive relation.

- The sun barely sets here in the summer, while in the winter, it barely rises.

  (Charles Platt, "Breaking the Law of Gravity," *Wired* online, Mar. 1998, paragraph 1)

  And would surely be a better choice here.

Therefore, do not use *while* to express a relationship of contrast or of addition in a sentence where it might unintentionally suggest simultaneity. Replacing *while* with *although* or *even though* in the next example would eliminate the undesired implication that Koop and Elders served together as surgeons general (Koop, in fact, preceded Elders in the post).

- While C. Everett Koop was tolerated when he thundered like some Old Testament prophet against the evils of tobacco, the indiscreet Dr. Elders was fired over comments sympathetic to masturbation.

  ("The Doctor Is In," editorial, *Pittsburgh Post-Gazette*, 16 Feb. 1998, p. A12)

Although or *even though* would also be a better choice in the following sentence, where the writer wants to emphasize contrast, not simultaneity.

- While the state troopers have said they don't choose the cars they stop based on the race of the drivers, a judge ruled last year that state troopers in South Jersey practiced "selective enforcement."

  (Jim Dwyer, "Bullets a Wakeup Call: Victim Lost Innocence in Turnpike Shooting," *New York Daily News*, 29 Apr. 1998, p. 8)

In the next excerpt, however, *while* appropriately expresses simultaneity.

- Granted, measuring the audience in traditional media is inexact. Television programs rely on a sampling of viewers, while newspapers and magazines report both circulation figures and readership levels.

  (Michael Newman, "For Advertisers, Tracking Web Site Visitors Is an Inexact Science," *Pittsburgh Post-Gazette*, 22 Feb. 1998, p. E4)

APPENDIX

SUBJECT GUIDE

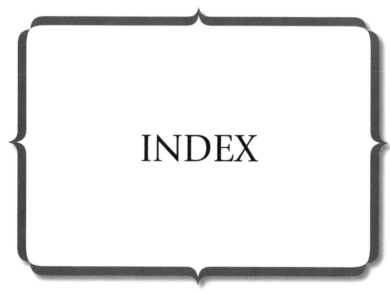

INDEX

adverbial compounds, 292

adverbial dependent clauses, 63–66
  because, beginning with, 226–228
  commas and, 66
  in complex sentences, 76, 300–301
  in compound-complex sentences, 299–301
  introductory, commas and, 66, 203–204
  as modifiers, 63–65
  nonrestrictive, commas and, 225–229
  placement of, 65–66, 127–133
  restrictive, commas and, 225–229

adverbs, 9–10, 35–38
  adjectives as, 36
  as adjectives, 36, 143
  dual form, 36–37, 147
  erroneous use of, as adjectives, 143
  flat, 147
  hyphenation of adjectival compounds beginning with, 275–280
  infinitive phrases as, 57
  introductory single-word, commas and, 200–201
  nouns as, 36
  phrases as, 44–45
  placement of, 35–36, 127–133, 143–144
  prepositional phrases as, 45
  relative, 63
  See also comparatives; conjunctive adverbs; superlatives

agreement, subject-verb. *See* subject-verb agreement

apostrophes, 248–256

appositives
  asyndeton vs., 97
  dangling, 138–139
  defined, 9–10, 45–46
  introductory, commas and, 203
  nonrestrictive, punctuating, 10–11, 45–46, 218–221
  nouns as, 9–11
  objective pronouns as, 150
  phrases as, 45–46
  placement of, 9–11, 45–46
  possessive, 254
  pronouns as, 149–150
  punctuating, 9–11, 45–46, 49–50, 218–221
  quotations as, 220–221
  reducing dependent clauses to, 69–70
  restrictive, punctuating, 10–11, 45–46, 218–221
  subjective pronouns as, 149
  subject-verb agreement and, 90

articles
  definite and indefinite, 32
  in parallel pairs or series, 114–115
  pluralization of noncount nouns and, 6
  the, capitalization of, in names, 307

asyndeton, 97, 297

auxiliary verbs
  erroneous use of, in perfect tenses, 19
  as modals, 23–24
  in a parallel pair or series, 117–120
  in past-perfect tense, 20
  in past-progressive tense, 17–18
  in perfect tenses, 16–17, 20
  in present-progressive tense, 17–18
  split infinitives and, 146

B

bad vs. badly, 37–38

be, to
  as auxiliary verb, 22
  conjugation of, 18, 22–23
  as linking verb, 18, 22, 28–29
  in passive voice, 29–30
  in progressive tenses, 17–18
  and subjunctive mood, 24–25

boldfaced type, 263–264

brackets, 267–268

C

can vs. could, 23–24

can vs. may, 24

capitalization, 303–311
  parentheses and, 243–244
  of proper nouns, 5, 304
  in quotations, 262–263

case
  noun, 8
  pronoun, 42, 148–151

clauses
  of attribution, punctuating, 211–213, 257–258, 299
  within clauses, 74
  concessive, commas and, 225–226
  defined, 61–62
  inverted, subject-verb agreement in , 99–100
  as modifiers, 63–70
  phrases vs., 661–62
  See also adjectival dependent clauses; adverbial dependent clauses; dependent clauses; independent clauses; infinitive phrases; nominative dependent clauses

collective nouns, 9
  pronoun-antecedent agreement and, 162–164
  subject-verb agreement and, 104–106

colons, 238–241
  clauses of attribution and, 212–213
  in compound sentences, 296
  independent clauses, joining, 296
  multisentence direct quotations and, 213
  with nonrestrictive appositives, 11

comma splices, 235–236, 295–296

commas, 200–234
    academic degrees and, 215
    adjectival dependent clauses and, 223–225
    in addresses, 214
    adverbial clauses beginning with because and, 226–228
    adverbial dependent clauses and, 66, 225–229
    appositives and, 10–11, 46, 49–50, 218–221
    asyndetonic compound sentences and, 297
    clauses of attribution and, 211–213, 257–258
    complex sentences and, 298–299
    compound sentences and, 293–296
    compound-complex sentences and, 299–301
    concessive clauses and, 225–226
    contrastive phrasing and, 209
    coordinate adjectives and, 206–207
    correlative conjunctions and, 208–209
    in correspondence, 217
    cumulative adjectives and, 207
    dates and, 213–214
    direct address and, 208
    direct quotations and, 211–213
    elliptical constructions and, 208
    erroneous use of with gerund phrases, 53
    etc. and, 216–217
    in greetings, 217
    in height measurements, 217
    identical words, between, 209, 232
    indirect quotations and, 212–213
    i.e. and, 209
    inc. and, 216–217
    interjections and, 208
    interruptive elements and, 210–211, 228–229
    introductory elements and, 46–47, 56, 66, 201–204
    job titles and, 215–216
    military titles and, 215
    misreading, preventing with, 209, 231–232
    in names, 221–222
    in numbers, 217
    no and, 217
    nonrestrictive adjectival dependent clauses and, 67–68
    nonrestrictive elements and, 49–50, 218–221
    official titles and, 215–216
    parenthetical elements and, 210–211, 229
    participial phrases and, 204, 223
    place names and, 214
    prepositional phrases and, 221–223
    quotation marks and, 211, 217–218
    quotations and, 211–213, 232–234
    restrictive elements and, 221–228
    restrictive elements, false, and, 228–229
    separating subject from verb, 47, 53, 231–232
    serial, 204–206, 230
    in a series, 204–206, 230
    that, dropped, and, 208
    transitional phrases and, 210

verbal phrases and, 46–50
yes and, 217

common nouns, 5–9

comparatives
    adjectival, 33–34
    adverbial, 37–38
    negative comparison and, 34
    proper use of, 141–142
    See also superlatives

complements, 11–12, 28–29, 54–55
    erroneous use of adverb as, 142–143
    hyphenation of adjectival compounds as, 283–285
    nominative dependent clauses as, 71–72
    objective pronouns as, 150
    subject-verb agreement and, 90
    See also objective complements; predicate adjectives; predicate nominatives; subjective complements

complex sentences, 76–77
    punctuating, 203–204, 297–299
    subordinating conjunctions in, 76

compound nouns, 8, 10
    hyphenation of, 270–271

compound sentences, 62, 74–76
    asyndetonic, 297
    conjunctive adverbs in, 75–76, 296
    coordinating conjunctions in, 75–76, 293–295
    punctuating, 75–76, 293–297
    transitional phrases in, 294–295

compound verbs, 271

compound-complex sentences, 77–78
    conjunctive adverbs in , 299
    coordinating conjunctions in, 299–301
    punctuating, 299–301

compounds. See adjectival compounds, adverbial compounds, compound nouns, compound verbs

concrete nouns, 4–6

conjunctions, 40–41
    adverbs as, 38
    beginning a sentence with, 41
    See also coordinating conjunctions; correlative conjunctions; subordinating conjunctions. See coordinating conjunctions

conjunctive adverbs, 38, 41
    in compound sentences, 295–296
    in compound-complex sentences, 299
    independent clauses, joining, 63–64, 76, 235–236, 295–296
    relationships expressed by, 63–64, 295

contractions, 249
    in a series, 119–120

coordinate adjectives, 32

punctuating, 206–207

coordinating conjunctions, 9, 40–41
  in compound sentences, 75–76, 295–296
  in compound-complex sentences, 299–301
  independent clauses, joining, 63, 75–76, 236, 295–297

correlative conjunctions, 41
  commas and, 208–209
  in a parallel pair, 121–125

count nouns, 4–5, 7–8

cumulative adjectives, 32–33
  punctuating, 207–208

D

dashes, em, 244–247
  appositives, nonrestrictive, and, 10–11, 46, 245–247
  in compound sentences, 296–297
  independent clauses, joining, 296–297
  interruptive elements and, 246

dashes, en, 247, 296

demonstrative pronouns, 32–33, 43, 166

dependent clauses, 61–70
  modifying, placement of, 127–133
  reducing to phrases for concision, 70
  as subjects, 83
  subordinating conjunctions introducing, 41
  See also adverbial dependent clauses; adjectival dependent clauses; nominative dependent clauses

determiners, 114–115

direct objects, 9, 12, 53–54
  gerunds and gerund phrases as, 53–54
  infinitive phrases as, 56, 58
  nominative dependent clauses as, 72
  objective pronouns as, 149–150

do, to, 20

double genitive, 253

E

ellipses, 265–267

elliptical constructions
  commas and, 208
  problems with, 187–190
  pronouns in, 149–150

emphasis
  capitalization for, 311
  dashes and, 245–246
  italics for, 261, 263
  quotation marks for, 261

essential elements, 49–50. See also restrictive elements and restrictive subentries under adjectival dependent clauses; adverbial dependent clauses; appositives; commas; participial phras-

es; prepositional phrases; verbal phrases

exclamation points, 41, 198–199

F

fewer/fewest vs. less/least, 5–6, 34

first-person pronouns, 14, 148–157
  verb conjugation and, 14–16

future tense, 14–16

future-perfect tense, 15–17

G

genitive, double, 253

gerund phrases, 46–48, 51–55
  as direct objects, 53–54
  as objects, 53–54
  participial phrases vs., 51–52
  punctuating, 53
  as subjective complements, 54–55
  as subjects, 51–52

gerunds
  defined, 51–52
  as direct objects, 53–54
  infinitives as objects of, 56
  nominative dependent clauses as objects of, 73–74
  as nouns, 47
  as objects, 53–54
  possessive nouns and pronouns preceding, 155–156, 254
  present participles vs., 52–53
  as subjective complements, 54–55
  in verbal phrases, 47

good vs. well, 37–38

H

have, to
  and past-perfect tense, 20
  and perfect tenses, 16, 18–21

hyphenation, 270–292
  of adjectival compounds preceding a noun, 272–283
  of adjectival compounds used as complements, 283–285
  of adverbial compounds, 292
  of compound adjectives, 34–35
  of compound nouns, 10, 270–271
  of compound verbs, 271
  of fractions, 285–286, 288–290, 314
  of multisyllabic words at a line break, 270
  of phrases and expressions with numbers, 285–290

hyphens. See also hyphenation
  within numbers, 314
  suspensive, 291–292

I

imperative mood, 24

indefinite pronouns, 32, 43
  antecedentless, 170–171
  in parallel pairs or series, 114–115
  possessive, 114, 253–254
  subject-verb agreement and, 92–93

independent clauses, 61–63
  conjunctive adverbs joining, 63, 76, 235–236, 296
  coordinate, 75–76
  dependent clauses, in relation to, 65
  patterns for joining, 62–63, 75–76, 293–299
  semicolons joining, 62–63, 75–76, 235–236, 294–295

indicative mood, 24–25

indirect objects, 12–13
  objective pronouns as, 149–150

infinitive clauses, 57–59
  pronoun-antecedent agreement in, 166–167
  See also infinitive phrases

infinitive phrases, 55–60
  as clauses, 57–59
  introductory, commas and, 203
  pronoun-antecedent agreement in, 166–167
  tenses of, 58–59

infinitives, 17, 55–60
  hyphenation of, 275
  split, 144–146
  in verbal phrases, 47

intensive pronouns, 42, 155

interjections, 41, 198–199, 208

interrogative pronouns, 32, 43

interruptive elements, 49–50, 71–72
  commas and, 210–211, 228
  compound-additive subjects vs., 99–100
  dangling, 137–138
  dashes and, 245–247
  parentheses and, 242, 246–247

intransitive verbs, 26–28

introductory elements
  commas and, 200–204
  See also specific elements

italics, 263–264

L

limiting adjectives, 31–32
  See also articles; pronouns

linking verbs, 11–12, 25–29, 54, 93

M

main clauses. *See* independent clauses

many vs. much, 5–6, 38

modals, 23–24

modifiers
  adjectival dependent clauses as, 66–69
  adverbial dependent clauses as, 63–66
  ambiguous, 139–140
  clauses as, 63–70
  dangling, 51, 133–139
  defined, 9
  infinitive phrases as, 57
  misplaced, 51
  nouns as, 9–11
  in a parallel series, 144
  participles as, 47
  past participles as, 33
  placement of, 127–133
  possessive nouns as, 10
  prepositional phrases as, 38–40
  present participles as, 33, 47
  See also adjectives; adverbs; articles; predicate adjectives

mood, 24–25
  avoiding illogical shifts in, 107

N

nominative dependent clauses, 63, 70–74
  punctuating, in complex sentences, 299
  in simple sentences, 76–77
  as subjects, 70–71, 83
  what, beginning with, and subject-verb agreement, 102–104

noncount nouns, 5–6

nonessential elements. *See* nonrestrictive elements; nonrestrictive subentries under adjectival dependent clauses; adverbial dependent clauses; appositives; colons; commas; dashes, em; parentheses; participial phrases; verbal phrases

nonrestrictive elements
  punctuating, 218–221, 242, 246–247
  See also nonrestrictive subentries under adjectival dependent clauses; adverbial dependent clauses; appositives; colons; commas; dashes, em; parentheses; participial phrases; verbal phrases

noun clauses. *See* nominative dependent clauses

nouns, 4–13
  as adverbs, 36
  attributive, vs. possessive, 253–254
  case and, 8
  collective, 9, 104–106, 162–164
  common, 5–8
  compound, 8, 10, 252, 270–271, 308
  concrete, 4–6
  count, 4, 7–8
  dependent clauses as, 70

functions of, 9–13
gender and, 8–9
gerunds as, 47
hyphenation of adjectival compounds beginning with, 272–273
-ics, ending in, 8, 96
mass, 5. *See also* nouns, noncount
as modifiers, 9–11
noncount, 5–6
plural-only, 8, 96
pluralization of, 4–8, 250–253
possessive, formation of, 8, 249–255
proper, 5, 304
See also abstract nouns; appositives; direct objects; indirect objects; objective complements; predicate nominatives; subjective complements; subjects

numbers
as adjectives, 32
hyphenation of, 287–290, 314
numerals as, 312–315
spelling out, 312–315

O

objective complements
adjectives as, 33
infinitive phrases as, 56–57
nouns as, 9, 13
placement of, 33
prepositional phrases as, 39–40

objective pronouns, 42, 149–150

objects
as antecedents of pronouns, 174–175
compound, pronouns in, 150
gerunds and gerund phrases as, 53–54
objective pronouns as, 149–150
pronouns as antecedentless, 173
whom and whomever as, 151–154
See also direct objects; indirect objects

P

pairs, parallel, 114, 117–126

parallelism, 111–126
articles and, 114
auxiliary verbs and, 117–120
contractions and, 114
correlative conjunctions and, 121–125
determiners and, 114–115
modifiers and, 144
of pairs, 114–115, 117–126
possessive pronouns and, 114–115
of a series, 111–120
that, as indefinite relative pronoun, and, 121

parentheses, 242–244
brackets, used with, 267–268
in compound sentences, 297
independent clauses, joining, 297

interruptive elements and, 246–247
nonrestrictive appositives and, 9–11, 246–247

parenthetical elements. *See* interruptive elements

participial phrases, 46–48
and concision, 48–49
dangling, 133–136
gerund phrases vs., 51–52
introductory, commas and, 202–203
misplaced, 136–137
nonrestrictive, punctuating, 205, 223–224
restrictive, commas and, 223–224
See also present-participial phrases; past-participial phrases

participles
hyphenation of adjectival compounds beginning with, 274
infinitives as objects of, 56
as modifiers, 46–47
objective pronouns preceding, 156
objects of, nominative dependent clauses as, 72–74
in verbal phrases, 46–47
See also present participles; past participles

parts of speech. *See* adjectives, adverbs, articles, conjunctions, interjections, nouns, prepositions, verbs

passive voice, 29–30, 107–108

past participles
erroneous use of, 19–20
formation of, 17–18
irregular, 18–19
as modifiers, 32
passive voice and, 29–30
past-perfect tense and, 20–21

past tense, 14–15
formation of, 17–18
indicative mood and, 24
irregular, 17–20
subjunctive mood and, 24–25

past-participial phrases
dangling, 135–136
See also participial phrases

past-perfect tense, 16, 19–21
in infinitive phrases, 58–59
past-progressive tense, 15, 17–18
perfect tenses, 16, 18–21
See also present-perfect tense; past-perfect tense

perfect-progressive tenses, 21–22

periods, 196–197, 316–317

person, 14, 157–158, 168

personal pronouns, 41–42, 148–158
case and, 41–42, 148–150
compound, 155
first-person, 14, 157–158, 168
intensive, 41–42, 155–157

solidus, 268–269

split infinitives, 144–147

subjective complements. *See* predicate adjectives;
    predicate nominatives

subjective pronouns, 41–42, 148–155

subjects
    adjectives as, 106
    asyndetonic compound, 97
    collective nouns as, 104–106
    compound, 9, 75, 97, 150
    compound-additive, 83–85, 99–100
    compound-alternative, 85–86, 98–99
    contrastive elements and, 101
    defined, 9
    dependent clauses as, 83
    distanced from verbs, 87–89
    elliptical, 104
    elliptical compound-additive, 100
    gerund phrases as, 52–53
    identifying, 40, 52, 82–83
    indefinite pronouns as, 92–93
    infinitive phrases as, 55–56
    in inverted clauses, 83, 98–100
    mismatched with predicates, 183–186
    nominative dependent clauses beginning with
        what as, 102–103
    nouns as, 9
    plural-only nouns as, 96
    pronouns as antecedentless, 170–173
    relative pronouns as, 97–98
    simple, 9
    subjective pronouns as, 148–149
    who and whoever as, 151–155
    See also subject-verb agreement

subject-verb agreement, 14, 82–106
    arithmetical operations as subjects and, 95
    asyndetonic compound subjects and, 97
    business names as subjects and, 95
    compound-additive subjects and, 83–85,
        99–100
    compound-alternative subjects and, 85–86
    contrastive elements and, 101
    couple as subject and, 105–106
    disease names as subjects and, 96
    distances as subjects and, 95
    each, following a plural subject, and, 87
    each, preceding a compound additive subject,
        and, 84–85
    elliptical compound-additive subjects and, 102
    elliptical subjects and, 101, 104
    events, names of, as subjects and, 95–96
    every, preceding a compound additive subject,
        and, 84–85
    fractions as subjects and, 94
    gerunds as subjects and, 89–90
    indefinite pronouns as subjects and, 92–93
    infinitive phrases following subjects and, 89

interruptive elements following subjects and,
    100–101
inverted clauses and, 99–100
linking verbs and, 93–94
measurements as subjects and, 94–95
names as subjects and, 95–96
nominative dependent clauses beginning with
    what, as subjects, and, 102–103
objects of prepositions and, 82, 87–89
organization names as subjects and, 95
parenthetical elements following subjects and,
    100–101
participial phrases following subjects and,
    88–89
percentages as subjects and, 91–92
performance groups, names of, as subjects
    and, 95
place names as subjects and, 96
plural-only nouns as subjects and, 96
prepositional phrases following subjects and,
    87–88
prepositions, objects of, and, 82, 91–93
quantities as subjects and, 94–95
relative pronouns, as subjects, within adjectival
    dependent clauses, and, 97–98
store names as subjects and, 95
there as expletive and, 83, 99–100
timespans as subjects and, 95
titles of works as subjects and, 95
troublesome single-word subjects and, 96–97

subjunctive mood, 24–25

subordinate clauses. *See* dependent clauses

subordinating conjunctions, 40–41
    in complex sentences, 76–77
    introducing adverbial dependent clauses,
        63–65
    introducing dependent clauses, 41
    relationships between clauses, expressing, 64

superlatives
    adjectival, 33–35
    adverbial, 37–38
    negative comparison and, 34
    proper use of, 141–142
    See also comparatives

T

tenses. *See* verb tenses

that
    avoiding redundant use of, 192–193
    clauses of attribution following, 212
    dropping, in adjectival dependent clauses, 67
    dropping, in nominative dependent clauses, 73,
        12–193, 208
    as indefinite relative pronoun, in a parallel pair
        or series, 121
    which vs., 69

there, as expletive, vs. subject, 83, 99–100

third-person pronouns, 14, 157–158
   verb conjugation and, 14

titles of works
   capitalization of, 307–308
   hyphenation in, 282
   italics and, 256
   possessive forms of, 255
   quotation marks and, 260

transitive verbs, 25–28
   and passive voice, 29

V

verb conjugations
   irregular, example, 17–19
   regular, example, 17

verb forms
   base, 14, 18
   emphatic, 20
   infinitives, 17
   past participles, 17–20
   past tense, 15, 17
   present participles, 17
   stem, 18

verb tenses, 14–25
   future, 14–17
   future perfect, 16–17
   historical present, 108
   illogical shifts in, avoiding, 108
   past, 14–15, 18–20, 25
   past perfect, 16, 20–21, 58–59
   past progressive, 15, 17–18
   perfect, 16, 19–21
   perfect progressive, 21–22
   present, 14–15
   present perfect, 16, 20–21, 58–59
   present progressive, 15, 17–18
   proper sequencing of, 108–110, 135
   in subjunctive mood, 24–25

verbal phrases, 46–50
   nonrestrictive, 49–50
   past participial, 50

past-perfect participial, 50–51
   placement of, 50
   present-perfect participial, 50–51
   punctuating, 46–47
   restrictive, 49–50
   tense in, 50–51

verbals, 46–47
   See also gerunds; infinitives; past participles;
      present participles; verbal phrases

verbs, 14–30
   abbreviations used as, 256
   action, 25–28
   apostrophes in abbreviations used as, 256
   compound, in simple sentences, 75
   conjugation of, 14
   defined, 4
   errors in the use of, 107–110
   hyphenation of adjectival compounds begin-
      ning with, 274–275
   intransitive, 25–27
   irregular, 17–19
   linking, 11, 28–29, 54, 93–94
   modals, 23–24
   mood, 24, 108
   number, 14
   passive voice and transitive, 29–30
   person and, 14, 157–158, 166–167
   transitive, 25–26
   voice, 29–30, 107–108
   See also auxiliary verbs; subject-verb agreement

virgules, 268–269

voice, 29–30, 107–108

W

which, and pronoun reference, 176–177

who/whoever vs. whom/whomever, 151–154

whom, in adjectival dependent clauses, 69–71

will, in formation of future tenses, 15–16

words, misused, 318–331